D0315768

WEEKEND OUTDOOR DIY

WEEKEND OUTDOOR DIY

40 step-by-step projects for garden **stonework, decking** and **ponds**

Bryan Hirst, Alan & Gill Bridgewater

NH
NEW
HOLLAND

This edition produced for
The Book People Ltd
Hall Wood Avenue, Haydock,
St Helens WA11 9UL

First published in 2006 by New Holland Publishers (UK) Ltd
London • Cape Town • Sydney • Auckland

Garfield House, 86-88 Edgware Road, London W2 2EA
www.newhollandpublishers.com

80 McKenzie Street, Cape Town 8001, South Africa

14 Aquatic Drive, Frenchs Forest, NSW 2086, Australia

218 Lake Road, Northcote, Auckland

ISBN 184537 2077

2 4 6 8 10 9 7 5 3 1

Editorial Direction: Rosemary Wilkinson
Project Editor: Clare Sayer
Production: Hazel Kirkman

Designed and created for New Holland by AG&G BOOKS
Project construction, planting and props: AG&G Books, Vana Haggerty and John Heming
Photography: John Freeman, AG&G Books and Ian Parsons
Illustrator: Gill Bridgewater Editors: Ian Keary and Fiona Corbridge Designer: Glyn Bridgewater

Printed by Times Offset, Malaysia

Conversion chart

To convert the metric measurements given in this book to imperial measurements, simply multiply the figure given in the text by the relevant number shown in the table alongside. Bear in mind that conversions will not necessarily work out exactly, and you will need to round the figure up or down slightly. (Do not use a combination of metric and imperial measurements – for accuracy, keep to one system.)

To convert	***Multiply by***
millimetres to inches	0.0394
metres to feet	3.28
metres to yards	1.093
sq millimetres to sq inches	0.00155
sq metres to sq feet	10.76
sq metres to sq yards	1.195
cu metres to cu feet	35.31
cu metres to cu yards	1.308
grams to pounds	0.0022
kilograms to pounds	2.2046
litres to gallons	0.22

Contents

Introduction

The three sections in the book – Decks and Decking, Garden Ponds and Stonework – contain simple and straightforward ideas that will transform your garden in a matter of days, whether you want to give your garden a swift makeover, take advantage of a splendid view, or simply expand your living space.

The exciting thing about building decking is its immediacy. It might be necessary to mix a small amount of concrete for the footings, but apart from that you can

This beautiful pond is the focal point in a classic garden. It requires careful planning and construction but is worth the effort (see page 230).

simply float the decking over an existing garden with all its problems.

It is now also relatively easy and inexpensive to build a pond in your garden. This book outlines the principles and practices of building, planting and maintaining ponds which uses both modern materials and traditional methods.

This strong, hardwearing path is enhanced by the use of colour in the terracotta Celtic knot strips. The path is long-lasting and would suit a formal garden (see page 116).

Stonework is an exciting craft: once you have tried it, you will see the world with fresh eyes. Take ideas and inspiration from the landscape and translate them into items that will enrich the beauty of your garden and give you many hours of pleasure.

There is no limit to what your imagination and hard work can achieve in a weekend. There are forty very different projects in this book, ranging from simple pieces to more formal constructions, all of which will be exciting to make and to use.

Health and safety

Many DIY procedures are potentially dangerous, so before starting work on the projects, check through the following list:

- ✔ Make sure that you are fit and strong enough for the task ahead of you. If you have doubts, ask your doctor for specific advice.
- ✔ Keep a first-aid kit and telephone within easy reach. If possible, avoid working alone.
- ✔ Never operate a machine such as a power drill, or attempt a difficult lifting or manoeuvring task, if you are overtired or using medication that makes you drowsy.
- ✔ Always use a safety electricity circuit breaker between the power socket and mains power tools. Never use a mains power tool if the lawn is wet. If possible, use battery-powered tools rather than those with cables, because they are safer for these types of outdoor project.
- ✔ When you are lifting heavy weights from ground level, minimize the risk of back strain by bending your knees, hugging the stone close to your body, and keeping the spine upright. If a weight looks too heavy to lift on your own, ask others to help. Don't risk injury.
- ✔ Wear gloves, a dust-mask and goggles when you are handling cement and lime, cutting stone with a hammer and chisel or when using a power tool such as a jigsaw, and when sanding pressure-treated wood, because it is impregnated with toxic preservative.
- ✔ Is it safe to build a pond in your garden if you have young children? (See page 185)
- ✔ Allow children to watch at a safe distance and help with small tasks, but never leave them unsupervised.
- ✔ Immobilise any equipment or lock it up and make sure that a safety barrier or tape stops anyone wandering unprepared into large excavations.

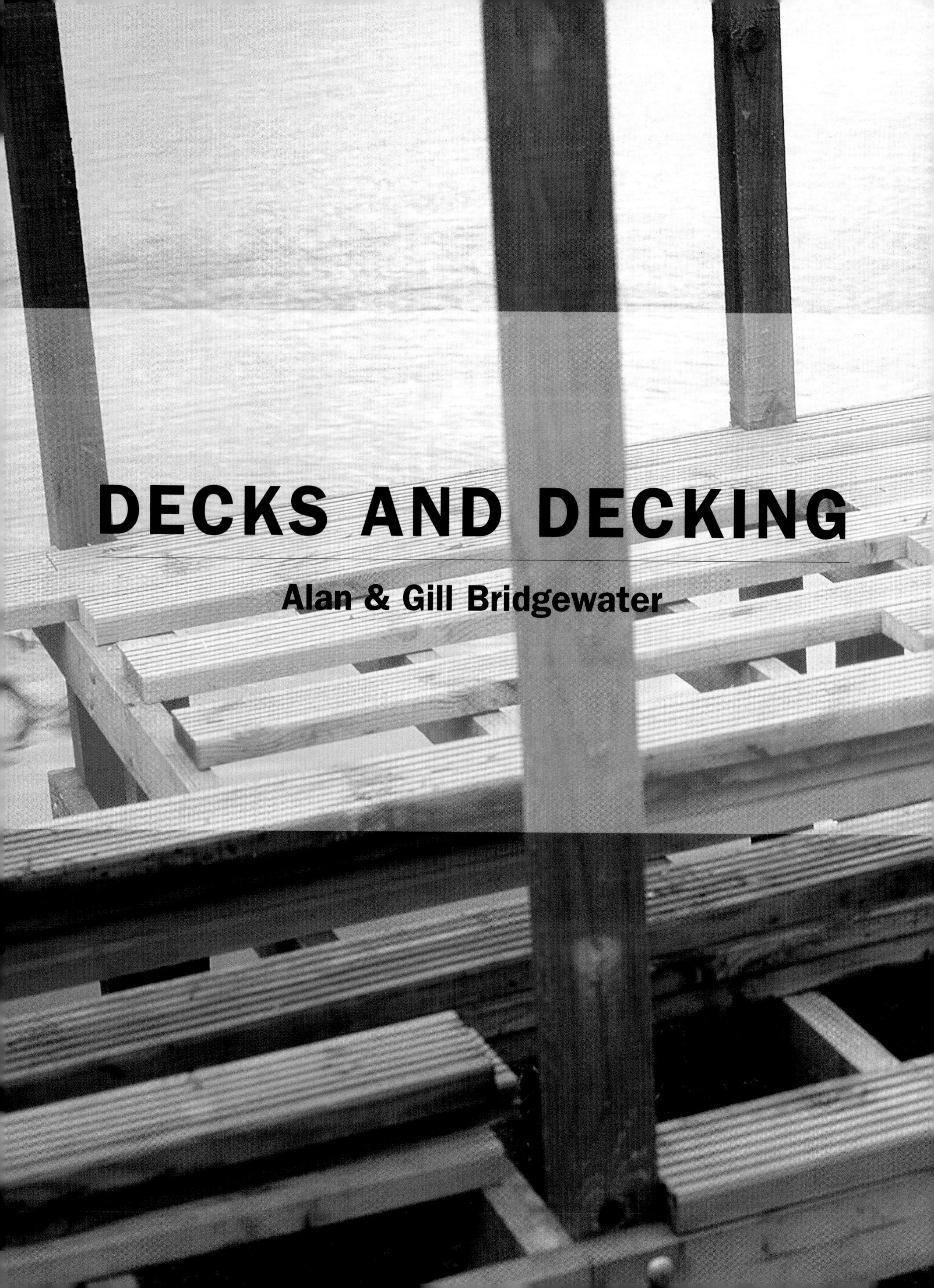

DECKS AND DECKING

Alan & Gill Bridgewater

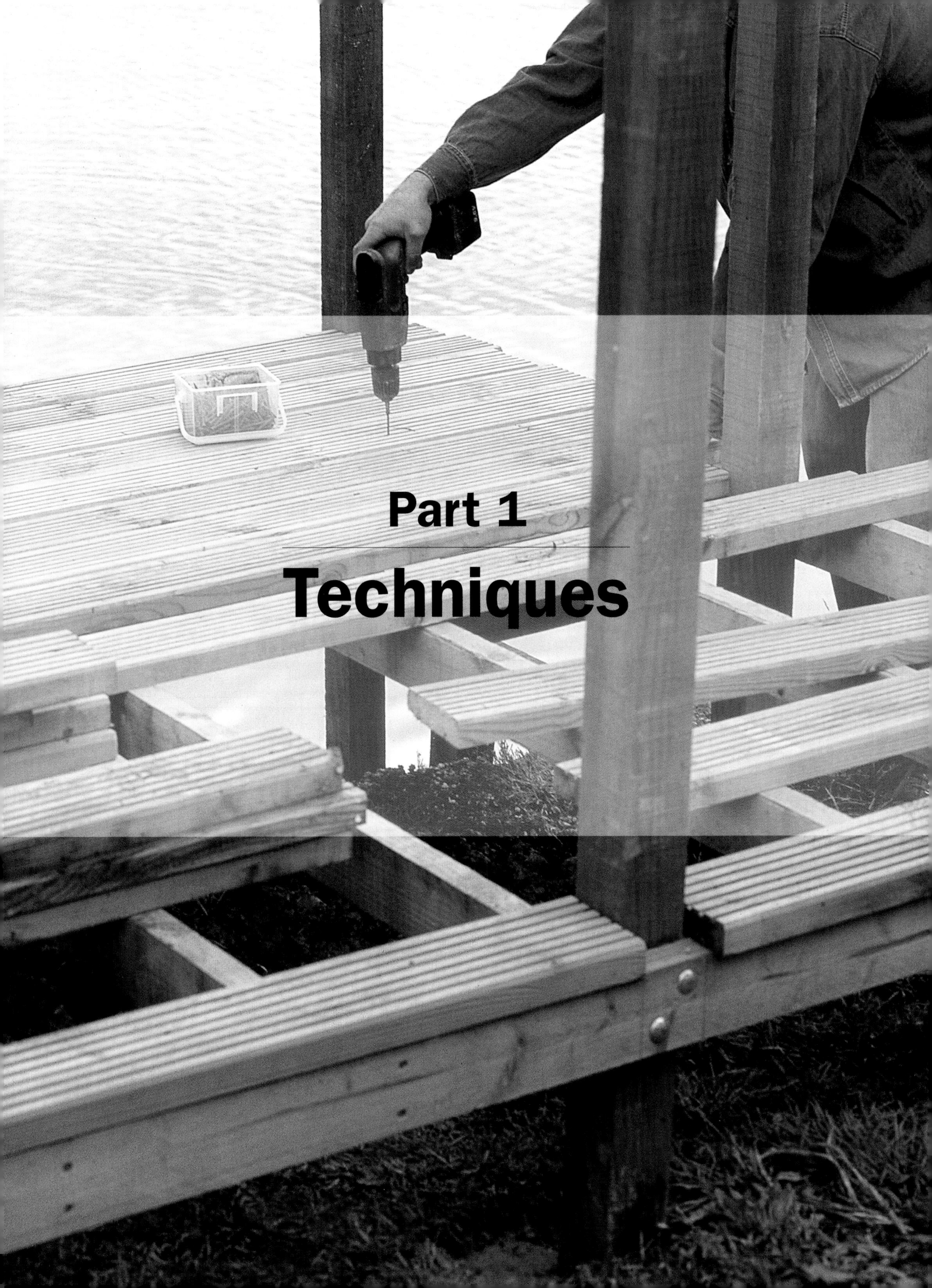

Part 1

Techniques

Designing and planning

Decking is fun to build, but only if you spend time carefully designing and planning all the details of the project. It is vital to study the site, ask other family members for their views, consult neighbours if the intended construction could conceivably affect them, draw up plans and list materials, before you start ordering wood. This section explains what you need to know.

Looking at your outdoor space

Assessing your garden

Walk around the garden and consider your requirements for the decking. How do you want to use it? Will it be an area for sunbathing or for sitting in the shade? Do you want it for evening barbecues, or for the children to play on? Do you want the decking to be physically linked to the house, or set in isolation? Look at the levels of the land, note the position of the sun at different times of day and the prevailing direction of the wind, and observe the way the family usually moves around the garden. Think about possible sites.

Style considerations

Take into account the style of your house and its setting. You may decide that the decking should continue the theme of the house, and look folksy or modern, for example. Alternatively, the decking could be a separate statement, providing a contrast to the style of the interior decor.

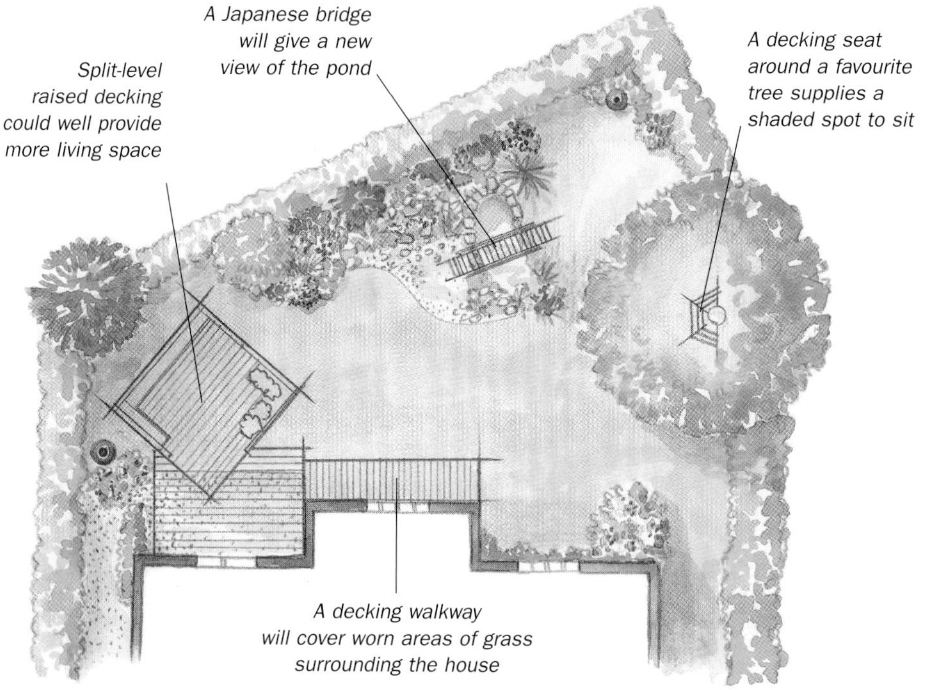

Split-level raised decking could well provide more living space

A Japanese bridge will give a new view of the pond

A decking seat around a favourite tree supplies a shaded spot to sit

A decking walkway will cover worn areas of grass surrounding the house

Whatever the size of your garden, there is a good chance that there is room for a decking feature – perhaps a patio or a decking bridge. Draw up a plan of your garden and consider the possibilities, using several copies to sketch in various options.

Design

Shape, form and structure

Once you have a clear idea of what you want to build, its site and overall style, you need to work out the design in more detail. What shape do you want it to be? Do you want the decking to be raised up high with feature stairs and decorative railings? Do the posts need to be set in concrete for stability? Does the decking have to wrap around the corner of the house, as for a Japanese engawa? Is the form so structurally complex that it will require lots of bolts and braces? Will the decking incorporate existing features such as trees and rocky outcrops?

Form and function

It is fine to allow form to dominate the design for a proposed project when it is no more than a plant tub or small patio, but for other projects, safety reasons dictate that function must be the main consideration. For example, when you are building raised decking with steps and railings, or a chair that has to bear your weight and also fold up for storage, function is much more important than form. The item has to be structurally sound and safe to use before pattern, texture and colour come into the picture.

Wood types

Always use the best wood that you can afford, especially when building more complex, time-consuming projects such as a large area of decking. If money is no object, select long-lasting woods such as redwood or oak. If you need to keep costs to a minimum, use pressure-treated pine. Either way, make sure that the wood is free from splits, twists, soft waney edges, decay, dead knots and insect infestation.

Drawing your designs

Phone three suppliers and ask about sizes and prices. Let's say, for example, that you need two 1.25 m lengths of wood. The cheapest option might be for you to order a single 3 m length and cut the wood to size yourself, rather than ordering two 1.25 m lengths. If this is the case, there will be some wastage, therefore would it be better to enlarge the project so that you use two 1.5 m lengths?

Once you have made all the decisions regarding length and cost, sketch the design on paper – the plan view, front and side views, and the details. Draw in the overall dimensions, the dimensions of the various sections, the number of pieces of wood, and any details concerning joints and fixings. Make a list of the component parts – the number of lengths of each type of wood, and the number of bolts and fixings required.

Before diving headlong into ordering wood and building, sit down in the garden with a piece of paper, inspirational pictures collected from magazines, and samples of decking materials. Spend some time considering the options. Design the project so that it suits all your needs.

Planning

First steps

Once you have ordered the wood, plan out the logistics of the project, from the moment the wood arrives through to the actual order of work. Decide where you are going to stack the wood and whether you will need to buy more tools or sharpen old ones. If concrete is required, establish whether you need to hire a cement mixer. If you are planning to work on a Sunday, find out if there is a nearby shop where you can replenish supplies if, for example, you run out of screws. Is it feasible to complete the project in a single weekend, or would it be better to spread the work over two weekends? Will you have to wait for concrete to cure, or can you plan the tasks so that the concrete dries out overnight?

Permission and safety

Check that there are no planning restrictions governing the type of structure you intend to build. Depending upon where you live, you might need permission before you can erect a "permanent structure", although the definition of this can vary. Some planning departments only define decking as permanent if it has a full concrete foundation slab; others make decisions based on height off the ground and number of steps.

Follow proper safety procedures and wear gloves to guard your hands against splinters and abrasion, goggles to protect your eyes, and strong boots to stop your feet being crushed. Wear a dust-mask if sanding pressure-treated wood or wood that has been brushed with preservative.

Planning checklist

- ✔ Are there any sawmills in your area? These will be the most economical source of materials.
- ✔ Can you save money by modifying the projects to suit a particular size or type of wood?
- ✔ Are local suppliers willing to deliver small quantities of wood?
- ✔ Is there adequate access to your garden, with a wide gateway and possibly room for a lorry to turn?
- ✔ If the wood is unloaded in your drive, or at your gate, will it cause problems or pose a danger?
- ✔ How are you going to move the wood from the drive to the site? Will you need help from friends?

Materials

The only reliable way to get top-quality wood is to go to the timberyard and choose it yourself, rather than ordering it unseen. Phone around for the best quotes first, then arm yourself with a detailed list of your needs – type of wood, quantity, and the various lengths and sections – and go to look at the wood on offer. Choose the boards yourself, one by one. The following section shows you how.

Using timber and other decking materials

Width, thickness and length

Timberyards sell wood that is termed "nominal rough-sawn" and "surfaced smooth". Sawn wood comes in exactly the sizes described, so a piece of 60 mm-wide rough-sawn wood is actually that size. However, a piece of 60 mm-wide surfaced-smooth wood measures something less. Wood is sold as standard sections, such as square, rectilinear or round, and comes in 2-, 3- and 4-metre lengths. Generally, you get a better deal if you buy long lengths and cut to fit.

Timber types and textures

Some timberyards offer various top-quality wood species such as redwood, cedar and oak, which are long-lasting and resistant to rot and insect attack. More commonly, timberyards tend to sell pine that has been pressure-treated with either brown or green chemical preservatives.

We favour using rough-sawn wood for the projects, which we swiftly sand to remove splinters, and then protect and colour with washes of garden paint, or with a traditional wash made from a mixture of lime and water.

Other materials

Woven plastic sheeting, gravel and shingle, ballast, sand and cement, and all manner of screws, nails and bolts are used in the projects. Gravel and shingle are used as decorative spreads and as a hardcore, and ballast (a mixture of sand and gravel) is used when making concrete. When selecting nails, screws and bolts, opt for plated or galvanized types. We generally prefer to use screws rather than nails, because they have more holding power. Bolts are good when you need an extra-strong joint, such as when fitting joists to posts, or building frames.

Buying wood

If you can get access to a flatbed truck for your visit to the timberyard, you can take the wood away with you, rather than waiting for it to be delivered. Take a tape measure and hand-pick every board, batten and post on your list. Don't be intimidated. Reject wood that is split, twisted or in any way less than perfect.

Caution
Pressure-treated timber
Wear gloves when handling newly treated wood, and avoid contact with the sawdust. Wash your hands before eating or drinking.

Opposite page: A selection of materials suitable for making the projects in this book. ***1*** *Gravel,* ***2*** *Plastic sheeting,* ***3*** *"Fence capping",* ***4*** *Preserved decking,* ***5*** *Pressure-treated decking,* ***6*** *Grooved decking,* ***7*** *Wide decking board,* ***8*** *Standard screws,* ***9*** *Decking screws,* ***10*** *Untreated decking,* ***11*** *Acorn finial,* ***12*** *Standard nails,* ***13*** *Coach bolt,* ***14*** *Joist,* ***15*** *Post,* ***16*** *Round-section post,* ***17*** *Wood chips.*

Concrete and other post fixing-materials

Most decking has to be set on some sort of foundation.

- For a small area of low-level decking: dig post holes, set posts on 100 mm of hardcore, fill up holes with gravel.
- For decking on solid ground: place pre-cast concrete pads on the ground, set the posts directly in position.
- For damp, compacted soil: dig post holes, add 100 mm of hardcore, insert posts, fill up with dryish concrete mix.
- For sandy soil: dig holes, line with plywood, add 100 mm of hardcore, insert posts, fill up with stiff concrete mix.
- For sandy soil, with the footing extended above ground level: dig post holes, set a fibre tube or former in the holes so that the top is at the desired level, put 100 mm of gravel into the former and top it up with concrete, and push the anchor-fixing into the wet concrete.

Caution
Cement and lime are both corrosive. Always wear a dust-mask, gloves and goggles. If you get the powder on your skin, especially if your skin is damp, wash it off immediately with copious amounts of water.

1
2
3
4
5
6
7
8
9
10
11
12
13
14
15
16
17

Tools

Tools are one of the main keys to successful woodwork. A few carefully chosen, medium-priced tools will make every task a pleasure to complete. But to save on costs, avoid splashing out on a complete new set of tools, and just start out by using the tools that you already have to hand. Buy new tools when you really need to. Here is a list of tools which, in an ideal world, would reside in your toolkit.

Useful tools for building decking

Tools for preparing the site

You need a large fibreglass tape measure for measuring the site, wooden pegs and string for setting out the limits of the decking, and a club hammer for banging in pegs. You also require a spade for cutting away turf and digging holes, and a bucket, wheelbarrow, shovel and rake for all the earth-moving tasks. Choose tools to suit your strength and height – for example, you can buy different sizes of spade and sledgehammer. A spirit level is neccessary for checking levels, both on the decking and when setting out pegs.

Measuring and marking

A small tape measure is used for measuring lengths and widths, a square for drawing and checking right angles, and a compass or a pair of dividers for drawing circle-based curves.

A clutch of good, strong carpenter's pencils is vital – they last longer than ordinary pencils, and don't roll off the workbench. If you are making decking with angles greater or smaller than 90°, you also need either a bevel gauge or an engineer's protractor square.

Sawing wood

A couple of hand saws are always useful. We use a crosscut saw for cutting wood to length across the grain, and a rip saw for cutting a board down its length.

When it comes to cutting curves, we use an electric jigsaw. Occasionally, we use a hand coping saw for cutting tight curves and little details. If you particularly enjoy using power tools, consider obtaining a small combination mitre saw, which is a really good tool for making a large number of identical cuts.

Drilling and screwing

We use a straightforward electric drill for drilling deep, large-diameter holes, and a cordless drill in conjunction with a cross-point screwdriver bit for driving in screws. However, if the weather is damp, or we are too lazy to unroll the cable for the electric drill, we might use the cordless drill both for drilling holes and driving in screws. If, by the end of the day, the cordless drill has run out of power, we might also use the electric drill to drive in screws. If you intend to build a lot of decking, it's a good idea to invest in two cordless drills, so that you can always have one charging up in readiness.

Nailing

Before nailing, you need one of the drills to drill pilot holes, and then a claw hammer to knock in the nails. If the workpiece needs to be supported, to stop it shaking or bouncing, hold a sledgehammer or a club hammer at the back of it. We generally have at least two or three claw hammers on site, so that there is always one near to hand – on the ground, on the decking, somewhere on the woodpile, or on the workbench.

Holding and securing

Ideally, you need two portable workbenches so that you can cut long lengths of wood comfortably, without asking for help. We use two very cheap benches, and don't worry about giving them a lot of heavy treatment. If you are trying to cut costs, you could even work on a couple of old teachests. If you are doing most of the work on your own, you will also need a couple of large-size clamps for holding the workpiece in place while you are drilling holes and screwing. It is important to keep your back straight while you work, to avoid strain.

Tool hire

If your main interest is in the end results of a particular project, rather than in taking up woodwork and decking construction as a future hobby, it might be best to borrow the larger and more expensive tools. If you need a large sander or a cement mixer, the most sensible course of action is to hire the piece of equipment.

Caution
Power tools

Electricity, early-morning dew, buckets of water and wet hands are a potentially dangerous combination. If you do decide to use an electric drill instead of a portable drill, or an electric cement mixer, make sure that you use it in conjunction with an electricity circuit breaker.

A basic tool kit

For making the projects in this book, you will need to buy or borrow the tools shown below. All these basic, everyday tools can be bought from a general DIY store. Larger pieces of equipment can be hired from specialist hire shops.

Items that are not illustrated include a portable workbench, wheelbarrow and bucket (the last two are for making concrete, which may be necessary for fixing posts in the ground to support areas of decking).

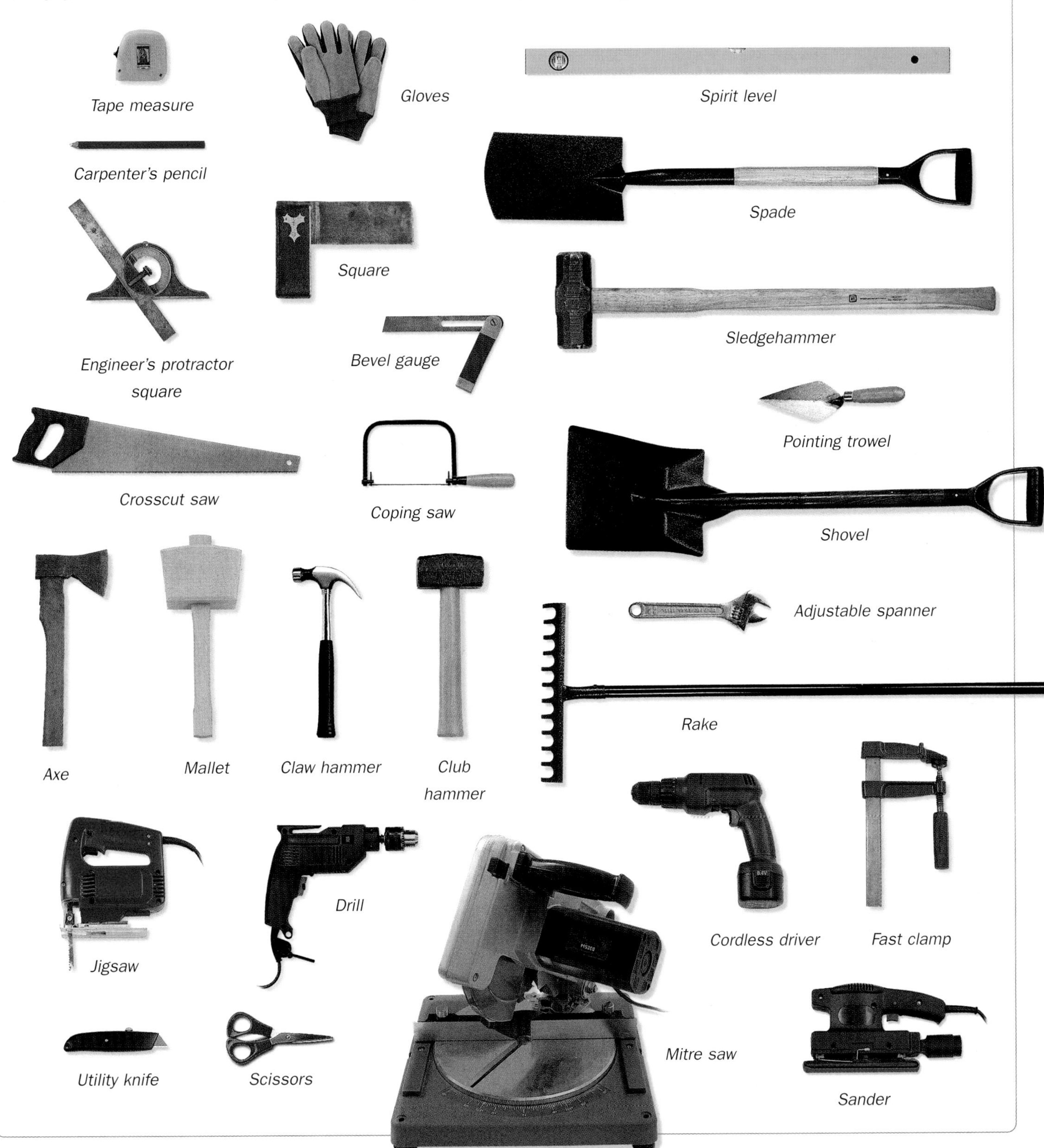
Tape measure
Gloves
Spirit level
Carpenter's pencil
Spade
Square
Engineer's protractor square
Bevel gauge
Sledgehammer
Pointing trowel
Crosscut saw
Coping saw
Shovel
Adjustable spanner
Axe
Mallet
Claw hammer
Club hammer
Rake
Jigsaw
Drill
Cordless driver
Fast clamp
Utility knife
Scissors
Mitre saw
Sander

Basic techniques

Once you have a clear understanding of the basic techniques, and you can handle the tools with confidence, building decking is an enjoyable experience. The secret is to work at an easy, comfortable pace, and not to rush things. Make sure you spend plenty of time assessing the intended site to ensure that it is suitable, measure accurately, and always double-check before you make a cut.

Marking out

Fixing the position of the posts

Once you have decided where you want to build the decking, establish the positions of the levels of decking and all the holes for the supporting posts. Fix a reference post in position and at the correct height, and then use pegs, string and the crossed diagonal method to relate all the other posts and levels to this point. We usually set the reference post on the high point of the site. The crossed diagonal method involves measuring each of the diagonals of a given rectangle (such as a marked-out site, or an area of decking), and ensuring that they are the same. If not, adjustments are made until they are.

Check that the diagonal measurements of the rectangle are identical
Check that the lengths of the rectangle's sides are equal

Due to the large scale of decking projects, it is often difficult to tell by eye alone if a rectangular structure – such as a decking framework – is square (has 90° corners). You need to use a tape measure to check the length, width and diagonal measurements.

Initial tasks

Preparing the site

Once you have worked out the precise position of the post holes, you need to make a decision about the existing foliage (lawn and plants) that is growing on the area that will be covered by the decking.

There is no problem if the decking is going to be high enough off the ground to walk under, but if it will be at a low level, remove the turf, roughly level the ground and lay a sheet of woven plastic over it, and then cover the plastic with gravel. This system not only controls the weeds, but also allows rainwater to drain away freely. If the decking is going to be positioned just clear of the ground, all you need do is level out the bumps, lay down a piece of woven plastic sheet and then simply rest the decking directly on short piles or concrete pads, so the joists are not in contact with the earth.

Setting posts in the ground

Dig a hole down to firm ground, or to the depth required by local planning regulations. It needs to be twice as big as the post. Shovel about 100 mm of hardcore in the hole, and set the post in position. Pour in concrete to surround the post, filling up the hole to ground level. Tamp the concrete with a beam to release air bubbles, check that the post is upright with a spirit level, and then fix it in place with temporary battens.

Coach bolts are used to fix a load-bearing joist to a post
Concrete is trowelled to a smooth finish to repel water

The decking framework (the main posts and joists) must be square, level and well secured. Concrete is used to fix the posts into the ground, so they do not move.

Cutting timber to size

Use an inexpensive, portable workbench to hold and support the workpiece. If you wish, use a clamp to grasp the wood firmly.

Cutting across the grain

A power saw is one option for cutting across the grain, but if you are a beginner it is best to use a new crosscut saw. Mark the line of cut with the square and pencil, and support the workpiece on the workbench. Place the saw to the waste side of the mark, draw the blade towards you to start the cut, and then continue sawing. When the saw is three-parts through the wood, hook your free hand round to support the waste, and complete the cut. A compound mitre saw is very useful when you need to repeat a large number of angled cuts, such as for laying decking at an angle to the frame.

Cutting curves

An electric jigsaw is a great tool for making curved cuts in wood up to about 50 mm thick. To use it, set the blade on the mark, switch on the power, and slowly advance to the waste side of the drawn line. To avoid dangerous kickbacks, always switch off the power before you draw the tool back from the workpiece.

Joints

Jointing with screws

There are various decking clips, fasteners and brackets on the market, but they are not the strongest, most attractive, or even the swiftest option. Also, many beginners find these fixings both expensive and confusing. For these reasons, we have opted for traditional joints held together either with cross-headed screws or with coach bolts. Occasionally, we use nails, but screws have more holding power and can be driven home or removed without damaging the wood. The order of work is to first drill a pilot hole, set the screw in place, and then drive it home with the cordless drill fitted with a cross-point screwdriver bit. If you are working with a partner, with one of you drilling the holes and the other driving in the screws, this technique can be just as fast as nailing.

A cordless driver is the best tool for putting in screws

When you are laying boards on a large structure, always stagger the joints because this gives the best effect visually.

Jointing with bolts

When an extra-strong joint is required, such as for fixing main joists to main posts, it is best to use a bolt. You can use a machine bolt with a washer at each end, or a coach bolt with a domed head and a square shoulder between the head and the shank. We prefer coach bolts, not only because the round head is more attractive, but they can also be fitted using a single spanner.

Washers are always used with coach-bolted joints, and a socket spanner or adjustable spanner to tighten up the nuts.

Finishing

Finishing

From the moment that your decking is completed, it will be subject to attack by the sun, rain and insects, so the wood needs to be protected. Traditionally, decking was limewashed or even tarred. There are many finishes on the market, from oils and resins to preservatives and varnishes. We generally prefer to start off with pressure-treated wood, and finish it with a colourwash. So we might mix lime with water, or thin down exterior-grade masonry paint until we have a wash. The resulting surface looks weathered, and instantly blends in with the garden.

Paths and patios

Wooden decking paths and patios look delightful and provide dry, level areas for safe and comfortable walking. They also attract your attention – the moment you see Japanese engawa decking running out of sight around the corner of a house, or a decking patio complete with a chair, you will be drawn to go and have a closer look. So for a striking, practical addition to your garden, opt for decking.

Constructing paths

Designing and planning

Walk around your garden and decide precisely where you want the path to be sited. Take note of the levels of the land, because these will have to be accommodated, and consider how the path will impact on your use of the garden.

Decide on the details of the decking's structure – the height off the ground and the position of the main beams – and use a tape measure, pegs and string to map out the site accordingly.

Building

Remove all large plants, level the ground, and dig out roots and large stones. Spread a layer of woven plastic weed-stop sheeting over the entire site and cover it with a generous layer of gravel. The wetter the site, the deeper the gravel needs to be, to ensure stability. Position the pressure-treated beams on the gravel and screw the decking boards in place.

A simple path that turns into a bridge complements the restrained planting scheme of this garden. The decking is supported on a concrete base and edged with log roll. The concrete supports for the three-board bridge are concealed behind the stacked slate walls.

INSPIRATIONS

A gently curving decking path, edged with cobbles, looks beautiful alongside a pond.

Decking boards lend themselves to crisp, geometrical layouts.

A path and water-crossing built from treated wood make an attractive feature.

Constructing a patio

Designing and planning

Think about how your garden looks over all the seasons, and then, in the light of your observations about sunshine, shade, being overlooked by neighbours, and so on, decide on the best place for siting the patio. Use a tape measure, pegs and string to mark out the boundaries of the site.

Building

If your garden is reasonably dry and level, and you want the patio close to the ground rather than raised up, you can use the same techniques as for building paths, and set the patio on a bed of plastic sheeting and gravel. Decking paths tend to consist of two tracks that run in straight or slightly curved lines, with decking boards bridging the tracks, but a patio offers you the opportunity to build a form that is both shapely and patterned. Once the plastic and gravel are in place, mark out the outer profile of the decking and divide it up with a pattern of joists set 300–450 mm apart at their centres. Make sure that the pattern of joists relates to the planned layout or pattern of your decking, so that there is plenty of support for the ends of the boards.

This patio and path uses a mix of straight boards and wedge-shaped segments. The decking is laid on gravel and set at the same depth as the lawn for easy mowing.

This generously sized ground-level decking looks ideally suited to the country house setting (New Orleans, USA). The owners needed a large seating area for barbecues and family gatherings. They wanted the patio to complement the existing tree, which offers some shade. The key to this type of decking patio is establishing a firm, level base (a low-lying framework).

A simple layout of decking tiles is perfectly suited to a small yard or balcony garden.

An octagonal patio is attention-grabbing. It is also easier to build than a circular patio.

A path linking the house to the garden. Well-trodden routes are prime sites for decking.

Decking

Decking can invigorate a family's use of their outdoor space, allowing many more activities to take place there. The space can be transformed by an area of raised decking standing high above the garden, or a subtle Japanese engawa running around the house, or even an island decking. Decking is also a crafty way of making a difficult-to-use area, such as a bank, participate fully in the life of the garden.

Constructing an engawa

Designing and planning

In a traditional Japanese garden, an *engawa* is a strip of low-level wooden decking that encircles the house, linking it to the garden. If you like the idea of having your own, walk around your house and have a good look at the levels of the land. Is it possible for an engawa to have a free passage around the house, or will it have to bridge immovable obstacles such as drainpipes? If you have to bridge drains, make sure that your decking includes inspection hatches. If there are existing paths, steps and trees, you will have to decide whether to leave them in place and run the decking over or around them, or whether to remove them. Use a tape measure, pegs and string to mark out the route of the engawa.

Building

Mark out the position of the footings at no more than 2 m apart, dig holes, and concrete short stub posts into place. Cover the site with plastic, topped off with gravel. Bridge the posts with beams and link the beams with joists. Bridge the beams with decking boards.

A Japanese teahouse with an engawa walkway in southern California, USA. The timber decking is minimal and practical, echoing the design of the building.

INSPIRATIONS

Stepped decking with an integral bench and railing, and under-seat storage space.

Low-level decking is ideal for a pond-side patio. A tree has been incorporated for shade.

Raised decking with steps and a handrail. The trellis screens off the neighbouring garden.

A simple island decking with an integral bench seat. The wood has been limewashed to create a cool, weathered effect (a welcome change to the popular red-brown finishes).

Island decking

Island decking can be built just about anywhere in the garden, so you can site it to take advantage of views, evening sunshine, afternoon shade, or whatever you wish. Use a tape measure, pegs and string to mark out the location of the footings. Dig holes and concrete the posts in position. Screw the main beams to the posts, make adjustments to correct the levels, and bolt the beams in place. Trim the tops off the posts, set joists on the beams and lay the decking as already described.

Raised decking with steps

Raised decking with steps is a great option for a home that is several steps above ground level, where there is a need to build decking that is close to the house but not actually attached to it.

Use a tape measure, pegs and string to establish the position of the footings and to mark out the total plan area. Concrete the posts into the ground. The secret of building decking of this type is to start by bolting a registration or ledger beam as close as possible to the house, and then use it as a marker for all the other levels.

Raised decking with steps in New Orleans, USA. The owners had to deal with the problem of varying ground levels in their garden, so the ideal solution was to lay decking to cover the entire area.

A decking porch with steps and railing provides an area for walking and sitting.

A porch walkway with a handrail. Trellis is used to cover the gap underneath.

Traditional raised decking overlooking the sea makes a perfect area for relaxation.

Decking additions

Once the decking is in place, additions such as railings, steps and benches offer you an opportunity for artistic expression in terms of pattern and form. If you like Japanese lattice screens, Swiss cottage fretwork, bold modernism or American folk colours, now is the time to incorporate them into your design. For sources of inspiration, have a root through the interior decor and architecture sections in a bookshop or library.

Constructing steps

A multi-level decking incorporating bench seating in Louisiana, USA. Steps are an obvious requirement for sloping sites and can be the most challenging aspect of the whole job of design and construction. Broad steps are more people-friendly than narrow stairways.

Designing and planning

Look at the site and use a tape measure, batten and pencil to establish the total distance along the ground that the flight of steps will cover, and the total height from one level to another. Decide on the riser height (between 100 mm and 180 mm), divide the total height by this number, and minus one to give the number of risers. Divide the horizontal distance along the ground by the number of risers to obtain the maximum depth of the treads.

Building

For the stringers (sides of the steps), you have a choice between zigzag stringers or solid planks. Start by measuring and cutting the two stringers so that they run parallel to each other, with their feet on the ground and their heads firmly fixed to the edge of the decking. Once the two stringers are in place, the rest is easy. A simple box dais does not have stringers.

INSPIRATIONS

This delightfully simple bridge or walkway draws inspiration from Japanese gardens.

Built-in seating with railings and planters, following a symmetrical arrangement.

Two planters bridged with boards provide a simple seat. A backrest is optional.

Railings

Ask your local planning department for advice and information about railing height, the recommended distance apart for the main posts, and other safety factors. The primary concern is that children cannot get their heads stuck between rails, or slip between the decking and the bottom horizontal rail. Consider your particular needs. Do the railings need to be especially safe because the decking is high off the ground, or are they more of a privacy screen or a windbreak? The order of work is to bolt the main posts in place, top them with the banister rail, and then fit the baluster rails or screen. The balusters afford you the opportunity to build in decorative details.

High railings combined with a lattice screen. The owners wanted to make sure that the raised decking was safe for their small children and pets to use.

A beautifully crafted bench makes this wonderful roofed decking even more enticing. Imagine sitting there and soaking up the view after a hard day's work.

Benches

Look at the seating in your house in order to decide on the height and depth for a bench (seats are likely to be about 400 mm above the ground). A bench can be fixed as part of the railings around the decking, or it can be freestanding so you have the option of moving it around. If a railing also forms the back of the bench, remember that children might climb on the bench, so the railing will need to be made higher. Once you have worked out the height of the seat, and the height and angle of the backrest, the actual building is very straightforward.

A bench built around a tree is a great place to sit – perfect for escaping from the sun.

What better way of enjoying decking than to stretch out on a home-made sun lounger?

A traditional American Adirondack chair is just the thing for a decking porch.

Part 2

Projects

Traditional boardwalk

★
Easy

Making time
One weekend
One day for putting the beams in place, and one day for fitting and fixing the decking

There is something very special about a traditional decking boardwalk – it looks spectacular in its simplicity, and feels good underfoot. The act of walking on the boards produces a characteristic drumming that will remind you of a seaside pier. This project is for the simplest kind of boardwalk – a straight path – but you could design one that turns corners, follows a curve or changes level.

Considering the design

The traditional boardwalk is very simple in construction – just two lines of posts banged directly into the ground, with beams lapped on to the posts to make two parallel rails, which are topped with weathered, rough-sawn decking boards. The tops of the 100 mm-square posts stand about 150 mm clear of the ground, allowing the boardwalk to skim over uneven land. This walkway is quick and easy to build, and suitable for various situations, such as over a lawn, or through an area of wooded scrub.

Getting started

Study your site and decide on the route of the boardwalk. Look at the ground and make checks with the spirit level to establish how far above ground level the decking needs to be, if your requirements are different to the specifications of the project (170 mm above ground level).

Measure the length of the proposed boardwalk from one end to the other to calculate the wood required. We have quoted quantities per 2 m length of boardwalk. Order the wood and when it is delivered, stack it as close as possible to the site. Set out your workbenches and tools, and you are ready to begin.

Overall dimensions and general notes

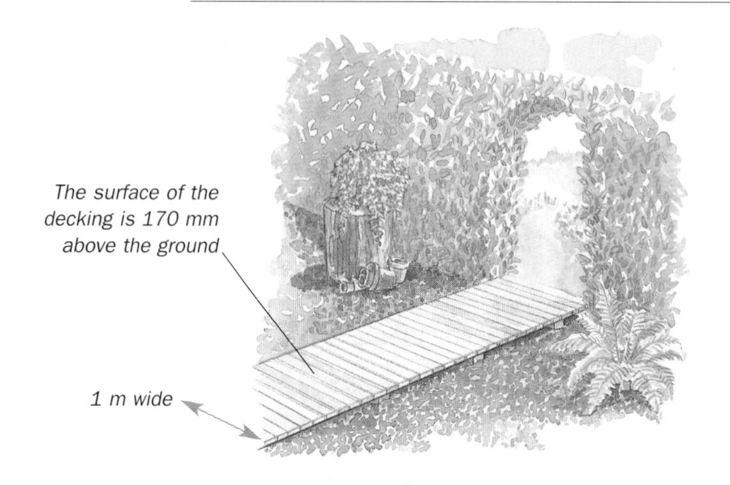
The surface of the decking is 170 mm above the ground
1 m wide

A traditional boardwalk will look good in just about any garden. It can be painted or left a natural colour.

You will need

Tools

- ✔ Two portable workbenches
- ✔ Pencil, ruler, tape measure and square
- ✔ Crosscut saw
- ✔ Wooden mallet
- ✔ Small hand axe
- ✔ Pegs and string
- ✔ Spade
- ✔ Sledgehammer
- ✔ Spirit level
- ✔ Cordless electric drill with a cross-point screwdriver bit
- ✔ Drill bit to match the size of the screws
- ✔ Two 5 mm-thick offcuts to use as spacers (either sawn wood or plywood)

Materials

(All rough-sawn pieces of pine include excess length for wastage. All the wood is pressure-treated with preservative.)

For approximately 2 m of boardwalk, 1 m wide

- ✔ Pine: 1 rough-sawn piece, 3 m long and 100 mm square section (posts)
- ✔ Pine: 2 rough-sawn pieces, 2 m long, 90 mm wide and 40 mm thick (beams)
- ✔ Pine: 10 rough-sawn pieces, 2 m long, 100 mm wide and 20 mm thick (decking boards)
- ✔ Zinc-plated, countersunk cross-headed screws: 100 x 90 mm no. 10

Exploded view of the traditional boardwalk

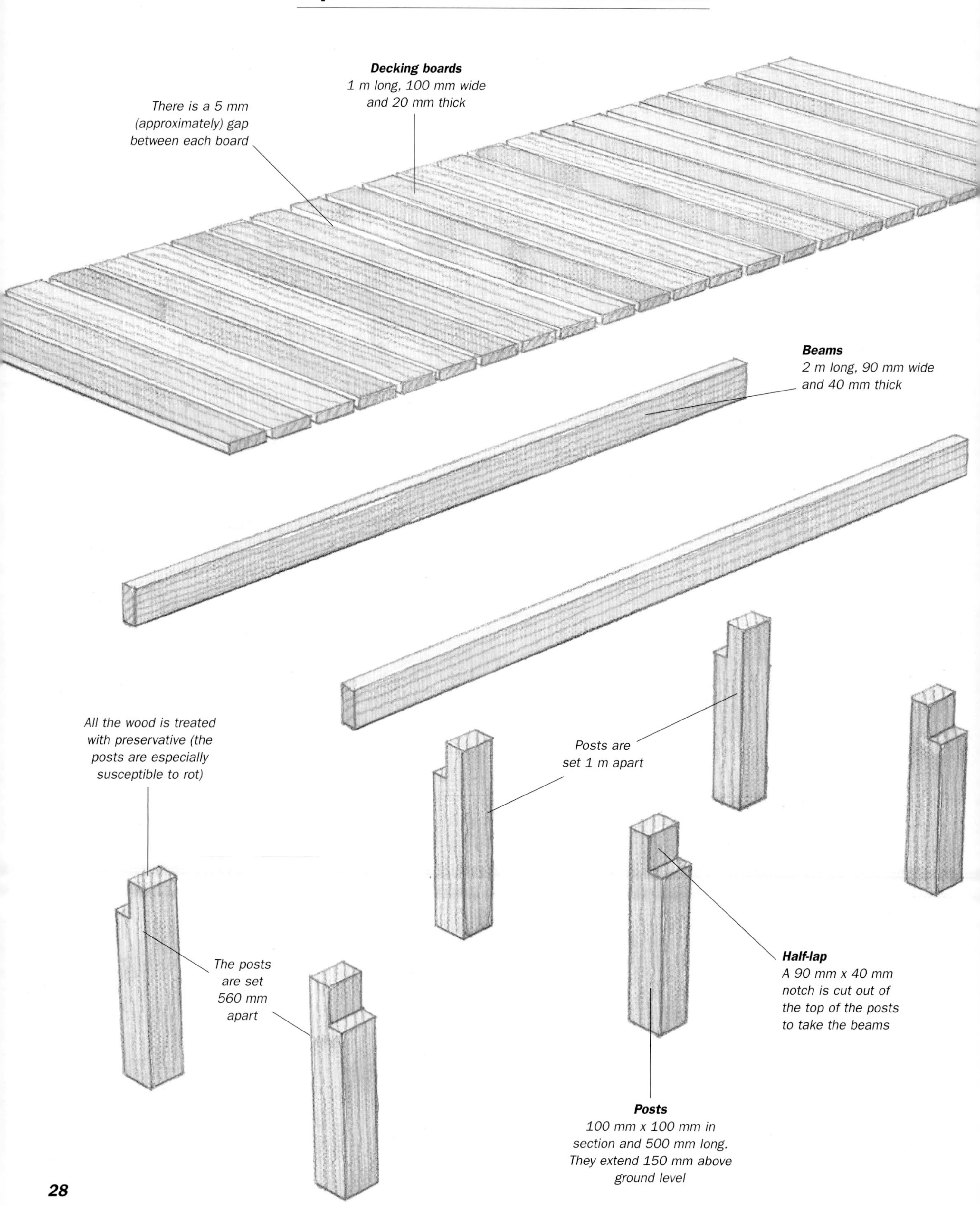
Decking boards
1 m long, 100 mm wide and 20 mm thick
There is a 5 mm (approximately) gap between each board
Beams
2 m long, 90 mm wide and 40 mm thick
All the wood is treated with preservative (the posts are especially susceptible to rot)
Posts are set 1 m apart
The posts are set 560 mm apart
Half-lap
A 90 mm x 40 mm notch is cut out of the top of the posts to take the beams
Posts
100 mm x 100 mm in section and 500 mm long. They extend 150 mm above ground level

Making the traditional boardwalk

1 Cutting the posts

Saw the 100 mm-square posts into 500 mm lengths and use the ruler and square to set out 90 mm x 40 mm half-laps. Saw across the grain to establish the length of the lap, and then use the mallet and axe to clear the waste.

2 Positioning the posts

Use the tape measure, pegs, string, spade and sledgehammer to set the posts in the ground. Place the centres of the posts 560 mm apart across the width and 1 m apart along the length of the boardwalk. They all extend 150 mm above the ground.

3 Fixing the beams

Set the beams for supporting the decking in position. Lay them on the half-laps in the posts, and fix them in place with 90 mm screws. (When fixing the beams end to end like this, make sure that they meet at the centre of the posts.)

4 Laying the decking

Cut the 100 mm-wide decking boards into 1 m lengths and screw them in place across the beams. Centre the boards on the beams and use the 5 mm-thick offcuts to space them apart.

Decking steps

★
Easy

Making time
One day
Two hours for planning and measuring, and the rest of the time for the woodwork

All too often, steps are not built to take account of the people who use them, and are difficult to negotiate for anyone using a walking stick, a shopping trolley or a pushchair. If you want to make a grand and easy entrance, decking steps are the perfect answer – and the great advantage of this project is that they can be built over existing steps to just about any size that you wish.

Considering the design

The decking steps fit over your existing steps in such a way that although they hardly change the height of the riser, they greatly increase the available standing area. You will, of course, have to modify the design to suit your particular steps, but we have made the design very flexible, so that it is easy to change.

Consider the attractions of the project. Perhaps you have an elderly relation who is unsteady on her feet and would like to be able to stand squarely on one very large step before moving to another. Alternatively, you might simply want to give your steps a makeover to give them a more generous and inviting feel, or provide a place for pot plants by the door.

Getting started

Study the design, and then carefully measure your existing steps and see how the design needs to be tweaked to fit them. The project is for a two-step unit, but you might have to change to a one- or three-step set-up. Check whether you need to make changes to the wood sizes, or perhaps to the overall dimensions.

You will need

Tools

- ✔ Two portable workbenches
- ✔ Pencil, ruler, tape measure, marking gauge and square
- ✔ Crosscut saw
- ✔ Cordless electric drill with a cross-point screwdriver bit
- ✔ Drill bits to match the sizes of the screws
- ✔ Spirit level
- ✔ Electric sander

Materials

(All rough-sawn pieces of pine include excess length for wastage. All the wood is pressure-treated with preservative.)

For steps 2 m wide and 1.22 m from front to back

- ✔ Pine: 8 rough-sawn pieces, 2 m long, 85 mm wide and 35 mm thick (joists)
- ✔ Pine: 2 rough-sawn pieces, 2 m long, 75 mm square section (main vertical supports)
- ✔ Pine: 20 rough-sawn pieces, 2 m long, 100 mm wide and 20 mm thick (decking and riser boards)
- ✔ Zinc-plated, countersunk cross-headed screws: 100 x 75 mm no. 8, 200 x 50 mm no. 8

Overall dimensions and general notes

The project is a good way of improving an existing doorstep that you consider to be too narrow or unattractive. The decking steps are built over the top of the existing steps.

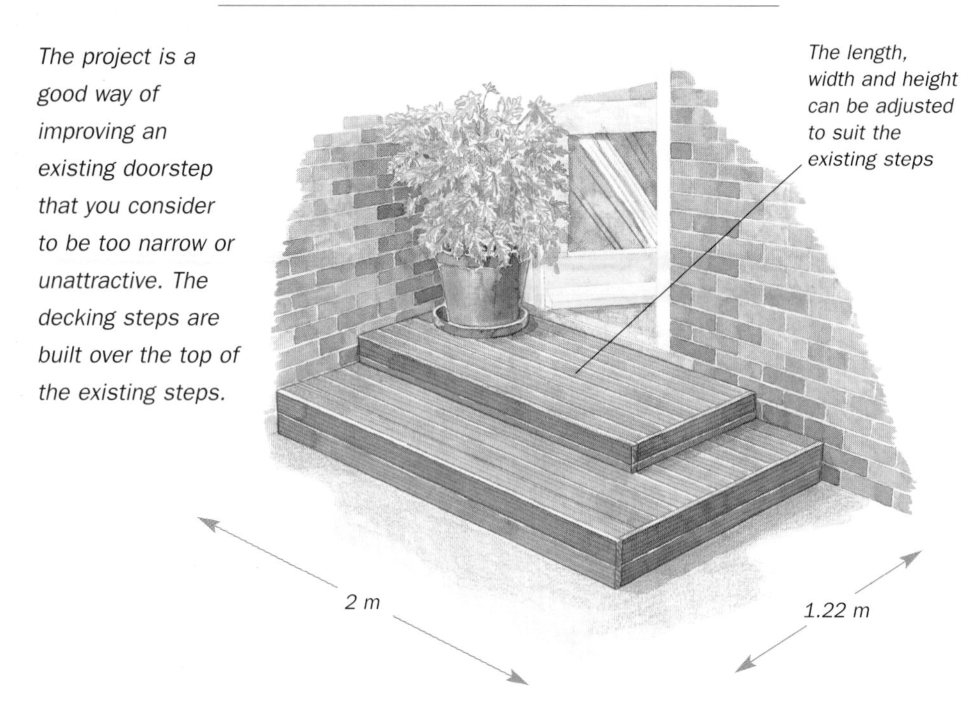
The length, width and height can be adjusted to suit the existing steps
2 m
1.22 m

Exploded view of the decking steps

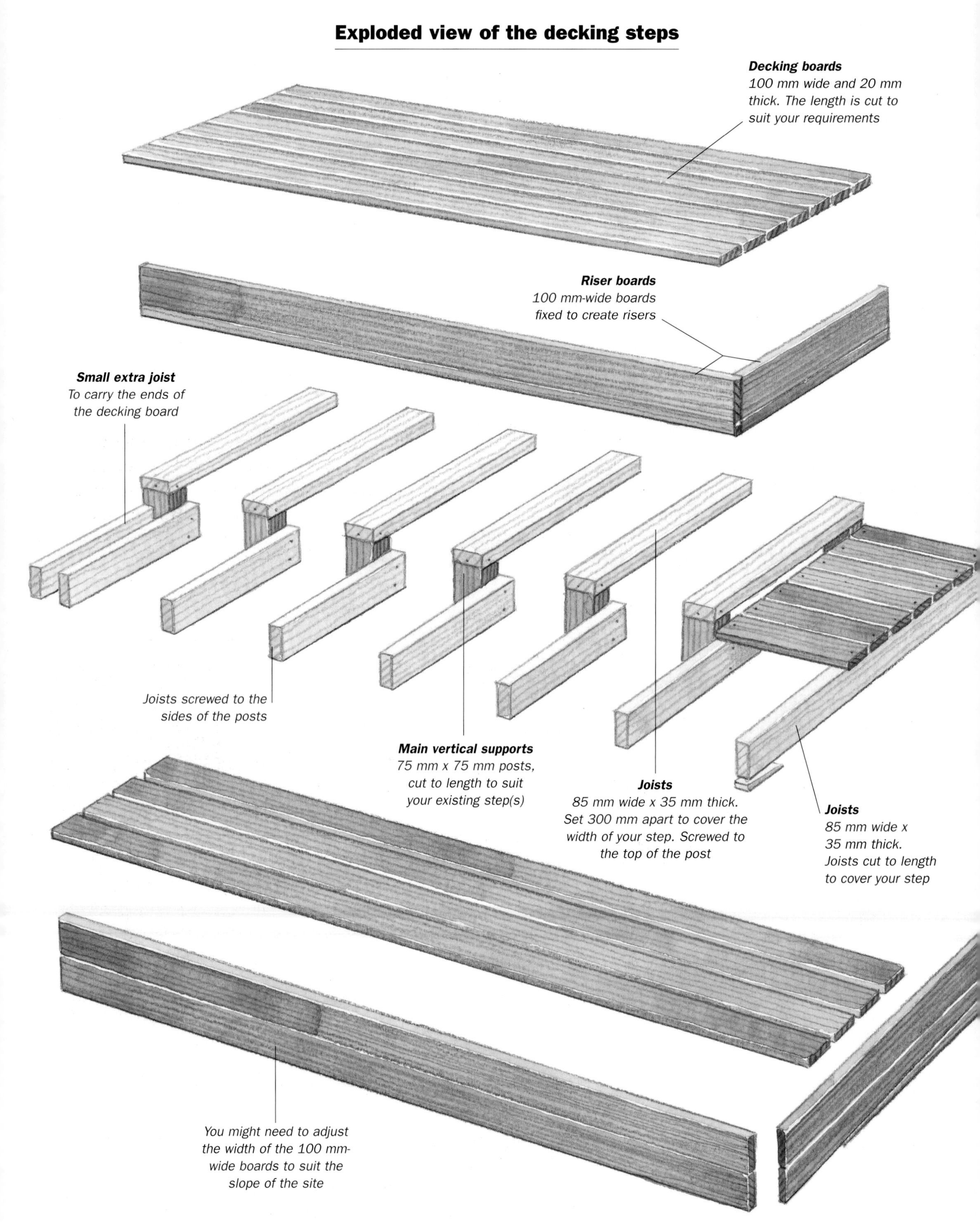
Decking boards
100 mm wide and 20 mm thick. The length is cut to suit your requirements
Riser boards
100 mm-wide boards fixed to create risers
Small extra joist
To carry the ends of the decking board
Joists screwed to the sides of the posts
Main vertical supports
75 mm x 75 mm posts, cut to length to suit your existing step(s)
Joists
85 mm wide x 35 mm thick. Set 300 mm apart to cover the width of your step. Screwed to the top of the post
Joists
85 mm wide x 35 mm thick. Joists cut to length to cover your step
You might need to adjust the width of the 100 mm-wide boards to suit the slope of the site

Making the decking steps

1 Fixing the joists
Measure your existing block of steps from front to back and cut the joists to length accordingly. Set the joists 300 mm apart (to match the full front to back measurement of your steps) and hold them in place with two lengths of decking. Use 50 mm screws.

2 Siting the frame
Place the joist frame over your steps and level it with scrap wood or whatever comes to hand. Use a spirit level to check the levels in all directions.

3 Fixing the vertical supports
Cut main vertical supports from the 75 mm square section posts. With 75 mm screws, fix them under the ends of the joists, so each joist has its own support.

4 Building the bottom step
Repeat the procedure already described to build a framework for the bottom step. Set the step at the right level and cut each main vertical support to suit the level of the ground.

5 Fitting the decking
When the two steps are in place, clad them with the decking boards, using 50 mm screws. When you come to fitting the riser boards on the bottom step, you will almost certainly have to adjust the width of the board along its length, tapering it to suit the run of the ground. Finally, sand the steps.

Japanese engawa

★
Easy

Making time
One weekend
One day for making the basic framing; one day for fixing the boards and making the steps

In a traditional Japanese garden, an *engawa* is low-level wooden decking that encircles the house, linking it to the garden and blurring the boundaries between the two. The engawa is made up of three component parts: a walkway which runs along the side of the building, a raised decking corner unit which sits at the corner of the building, and a set of steps that runs from the corner unit down to the ground.

Considering the design

By using combinations of these three basic units, you can design a scheme to suit your own requirements.

Getting started

Decide how many basic units you need. The details for the steps are in the project Garden Decking with Steps (page 58). Measure the total length of your walkway, and divide it into the 2.4 m-long modules we have given quantities for.

Overall dimensions and general notes

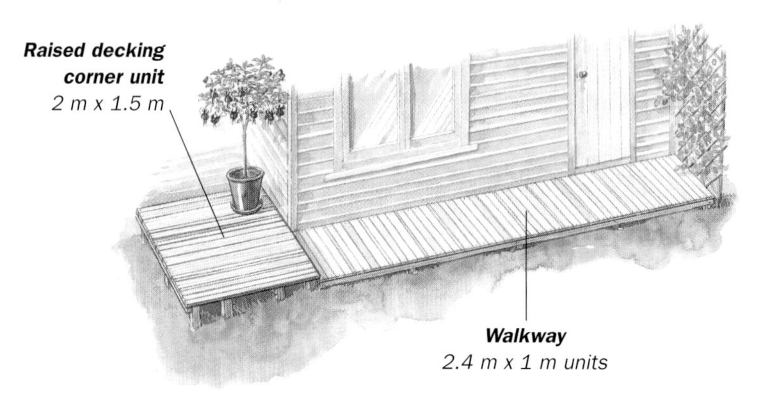
Raised decking corner unit
2 m x 1.5 m
Walkway
2.4 m x 1 m units

Using a combination of straight walkways and raised corner units, the engawa can be adapted to suit your situation.

You will need

Tools

- Pencil, ruler, tape measure and square
- Pegs and string
- Two portable workbenches
- Crosscut saw
- Cordless electric drill with a cross-point screwdriver bit
- Drill bits to match the sizes of the screws
- Craft knife
- Staple gun
- Spade and shovel
- Wheelbarrow and bucket
- Spirit level
- Electric sander
- Paintbrush

Materials

(All rough-sawn pieces of pine include excess length for wastage. All the wood is pressure-treated with preservative.)

For each 2.4 m length of walkway

- Pine: 3 rough-sawn pieces, 3 m long, 90 mm wide and 40 mm thick (joists)
- Pine: 1 rough-sawn piece, 3 m long, 75 mm square (posts)
- Pine: 8 rough-sawn pieces, 3 m long, 90 mm wide and 20 mm thick (decking boards)
- Pine: 3 rough-sawn pieces, 3 m long, 35 mm wide and 20 mm thick (decking boards)

For each 2 m x 1.5 m corner unit

- Pine: 4 rough-sawn pieces, 2 m long, 90 mm wide and 40 mm thick (joists)
- Pine: 4 rough-sawn pieces, 2 m long, 75 mm square (posts)
- Pine: 7 rough-sawn pieces, 3 m long, 90 mm wide and 20 mm thick (decking boards)
- Pine: 1 rough-sawn piece, 3 m long, 250 mm wide and 25 mm thick (decking boards)
- Pine: 3 rough-sawn pieces, 3 m long, 35 mm wide and 20 mm thick (decking boards)

General

- Zinc-plated, countersunk cross-headed screws: 200 x 75 mm no. 8, 100 x 90 mm no. 10
- Galvanized staples: 100 x 10 mm
- Concrete: 1 part (20 kg) cement, 5 parts (100 kg) ballast (for every 9 posts)
- Woven plastic weed-stop sheeting (large enough for the total decking area of the ground-level walkways)
- Exterior-grade matt white paint

Exploded view of the Japanese engawa

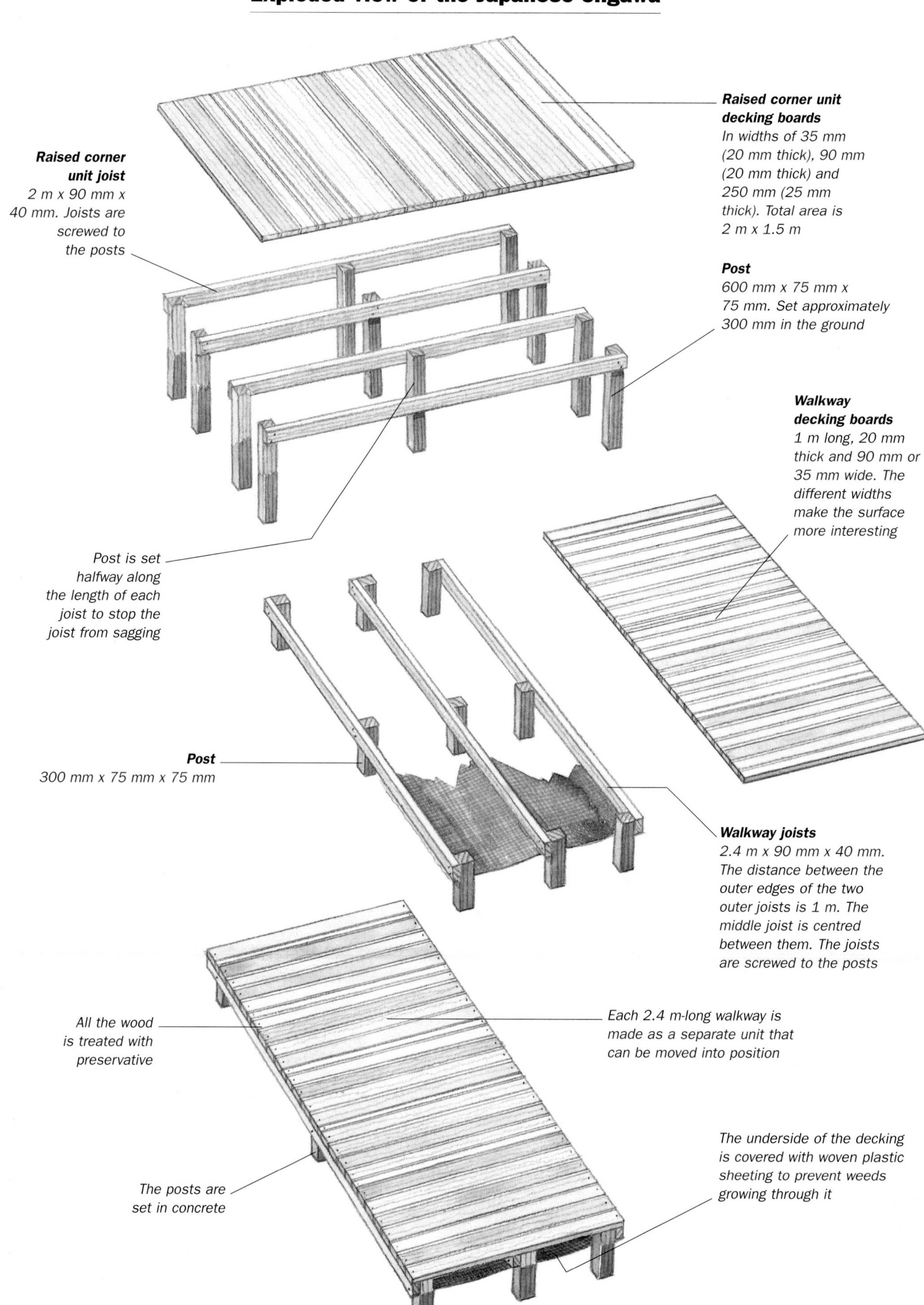
Raised corner unit decking boards
In widths of 35 mm (20 mm thick), 90 mm (20 mm thick) and 250 mm (25 mm thick). Total area is 2 m x 1.5 m
Raised corner unit joist
2 m x 90 mm x 40 mm. Joists are screwed to the posts
Post
600 mm x 75 mm x 75 mm. Set approximately 300 mm in the ground
Walkway decking boards
1 m long, 20 mm thick and 90 mm or 35 mm wide. The different widths make the surface more interesting
Post is set halfway along the length of each joist to stop the joist from sagging
Post
300 mm x 75 mm x 75 mm
Walkway joists
2.4 m x 90 mm x 40 mm. The distance between the outer edges of the two outer joists is 1 m. The middle joist is centred between them. The joists are screwed to the posts
All the wood is treated with preservative
Each 2.4 m-long walkway is made as a separate unit that can be moved into position
The underside of the decking is covered with woven plastic sheeting to prevent weeds growing through it
The posts are set in concrete

Making the Japanese engawa

1 Building the walkway frame
Take three 2.4 m lengths of wood for the joists, and position them as shown on the drawing to make the basic three-joist frame. Screw a 1 m-long piece of 20 mm-thick decking board at each end to hold the frame square, using 75 mm screws.

2 Fixing the plastic
Turn the frame upside-down, and cut a piece of the woven plastic sheet to fit. Staple it to what will be the underside of the joists.

3 Screwing on the posts
Cut nine 300 mm lengths of 75 mm square-section wood and screw them to the joists with 90 mm screws to make the posts (cut the plastic to fit around each post). Put one at each end of the joists, and one halfway along their length to provide a central support.

4 Concreting the posts
Set the frame on the ground and establish the position of the posts. Dig holes 210 mm deep. (The walkway sits at ground level.) Make a dryish mix of concrete, put it in the holes and lower the frame into place. Tamp the concrete around the posts with a piece of wood.

5 Building other frames
Follow the same procedures for all the walkway frames, all the while using the spirit level to ensure that the frames are level with each other. Build the raised decking corner units in the same way, concreting the 600 mm-long posts into holes 300 mm deep.

6 Fixing the decking on all frames
Screw the decking boards across the joists with 75 mm screws. To complete the engawa, sand down the whole structure. Mix the white paint with a good quantity of water to make a thin wash, and give the engawa two coats. See page 58 for how to build the steps.

Circular patio

The circular patio is intriguing to look at – reminiscent of a waterwheel, or maybe part of a windmill. Its arresting appearance makes the perfect setting for a water feature or a flower display, and the rugged decking provides a good, level surface for all manner of other garden activities. You can easily save on material costs by using salvaged wood, such as old floorboards, if necessary.

★
Easy

Making time
One weekend
One day for building the hexagonal frames; one day for putting it together and finishing

Considering the design

The patio is constructed from wedge-shaped segments cut from eighteen pine planks, measuring 1.05 m long, 250 mm wide and 25 mm thick. This provides 35 wedges and allows a spare one left over for good measure. The diameter of the patio is about 2.5 m.

We set the patio in an existing circle of pea gravel. If you want to create a similar gravel area specifically for your patio, you will need about eight wheelbarrow loads of fine pea gravel. The wedge-shaped decking boards are screwed to three hexagonal under-frames. When the whole patio construction is in place, the frames are held secure by the gravel, and the boards are supported and displayed to their best advantage.

Getting started

Have a look at your site, and decide whereabouts you want the patio to be placed. Use pegs and string to set out a circular area something over 2.5 m in diameter, and cover it with gravel. Edge the circle with a material of your choice. We have used log roll edging, and arranged a few cobbles in the space between the patio and the edging.

You will need

Tools

- Pencil, ruler, tape measure and square
- Pegs and string
- Two portable workbenches
- Electric mitre saw
- Rip saw
- Cordless electric drill with a cross-point screwdriver bit
- Drill bits to match the sizes of the screws
- Rake

Materials

(All rough-sawn pieces of pine include excess length for wastage. All the wood is pressure-treated with preservative.)

For a patio 2.5 m in diameter

- Pine: 9 rough-sawn pieces, 2.1 m long, 250 mm wide and 25 mm thick (wedge boards)
- Pine: 8 rough-sawn pieces, 2 m long, 75 mm wide and 30 mm thick (hexagonal frames)
- Zinc-plated, countersunk cross-headed screws: 50 x 75 mm no. 10, 200 x 50 mm no. 8

Overall dimensions and general notes

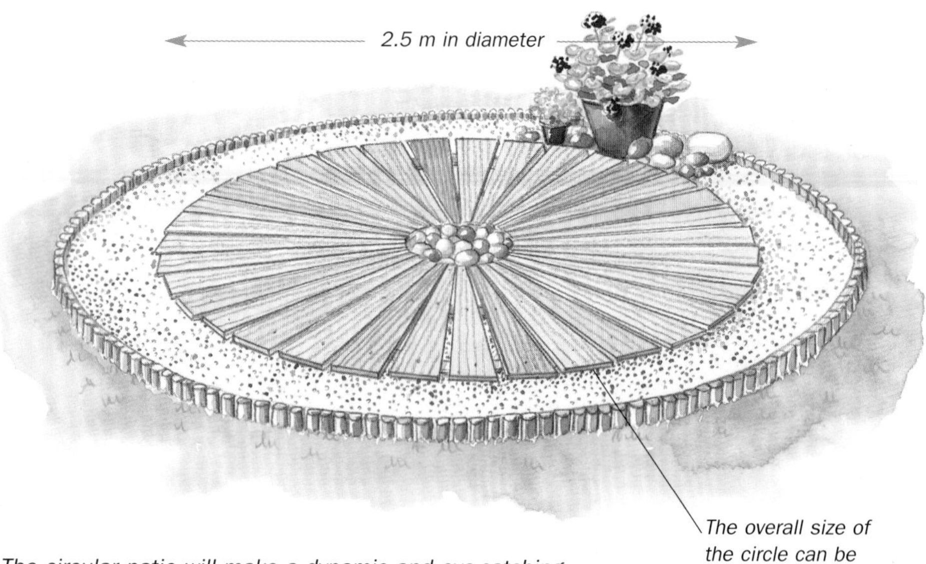
2.5 m in diameter
The overall size of the circle can be easily adapted to suit any garden

The circular patio will make a dynamic and eye-catching feature, whether in a small town plot or a larger garden.

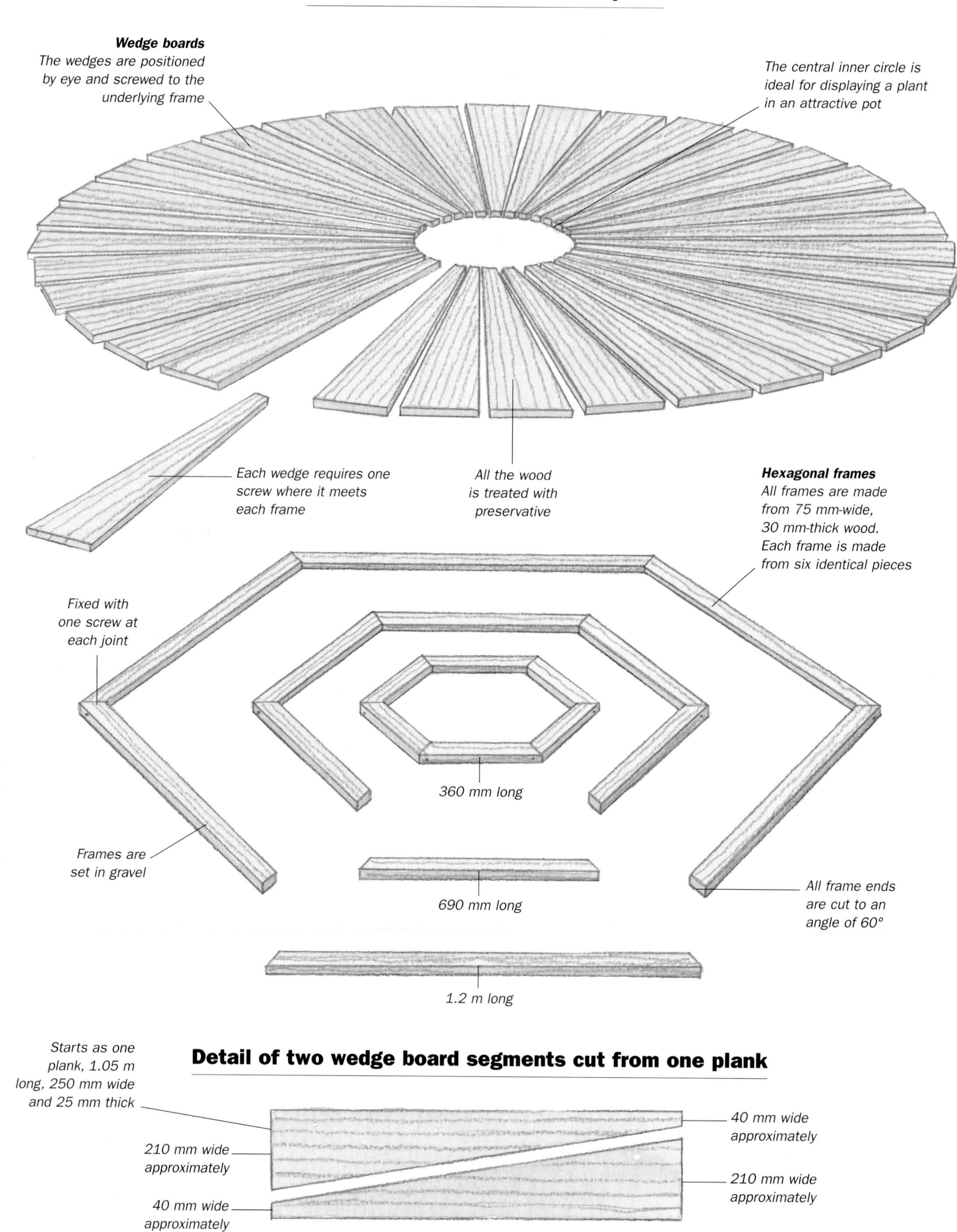
Exploded view of the circular patio
Wedge boards
The wedges are positioned by eye and screwed to the underlying frame
The central inner circle is ideal for displaying a plant in an attractive pot
Each wedge requires one screw where it meets each frame
All the wood is treated with preservative
Hexagonal frames
All frames are made from 75 mm-wide, 30 mm-thick wood. Each frame is made from six identical pieces
Fixed with one screw at each joint
360 mm long
Frames are set in gravel
690 mm long
All frame ends are cut to an angle of 60°
1.2 m long
Starts as one plank, 1.05 m long, 250 mm wide and 25 mm thick
Detail of two wedge board segments cut from one plank
40 mm wide approximately
210 mm wide approximately
210 mm wide approximately
40 mm wide approximately

Making the circular patio

1 Cutting the wedges
Cut the wedge boards into 1.05 m lengths, and mark them off into two parts, as shown on page 40. Use the rip saw to cut them diagonally along their length, so that you have two wedges.

2 Cutting the frames
Mark out the pieces that make the three hexagonal frames. Set the mitre saw to make a 60°/30° cut and saw the wood to length. You need six identical lengths for each hexagon.

3 Screwing the frames
Lay out the pieces for each frame and fix them together with 75 mm screws. Drill pilot holes before screwing so that you do not split the wood.

4 Positioning the frames
Position the three frames, one within another, on the gravel circle. Stand back and look at them from several angles to ensure that they are centred and correctly aligned, and then rake the gravel level with the top of the frames.

5 Fixing the wedges
Set all the wedge-shaped boards in place. Check by eye and make adjustments until you are happy with the arrangement, then fix them with 50 mm screws, using one screw for each board–frame intersection.

Country walk path

This sweeping path looks good in both country and urban settings, and will remain dry, firm and level despite assault by the weather and wear and tear by humans. It is simplicity itself – there is no need to mix concrete for securing posts or to lay plastic sheet to stop the growth of weeds. If you like the notion of a low-key path, and you want to build it quickly and easily, this is a good project to try.

★
Easy

Making time
One weekend for a 6 m path
One day for trenches and cutting wood; one day for construction

Considering the design

The path measures approximately 1 m wide. It is made from two types of post – 500 mm lengths of turned, round-section wood (150 mm in diameter) for the edging, and 500 mm lengths of 100 mm square-section wood for the walkway blocks. Once the edging is in place, the walkway blocks are carefully positioned about 50 mm apart on a base of large-size gravel or shingle, and then the spaces in and around the blocks are topped up with fine pea gravel. The blocks are firm and level, making a good, safe path, which is perfect for all users of the garden and their activities, whether it is strolling, pushing a wheelbarrow, or playing.

Getting started

Use the tape measure, pegs and string to set out the route of the path. Note that you need six round-section posts (1 m long), and three square-section posts (1 m long) for each metre length of path (all posts will be cut in half). Clear the route of plants, and dig out the area to a depth of 200 mm. Establish the position of the two trenches.

You will need

Tools

- Pencil, ruler, tape measure and square
- Spade and shovel
- Two portable workbenches
- Crosscut saw
- Sledgehammer
- Rake
- Wheelbarrow

Materials

(All rough-sawn pieces of pine include excess length for wastage. All the wood is pressure-treated with preservative.)

For 1 m of path, 1 m wide

- Pine: 6 round-section turned posts, 1 m long, 150 mm in diameter (posts)
- Pine: 3 rough-sawn pieces, 1 m long, 100 mm square section (walkway blocks)
- Shingle: 1 wheelbarrow load of large-size shingle
- Pea gravel: 1 wheelbarrow load

Overall dimensions and general notes

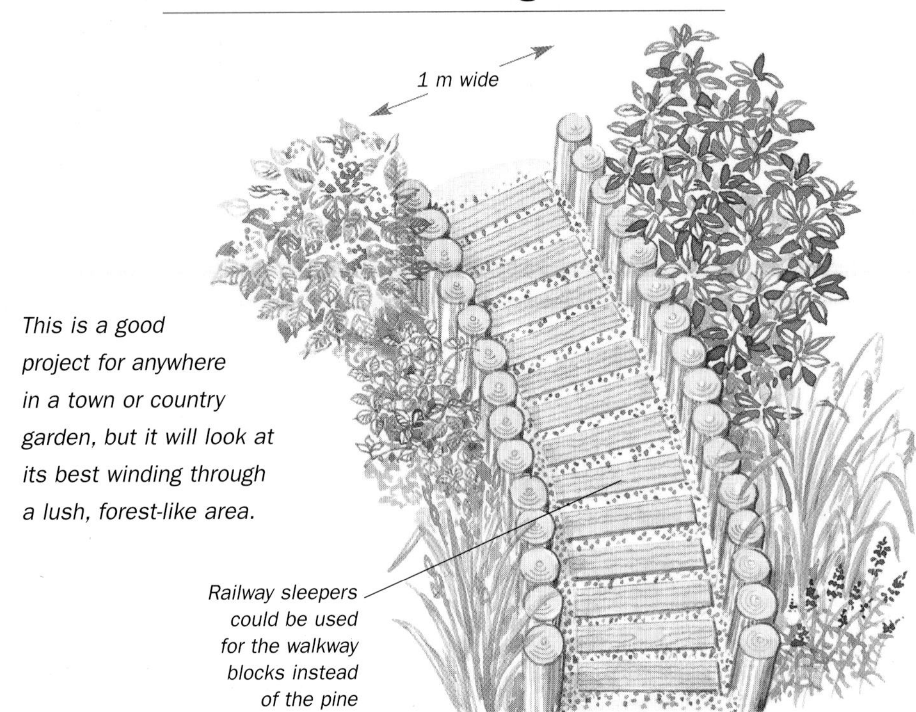
1 m wide
Railway sleepers could be used for the walkway blocks instead of the pine

This is a good project for anywhere in a town or country garden, but it will look at its best winding through a lush, forest-like area.

Exploded view of the country walk path

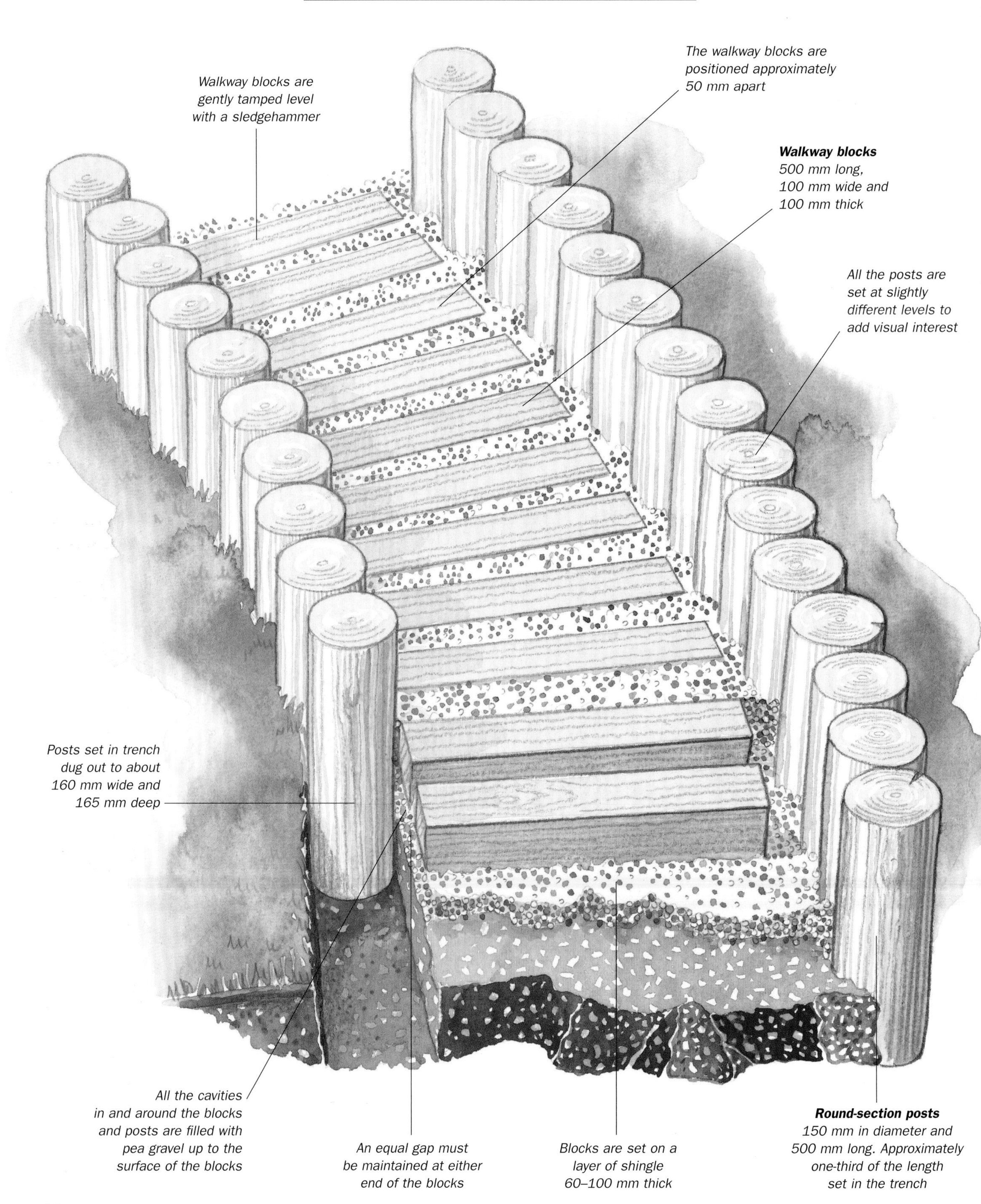
Walkway blocks are gently tamped level with a sledgehammer
The walkway blocks are positioned approximately 50 mm apart
Walkway blocks
500 mm long, 100 mm wide and 100 mm thick
All the posts are set at slightly different levels to add visual interest
Posts set in trench dug out to about 160 mm wide and 165 mm deep
All the cavities in and around the blocks and posts are filled with pea gravel up to the surface of the blocks
An equal gap must be maintained at either end of the blocks
Blocks are set on a layer of shingle 60–100 mm thick
Round-section posts
150 mm in diameter and 500 mm long. Approximately one-third of the length set in the trench

Making the country walk path

1 Setting out the path
Use the tape measure, pegs and string to set out the route of the path. Dig out the area to a depth of 200 mm and a total width of 1 m. Dig a trench along one side of the path about 160 mm wide and 165 mm deep and set in a row of 500 mm-long round-section posts.

2 Completing the posts
Repeat the procedure for the other side of the path. Use the excavated earth to fill around the posts and to generally level the area. Tamp with the sledgehammer.

3 Spreading shingle
Shovel a layer of shingle over the ground between the posts, and then spread and level it with the rake, making it 60–100 mm thick. Tamp the shingle into the earth until it is firm underfoot.

4 Laying the walkway blocks
Take the 500 mm-long walkway blocks of 100 mm square-section wood and place them on the gravel, about 50 mm apart and centred within the width of the path. Adjust them so that they radiate around the curves. Lay the pea gravel.

Japanese bridge

The Japanese bridge allows you to cross over a narrow expanse of water. It is made by spanning the water with two beams 100 mm in diameter, which are covered with 85 mm-wide, 40 mm-thick decking. There is a handrail to one side of the bridge made from bamboo. The handrail posts are bolted directly to the side of one beam, and braced and triangulated to the underside of the other.

Intermediate

Making time
One weekend
One day for the main beams and decking, and one day for the bamboo handrail

Considering the design

The bridge is 3.6 m long – if you wish, you can make it shorter, but for reasons of safety it cannot be made any longer. The handrail is fixed to the posts with mortise and tenon joints, pegs are driven into the sides of the posts, and then the joints are lashed together with cord.

Getting started

Clear the foliage from the bank sides and check that the ground is firm. Inspect the main beams to make sure that they are free from splits and deep knots.

Overall dimensions and general notes

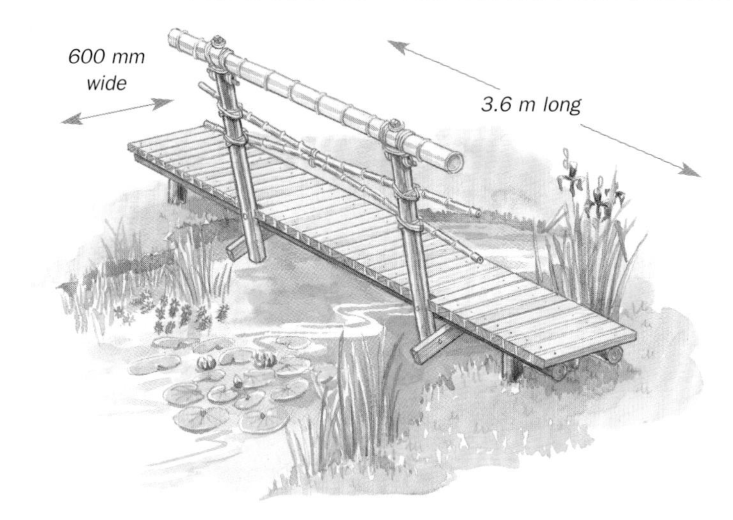
600 mm wide
3.6 m long

We have chosen to build this bridge over a pond, but it would also look good built over a dry "river" of gravel in the Japanese tradition.

You will need

Tools

- Pencil, ruler, tape measure and square
- Pegs and string
- Two portable workbenches
- Crosscut saw
- Spade and sledgehammer
- Claw hammer
- Axe
- Wrench to fit the bolts
- Cordless electric drill with a cross-point screwdriver bit, 25 mm flat bit
- Drill bits to match the sizes of the screws, nails and bolts
- Electric jigsaw
- Electric sander

Materials

(All rough-sawn pieces of pine include excess length for wastage. All the wood is pressure-treated with preservative. Nails are purchased to the nearest kg measure.)

For a bridge 3.6 m long and 600 mm wide

- Pine: 2 round-section pieces, 4 m long, 100 mm in diameter (main beams)
- Pine: 2 round-section pieces, 3 m long, 100 mm in diameter (support piles, handrail posts and rail pegs)
- Pine: 15 rough-sawn pieces, 2 m long, 85 mm wide and 40 mm thick (decking and bracing)
- Pine: 1 rough-sawn piece, 4 m long, 30 mm wide and 20 mm thick (temporary batten)
- Bamboo: 1 piece, 3 m long, 100 mm in diameter (handrail)
- Bamboo: 2 pieces, 3 m long (secondary rails)
- Cord: 20 m of heavy-duty natural fibre cord (for binding the joints)
- Nails: 1 kg of 150 mm x 6 mm (for fixing the main beams to the piles)
- Nails: 2 kg of 125 mm x 5.6 mm (for fixing the decking to the beams)
- Zinc-plated, countersunk cross-headed screws: 50 x 90 mm no. 10
- Coach bolts: 2 x 250 mm long, with nuts and washers to fit

Exploded view of the Japanese bridge

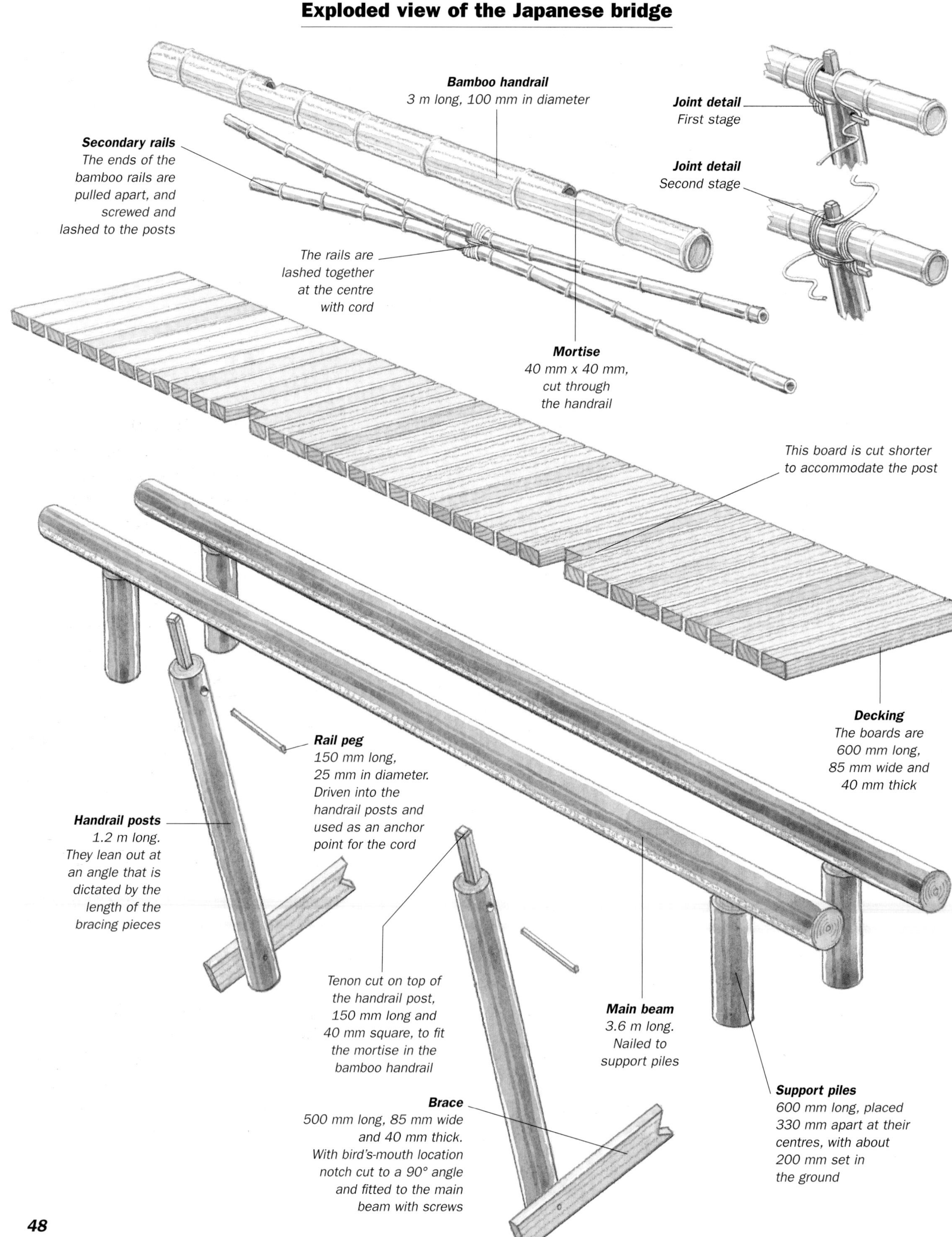
Bamboo handrail
3 m long, 100 mm in diameter
Joint detail
First stage
Joint detail
Second stage
Secondary rails
The ends of the bamboo rails are pulled apart, and screwed and lashed to the posts
The rails are lashed together at the centre with cord
Mortise
40 mm x 40 mm, cut through the handrail
This board is cut shorter to accommodate the post
Decking
The boards are 600 mm long, 85 mm wide and 40 mm thick
Rail peg
150 mm long, 25 mm in diameter. Driven into the handrail posts and used as an anchor point for the cord
Handrail posts
1.2 m long. They lean out at an angle that is dictated by the length of the bracing pieces
Tenon cut on top of the handrail post, 150 mm long and 40 mm square, to fit the mortise in the bamboo handrail
Main beam
3.6 m long. Nailed to support piles
Support piles
600 mm long, placed 330 mm apart at their centres, with about 200 mm set in the ground
Brace
500 mm long, 85 mm wide and 40 mm thick. With bird's-mouth location notch cut to a 90° angle and fitted to the main beam with screws

Making the Japanese bridge

1 Fixing the main beams

Cut four 600 mm-long support piles and dig them in at either side of the water, so that they are level and 330 mm apart at their centres, and 400 mm above ground level. Nail the main beams directly to the top of the posts with 150 mm nails.

2 Fixing the decking

Centre and nail one 600 mm-long decking board at either end of the main beams. Nail the temporary batten to the ends of the boards to act as a guide, and then nail all the decking boards in place. Leave two gaps for the handrail posts. Use 125 mm nails throughout.

3 Making the handrail

Cut the handrail posts to length. Use the saw and axe to cut tenons 150 mm long and 40 mm square on what will be the top end of each post. Use coach bolts to bolt the handrail posts securely to the main beams (see illustration, step 4).

4 Bracing

Cut the two braces to length. Cut a right-angled bird's-mouth location notch on one end of each brace. Screw the braces between the end of the posts and the underside of the beams.

5 Fixing the handrail

Mark in the position of the mortise holes on the bamboo handrail, and cut them out with the drill and jigsaw. Sit the handrail on the tenons. Drill holes and bang in the rail pegs, and lash the joints with the cord.

6 Adding secondary rails

Lash the two bamboo secondary rails together at the centre, and drill and screw them to the posts. Finally, bind over the screws with the cord. Sand everything to a good finish.

Planter tubs

Intermediate

Making time
One weekend
One day for building the frames and cutting the pickets, and one day for putting together

Planter tubs make a great addition to any outdoor space. They can be filled with an ever-changing display to inject colour into the garden throughout the year. Wood has an instant appeal when combined with plants – as a natural material, it instantly harmonizes. These planters are built with variously cut and curved pickets, in folksy style, or with square pickets topped with a mitred frame, for a clean, modern look.

Considering the design

Each of the three planters is built from two horizontal frames, with pickets fixed vertically to the outside so that the frames are hidden from view.

We have made a large planter with square pickets, trimmed on top with a decorative mitred frame, a medium planter with rounded pickets, and a small planter with pointed pickets. If you follow our suggestions exactly, this assortment of styles will provide an eclectic look for your patio. Alternatively, you can opt for a more traditional look and make a set of three planters to the same design.

The frames are built from battens, 35 mm wide and 20 mm thick, the pickets are cut from boards, 70 mm wide and 16 mm thick, and the right-angled corner fillet pieces are cut from wood 60 mm wide and 30 mm thick.

Getting started

If you want to vary the design, shape, size and quantity of the planters, sit down with a pencil and paper and work out the materials, and then order the wood accordingly. You have to decide on the design of the top, the total height, and the length and width of the sides.

Overall dimensions and general notes

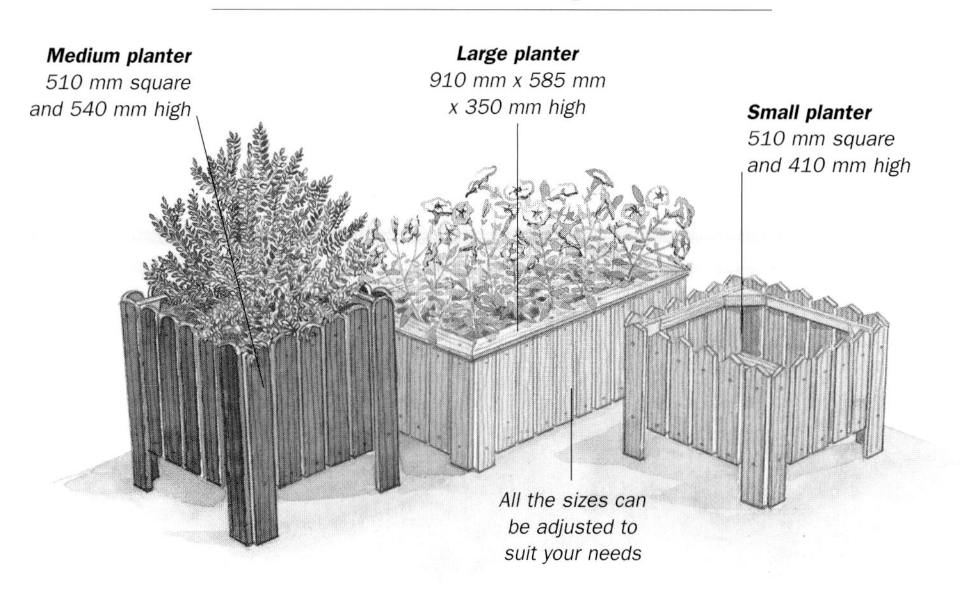
Medium planter
510 mm square
and 540 mm high
Large planter
910 mm x 585 mm
x 350 mm high
Small planter
510 mm square
and 410 mm high
All the sizes can
be adjusted to
suit your needs

Planter tubs can brighten up an area of decking, a patio, or a balcony garden. They can be filled directly with earth; alternatively, plants in pots can be arranged in them.

You will need

Tools

- Pencil, ruler, compass, tape measure, bevel gauge and square
- Two portable workbenches
- Crosscut saw
- Cordless electric drill with a cross-point screwdriver bit
- Drill bits to match the sizes of the screws
- Claw hammer
- Electric jigsaw and electric sander

Materials

(All rough-sawn pieces of pine include excess length for wastage. All the wood is pressure-treated with preservative. Make sure this is of a type that is not harmful to plants.)

For a large, medium and small planter tub

- Pine: 5 rough-sawn pieces, 3 m long, 35 mm wide and 20 mm thick (frames)
- Pine: 1 rough-sawn piece, 2 m long, 60 mm wide and 30 mm thick (corner fillets)
- Pine: 15 rough-sawn pieces, 3 m long, 70 mm wide and 16 mm thick (pickets, decorative mitred frame, floorboards)
- Zinc-plated, countersunk cross-headed screws: 200 x 30 mm no. 8, 200 x 50 mm no. 8
- Galvanized nails: 2 kg of 40 mm-long nails

Exploded view of the large planter tub

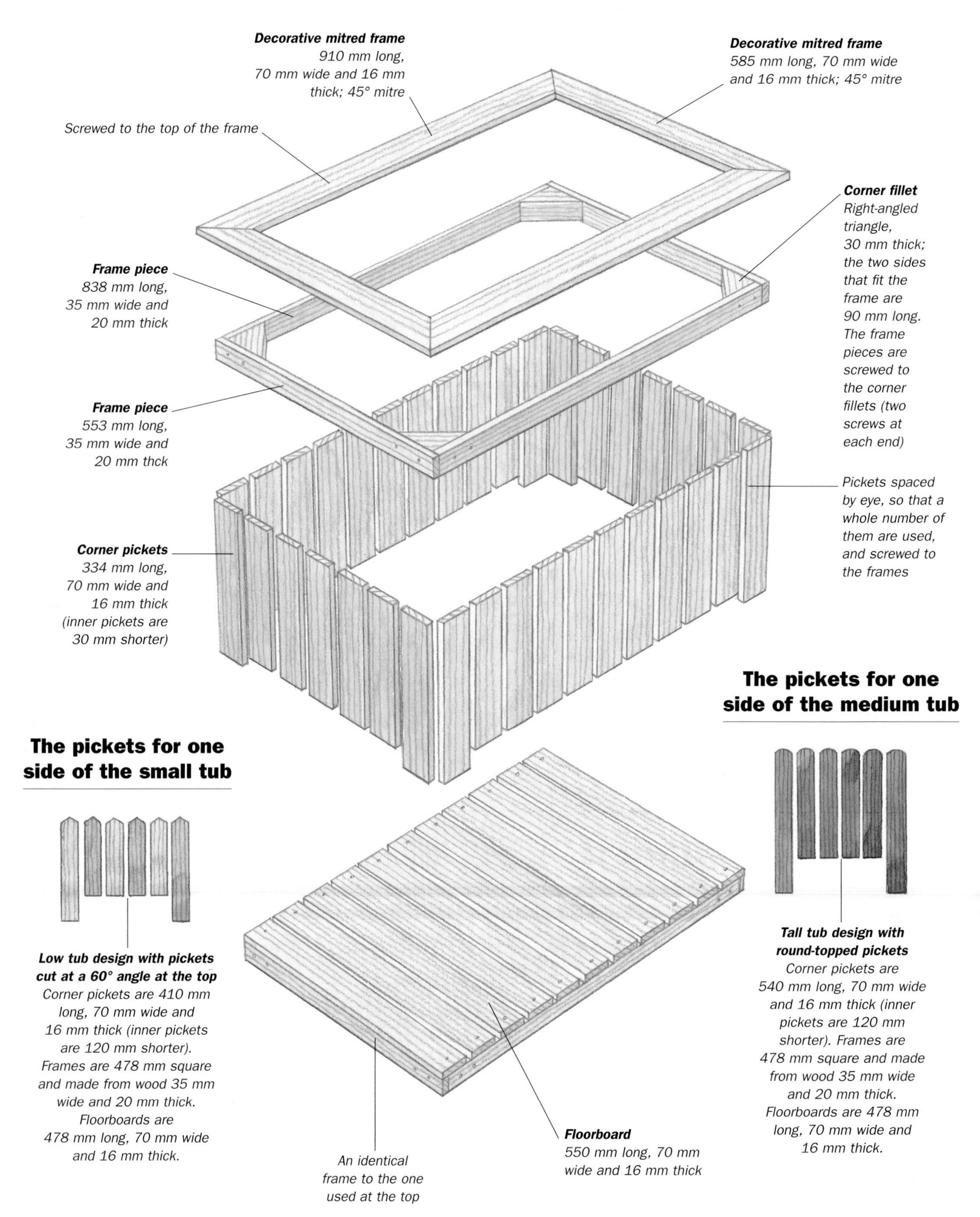
Decorative mitred frame
910 mm long,
70 mm wide and 16 mm
thick; 45° mitre
Decorative mitred frame
585 mm long, 70 mm wide
and 16 mm thick; 45° mitre
Screwed to the top of the frame
Corner fillet
Right-angled
triangle,
30 mm thick;
the two sides
that fit the
frame are
90 mm long.
The frame
pieces are
screwed to
the corner
fillets (two
screws at
each end)
Frame piece
838 mm long,
35 mm wide and
20 mm thick
Frame piece
553 mm long,
35 mm wide and
20 mm thck
Pickets spaced
by eye, so that a
whole number of
them are used,
and screwed to
the frames
Corner pickets
334 mm long,
70 mm wide and
16 mm thick
(inner pickets are
30 mm shorter)
An identical
frame to the one
used at the top
Floorboard
550 mm long, 70 mm
wide and 16 mm thick

The pickets for one side of the small tub

Low tub design with pickets cut at a 60° angle at the top
Corner pickets are 410 mm long, 70 mm wide and 16 mm thick (inner pickets are 120 mm shorter). Frames are 478 mm square and made from wood 35 mm wide and 20 mm thick. Floorboards are 478 mm long, 70 mm wide and 16 mm thick.

The pickets for one side of the medium tub

Tall tub design with round-topped pickets
Corner pickets are 540 mm long, 70 mm wide and 16 mm thick (inner pickets are 120 mm shorter). Frames are 478 mm square and made from wood 35 mm wide and 20 mm thick. Floorboards are 478 mm long, 70 mm wide and 16 mm thick.

Making the planter tubs

1 Constructing the frames
Cut the component parts for the frames, and the corner fillets, to length. Set the parts together, drill pilot holes and fix them with 50 mm screws. Make two frames for each tub.

2 Fixing the corner pickets
Cut the corner pickets to length and screw them to the corners of the top frame with 30 mm screws. Note how the extended length of the corner pickets creates the leg feature.

3 Making the floor
Cut the floorboards to length and nail them to the bottom frame. Drill pilot holes for the nails, to avoid splitting the wood. Space the floorboards by eye so that you use a complete number to cover the frame.

4 Putting together
Screw the bottom frame to the corner pickets. Check that the structure is square and screw all the inner pickets in place on both frames. Use 30 mm screws throughout. Space the pickets by eye so that you use a complete number to cover each side of the planter.

5 Decorative frame for large tub
The large planter has a decorative mitred frame on the top. Cut pieces of wood to fit both the length and width of the tub. Mitre the corners with the jigsaw and screw the resultant frame to the top of the tub with 30 mm screws, to cover the tops of the pickets.

6 Shaped pickets
If you are going to fit shaped pickets (curved for the medium planter and pointed for the small planter), draw curves or mark centre points on the pickets with the compass. Use the jigsaw to fret out the profile. Finally, sand all the planters to a good finish.

Chequerboard decking patio

Intermediate

Making time
One weekend
One day for building the gridded frame, and the rest of the time for fitting the decking

The good thing about the chequerboard patio is its flexibility. The design allows it to be square, rectilinear, castellated, or just about any shape that inspires you, as long as the sum total shape can be made up from a square grid. The chequerboard grid construction also permits you to miss out selected squares in order to plant flowers, or site a bench seat, sandpit, water feature, tree or area of soft grass.

Considering the design

The frame is set face down on a bed of gravel. It is made up of eight joists spaced 365 mm apart in one direction, topped by a second layer set at right angles in the other direction. The resulting grid is secured and held square by screwing 300 mm-long filler pieces to the bottom layer. Finally, the decking boards are simply screwed to the gridded frame.

The techniques are straightforward – there are no difficult-to-use tools involved or complex jointing to do – but this very simplicity calls for extra care and effort at the designing and planning stage in order to get good results.

Getting started

Look at your site and decide whether you want the patio to follow the dimensions of the project (2.62 m square). Use a tape measure, pegs and string to mark it out. Transfer the shape to gridded paper, so that the joists are 365 mm apart at their centres. Work out how much wood is needed if dimensions have altered.

Overall dimensions and general notes

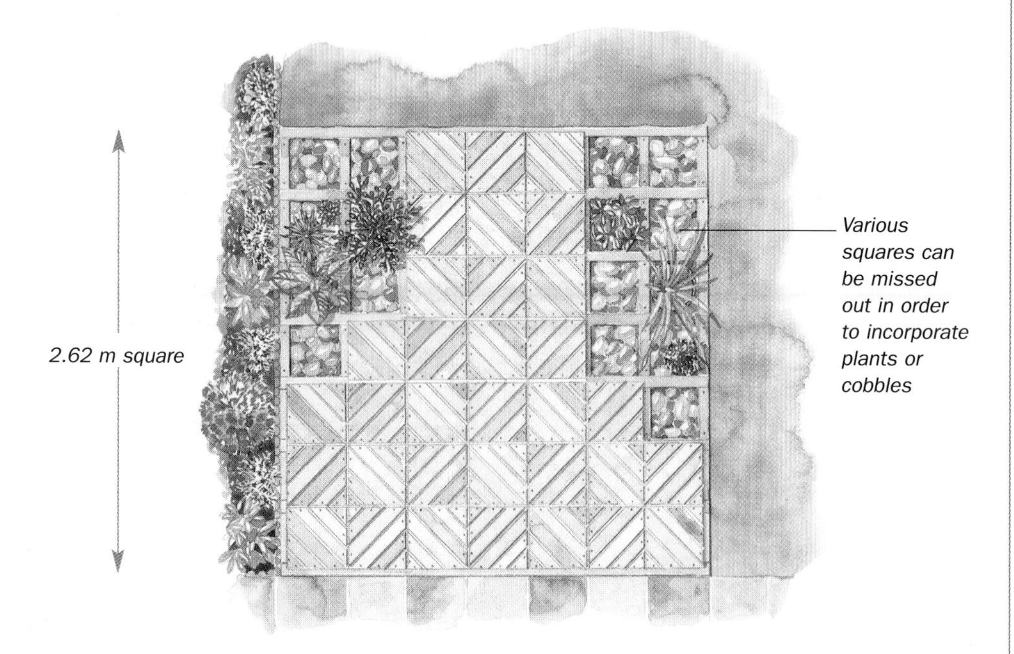
2.62 m square
Various squares can be missed out in order to incorporate plants or cobbles

This is an excellent project when space is limited. The patio can also be used to reduce the monotony of a large area of lawn. It could even be painted in bold colours.

You will need

Tools

- ✓ Pencil, ruler, tape measure, square, bevel gauge, gridded paper
- ✓ Pegs and string
- ✓ Spade and wheelbarrow
- ✓ Cordless electric drill with a cross-point screwdriver bit
- ✓ Drill bits to match the sizes of the screws
- ✓ Crosscut saw
- ✓ Two portable workbenches
- ✓ Electric sander
- ✓ Paintbrush

Materials

(All rough-sawn pieces of pine include excess length for wastage. All the wood is pressure-treated with preservative.)

For a patio 2.62 m square

- ✓ Pine: 24 rough-sawn pieces, 3 m long, 65 mm wide and 30 mm thick (frame and filler pieces)
- ✓ Pine: 33 rough-sawn pieces, 3 m long, 75 mm wide and 16 mm thick (decking boards)
- ✓ Zinc-plated, countersunk cross-headed screws: 100 x 55 mm no. 8, 200 x 35 mm no. 8
- ✓ Woven plastic sheeting: 3 m x 3 m
- ✓ Gravel: 10 wheelbarrow loads
- ✓ Exterior-grade decking paint

Exploded view of the chequerboard decking patio

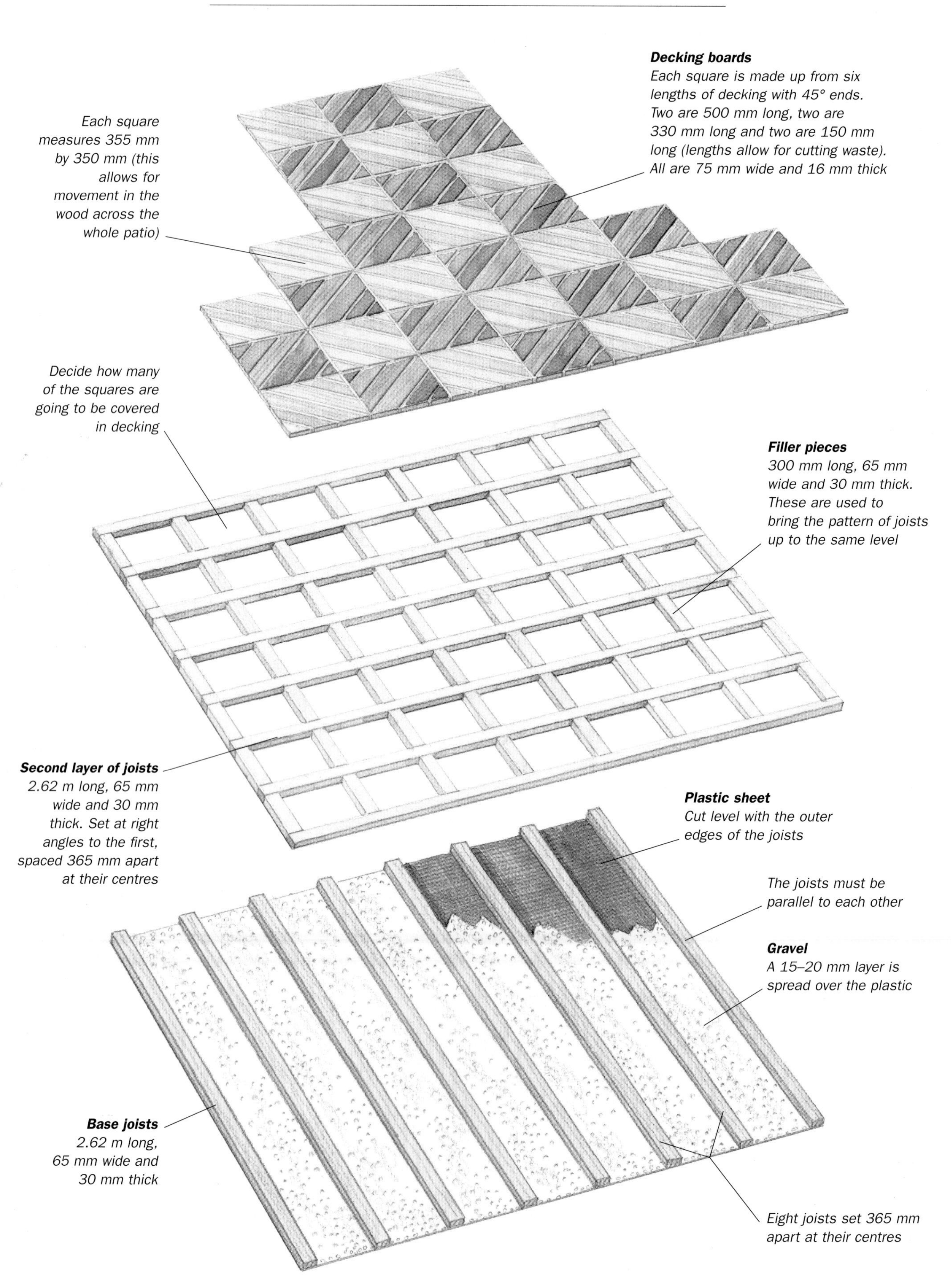
Decking boards
Each square is made up from six lengths of decking with 45° ends. Two are 500 mm long, two are 330 mm long and two are 150 mm long (lengths allow for cutting waste). All are 75 mm wide and 16 mm thick
Each square measures 355 mm by 350 mm (this allows for movement in the wood across the whole patio)
Decide how many of the squares are going to be covered in decking
Filler pieces
300 mm long, 65 mm wide and 30 mm thick. These are used to bring the pattern of joists up to the same level
Second layer of joists
2.62 m long, 65 mm wide and 30 mm thick. Set at right angles to the first, spaced 365 mm apart at their centres
Plastic sheet
Cut level with the outer edges of the joists
The joists must be parallel to each other
Gravel
A 15–20 mm layer is spread over the plastic
Base joists
2.62 m long, 65 mm wide and 30 mm thick
Eight joists set 365 mm apart at their centres

Making the chequerboard decking patio

1 Placing the base joists
Spread the plastic sheeting over the site and cover it with a 15–20 mm layer of washed gravel. Take eight joists and position them side by side, so that they are parallel to each other and set 365 mm apart at the centres.

2 Placing the second layer
Take eight more joists and position them on top of the base joists in the manner just described, so that they are side by side in a grid pattern and set 365 mm apart at the centres. Run 55 mm screws down through the intersections to fix the layers together.

3 Adding filler pieces
Cut 300 mm lengths of the 65 mm x 30 mm wood to make filler pieces for the grid. Place these over the visible parts of the first layer of joists to bring them up to the level of the second layer. Screw the filler pieces in place with 55 mm screws.

4 Cutting the decking
Look at the gridded frame, decide on the edge profile and where you want the planting holes to occur, and calculate how many squares you need to cover with decking. Cut and mitre six lengths of decking board (see page 56 for measurements) for each square.

5 Fitting the decking
Set the decking boards on the frame in the pattern and configuration that you have planned, and fix them in place with 35 mm screws. Sand the structure. Finally, thin the paint with water to create a colourwash, and brush on.

Garden decking with steps

Intermediate

Making time
Two weekends
One day for casting the foot pads, two days for building the decking, one day for finishing

Decking is great for a sloping site. You don't have the task of moving vast quantities of earth to create a level area, because you simply float the decking over the problem by adjusting the length of the legs to accommodate the slope of the ground. Once the decking is in place, you will suddenly be able to see the garden in a whole new light – the experience is rather like sitting on a flying carpet.

Considering the design

This large, square platform has a post at each corner, and a small flight of steps centred on one side. The platform frame is bolted directly to the legs, which are socketed into concrete pads.

Getting started

Measure out the site, clear the ground and establish where the concrete pads will go. Decide where you want the steps to be fixed. Arrange the wood in ordered stacks, and recruit friends for future help at the levelling stage, when you will have to bolt the frame to the legs.

Overall dimensions and general notes

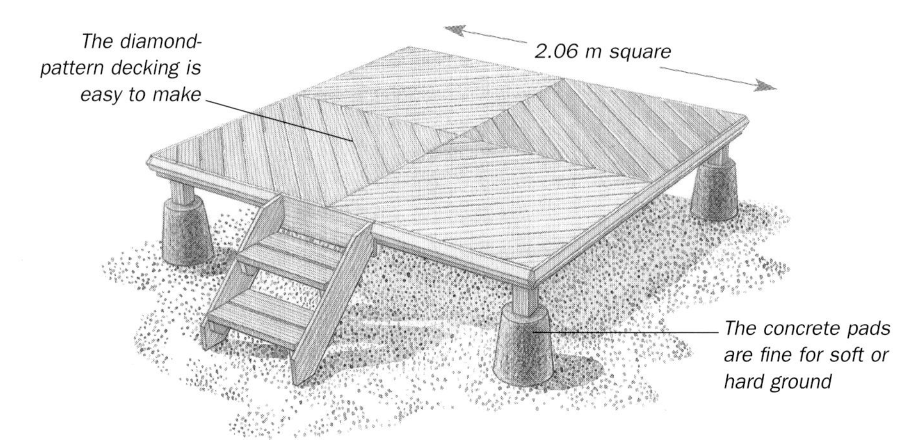
The diamond-pattern decking is easy to make
2.06 m square
The concrete pads are fine for soft or hard ground

This decking is suitable for a level or sloping site (the lengths of the posts are varied accordingly) and is ideal for sunbathing or as the site for a table and a couple of chairs.

You will need

Tools

- Pencil, ruler, tape measure, marking gauge and square
- Two portable workbenches
- Crosscut saw, spade, shovel
- Wheelbarrow, bucket, spirit level
- Cordless electric drill with a cross-point screwdriver bit
- Drill bits to match the sizes of the nails, screws and bolts
- Claw hammer, ratchet spanner
- Electric sander

Materials

(All pieces of rough-sawn wood include excess length for wastage. All the wood is pressure-treated with preservative.)

For decking 2.06 m square and about 500 mm high

- Pine: 1 rough-sawn piece, 2 m long, 75 mm square section (leg posts, support blocks and moulding blocks)
- Pine: 10 rough-sawn pieces, 2 m long, 70 mm wide and 40 mm thick (framework and joists)
- Pine: 25 pieces of planed, grooved decking boards, 2 m long, 95 mm wide and 25 mm thick (floor)
- Pine: 4 pieces of rough-sawn, pitch-top fence capping, 2 m long, 65 mm wide and 30 mm thick (frame trim)
- Pine: 1 rough-sawn piece, 3 m long, 150 mm wide, 20 mm thick (stringers)
- Pine: grooved decking, 3 m long, 120 mm wide, 35 mm thick (treads)
- Pine: 1 rough-sawn piece, 1 m long, 65 mm wide, 30 mm thick (brackets)
- Zinc-plated coach bolts with washers and nuts to fit: 8 x 150 mm
- Zinc-plated, countersunk cross-headed screws: 300 x 100 mm no. 8, 300 x 75 mm no. 10, 50 x 50 mm no. 8
- Steel nails: 1 kg, 125 mm x 5.6 mm
- Concrete: 1 part (25 kg) cement, 2 parts (50 kg) sharp sand, 3 parts (75 kg) aggregate
- Six plastic flowerpots: about 250 mm high, 235 mm wide at the rim, and 175 mm wide at the base
- Sticky tape

Exploded view of the garden decking with steps

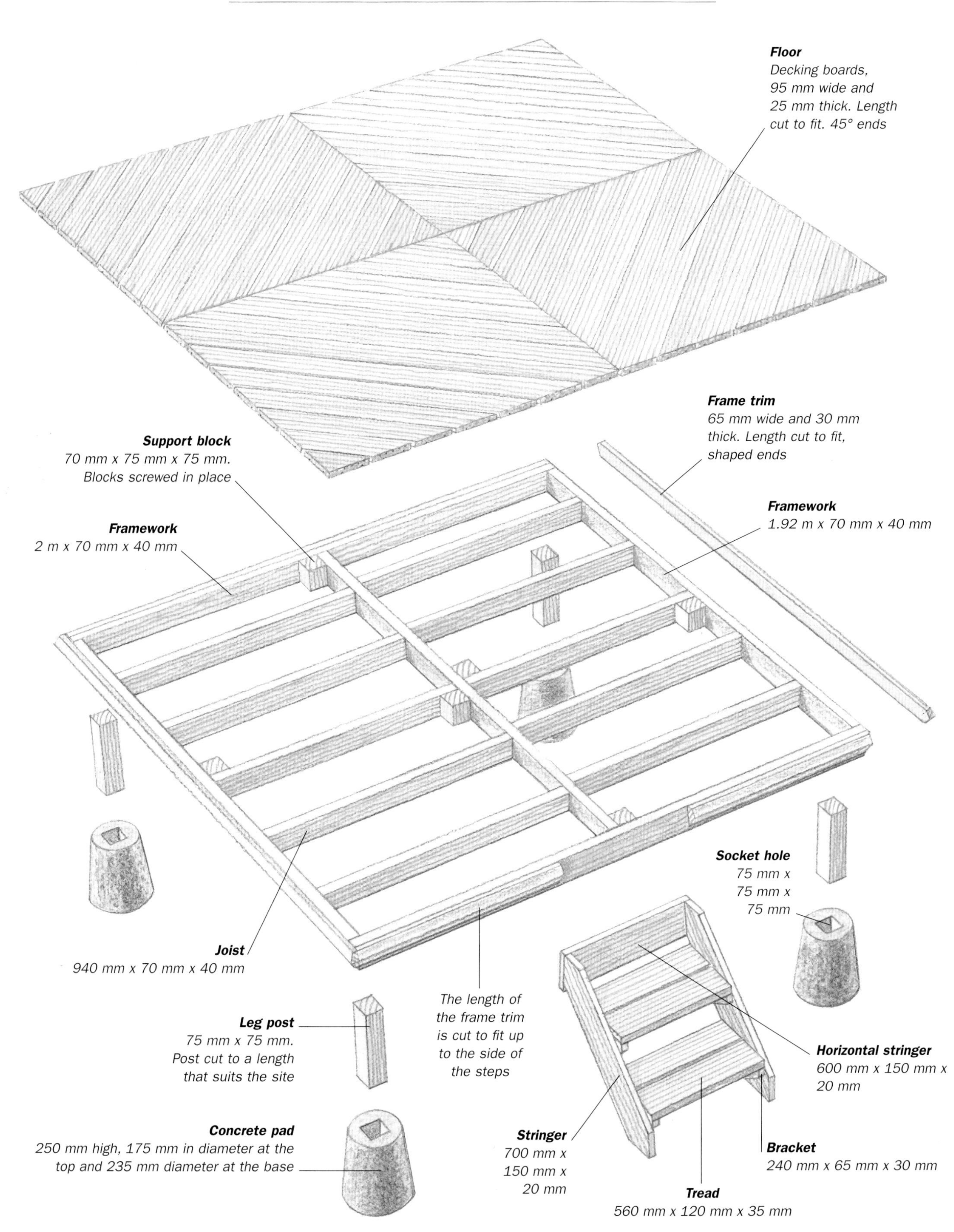
Floor
Decking boards, 95 mm wide and 25 mm thick. Length cut to fit. 45° ends
Frame trim
65 mm wide and 30 mm thick. Length cut to fit, shaped ends
Support block
70 mm x 75 mm x 75 mm. Blocks screwed in place
Framework
1.92 m x 70 mm x 40 mm
Framework
2 m x 70 mm x 40 mm
Socket hole
75 mm x 75 mm x 75 mm
Joist
940 mm x 70 mm x 40 mm
Leg post
75 mm x 75 mm. Post cut to a length that suits the site
The length of the frame trim is cut to fit up to the side of the steps
Horizontal stringer
600 mm x 150 mm x 20 mm
Concrete pad
250 mm high, 175 mm in diameter at the top and 235 mm diameter at the base
Stringer
700 mm x 150 mm x 20 mm
Bracket
240 mm x 65 mm x 30 mm
Tread
560 mm x 120 mm x 35 mm

Making the garden decking with steps

1 Making the concrete pads
Cut six 75 mm-long moulding blocks from the 75 mm-square wood and set one in the bottom of each plastic flowerpot. Cover the hole at the bottom with sticky tape and fill the pots with concrete. (Two extra pots have been allowed in case of mistakes.)

2 Making the framework
Cut the wood for the framework (see page 60). Build a frame 2 m square, with a central joist crossing between opposite sides. Screw on 75 mm-square support blocks (see diagram) to strengthen the primary T-junction joints. Use 100 mm screws throughout.

3 Fixing the secondary joists
Set the secondary joists in place in each quarter of the frame – so that they are a tight wedge fit – and spike them in place with nails. Ease the concrete foot pads out of the flowerpots and remove the wood to reveal the sockets.

4 Setting the frame on its legs
With friends to help, cut one post for each leg, and push them into the sockets in the concrete pads. Bolt the legs inside the corners of the frame, and check that the frame is level. Saw the top of the leg posts level with the top edge of the frame.

5 Making the steps
Construct the steps from the treads, stringers and brackets, and fix to the frame, using 75 mm screws. Cut the frame trim to fit, shaping the ends to create neat corners to cover the sawn ends of the decking. Screw it in place on the frame with 50 mm screws.

6 Making the floor
Cut the decking boards for the floor to size and screw them to the top surface of the joists with 75 mm screws. Finally, use the sander to rub all the sawn ends to a slightly rounded, splinter-free finish.

Bench seat and safety rail

Intermediate

Making time
Two weekends
Two days for the bench seat and two days for the rail

If you fancy having a bench seat to put on an area of decking, try this project. Because it is potentially dangerous if a bench is placed near the edge of the decking, we have designed a rail to act as a safety barrier. The rail and baluster design can easily be modified to match the style of existing decking. If you wish, the bench can be bolted to both the decking and the rail to make an extra-strong structure.

Considering the design

Both items have been designed so that they can be made from off-the-shelf sections. In many of our projects, function follows form, meaning that the way the design looks in the garden is as least as important as the way the project functions, so that it doesn't matter too much if you make changes to the design.

However in this instance, function is all-important, and both the bench and rail must be safe before any other considerations. (This is especially true for rails. They must be just the right height, and fitted so that they can stand a fair amount of wear and tear.) So you must think very carefully before you make any major structural changes to the designs.

Finally, we used exterior-grade paint to add an attractive finish to the design.

Getting started

Look at your decking and consider the best site for the bench and rail. The weight of the bench must be equally distributed over the joists of the decking, and the rail must be bolted to one or more of the primary joists. We have fixed rails to two sides of a relatively low decking patio, but if you have an area of decking that is raised high off the ground, it is best to fit rails on all sides.

Overall dimensions and general notes

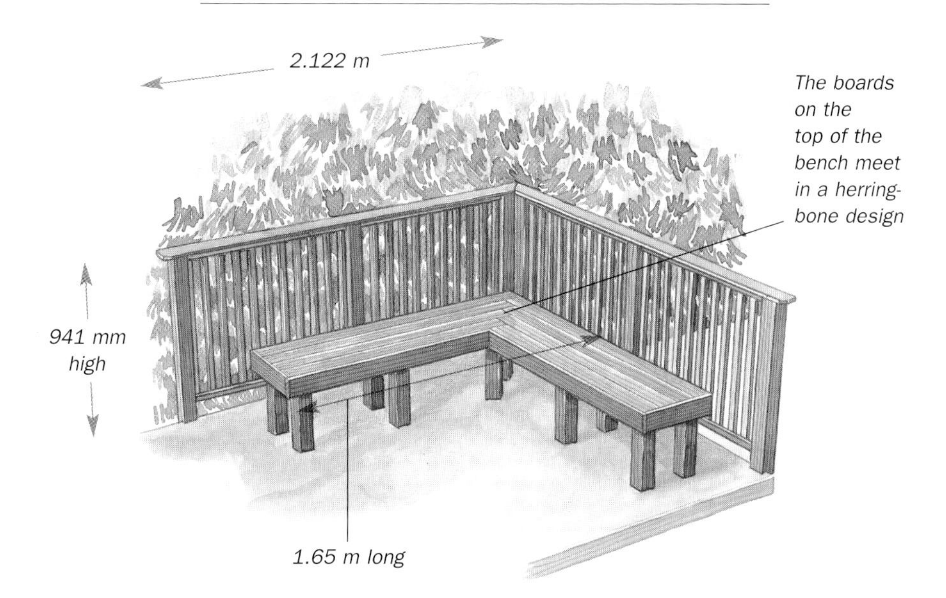
2.122 m
The boards on the top of the bench meet in a herring-bone design
941 mm high
1.65 m long

This bench and safety rail combination is suitable for adding to a wide range of decking patios, and is simple to build. It makes a safe place for all the family to relax.

You will need

Tools

- Pencil, ruler, tape measure, square
- Two portable workbenches
- Crosscut saw
- Cordless electric drill with a cross-point screwdriver bit
- Drill bits to match the sizes of the screws and bolts
- Ratchet wrench and spirit level
- Electric sander

Materials

(All rough-sawn pine includes excess length for wastage. All wood is pressure-treated with preservative.)

For a bench with sides 1.65 m long; rails 2.122 m long, 941 mm high

- Pine: 3 rough-sawn pieces, 2 m long, 75 mm square section (posts and bench legs)
- Pine: 26 rough-sawn pieces, 2 m long, 40 mm wide and 20 mm thick (balusters and baluster rails)
- Pine: 7 rough-sawn pieces, 3 m long, 100 mm wide and 20 mm thick (rails, seat boards, fascia)
- Pine: 1 rough-sawn piece, 3 m long, 80 mm wide and 35 mm thick (under-seat stretcher)
- Zinc-plated, countersunk cross-headed screws: 50 x 90 mm no. 10, 100 x 35 mm no. 8
- Coach bolts: 12 x 150 mm long, with nuts and washers to fit

Exploded view of the bench seat and safety rail

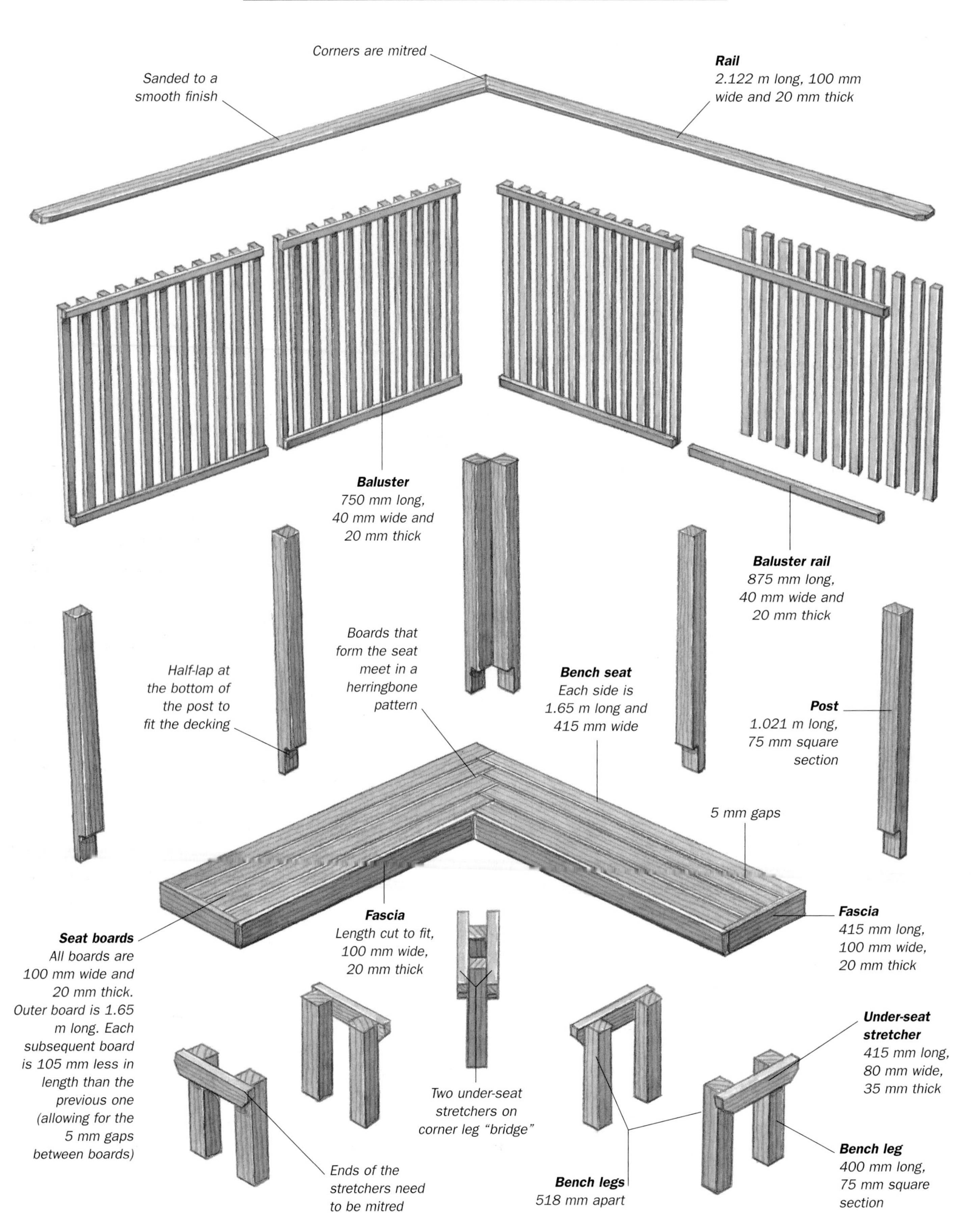

Corners are mitred
Sanded to a smooth finish
Rail
2.122 m long, 100 mm wide and 20 mm thick
Baluster
750 mm long, 40 mm wide and 20 mm thick
Baluster rail
875 mm long, 40 mm wide and 20 mm thick
Half-lap at the bottom of the post to fit the decking
Boards that form the seat meet in a herringbone pattern
Bench seat
Each side is 1.65 m long and 415 mm wide
Post
1.021 m long, 75 mm square section
5 mm gaps
Fascia
Length cut to fit, 100 mm wide, 20 mm thick
Fascia
415 mm long, 100 mm wide, 20 mm thick
Seat boards
All boards are 100 mm wide and 20 mm thick. Outer board is 1.65 m long. Each subsequent board is 105 mm less in length than the previous one (allowing for the 5 mm gaps between boards)
Two under-seat stretchers on corner leg "bridge"
Under-seat stretcher
415 mm long, 80 mm wide, 35 mm thick
Ends of the stretchers need to be mitred
Bench legs
518 mm apart
Bench leg
400 mm long, 75 mm square section

Making the bench seat and safety rail

1 Cutting the posts
Cut the six posts for the uprights of the safety rail assembly to length, cutting half-laps on one end to fit the ring joist (outer frame) of the existing decking. Set the posts in position.

2 Fixing the posts and rails
Fix the posts to the decking joists using 90 mm screws and 150 mm coach bolts. Use the spirit level to ensure that the posts are upright. Cut the two rails to length, complete with a 45° mitre at the corner, and screw them to the top of the posts with 90 mm screws.

3 Building the balusters
With the baluster rails and balusters, build four frames. Set them in place between the posts, and screw them in position. Run screws down through the rails and into the top of the baluster frames. Use 90 mm screws throughout.

4 Making the bench legs
Build the five "bridge" frames that make the legs of the bench – the four frames for the straight sides, and the double-top frame for the corner of the bench. Use 90 mm screws throughout.

5 Fixing the bench legs and seat
Set the leg "bridge" frames in place on the decking and link them with the seat boards, using 35 mm screws. Note the way the boards are cut and fixed in a herringbone pattern at the corner.

6 Making a fascia
Cap the front edges and ends of the bench with a fascia that runs flush to the surface of the bench. Use 35 mm screws throughout. Finally, sand everything to a good finish.

Tree ring seat

Advanced

Making time
One weekend
One day for making the parts and one day for assembling the seat around the tree

When I was a child I used to love sitting on an old ring seat under an apple tree in my grandparents' orchard. I can picture the scene now – the trunk of the old tree to my back, a dappled canopy of leaves overhead, and long, lush grass underfoot. If you have a suitable small tree, this seat will come into its own in summer when you can use it to relax under the leafy shade. Remember to allow room for the trunk to grow.

Considering the design

The seat is based on a hexagon and built in easy-to-make sections. The idea is that the sections can be prepared in a convenient location – perhaps in the workshop or the garage – and then put together around your chosen tree.

The seat stands about 420 mm above ground level. The legs are built from 50 mm-wide, 32 mm-thick sections, and each pair of legs is bridged with top stretchers. These leg units are in turn joined to each other with linking stretchers, making the hexagonal design seen in plan view. The construction is topped with a seat made from 94 mm-wide grooved decking boards, and the front edge of the seat is trimmed with a decorative wavy frieze or apron.

Getting started

Search out an appropriate tree, and decide whether or not the project needs to be modified according to the dimensions of the trunk. Cut all the wood to length, tidy up the sawn ends with sandpaper, and stack it in readiness. Set out the two workbenches in your chosen working area and generally arrange your tools for the task ahead.

Overall dimensions and general notes

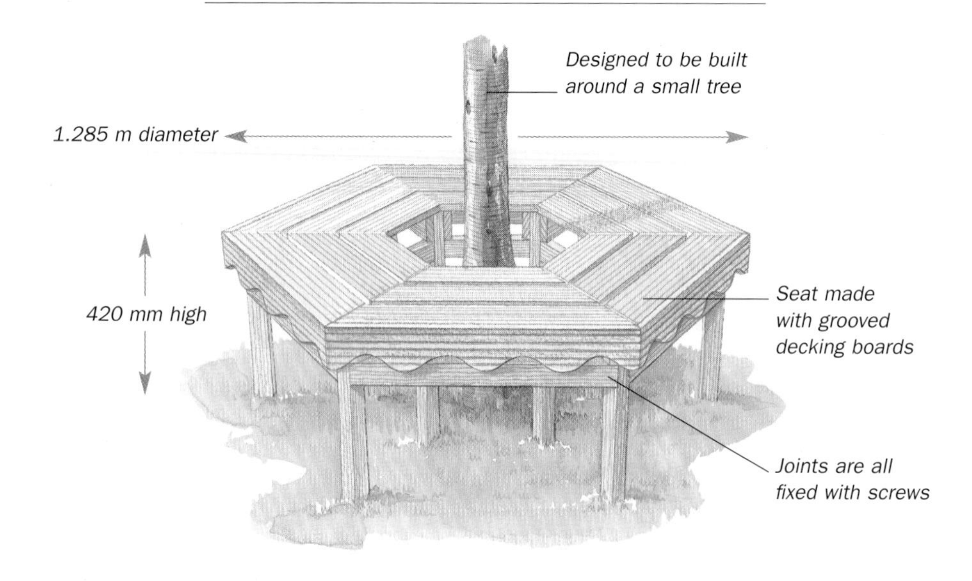
Designed to be built around a small tree
1.285 m diameter
420 mm high
Seat made with grooved decking boards
Joints are all fixed with screws

This is a traditional design for freestanding seating to fit around a tree, and it works best on a level site. It could be used to complement the Patio with Sandpit on page 76.

You will need

Tools

- Pencil, ruler, tape measure, square and tracing paper
- Two portable workbenches
- Crosscut saw
- Cordless electric drill
- Drill bits to match the screw size
- Hand cross-point screwdriver
- Electric jigsaw and electric sander
- Pair of clamps

Materials

(All rough-sawn pine includes excess length for wastage. All the wood is pressure-treated with preservative.)

For a seat 1.285 m in diameter

- Pine: 2 rough-sawn pieces, 3 m long, 50 mm wide and 32 mm thick (legs)
- Pine: 2 rough-sawn pieces, 3 m long, 75 mm wide and 20 mm thick (top stretchers)
- Pine: 2 rough-sawn pieces, 3 m long, 50 mm wide and 37 mm thick (linking stretchers)
- Pine: 2 pieces planed and grooved decking, 3 m long, 94 mm wide, 20 mm thick (decorative frieze)
- Pine: 3 pieces planed and grooved decking, 3 m long, 94 mm wide and 20 mm thick (seating boards)
- Zinc-plated, countersunk cross-headed screws: 200 x 55 mm no. 8

Exploded view of the tree ring seat

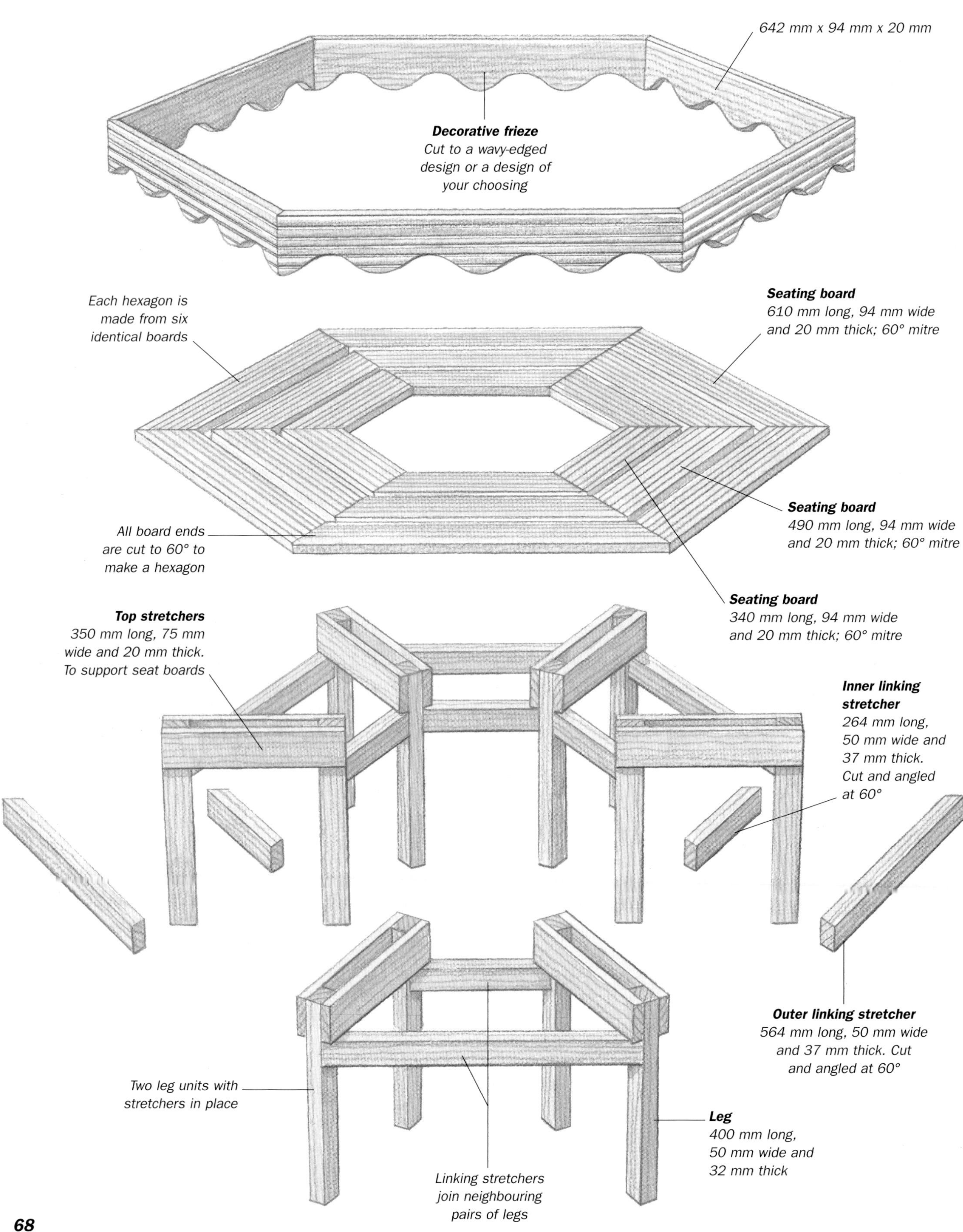
642 mm x 94 mm x 20 mm
Decorative frieze
Cut to a wavy-edged design or a design of your choosing
Each hexagon is made from six identical boards
Seating board
610 mm long, 94 mm wide and 20 mm thick; 60° mitre
Seating board
490 mm long, 94 mm wide and 20 mm thick; 60° mitre
All board ends are cut to 60° to make a hexagon
Seating board
340 mm long, 94 mm wide and 20 mm thick; 60° mitre
Top stretchers
350 mm long, 75 mm wide and 20 mm thick. To support seat boards
Inner linking stretcher
264 mm long, 50 mm wide and 37 mm thick. Cut and angled at 60°
Outer linking stretcher
564 mm long, 50 mm wide and 37 mm thick. Cut and angled at 60°
Two leg units with stretchers in place
Leg
400 mm long, 50 mm wide and 32 mm thick
Linking stretchers join neighbouring pairs of legs

Making the tree ring seat

1 Making the leg units
Sandwich two legs between two top stretchers, so that you have a frame 400 mm high and 350 mm wide. Fix each end of each stretcher to the leg with two screws, with the screws offset (see photo). Build six such frames.

2 Fixing the stretchers
When you have made all six leg units, take the inner and outer linking stretchers (all cut to length and angled at 60°) and screw the units together in pairs. You should finish up with three identical angle-ended bench units.

3 Joining the structure
Set the three identical bench units around your chosen tree, spacing them to make a hexagon. Screw the remaining linking stretchers in place to join neighbouring bench units.

4 Fitting the seat
Take the seating boards (three different lengths for each of the six sections) and screw them on top of the frame. Make sure that the sawn ends are centred on the leg frames.

5 Making the decorative frieze
Draw the wavy design on tracing paper and with a pencil, press-transfer the drawn lines through to the 94 mm-wide frieze boards. Cut out the design with the jigsaw and use the sander to tidy up the sawn edges.

6 Finishing
Finally, clamp and screw the frieze boards around the seat so that the top edge is flush with the top of the seat. Use the sander to rub down the whole seat area to a smooth finish.

Adirondack chair

★★★
Advanced

Making time
One weekend
One day for building the basic chair, and one day for finishing

This beautiful folk art chair gets its name from the Adirondack Mountains in north-east New York State in America, where, in the middle of the nineteenth century, chairs of this type were first made. It is characterized by the flowing shape of the side boards, the roll of the seat, the fan back and the broad, flat arms. These chairs were originally made from scrap such as crates, salvaged wood, or waste from sawmills.

Considering the design

We have modified the basic Adirondack chair design by hinging the arms to the front legs and the seat back, and by fixing a swivel pin between the arms and the fretted side boards so that the chair can be packed flat for winter storage. The design uses only rough-sawn wood, and cutting has been kept to the minimum.

Getting started

Note the various lengths and sections in the working drawings, and then saw your wood to size. Stack the wood in four groups: for the basic seat unit, the front legs and arms, the seat back, and the little pieces needed under the seat.

Overall dimensions and general notes

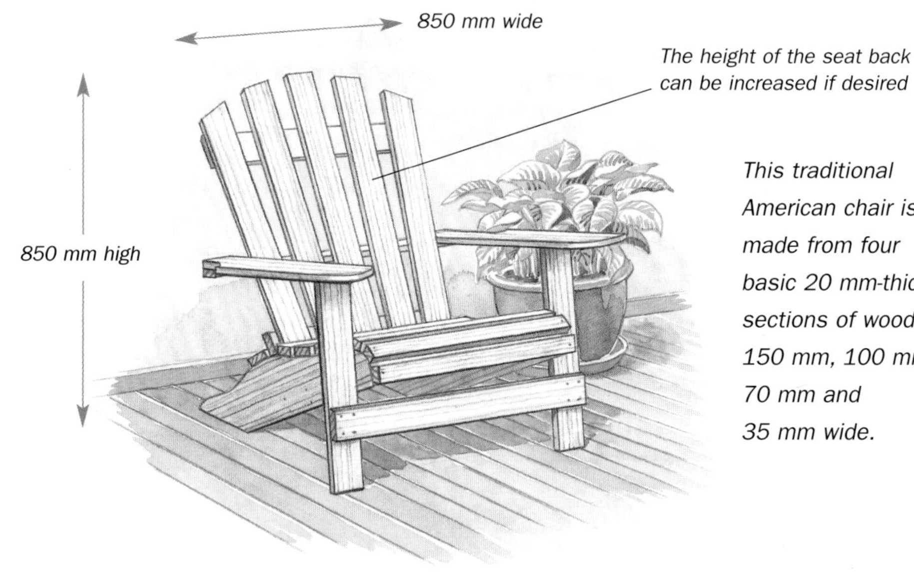
850 mm wide
850 mm high
The height of the seat back can be increased if desired

This traditional American chair is made from four basic 20 mm-thick sections of wood, 150 mm, 100 mm, 70 mm and 35 mm wide.

You will need

Tools

- Pencil, ruler, tape measure, compass and square
- Two portable workbenches
- Crosscut saw
- Electric jigsaw
- Cordless electric drill with a cross-point screwdriver bit
- Drill bits to match the sizes of the screws
- Electric sander
- Paintbrush

Materials

(All rough-sawn pieces of pine include excess length for wastage. All the wood is pressure-treated with preservative.)

For one chair, 850 mm wide and 850 mm high

- Pine: 2 rough-sawn pieces, 2 m long, 150 mm wide and 20 mm thick (side and arm boards)
- Pine: 3 rough-sawn pieces, 2 m long, 100 mm wide and 20 mm thick (front legs, stretcher board, stop boards)
- Pine: 6 rough-sawn pieces, 2 m long, 70 mm wide and 20 mm thick (seat back, back supports, fan support bar and wide seat boards)
- Pine: 1 rough-sawn piece, 2 m long, 35 mm wide and 20 mm thick (narrow seat boards)
- Pine: 1 rough-sawn piece, 1 m long, 35 mm square (under-seat fixing blocks)
- Zinc-plated, countersunk cross-headed screws: 100 x 35 mm no. 8, quantity of 15 mm no. 8 (number to fit your chosen hinges), 2 x 100 mm no. 10 (with washers to fit)
- Hinges: 4 painted 200 mm-long T-hinges (the type used for gates)
- Exterior-grade white masonry paint in a matt finish
- Danish oil

Perspective view of the Adirondack chair

The chair folded

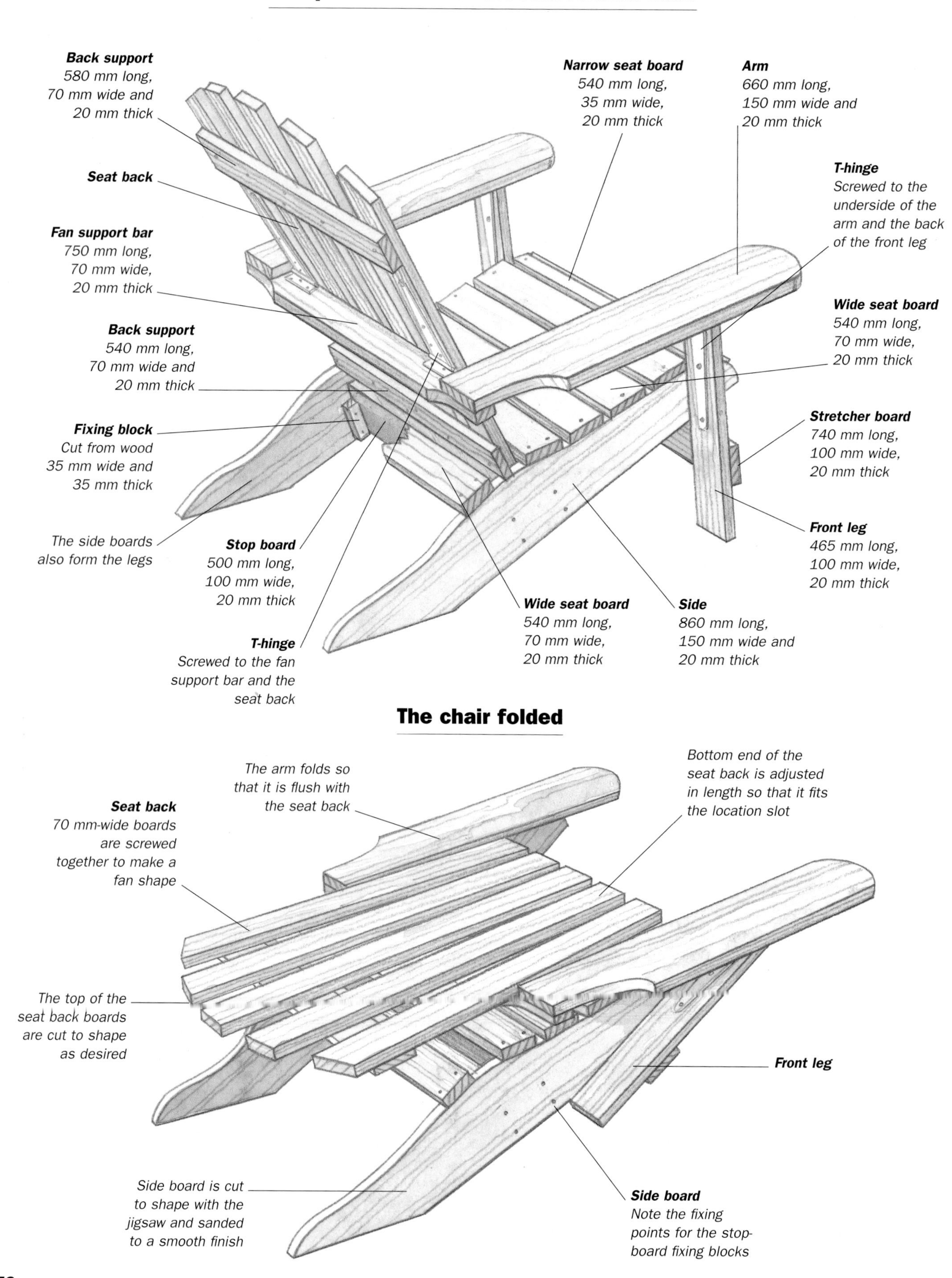
Back support
580 mm long,
70 mm wide and
20 mm thick
Seat back
Fan support bar
750 mm long,
70 mm wide,
20 mm thick
Back support
540 mm long,
70 mm wide and
20 mm thick
Fixing block
Cut from wood
35 mm wide and
35 mm thick
The side boards
also form the legs
Stop board
500 mm long,
100 mm wide,
20 mm thick
T-hinge
Screwed to the fan
support bar and the
seat back
Narrow seat board
540 mm long,
35 mm wide,
20 mm thick
Arm
660 mm long,
150 mm wide and
20 mm thick
T-hinge
Screwed to the
underside of the
arm and the back
of the front leg
Wide seat board
540 mm long,
70 mm wide,
20 mm thick
Stretcher board
740 mm long,
100 mm wide,
20 mm thick
Front leg
465 mm long,
100 mm wide,
20 mm thick
Wide seat board
540 mm long,
70 mm wide,
20 mm thick
Side
860 mm long,
150 mm wide and
20 mm thick
Seat back
70 mm-wide boards
are screwed
together to make a
fan shape
The arm folds so
that it is flush with
the seat back
Bottom end of the
seat back is adjusted
in length so that it fits
the location slot
The top of the
seat back boards
are cut to shape
as desired
Front leg
Side board is cut
to shape with the
jigsaw and sanded
to a smooth finish
Side board
Note the fixing
points for the stop-
board fixing blocks

The chair components

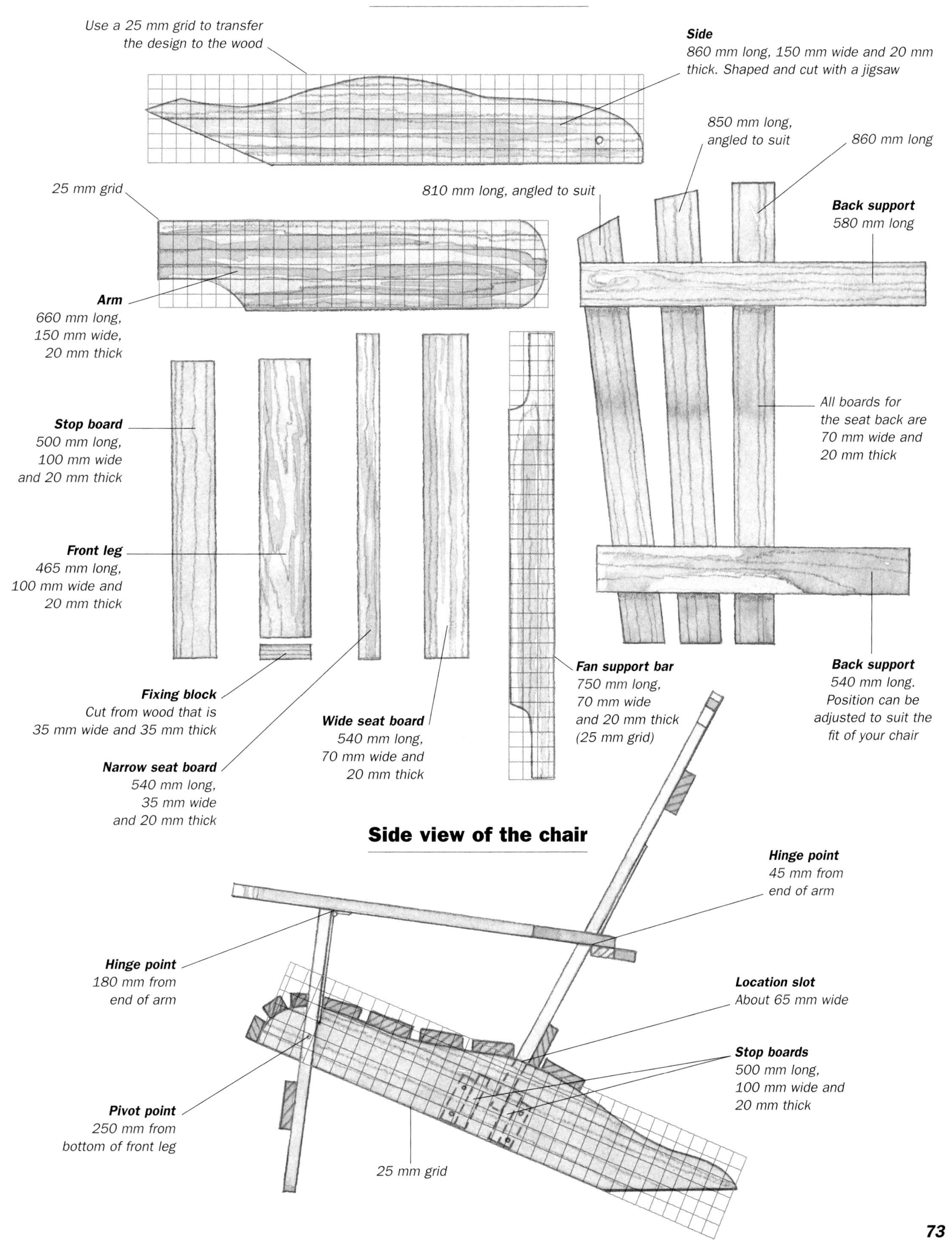

Use a 25 mm grid to transfer the design to the wood
Side
860 mm long, 150 mm wide and 20 mm thick. Shaped and cut with a jigsaw
850 mm long, angled to suit
860 mm long
25 mm grid
810 mm long, angled to suit
Back support
580 mm long
Arm
660 mm long, 150 mm wide, 20 mm thick
All boards for the seat back are 70 mm wide and 20 mm thick
Stop board
500 mm long, 100 mm wide and 20 mm thick
Front leg
465 mm long, 100 mm wide and 20 mm thick
Fan support bar
750 mm long, 70 mm wide and 20 mm thick (25 mm grid)
Back support
540 mm long. Position can be adjusted to suit the fit of your chair
Fixing block
Cut from wood that is 35 mm wide and 35 mm thick
Wide seat board
540 mm long, 70 mm wide and 20 mm thick
Narrow seat board
540 mm long, 35 mm wide and 20 mm thick
Side view of the chair
Hinge point
45 mm from end of arm
Hinge point
180 mm from end of arm
Location slot
About 65 mm wide
Stop boards
500 mm long, 100 mm wide and 20 mm thick
Pivot point
250 mm from bottom of front leg
25 mm grid

Making the Adirondack chair

1 Cutting the boards
Draw curves on the appropriate boards for the two arms, the two side boards, the five seat back boards, and the single fan support bar that links the ends of the arms across the chair back. Use the jigsaw to fret out the shapes.

2 Making the seat
To form the seat, take three narrow seat boards and four wide seat boards, and screw them to the two side boards with 35 mm screws. (A final wide seat board is added later.) The two sides must be parallel to each other and square with the seat.

3 Making the legs
Take the two boards that make the front legs, link them with the stretcher board – to make the characteristic H-frame – and fix them with four 35 mm screws at each intersection.

4 Hinging the arms
Set the two arms face down, and hinge them to the front H-frame. Note that the stretcher board is placed so that it lies across the front of the legs.

5 Attaching the fan support
Screw the fan support bar to the back ends of the two arm boards, all the while making sure that all the components are square to each other.

6 Pivoting the seat
Drill pivot holes through the side boards. Slide the washers on the 100 mm screws and run the screws through the side board holes and on into the thickness of the front legs.

7 Making the location slot
Position the chair so that the top of the seat is uppermost, and screw the eighth seat board in place with 35 mm screws. Leave a 65 mm gap between the eighth board and the one before it to make the location slot for the seat back.

8 Fixing the stop boards
With the underside of the seat uppermost, fix the two stop boards (to secure the seat back in the location slot) in place with 35 mm screws and the under-seat fixing blocks. Screw the blocks to the stop boards first, then screw the blocks to the side boards.

9 Making the back
Take the five seat back boards, and place them best face down, arranging them into a fan shape. Spread of fan at position of bottom edge of back support bar must not exceed 500 mm. Screw the two back supports in place with 35 mm screws.

10 Fixing the back
Slide the seat back into the location slot, raise the arms up so that it is supported, and hinge the seat back to the fan support bar with 15 mm screws. Paint the chair, let it dry, rub it down so that it looks worn at the edges and ends, and then give it a coat of Danish oil.

Patio with sandpit

Picture this... the sun is shining, you are relaxed and stretched out on wooden decking, there is a dappled canopy of leaves overhead, and there is a child at your side happily playing in a sandpit. If you choose this project, that scene could become reality after a weekend's work. The structure measures 2.9 m long by 2 m wide, but there is no reason why you cannot make it bigger or smaller to suit your garden situation.

Advanced

Making time
One weekend
One day for the basic structure, and one day for fixing the decking and finishing

Considering the design

There are holes to accommodate the sandpit and a tree. The decking boards are slightly cut back around the sandpit, so that the resultant board-thickness step between the surface of the decking and the top face of the beam becomes the lip for the pet-proof hatch cover. Because children will be crawling over the decking, make sure that a sealant is used over the preserved wood.

Getting started

Look at your site and choose a level area with a suitable tree. Measure the girth of the tree, and decide just where the sandpit will be placed. Choose your wood with extra care, and make sure that it is free from loose knots and splits.

Overall dimensions and general notes

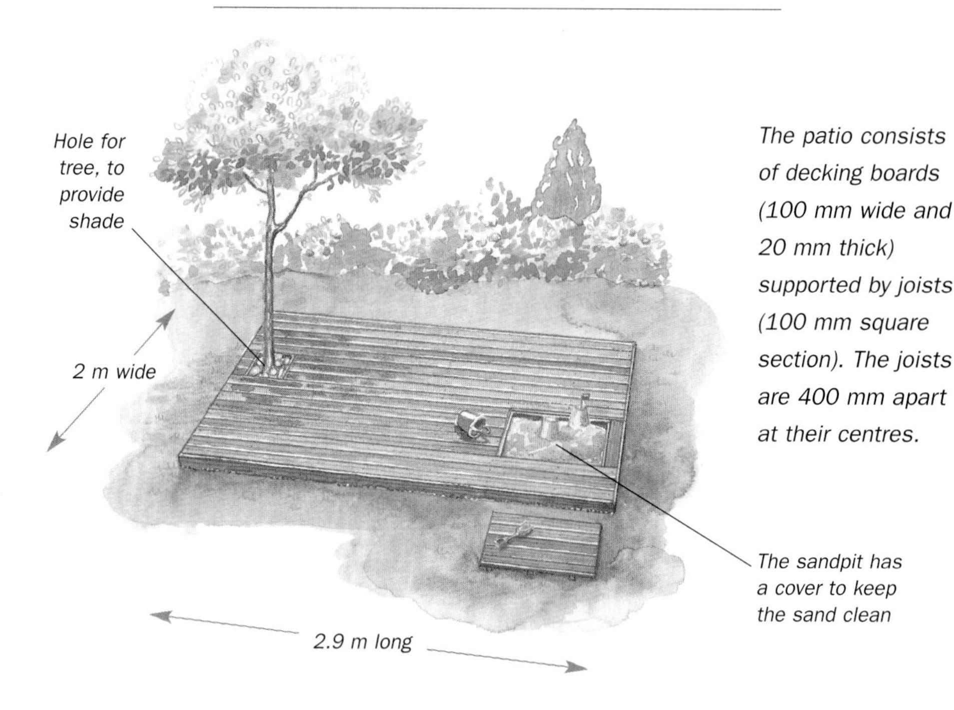
Hole for tree, to provide shade
2 m wide
2.9 m long
The sandpit has a cover to keep the sand clean

The patio consists of decking boards (100 mm wide and 20 mm thick) supported by joists (100 mm square section). The joists are 400 mm apart at their centres.

You will need

Tools

- ✔ Pencil, ruler, tape measure and square
- ✔ Pegs and string
- ✔ Two portable workbenches
- ✔ Crosscut saw
- ✔ Cordless electric drill with a cross-point screwdriver bit
- ✔ Drill bit to match the size of the screws
- ✔ Claw hammer
- ✔ Electric sander
- ✔ Paintbrush

Materials

(All rough-sawn pieces of pine include excess length for wastage. All the wood is pressure-treated with preservative)

For a patio 2.9 m long and 2 m wide

- ✔ Pine: 8 rough-sawn pieces, 2 m long, 100 mm square section (joists)
- ✔ Pine: 22 rough-sawn pieces, 3 m long, 100 mm wide and 20 mm thick (decking boards, frames and fascias)
- ✔ Pine: 1 rough-sawn piece, 2 m long, 40 mm wide and 20 mm thick (sandpit hatch cover battens)
- ✔ Woven plastic sheet: 3 m long and 2 m wide (to go under the decking)
- ✔ Nails: 1 kg of 125 mm x 5.6 mm
- ✔ Zinc-plated, countersunk cross-headed screws: 300 x 50 mm no. 8, 50 x 35 mm no.8
- ✔ Matt decking sealant
- ✔ Soft sand: 50 kg washed soft sand

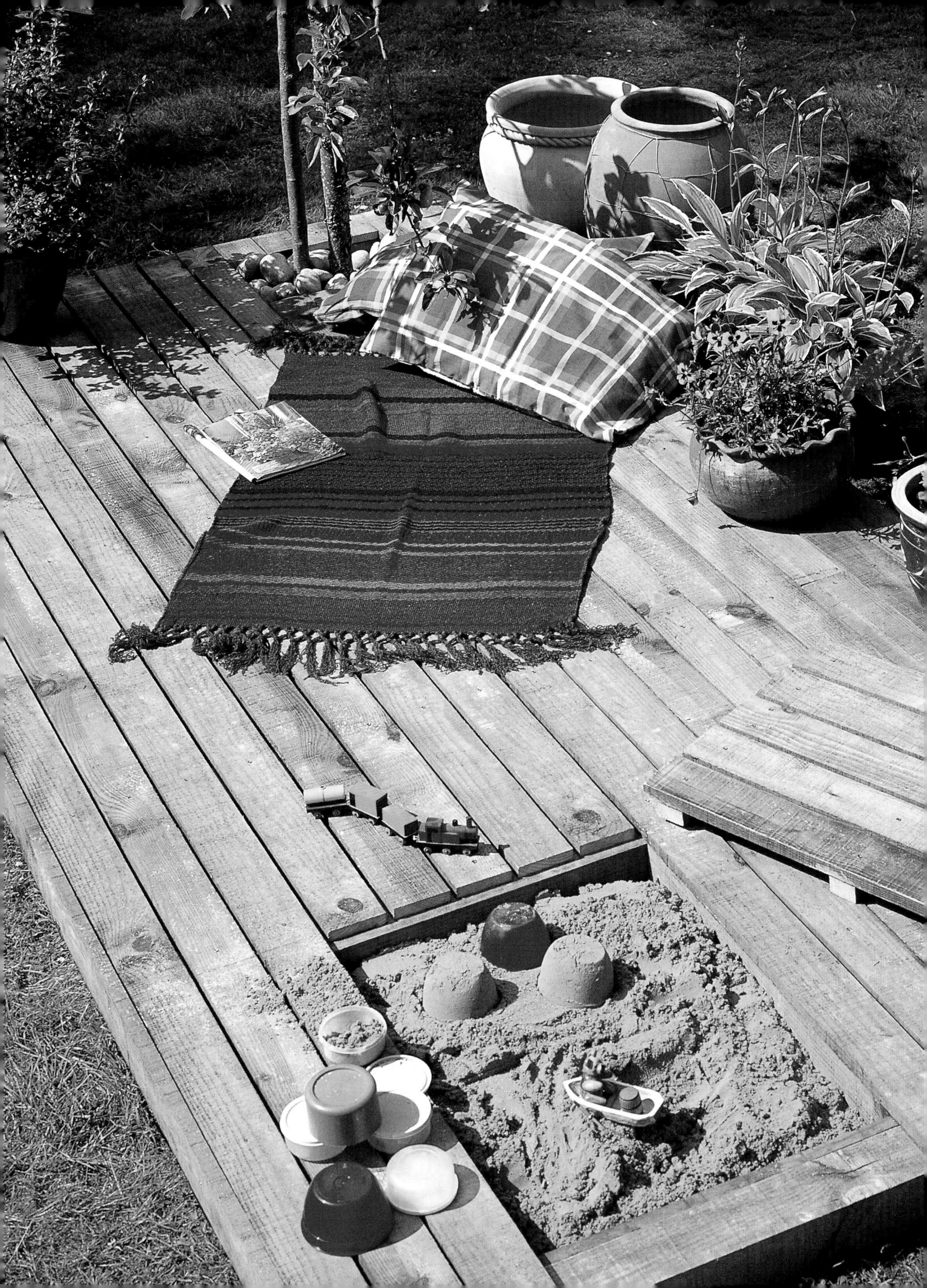

Exploded view of the patio with sandpit

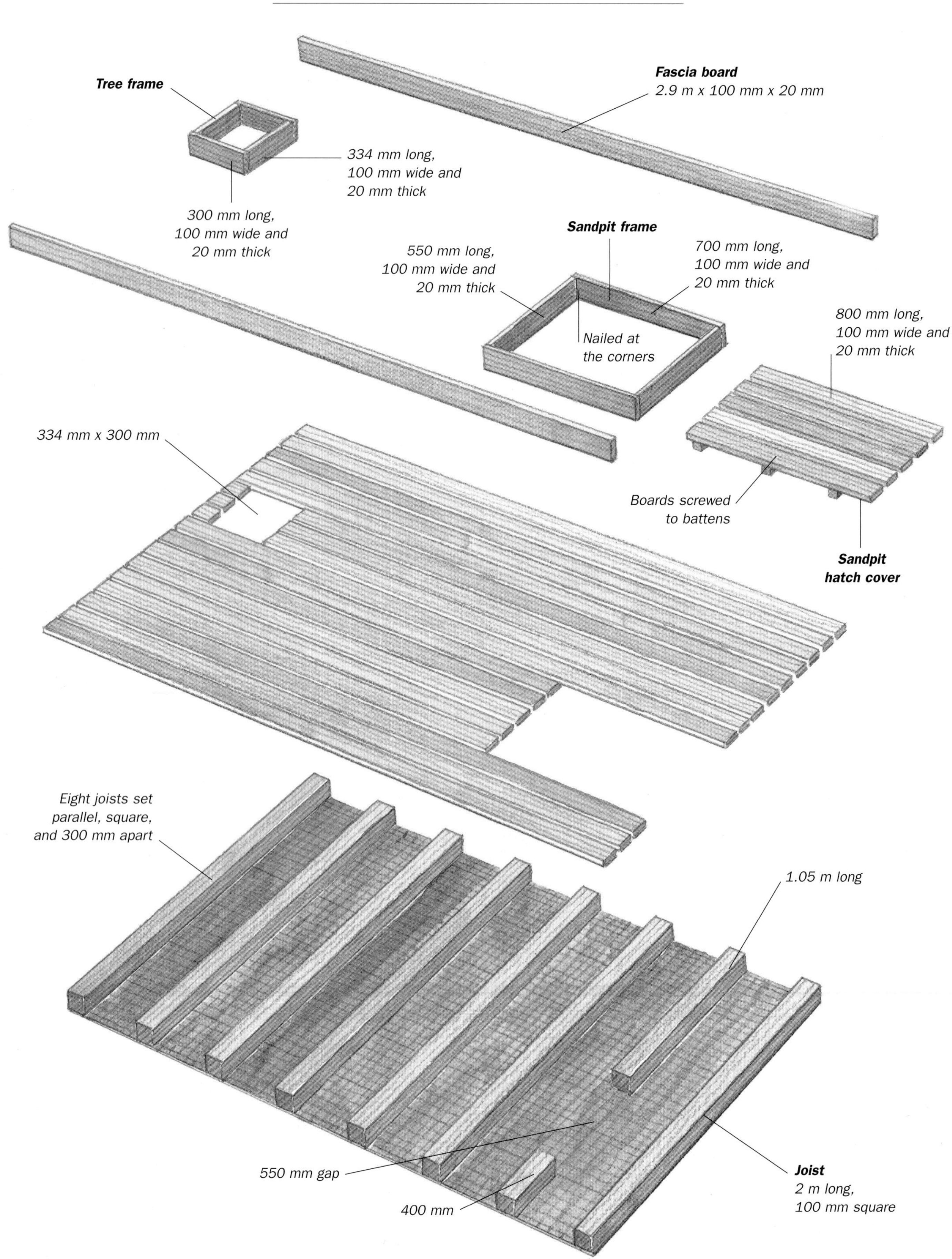
Fascia board
2.9 m x 100 mm x 20 mm
Tree frame
334 mm long,
100 mm wide and
20 mm thick
300 mm long,
100 mm wide and
20 mm thick
Sandpit frame
550 mm long,
100 mm wide and
20 mm thick
700 mm long,
100 mm wide and
20 mm thick
Nailed at
the corners
800 mm long,
100 mm wide and
20 mm thick
334 mm x 300 mm
Boards screwed
to battens
Sandpit
hatch cover
Eight joists set
parallel, square,
and 300 mm apart
1.05 m long
550 mm gap
400 mm
Joist
2 m long,
100 mm square

Exploded view of the patio with sandpit

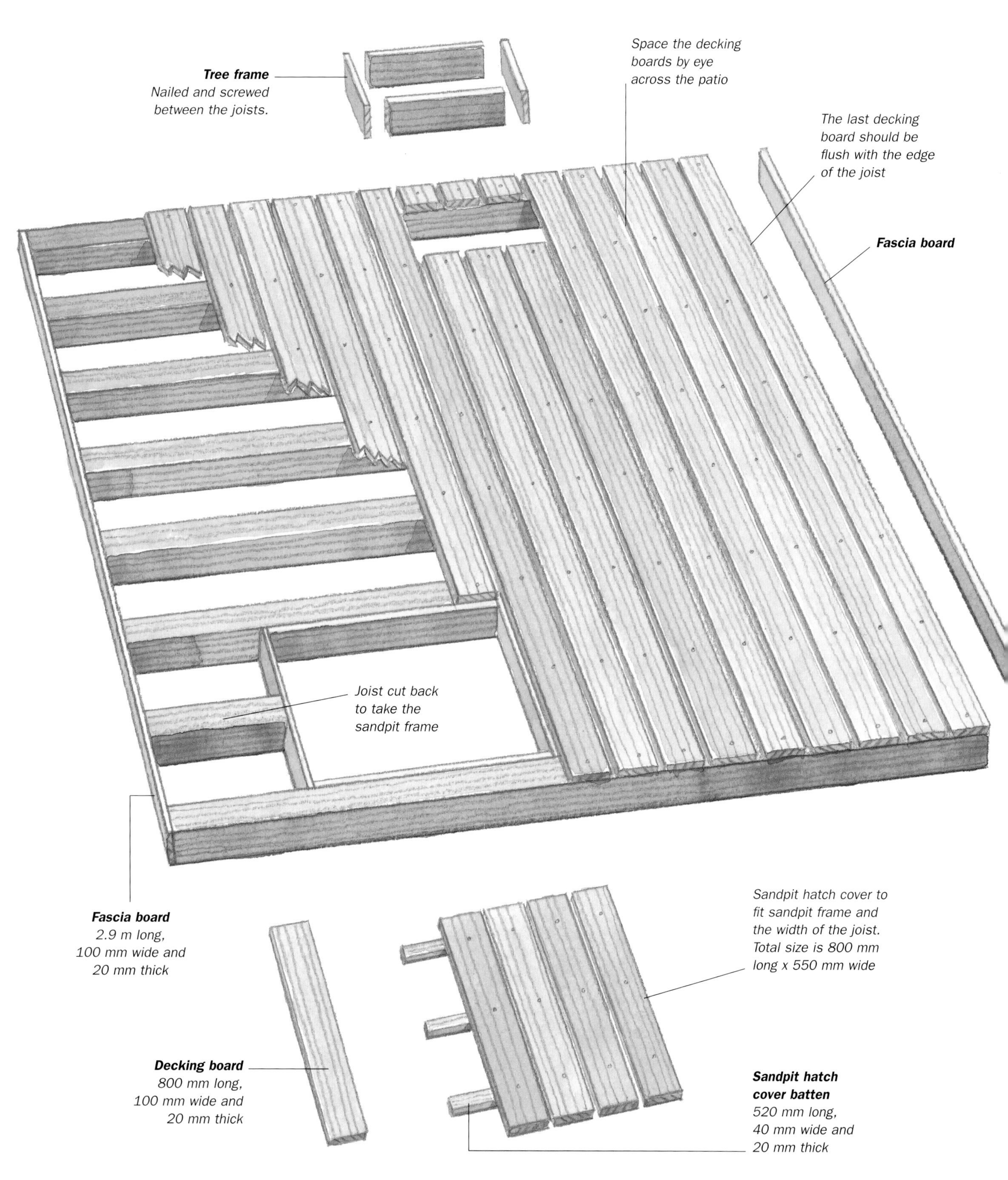
Tree frame
Nailed and screwed between the joists.
Space the decking boards by eye across the patio
The last decking board should be flush with the edge of the joist
Fascia board
Joist cut back to take the sandpit frame
Fascia board
2.9 m long, 100 mm wide and 20 mm thick
Sandpit hatch cover to fit sandpit frame and the width of the joist. Total size is 800 mm long x 550 mm wide
Decking board
800 mm long, 100 mm wide and 20 mm thick
Sandpit hatch cover batten
520 mm long, 40 mm wide and 20 mm thick

Making the patio with sandpit

1 Cutting the joists
Cut the joists to length (allowing for the sandpit area) and set them in position on the site, together with a couple of decking boards, to give you an idea of how the finished project will look. Decide exactly where they will lie in relation to the tree.

2 Fixing the joists
Cover the whole site with the woven plastic sheeting, leaving a hole around the tree. Position the joists, setting them square with the plastic and parallel to each other. Fix them in place with a decking board at each side, using one screw at each intersection.

3 Squaring the frame
To ensure that the frame is square, measure the diagonals and make adjustments to the frame until both diagonals are equal. Drive in a second screw at each corner.

4 Making the frames
Build two frames – a tree frame to go around the tree, and a sandpit frame for the sandpit. Nail and screw the frames in place between the joists.

5 Fixing the decking
Cut and fit all the long decking boards, which run the full length of the frame. Screw them to the joists. Set them flush with the sides of the two frames. Leave a 550 mm gap between the boards for the sandpit, and a 334 mm gap for the tree.

6 Completing the decking
Cut and fit all the other shorter decking boards, spacing them as before. They should be stepped back around the sandpit frame to provide a lip for the sandpit hatch cover, and flush with the tree frame. Cut boards for the sandpit hatch cover.

7 Fixing the fascia boards
Fit the fascia boards along the two long sides of the decking, covering the ends of the joists. Position the edges of the boards so that they are flush with the surface of the decking.

8 Making the sandpit hatch cover
Fix the boards for the sandpit hatch cover to the three battens. Space them to match the rest of the decking. Finally, rub down the structure with the sander, give all the surfaces two or three coats of matt sealant and fill the sandpit.

Hillside decking

★★★
Advanced

Making time
One long weekend
One day for the basic frames and one day for fixing and fitting the posts, and finishing

This decking is designed specifically to be built on a piece of gently sloping ground. You simply cut the posts to length to suit the slope, and then bolt them to the platform and set them in concrete. Working in this way, it is easy to adapt the structure to suit just about any situation. The project is made up from three basic platforms: one set at ground level, one set higher up the slope, and a mini platform that is used as a step.

Considering the design

The joists are butted and screwed at the corners, and then bolted to the posts. The upper platform has been set at a 45° angle to the lower one. The three platforms are built as separate units, which allows you to change things around to suit the slope and layout of your garden.

Getting started

Work out how you want the platforms to be positioned in relation to each other. If you find it difficult to picture, build the lower one and set it in the ground, then build the upper one and move it around until you find a suitable position.

Overall dimensions and general notes

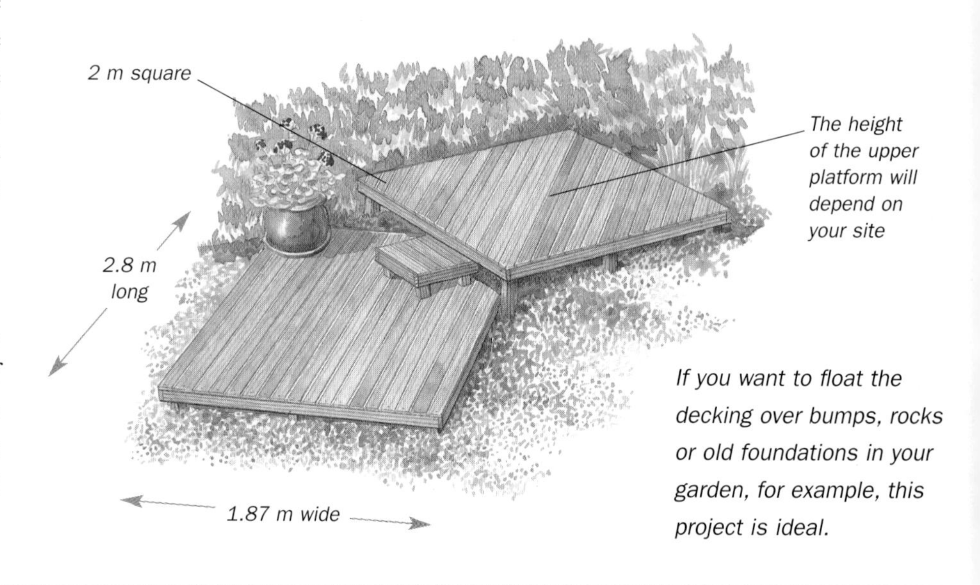
2 m square
The height of the upper platform will depend on your site
2.8 m long
1.87 m wide

If you want to float the decking over bumps, rocks or old foundations in your garden, for example, this project is ideal.

You will need

Tools

- Pencil, ruler, tape measure and square
- Two portable workbenches
- Crosscut saw
- Cordless electric drill with a cross-point screwdriver bit
- Drill bits to match the sizes of the screws and bolts
- Spade
- Wrench to fit the bolts
- Wheelbarrow
- Bucket
- Shovel and pointing trowel
- Spirit level
- Sledgehammer
- Electric sander

Materials

(All rough-sawn pieces of pine include excess length for wastage. All the wood is pressure-treated with preservative.)

For two areas of decking: 2.8 m x 1.87 m, and 2 m square

- Pine: 5 rough-sawn pieces, 2 m long, 75 mm square section (posts)
- Pine: 22 rough-sawn pieces, 2 m long, 85 mm wide and 40 mm thick; 2 pieces, 3 m long, 85 mm wide and 40 mm thick (joists, frames and noggings)
- Pine: 34 rough-sawn pieces, 3 m long, 100 mm wide and 20 mm thick (decking boards)
- Pine: 2 rough-sawn pieces, 3 m long, 35 mm wide and 20 mm thick (temporary battens)
- Zinc-plated, countersunk cross-headed screws: 300 x 40 mm no. 8, 100 x 90 mm no. 10
- Zinc-plated coach bolts with nuts and washers to fit: 30 x 150 mm
- Concrete: 1 part (50 kg) cement, 2 parts (100 kg) sharp sand, 3 parts (150 kg) aggregate

Exploded view of the hillside decking

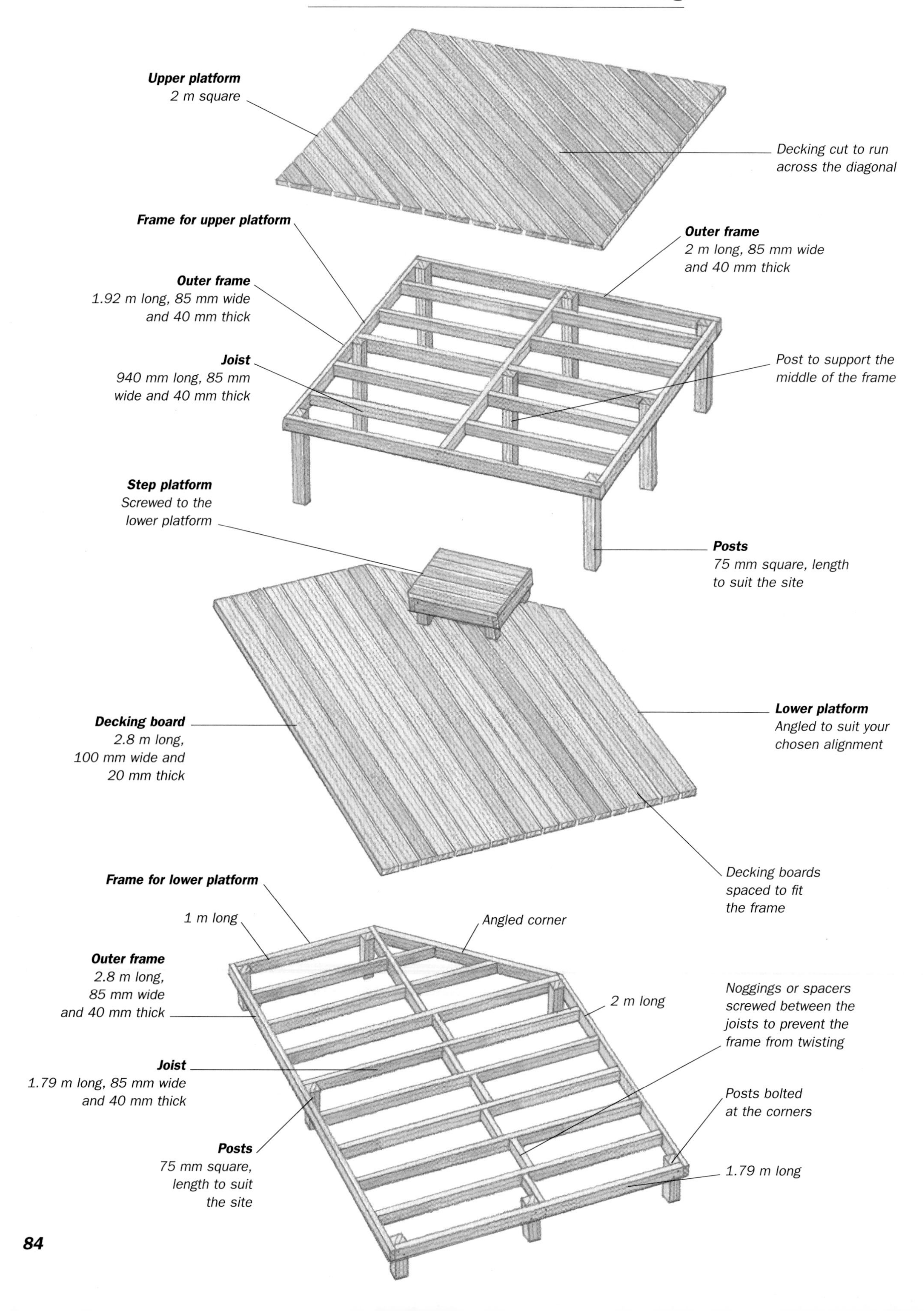
Upper platform
2 m square
Decking cut to run across the diagonal
Frame for upper platform
Outer frame
2 m long, 85 mm wide and 40 mm thick
Outer frame
1.92 m long, 85 mm wide and 40 mm thick
Joist
940 mm long, 85 mm wide and 40 mm thick
Post to support the middle of the frame
Step platform
Screwed to the lower platform
Posts
75 mm square, length to suit the site
Decking board
2.8 m long, 100 mm wide and 20 mm thick
Lower platform
Angled to suit your chosen alignment
Decking boards spaced to fit the frame
Frame for lower platform
1 m long
Angled corner
Outer frame
2.8 m long, 85 mm wide and 40 mm thick
2 m long
Noggings or spacers screwed between the joists to prevent the frame from twisting
Joist
1.79 m long, 85 mm wide and 40 mm thick
Posts bolted at the corners
Posts
75 mm square, length to suit the site
1.79 m long

Plan view of the hillside decking

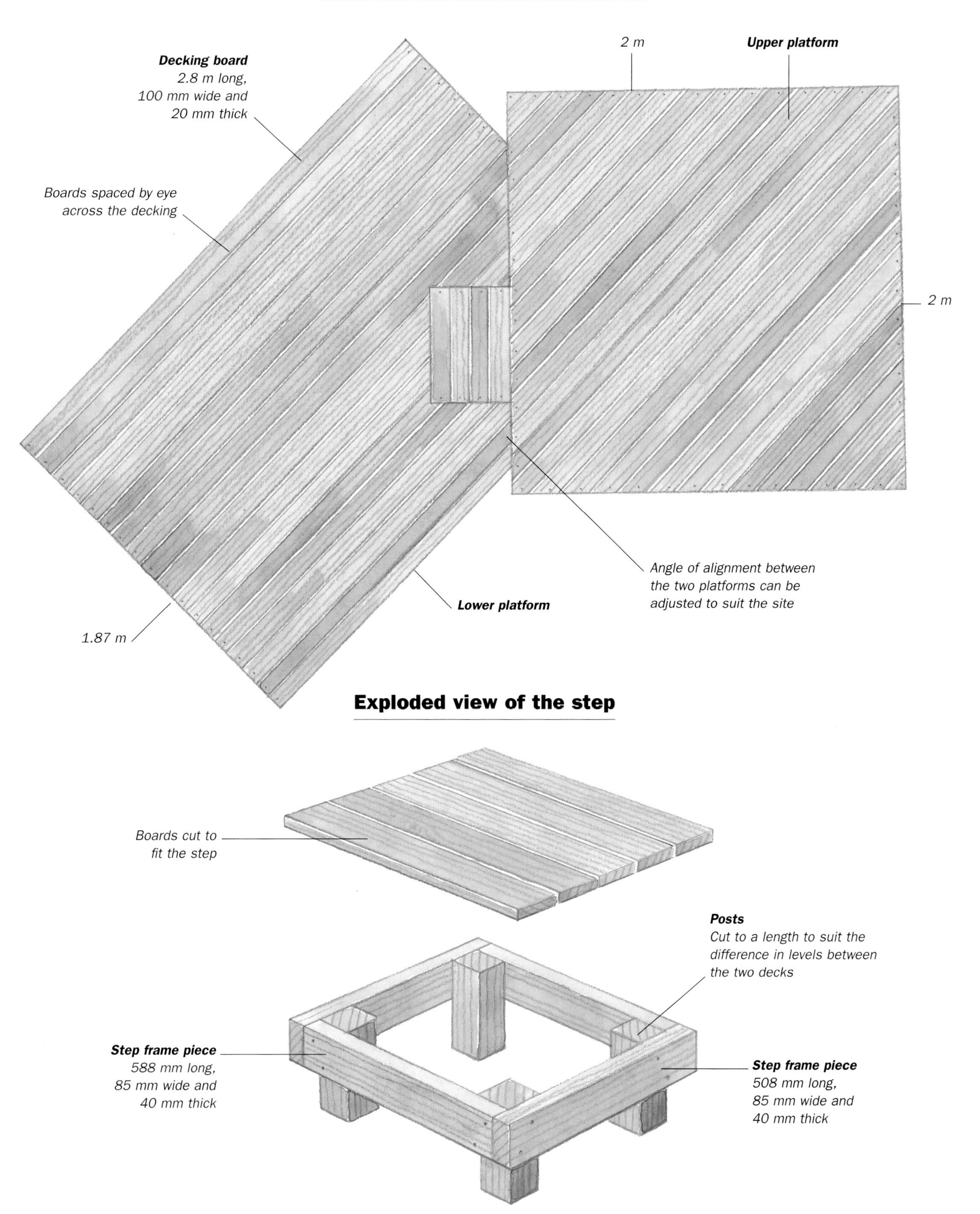
2 m
Upper platform
Decking board
2.8 m long,
100 mm wide and
20 mm thick
Boards spaced by eye
across the decking
2 m
Angle of alignment between
the two platforms can be
adjusted to suit the site
Lower platform
1.87 m
Boards cut to
fit the step
Posts
Cut to a length to suit the
difference in levels between
the two decks
Step frame piece
588 mm long,
85 mm wide and
40 mm thick
Step frame piece
508 mm long,
85 mm wide and
40 mm thick

Exploded view of the step

Making the hillside decking

1 Planning
Use the joists to plan out the total design on the ground. Work out the precise dimensions of the lower platform and the position of the post holes.

2 Lower platform frame
Cut the wood for the outer frame, butt the pieces at the corners and fix with 90 mm screws. Cut the diagonal piece for the angled corner to suit the frame. Fit in place. With 40 mm screws, screw temporary battens across the diagonals to hold the frame square.

3 Fitting the joists
Cut the joists and place them inside the outer frame so that they are set a little over 300 mm apart at their centres. Fix each joint with two 90 mm screws.

4 Digging the post holes
Set the frame level on the ground and establish the position of the posts within the frame. Dig a 300 mm-deep hole for each post. Set the posts in place and trim them to length to suit the height of the frame off the ground.

5 Attaching the posts
Bolt the posts to the frame, so that the tops are just level with the top of the frame. Repeat all the procedures just described to make the upper platform, and then set it in place.

6 Checking levels

Check each frame with the spirit level to make sure that it is horizontal, and make any small adjustments either by using the sledgehammer to tap down the posts, or by wedging the frames with offcuts.

7 Concreting the posts

Set both frames in their post holes. Mix a stiff batch of concrete and tamp it into the holes around the posts, filling them almost up to ground level. Trowel the concrete flush with the ground and shape it so that rainwater will flow away from the posts.

8 Fixing the decking

Screw the decking boards across the upper platform frame with 40 mm screws, so that they are at 45° to the sides. Use the crosscut saw to trim the waste ends so that the edge runs parallel to the frame. Fix decking boards to the lower platform.

9 Building the step

Repeat the procedures in Steps 1–8 to build a small platform to act as a step (modify to suit your decking). Screw the step to the lower platform with 90 mm screws, running the screws down through the legs at a sharp angle. Finally, sand everything to a good finish.

Waterside raised decking

Advanced

Making time
Two weekends
One weekend for the basic frame; second weekend for the balusters and details

Raised decking is a wonderfully exciting feature for a garden that backs on to a stretch of water. It's a magical feeling to be raised up high and looking out over a lake, river or the sea. This project is time-consuming and a challenge, but the design is easy to understand. The order of work is to first set the posts in concrete, then bolt a frame to the posts to establish the level of the decking, and fill in the frame with joists.

Considering the design

Decking is laid over the joists, the posts are trimmed to establish the level of the handrail, then the balusters are made.

Getting started

Only six of the ten posts are set in the ground, but in your particular situation this may vary: study your site, decide where the decking is going, and see how many posts need to be set in concrete.

Overall dimensions and general notes

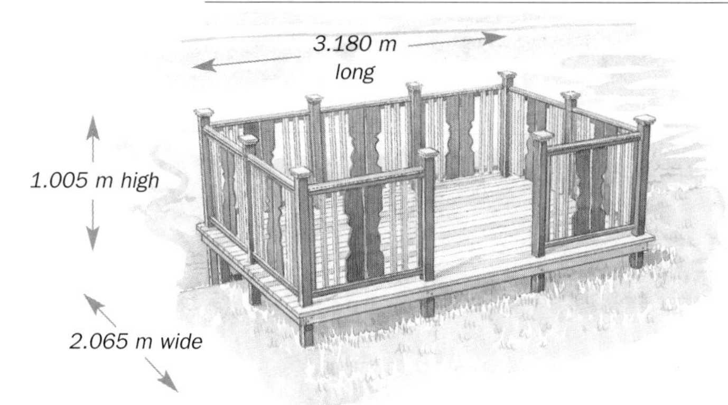
3.180 m
long
1.005 m high
2.065 m wide

This decking is designed to be built on a riverbank, or could overhang a pond. You can choose where the baluster rail panels go – the entrance can be moved.

You will need

Tools

(Warning. Because you are working by water, mains power tools must be used in conjunction with an electricity circuit breaker.)

- Pencil, ruler, tape measure and square
- Two portable workbenches
- Crosscut saw
- Spade and shovel
- Wrench to fit your chosen nuts
- Sledgehammer
- Spirit level
- Cordless electric drill with a cross-point screwdriver bit
- Drill bits to match the sizes of the screws and bolts
- Wheelbarrow, bucket and trowel
- Electric jigsaw
- Pair of clamps
- Electric sander

Materials

(All rough-sawn pieces of pine include excess length for wastage and design modifications. All the wood is pressure-treated with preservative.)

For raised decking 3.180 m long, 2.065 m wide, and 1.005 m high

- Pine: 14 rough-sawn pieces, 3 m long, 75 mm square section (ten main posts and secondary posts, joist supports, bracing beams)
- Pine: 15 rough-sawn pieces, 3 m long, 87 mm wide and 40 mm thick (joists, noggings, temporary battens)
- Pine: 27 pieces planed and grooved decking board, 3 m long, 120 mm wide and 30 mm thick (floor and any steps that might be needed)
- Pine: 15 rough-sawn pieces 3 m long, 50 mm wide and 30 mm thick (baluster rails and fixing battens)
- Pine: 4 rough-sawn pieces, 3 m long, 60 mm wide and 30 mm thick (pitch-topped rail capping)
- Pine: 15 rough-sawn pieces, 2 m long, 40 mm wide and 20 mm thick (slender balusters or vertical rails)
- Pine: 12 rough-sawn pieces, 3 m long, 150 mm wide and 20 mm thick (wide fretted baluster boards and newel post caps)
- Zinc-plated coach bolts with washers and nuts to fit: 36 x 120 mm, 16 x 180 mm
- Zinc-plated, countersunk cross-headed screws: 400 x 90 mm no. 8, 400 x 75 mm no. 10
- Concrete: 1 part (50 kg) cement, 2 parts (100 kg) sharp sand, 3 parts (150 kg) aggregate
- Hardcore: 1 bucket for each post

Exploded view of the waterside raised decking

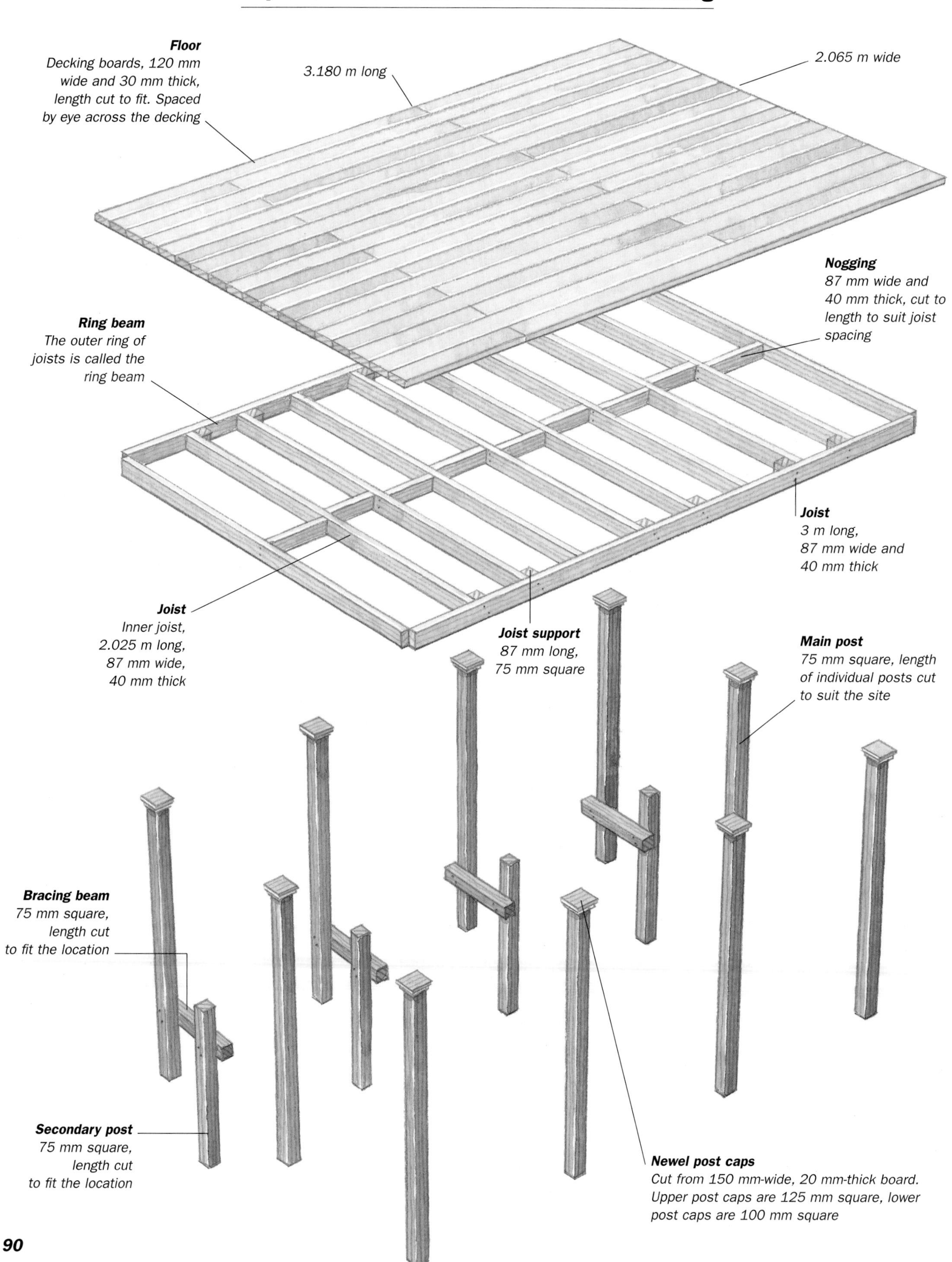
Floor
Decking boards, 120 mm wide and 30 mm thick, length cut to fit. Spaced by eye across the decking
3.180 m long
2.065 m wide
Nogging
87 mm wide and 40 mm thick, cut to length to suit joist spacing
Ring beam
The outer ring of joists is called the ring beam
Joist
3 m long, 87 mm wide and 40 mm thick
Joist
Inner joist, 2.025 m long, 87 mm wide, 40 mm thick
Joist support
87 mm long, 75 mm square
Main post
75 mm square, length of individual posts cut to suit the site
Bracing beam
75 mm square, length cut to fit the location
Secondary post
75 mm square, length cut to fit the location
Newel post caps
Cut from 150 mm-wide, 20 mm-thick board. Upper post caps are 125 mm square, lower post caps are 100 mm square

Front view of the waterside raised decking (viewed from the water)

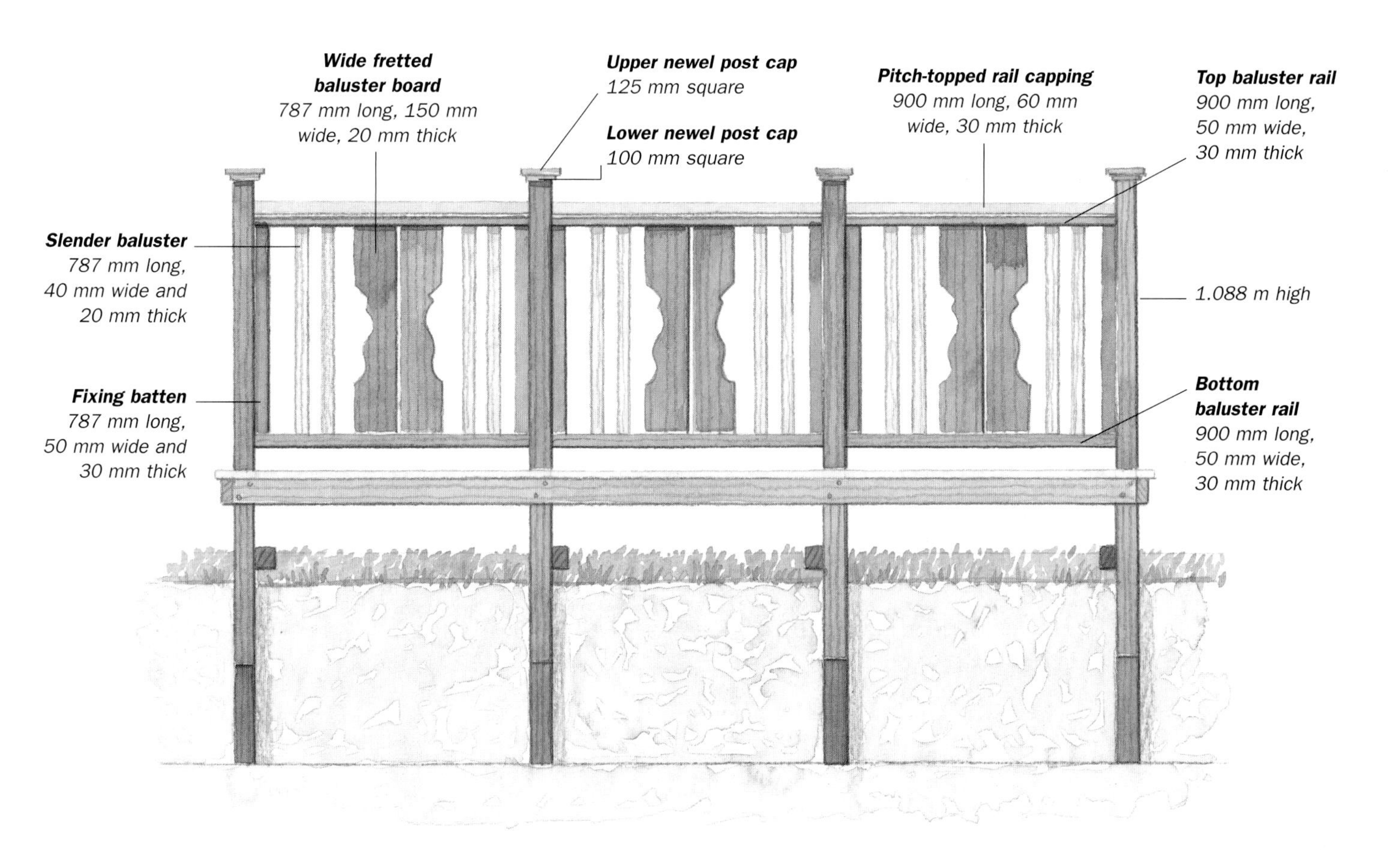
Wide fretted baluster board
787 mm long, 150 mm wide, 20 mm thick
Upper newel post cap
125 mm square
Lower newel post cap
100 mm square
Pitch-topped rail capping
900 mm long, 60 mm wide, 30 mm thick
Top baluster rail
900 mm long, 50 mm wide, 30 mm thick
Slender baluster
787 mm long, 40 mm wide and 20 mm thick
1.088 m high
Fixing batten
787 mm long, 50 mm wide and 30 mm thick
Bottom baluster rail
900 mm long, 50 mm wide, 30 mm thick

Side view of the waterside raised decking

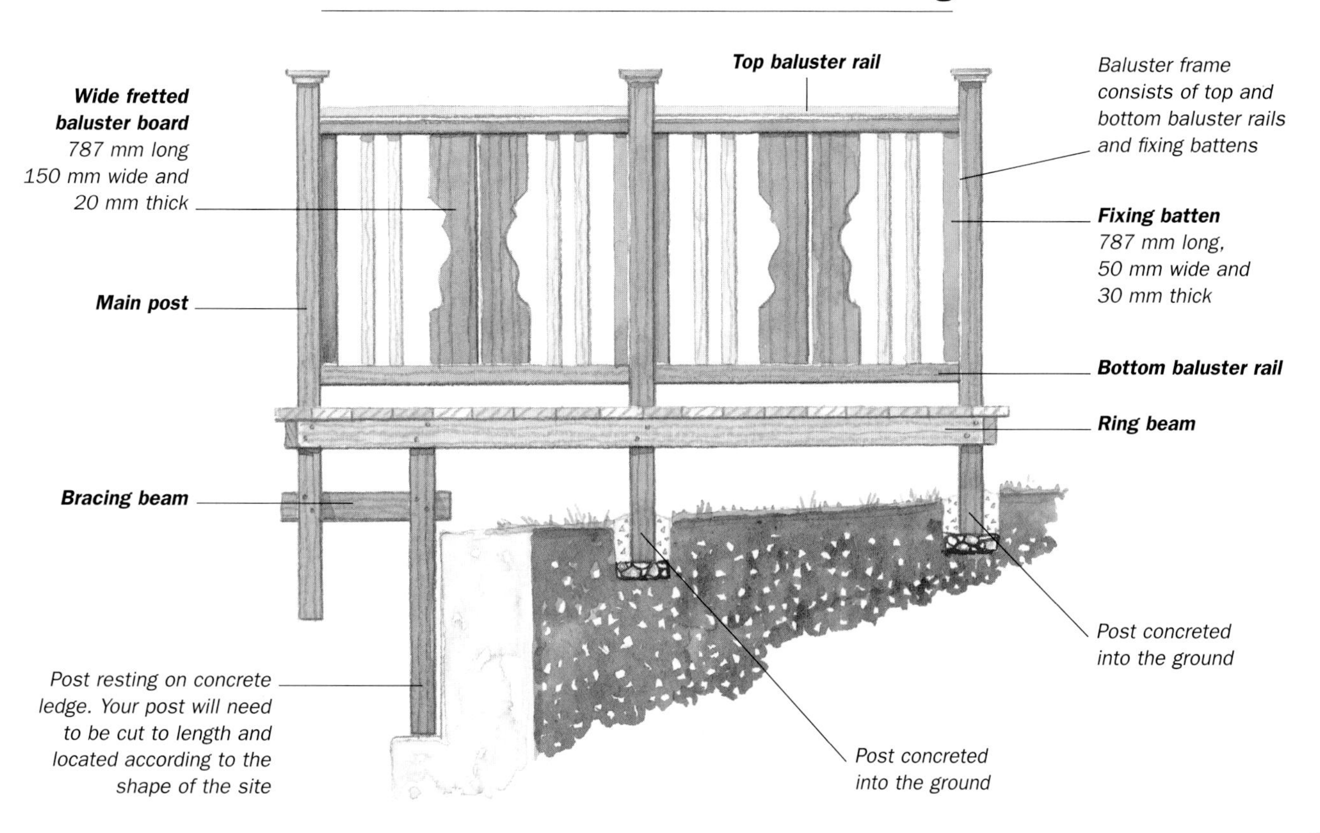
Top baluster rail
Baluster frame consists of top and bottom baluster rails and fixing battens
Wide fretted baluster board
787 mm long
150 mm wide and
20 mm thick
Fixing batten
787 mm long,
50 mm wide and
30 mm thick
Main post
Bottom baluster rail
Ring beam
Bracing beam
Post concreted into the ground
Post resting on concrete ledge. Your post will need to be cut to length and located according to the shape of the site
Post concreted into the ground

Making the waterside raised decking

1 Digging post holes
Dig holes for the main posts that require them, to a depth of 300 mm. Set the main posts in them. Loosely bolt the outer ring of joists (ring beam) to the main posts and outer secondary posts to create the frame.

2 Levelling
With the spirit level, check that the ring beam is level. Adjust the height of individual posts if necessary, by standing them on hardcore. (Compact the hardcore with the sledgehammer.) Use the wrench to tightly clench the bolts holding the posts to the ring beam.

3 Concreting the posts
Screw the inner joists in place in the frame with 90 mm screws, complete with noggings and joist supports. Check that the whole structure is square. Make a fairly stiff mix of concrete and pour it into the post holes around the posts. Trowel to a good finish.

4 Fitting the secondary posts
Using coach bolts, fix the secondary posts, bracing beams, and braces. Saw off the secondary posts level with the joists. Saw off the main posts level with each other and screw a temporary batten across the top to hold them square.

5 Fixing the floor
Screw the decking boards across the framework of joists with 75 mm screws, making sure that the joints between boards are staggered. Cut and fix the leading boards so that you see a nosing as you approach the decking from the garden.

6 Cutting the wide balusters
Draw the decorative profile on the 150 mm-wide boards and use the jigsaw to fret out the shape. Rub the sawn edges to a smooth finish.

7 Making the baluster frames
Make up the baluster frames on the ground, complete with fixing battens, top and bottom baluster rails, pitch-topped rail capping, slender balusters and wide fretted balusters. Fix together with 75 mm screws.

8 Finishing
Clamp the baluster frames between the posts and fix them with 90 mm screws. Cut and fix the upper and lower newel post caps to the top of the posts with 75 mm screws. Finally, rub down the whole structure with the sander.

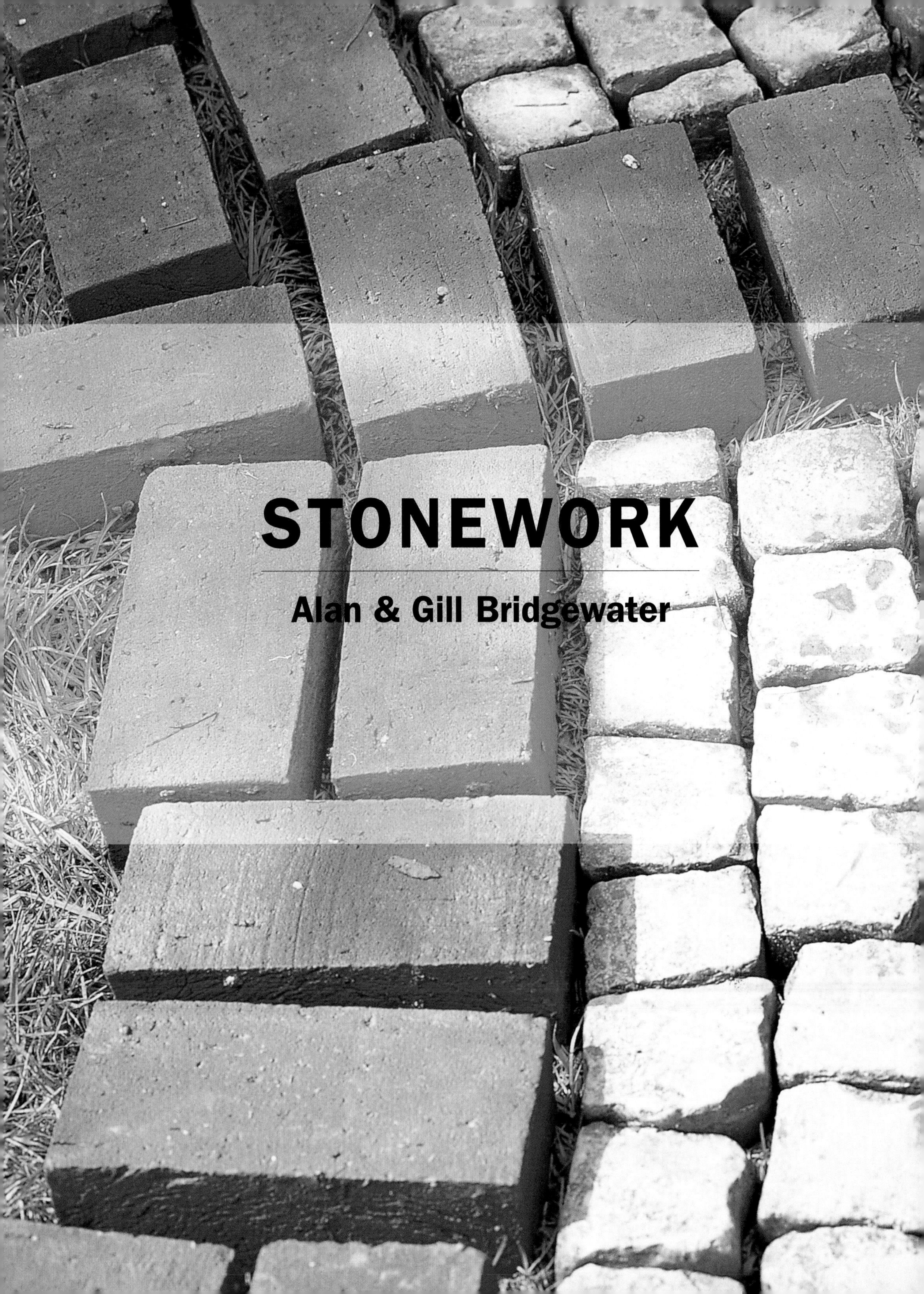

STONEWORK

Alan & Gill Bridgewater

Part 1

Techniques

Designing and planning

The secret of good stonework lies in the detail. If you are painstaking, and prepared to spend time thinking through the whole operation involved in a project – from measuring the site and making drawings, to ordering and buying stone, and considering how a seemingly immovable stone can be moved – then not only are you going to enjoy this activity, but your garden will be magically transformed.

Looking at your outdoor space

Assessing your garden

Wander through your garden and observe how the position of the sun – the intensity of the light, and the depth of the shade – changes the mood of the space. Consider the possibilities. Could you blur the difference between indoor and outdoor space by constructing a stone patio right next to the house? Or change the way the garden is used by running a path in a new direction? Or encourage a different use of the space by building walls, tables and benches? There are many exciting alternatives.

Style considerations

Just as you style your interior decor – it might be modern, ethnic or period, for example – you need to do the same for your outdoor space. Do you simply want it to mirror the character of your indoor space? Or do you want it to be an adventurous reflection of nature?

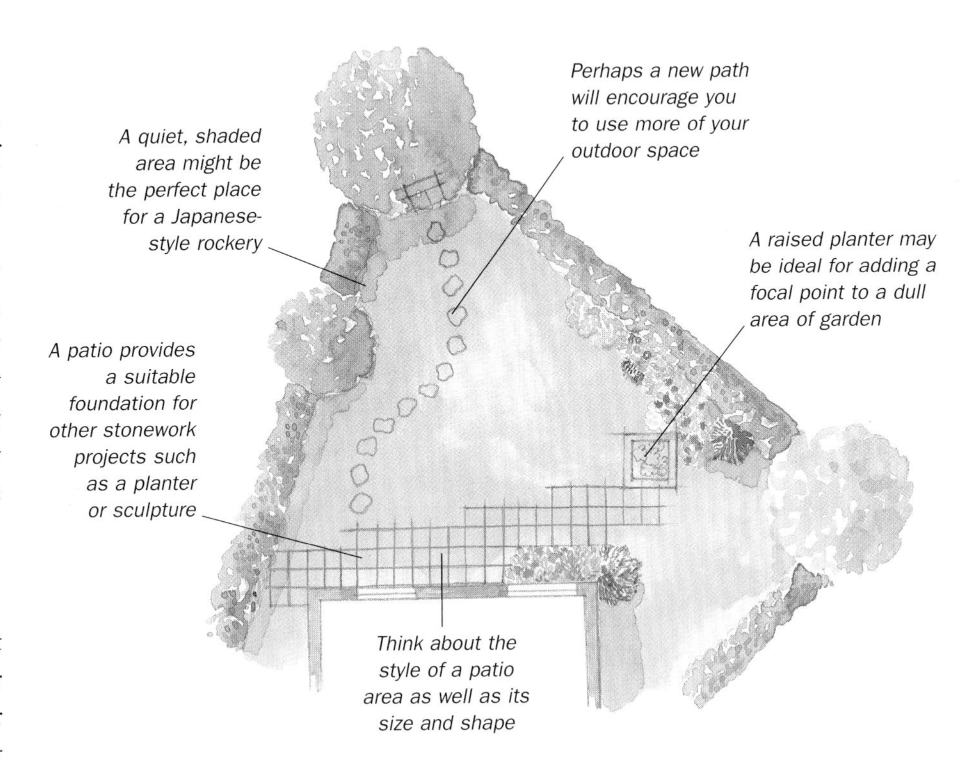
A quiet, shaded area might be the perfect place for a Japanese-style rockery
Perhaps a new path will encourage you to use more of your outdoor space
A raised planter may be ideal for adding a focal point to a dull area of garden
A patio provides a suitable foundation for other stonework projects such as a planter or sculpture
Think about the style of a patio area as well as its size and shape

Whatever the size, shape and style of your outdoor space, there are likely to be areas that you wish to improve. A patio may be essential, or you may want to build a dramatic stonework sculpture. Sketch out the possibilities on a plan of your garden.

Design

Deciding what to build

Once you have considered your outdoor space in terms of sunlight, mood and style, you can immerse yourself in the exciting business of deciding just what you want to build. The best way to proceed is to tackle the infrastructure first, and then take it from there. So if, for example, your garden lacks paths and paving, perhaps now is the time to do something about it. Then again, if you have always had an urge to build an arch or a wall, indulge in your dream.

Form and function

In many ways, it is true to say that form follows function – in the sense that you need to ensure that a bench is comfortable before you start to worry about the designer curlicues. However, don't let that stop you using your imagination. For example, if you like our Roman Arch Shrine (see page 174), but would prefer to build a whole row of shrines the full length of the garden, go ahead.

Choosing stone

Any stonework project has certain essential requirements – such as for thin slabs of stone or squarish blocks – but apart

from that, various materials are usually suitable. To see what is on offer, visit suppliers who sell quarry stone, salvaged stone and reconstituted stone.

Drawing your designs

Once you have looked at your garden, and considered your needs in terms of design, size, function, stone supply and costs, turn to the projects. If you do not see exactly what you are looking for, sketch out your ideas and then work out how a project might be modified. Draw your design to a rough scale, complete with the number of courses of stone. A good way of planning out the building stages is to slice up the project into layers – the foundation slab, the first course of stone, the next course, and so on – and then draw the layers on paper. This will not only help clarify the order of work, but also reveal potential problems.

It is helpful to build up a picture scrapbook of stone structures, augmented by garden ephemera such as planters, that appeal to you. Use it for ideas and inspiration when planning a stonework design.

Planning

First steps

Plan out the logistics of the project. Firstly, decide where all the materials are going to be stored. If you are having stone delivered, ask if it will be offloaded on a pallet or whether you will be expected to help unload it by hand. Sometimes sand and gravel are delivered in huge bags, and unloaded with a hoist, so check that there is an adequate accessible space for them to live in. Where are you going to put the removed turf and waste earth?

Will the building procedures get in the way of all the other activities of the household, such as getting the car out, or children playing? Will you require help when it comes to mixing concrete or moving stone? Will you need to cover the project with a plastic sheet if it starts to rain? Try to visualize every eventuality and forestall potential problems.

Permission and safety

Check that there are no planning restrictions governing the type of structure you are intending to build. If a project is constructed against a garden wall, check that the wall belongs to you. If it belongs to your neighbours, make sure that they have no objections before you go ahead.

For safety's sake, dress properly for the task ahead. You must protect your hands with strong gloves and your feet with heavy boots. Make sure that children are out of harm's way when you come to lifting heavy stones and slabs.

Planning checklist

- ✓ Is there a stone quarry in your area? This is likely to be the most economical source of materials.
- ✓ Is there adequate access to your garden? If the stone is unloaded in your driveway, or at your gate, will it cause problems or pose a danger?
- ✓ How are you going to move the stone to the site? Can you do it, or do you need friends to help?
- ✓ Is your garden reasonably level, with paths wide enough for a wheelbarrow? Or does it have soft, squashy lawns and very few pathways – if so, what arrangements do you need to make to move the materials?

Materials

For the projects in this book, all you really need to know about the primary materials – stone and sand – are their common names, colour and working characteristics. Once you know that sandstone splits into easy-to-work slices, and salvaged roof stone is good when you want to build a structure in thin courses, the rest is easy.

Caution
Stoneworkers risk injury from stones dropped on fingers or toes, and from muscle strain. Wear sturdy gloves and boots, lift carefully, and get help to move large stones.

Stone, concrete and mortar

Stone shape and colour

All the projects involve breaking stone with a chisel (rather than cutting with an angle grinder), so the two best types of stone to use are sandstone, which breaks into thin sheets, and limestone, which breaks into squarish blocks. Explain your needs to the supplier, see what stone is on offer, check its working characteristics, and then search around for pieces in the colour of your choice.

Natural stone versus reconstituted stone

The colour and texture of natural stone cannot be beaten; however, it is more expensive than reconstituted stone. For the most part, we prefer to use natural stone for walls and arrangements, and reconstituted stone when we need large, square-cut slabs or pavers. We did use reconstituted blocks for walling in the Dry-stone Border Wall (see page 132), but this is with the hope that once you have tried your hand with blocks, you will have the confidence to build a more complex wall project using natural stone.

Other materials

Soft sand (also known as builder's sand) is usually used for making smooth mortar, and sharp sand for making concrete and coarse-textured mortar. However, we use soft sand for most of the mortar mixes, and sharp sand in the form of ballast (a mixture of sand and gravel) when making concrete. This way of working enables you to buy the sand in bulk. Gravel and shingle are used both as decorative spreads and as a hardcore.

Buying stone

Decide on the colour and character of stone required for the project, and then visit a quarry or stoneyard and buy the stone as seen. Most stone is sold by the square metre or cubic metre. Pick out the pieces and spread them on the ground to fill up a square metre – this allows you to see how the pieces relate to each other for the purposes of the project. Never buy stone without looking at it first.

Opposite page: A selection of materials suitable for making the projects in this book (reconstituted stone products are available at builders' merchants): ***1*** *Reconstituted stone block,* ***2*** *Concrete block,* ***3*** *Reconstituted stone rope-top edging,* ***4*** *Corner post* ***5*** *Celtic pattern paver and square paver,* ***6*** *Ceramic roof tile,* ***7*** *Limestone,* ***8*** *Sandstone,* ***9*** *Brick,* ***10*** *Roof stone,* ***11*** *Flagstone,* ***12*** *Medium-sized cobble,* ***13*** *Reconstituted stone paver,* ***14*** *York stone,* ***15*** *Statue,* ***16*** *Rock,* ***17*** *Slate chippings,* ***18*** *Radius paving,* ***19*** *Pea gravel,* ***20*** *Feature stone,* ***21*** *Reconstituted stone paver,* ***22*** *Reconstituted grey stone setts.*

Concrete and mortar mixes

Mortar and concrete both contain aggregates, cement and water, but are made according to quite different recipes. Most stoneworkers have their own favourite blends. For example, some people make mortar using 1 part cement, 5 parts coarse sharp sand and 1 part lime; others use 1 part cement, 6 parts soft sand, and don't bother with the lime. The quantities we give in the projects are generous and allow for wastage. We use the following mixes:

Caution
Cement and lime are both corrosive
Always wear a dust-mask, gloves and goggles. If you get cement or lime powder on your skin – especially if your skin is damp – wash it off immediately with copious amounts of water.

- ✔ Concrete for general foundations: 1 part Portland cement to 5 parts ballast (ranging from small stones down to sharp sand).
- ✔ Concrete for paths: 1 part Portland cement to 4 parts ballast.
- ✔ Mortar for a general mix: 1 part Portland cement to 4 parts soft sand.
- ✔ Mortar for a smooth, strong mix: 1 part Portland cement, 1 part lime, and 3–4 parts soft sand.

1
2
3
4
5
6
7
8
9
10
11
12
13
14
15
16
17
18
19
20
21
22

Tools

Tools are one of the main keys to successful stonework. Although the best tools are no substitute for enthusiasm and determination, carefully chosen, top-quality tools will ensure that each and every task is accomplished with minimum effort and maximum efficiency, in the shortest possible time. However, it is fine to begin by using existing tools for the projects – just buy new ones if and when the need arises.

Choosing and using the correct tools

Measuring and marking

You need a flexible tape measure and a straight-edge for measuring the site, a rule for taking smaller measurements within the project, pegs and string for setting out the shape of the project on the ground, a spirit level to check that the project is both vertically and horizontally level, and a piece of chalk for drawing registration marks. It will make your life easier if you have two tape measures – a small, steel one for making measurements up to 3 m, and a large, wipe-clean fibreglass tape for measuring over longer distances in the garden.

Moving earth

Get yourself a spade for slicing into grass and for digging holes, and a fork for picking up turf. To move earth from one spot to another, you need a shovel, a wheelbarrow, and one or more buckets. If you are moving a lot of earth, it is a good idea to obtain a rake for spreading out the earth on the site.

Cutting and breaking stone

Apart from strong gloves to safeguard your hands and stout boots to protect your feet, you will require a sledgehammer for compacting hardcore level, a club hammer and bolster chisel for cutting and splitting stone, and a mason's hammer for the more precise task of cutting and pecking small pieces of stone to shape. An old piece of carpet makes a good surface to work on. For cleaning the stone and tidying up the site at the end of work, it is handy to have a wire brush, broom and a small hand brush. If you are prone to suffer from aches and pains, especially in your knees, it is a good idea to use an old cushion or padded kneeling mat to kneel on while you work.

Mixing concrete and mortar

You need a shovel for moving the sand, cement and ballast, a bucket for carrying water and small amounts of the concrete or mortar mixture, and a wheelbarrow for moving large amounts of the mixture around the garden. If you discover that you really enjoy working with stone and intend to do a lot of it, a small electric mixer will make the task of mixing concrete and mortar a lot easier. Always wash mortar and concrete off tools as soon as you have finished working, especially in hot weather when the mixtures are liable to harden quickly.

Laying stone

Once the concrete and mortar have been moved to the site, you must have a bricklayer's trowel (a large trowel) for handling large amounts of mortar, and a pointing trowel (a small trowel) for tidying up the joints and making good. We also use the bricklayer's trowel to carry the mortar when we are using the pointing trowel to do the pointing. When the stone is nicely bedded on the mortar, it is tapped into place with a club hammer or a rubber mallet. The measurements and levels are checked to make sure that they are correct. Finally, about an hour after the stone has been laid, when the mortar has started to cure, the excess mortar is removed with a trowel.

General tasks

At various points along the way, we use a claw hammer for banging in and pulling out nails, a crosscut saw for sizing lengths of wood, a portable drill in conjunction with drill bits for drilling holes and a screwdriver bit for driving in screws, and a craft knife to cut string and plastic sheet. We use all manner of odd-shaped pieces of plywood and board for protecting the site and as workboards to hold piles of mortar. If you value your existing lawn, start the project by surrounding the site with workboards so that the grass is covered and safeguarded from damage by feet, wheelbarrows and tools.

Caution

Power tools

Electricity, early-morning dew, buckets of water and wet hands are a potentially dangerous combination. If you do decide to use a power drill instead of a portable drill, or an electric cement mixer, make sure that you use them in conjunction with an electricity circuit breaker, which will protect you against possible electric shock.

A basic tool kit

For making the projects in this book, you will need the tools shown below. All of these can be bought from a local general DIY superstore, or hired from a hire shop. The angle grinder is optional – it is quite expensive and not essential for the projects. However, if you are planning to do a lot of stonework projects in the future which involve cutting stone, it may be a worthwhile investment. Likewise, an electric cement mixer (not illustrated) may also be useful.

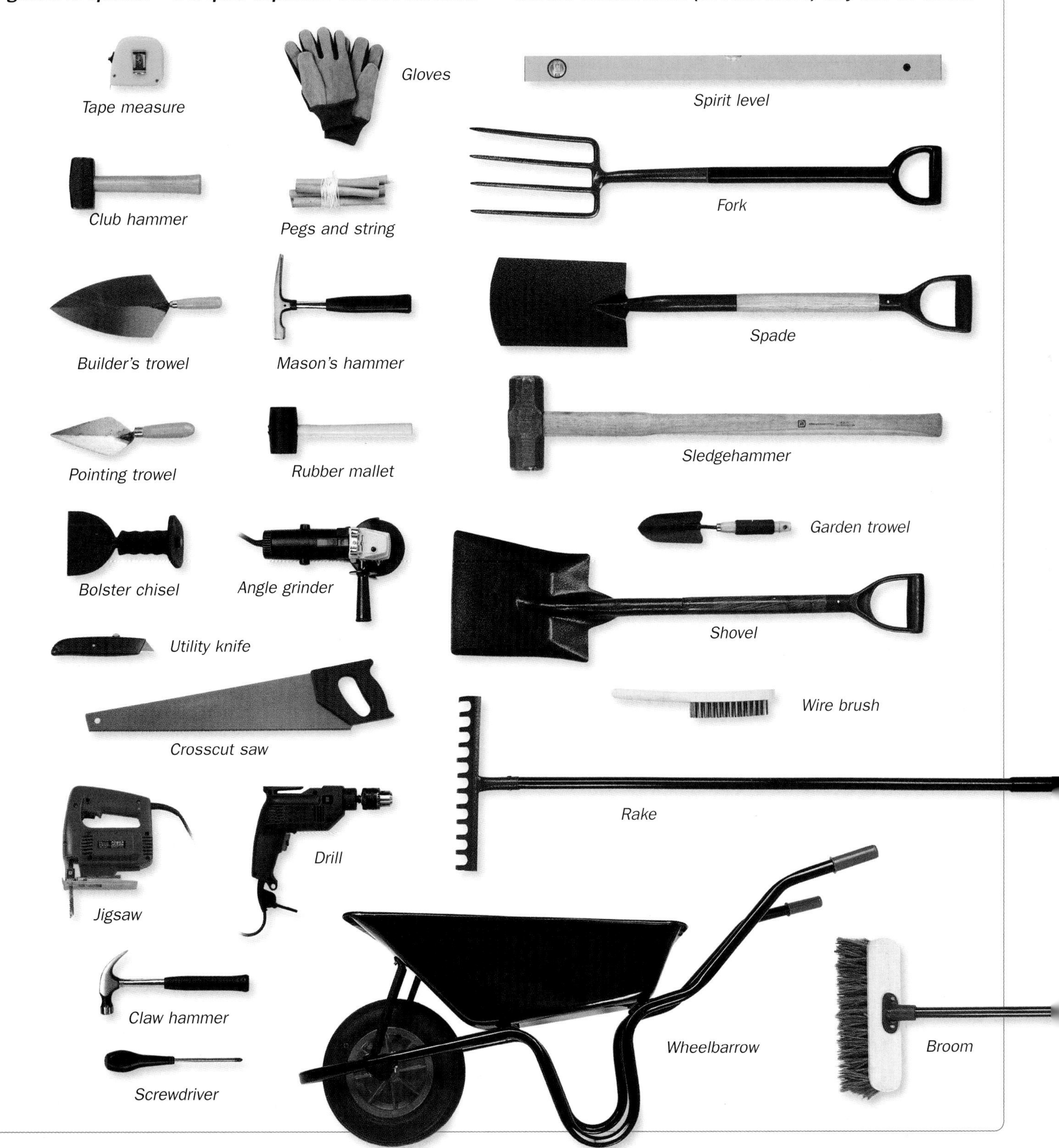
Tape measure
Gloves
Spirit level
Club hammer
Pegs and string
Fork
Builder's trowel
Mason's hammer
Spade
Pointing trowel
Rubber mallet
Sledgehammer
Garden trowel
Bolster chisel
Angle grinder
Shovel
Utility knife
Crosscut saw
Wire brush
Rake
Jigsaw
Drill
Claw hammer
Screwdriver
Wheelbarrow
Broom

Basic techniques

Once you have mastered the basic techniques, working with stone is a wonderfully therapeutic experience. After a day or so of practising the basic techniques, such as cutting stone and mixing mortar, you will be able to tackle any of the projects in this book. And after a weekend of putting your skills into practice, you will see a fascinating structure emerge from a heap of stone and a pile of sand.

Marking out

When you have chosen your site and made sure that it is right for the project, measure out the area needed and mark it with pegs and string. If the foundation is square or rectilinear, check that corners are at right angles by making sure that the two diagonal measurements are identical. The two-peg technique at the corners (see photo on the right) not only allows you to set out the shape without cutting the string, but also to dig the trench without the pegs getting in the way. Use a natural-fibre string that is less likely to twist and knot itself.

Make sure the strings cross at right angles

You can choose to wet the string prior to use so that it shrinks and tightens on the pegs

Use pegs and string to mark out the size and shape of a site. Double-check your measurements every step of the way.

Preparing a foundation

Rock the ends of the batten against the top edge of the formwork

You may need to add or remove concrete to achieve the correct level

Use a frame of wood (formwork) set level in the ground to establish the area for the concrete slab. Fill the formwork with concrete and tamp and scrape it level.

Building formwork

With the shape of the foundation marked with pegs and string, dig out the earth to the required depth and move it from the site. Take the formwork boards and formwork pegs, and set to work building a frame within the recess. Bang two pegs in the ground, set one board level against the pegs and screw it in place. Position the second board against the first and fix it with pegs, then continue until the frame is complete.

Use the spirit level to check that the top edge of the frame is level. If it is necessary to hit the frame slightly to adjust the level, be sure to remove the spirit level first so that it doesn't get hit with the hammer by accident.

Laying the concrete slab

When the formwork has been built, spread your chosen hardcore – it might be broken stone or builder's rubble – within the frame and use the sledgehammer to stamp it into the ground. Avoid using rubble that contains vegetable matter, bits and pieces of rusty iron or glass. Never use anything that contains asbestos. Continue until you have a firm, compact layer of hardcore.

Starting from one end of the formwork, pour concrete over the hardcore. Spread it roughly with the shovel, and use a length of wood to tamp it level with the top of the formwork. The general rule with concrete is the dryer the mix, the stronger the finished concrete slab.

Cutting stone

Use a bolster chisel and a club hammer to cut (break) pieces of stone. Hold the chisel upright and hit it several times.

Using a bolster chisel

A bolster chisel and club hammer are used to break stones in two. Mark the line of cut with a straight-edge and a piece of chalk. Wear gloves to guard your hands and goggles to protect your eyes. Keep children and pets out of the way because of the danger of flying shards of stone. Place the stone on a block of wood, a pad of old carpet or even a pile of sand, set the bolster chisel on the line, and give it a series of taps with the club hammer. Repeat this procedure on both sides of the stone to score a line. Now increase the force of the blow until the stone breaks in two. Don't be tempted to try and break the stone with a single, crashing blow – it rarely works!

Using a mason's hammer

A mason's hammer is used to trim stones to shape. Hold the stone firmly in one hand, so that the edge to be trimmed is furthest away from you. Take the mason's hammer and use the chisel end of the head to clip the edge into shape.

Building

Laying courses of stone

Mix the mortar to a smooth, buttery consistency, so that it is firm without being watery. Dampen the pile of stone. Trowel mortar on the foundation slab and set the first stone in place. Butter the end of the next stone with mortar and bed it into the mortar on the slab, with its end butted hard up against the first stone. When you have a line of stones, take a club hammer or rubber mallet and gently tap the stones into line. Don't fuss around with the mortar that oozes out, other than to gather it up and throw it back on the pile. Make sure that bits of hard mortar and stone do not get thrown back into the mortar heap.

Levelling the courses

When you have put down a group of stones, it is necessary to check and adjust the vertical and horizontal levels. Stand back and try to identify problems, then put a wooden batten on the stones, and tap it with the hammer until the offending stones get into line. Place the spirit level against the batten to take a reading, then make further adjustments if needed.

When you are laying courses of stone, remember to stagger the joints and check each course is level before proceeding.

Filling joints

After filling crazy-paving joints with mortar, use a pointing trowel to shape the mortar into an angled or slightly peaked finish.

Filling joints

When you have finished a section of wall, the cavities need to be filled or pointed. Use the small pointing trowel to spread a 10 mm layer of buttery mortar over the back of the large bricklayer's trowel. Using the large trowel as your palette and the small trowel like a spatula, slice through the mortar to reveal a straight edge, and then pick up a 10 mm-wide strip on the back edge of the small trowel (so that you have a square-section worm) and wipe it into the cavity. Follow the procedure on all open joints. This is a skill that needs to be practised. Hold the trowels in the way that is most comfortable for you, and you will be more likely to get good results.

Pointing and raking joints

You can either wait until the mortar is firm and then use the trowel to tool it to a smooth, shaped finish, or you can wait until the mortar is hard and rake out the joints to reveal the edges of the stone. Most projects in this book favour the raking option. Do not be tempted to rake out mortar while it is still soft.

Paths, steps and patios

Paths, steps and patios are functionally desirable in that they provide dry, level areas enabling us to move around the garden in comfort. They are also visually desirable – who can resist exploring a path that curves out of sight, or climbing steps that lead up a slope, or sitting on a shaded patio? Visit parks, gardens and stately homes to get an idea of possibilities for schemes varying from the simple to the grandiose.

Constructing paths

Designing and planning

Study the site and decide on the route and the type of path, including the depth and structure of the foundation, and the type of surface material and edging required. Use the tape measure, pegs and string to mark out the route on the ground. Make sure that the layout does not upset the balance of the garden.

Building

Dig out the earth to the required depth, spread compacted hardcore over the site and top it with your chosen surface – sand, ballast or concrete. If the ground is soft and/or wet, a firmer foundation is needed, so dig out the earth to a greater depth, increase the thickness of the hardcore, and use concrete rather than sand or ballast. Bed the stone, pavers or slabs on generous blobs of mortar. Dig a trench and bed the edging in mortar. Finally, fill the joints with sand or mortar.

This beautifully crafted, natural-looking path is built from Gloucestershire stone. The stones are set on edge (a traditional technique) in a mixture of clay and crushed stone. The path may be a little bumpy to walk on, but would look good in a traditional garden. Curved or undulating paths can also be built using the same technique.

INSPIRATIONS

A mixture of brick pavers and stone lends itself to rectangular layouts.

The precise shapes of moulded concrete slabs allow you to create complex patterns.

Natural stone steps edged by rockery stones are ideal for a fairly informal garden.

Constructing steps

Designing and planning

Decide on the number and height of the risers, and the depth of the treads. Measure the average thickness of the stone you intend to use and see how many courses you need for each riser.

Building

Use pegs and string to set out the foundation, then dig to the required depth, set the formwork in the recess and fill it with hardcore and concrete. Build the first riser and side walls and back-fill with hardcore. Set the first tread in place. Build subsequent steps in the same way.

These rockery steps are like stepping stones and seem to be part of the landscape. The design of more formal steps needs careful planning with a tape measure, batten and spirit level.

Constructing a patio

This blue-grey patio is made of random pieces of slate laid as crazy paving. It includes a circular feature made of stones set on edge in a radiating pattern, looking like a fossilized ammonite.

Designing and planning

Use the tape measure, string and pegs to describe the shape of the patio on the ground. If you are using cast concrete pavers, do your best to make sure that the patio is made up from a number of whole units, so that you don't have to cut slabs.

Building

Dig the foundation to the required depth and set the formwork in place. Check the levels and adjust the formwork so that there is a very slight fall to one side, so the patio will shed surface water. Spread the hardcore and sand, ballast or concrete. Bed the surface material on mortar.

Recessed steps, together with symmetrical decorative urns, give a classical feel to an area.

A patio area and path made from stone pavers, stepping stones, cobbles and gravel.

A circular patio and a radiating design attract attention and so become a focal point.

Walls and other structures

Walls, containers, pedestals and other freestanding structures are usually built from courses of stone and extra care is needed to build strong, safe structures that will not fall down. Once completed, there is a good chance that they will still be in existence in a hundred years' time. Walls are capable of making a powerful statement in your garden, with aesthetic possibilities as well as practical advantages.

Constructing walls

Designing and planning

Decide where you want the wall. Do you want a dry-stone wall or are you going to use mortar? Do you want an easy-to-build low wall (such as a three-course wall across the corner of the garden), or a more complex freestanding structure that needs a substantial foundation?

Once you have decided on the height, form and construction, sit down with a pencil and paper and work out the quantities of stone, sand and cement.

Building

Use a tape measure, pegs and string to establish the shape of the foundation trench. Dig the trench, half-fill it with hardcore and top it with concrete. Select stone for the first two or three courses and have a dry run to test placement. Then either lay the stones with mud pug if it is a dry-stone wall (see the Dry-stone Border Wall on page 132), or use mortar.

This dry-stone wall in Wales is made from chunky slabs of slate. Note how the builder has selected and placed the stones to create a strong and attractive pattern.

INSPIRATIONS

Mixed materials and built-in shelves provide a beautiful backdrop for pot plants.

This stone wall with decorative coping (top pieces) could make a good garden boundary wall.

A seating area achieved by incorporating large, outward-extending slabs into the wall.

Constructing containers

A container made from a single piece of found stone. Not everyone is lucky enough to find a piece of naturally hollowed stone such as this, but it is possible to make your own using hypertufa (see the Japanese Suiseki Stone on page 120).

Designing and planning

Establish the shape, height and composition of the container. Decide whether it needs a foundation, such as a slab, a trench full of hardcore, or a trench with hardcore and concrete, and then use the tape measure, pegs and string to mark the shape of the foundation on the ground.

Building

Once the foundation is in place, take your chosen stone and set out the first two or three courses dry, choosing the best possible stones for the corners. Fix the courses in place with mortar.

Constructing columns and pedestals

Designing, planning and building

Columns and pedestals are really just small containers with the centres filled in, so you can follow the same designing, planning and building procedures already described. Build with extra care and attention, especially when it comes to checking the horizontal and vertical levels, because tiny inaccuracies are swiftly accentuated and highlighted by the modest size of the structure. Remember that there is always a correlation between the height of the structure and the size of the foundation. If you want to build a tall structure (more than 1 m high) the foundation needs to be proportionally wider.

As an alternative to building a pedestal from lots of small pieces of stone, you can search around for large, ready-made pieces. Here, saddle stones (used for the base of a haystack) form striking pedestals for displaying plant pots or ornaments.

Decorative stone containers, full of plants, add interest and warmth to a plain paved area.

A bold stone structure is sometimes all that is needed to decorate your yard.

A two-tier pedestal for displaying plants, which could also form a retaining wall.

Rockeries and other stone arrangements

Rockeries are built in direct imitation of nature; other garden stone arrangements are often built as a contrast or may even have a symbolic purpose, containing spheres, cones or Japanese lanterns, for example. Look at stones in nature, art and architecture, and then draw inspiration from your observations.

Constructing a rockery

A striking rockery and waterfall. The large rocks have been positioned in imitation of a natural rocky slope. (If you want to make a rockery avoiding the use of huge rocks, see the Traditional Rockery project on page 112, which uses thin layers of stone instead.)

Designing and planning

To give you ideas for constructing a natural-looking rockery, think about the beaches and mountains you have visited. Use a tape measure, pegs and string to map the shape of the rockery on the ground. Remember that if you are going to use huge rocks, you have to find some way of getting them to the site. It may be easier to group small rocks, which are relatively easy to move, so that they look like large outcrops.

Building

Clear the site of all weeds and cover it with shale, hardcore or shingle. Arrange the rocks in groups or stacks, and tilt them so that they rear up at an angle. Create small pockets of rich soil all over the site, for filling with rockery plants. Cover a good proportion of the rocks and soil with your chosen grit, pea gravel or crushed shell.

INSPIRATIONS

A miniature version of a stony landscape will blend well into almost any small garden.

This arrangement of bold plants bordered by large rocks looks like a natural outcrop.

A design using ground-covering stone, plants and rocks to mimic a river and its banks.

An award-winning Japanese-style garden (Gold medal winner at the Hampton Court Flower Festival, England, 1995). A "river" of stone flows beneath a simple stone bridge and around other small feature stones – a landscape in miniature.

A beautifully built cone, which may not be particularly useful, but is a great piece of sculpture for the garden! Any bold shape like this will probably dominate a small garden, so make sure you really want one.

Japanese-style arrangements

Designing and building

For the Japanese, the art of rock arrangement is concerned with using a small number of stones to create a blend of nature and symbolism, and each and every stone that plays a part needs to be chosen with great care. When creating your own version try, if possible, to use timeworn stones covered in moss and lichen, which impart subtle colour, shape and character to the arrangement.

Sculptures and other found objects

Designing and building

The wonderful thing about using stone sculptures and found stones is that you can follow your intuition and create an arrangement that is uniquely your own. If you like stone frogs or gnomes, or have a passion for collecting pebbles, you are halfway to having a very special rock garden. Set aside a corner – perhaps an area ringed with rocks – and then simply set out your sculptures and found stones, allowing the arrangement to evolve.

A traditional Japanese design that uses bamboo to deliver water to a stone basin.

A simple path design is remarkably powerful when placed in stark surroundings.

A "river" of randomly shaped stones forms an attractive path and is also easy to build.

Part 2

Projects

Traditional rockery

Easy

Making time
One weekend
One day for clearing the site and setting the rocks in place, and one day for planting

Anyone who is lucky enough to have a natural outcrop of rock in the garden has the perfect place for planting beautiful heathers, alpines and lichens. You can create the same effect by building a rockery with lots of nooks and crannies for rock plants. The great thing about this project is the fact that the rockery is made from small, easy-to-handle stones, which can be transported in your car without difficulty.

Considering the design

It would be nice if you could wave a magic wand and conjure up a series of dramatic monolithic rocks in your garden. However, the expense, physical challenge and access difficulties involved in moving large single rocks into an established garden make most people shy away from the prospect. It's much easier to build a rockery from small, manageable rocks, and we have designed the project with this in mind.

The slices of rock are stacked like slices of bread, and arranged to resemble the tip of a sloping outcrop of stone breaking through the ground. Note how the groups of stones are placed in steps, and the line of steps both rears up and angles across the bed. The borders of the rockery are defined by stones set on edge.

Getting started

Walk around your garden and look at the various possible sites. Ideally, you need a site that is gently sloping, well drained, and has no overhanging trees. It should receive plenty of sun, because many rockery plants prefer these conditions.

You will need

Tools

- Tape measure
- Pegs and string
- Spade, fork, rake and shovel
- Wheelbarrow and bucket
- Club hammer

Materials

For a rockery 2 m long and 1 m wide

- York stone: about 3 sq. m of split sandstone, in the largest sizes that you can manage (rockery stones)
- York stone: about 2 sq. m of split sandstone in random small sizes (coping edging)
- Shingle: 300 kg of large-size, well-washed shingle
- Pea gravel: 100 kg of well-washed gravel in a colour to match the stone
- Planting mixture: 1 part (50 kg) topsoil, 1 part (50 kg) fine grit, gravel or stone chippings, 1 part (50 kg) leaf mould
- Rockery plants (such as erica, sedum, alyssum, aubretia, campanula, cerastium, erigeron, primula, saponaria, sempervivum, saxifrage, thyme; bulbs such as dwarf narcissus, crocus, cyclamen, chionodoxa, muscari, galanthus and convallaria)

Overall dimensions and general notes

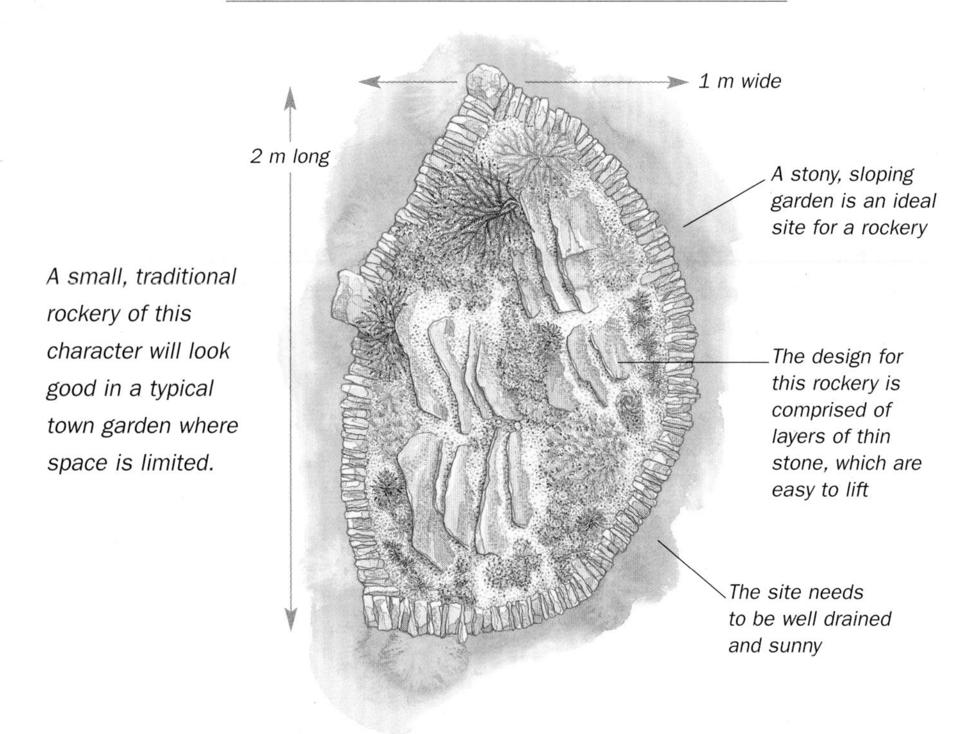
1 m wide
2 m long
A stony, sloping garden is an ideal site for a rockery
The design for this rockery is comprised of layers of thin stone, which are easy to lift
The site needs to be well drained and sunny

A small, traditional rockery of this character will look good in a typical town garden where space is limited.

Cut-away view of the traditional rockery

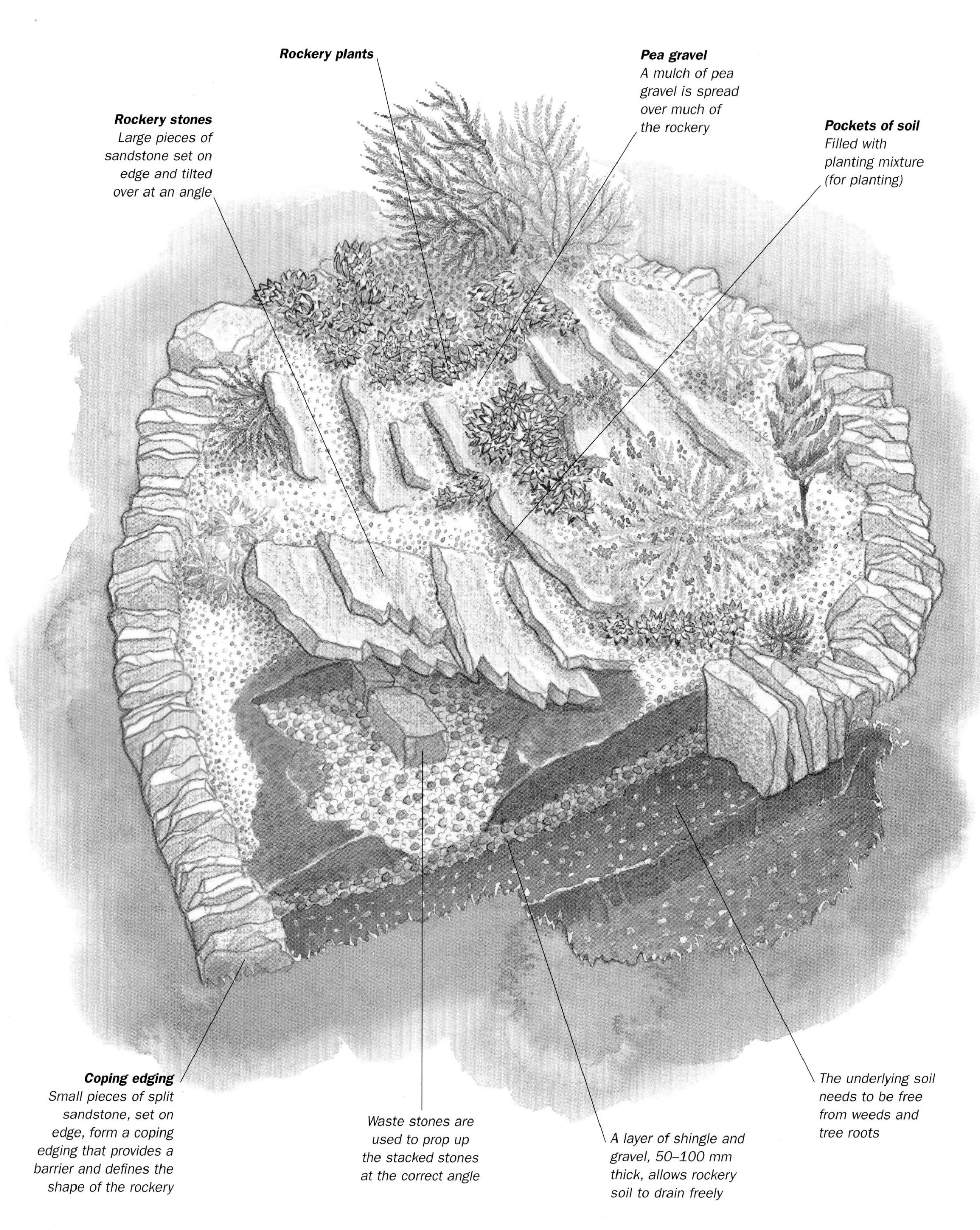
Rockery plants
Pea gravel
A mulch of pea gravel is spread over much of the rockery
Rockery stones
Large pieces of sandstone set on edge and tilted over at an angle
Pockets of soil
Filled with planting mixture (for planting)
Coping edging
Small pieces of split sandstone, set on edge, form a coping edging that provides a barrier and defines the shape of the rockery
Waste stones are used to prop up the stacked stones at the correct angle
A layer of shingle and gravel, 50–100 mm thick, allows rockery soil to drain freely
The underlying soil needs to be free from weeds and tree roots

Making the traditional rockery

1 Measuring out
Measure out the area for the rockery, clear the turf and weeds, and define it with a simple coping made from stones set on edge. Dig over the site and increase the drainage by adding a small amount of shingle and pea gravel to the earth.

2 Covering with shingle
Rake shingle and pea gravel over the whole site to a depth of about 50–100 mm. Tread it into the soil, until the entire area feels firm underfoot.

3 Stacking the stone
Stack the split sandstone rockery stones side by side, in groups of three or four slices. Arrange the leading edges of the stones so that the profiles look natural in relation to each other.

4 Stabilizing the rockery
Use pieces of waste stone to prop up the stacks of stone so that they all rear up at the same angle. Pack additional shingle under the stacks to make them stable and firm.

5 Adding soil
Rake the planting mixture over the whole arrangement and pack it under the stones. Look for natural planting areas, and make sure that they are covered by a generous thickness of soil.

6 Planting
Purchase suitable rockery plants. Spend time considering the best possible arrangement before you plant them. Water them in, and water regularly until established.

Magic knot path

★
Easy

Making time
Two weekends
Two days for laying the concrete, and two days for laying the slabs and making good

If you enjoy colour and Celtic imagery, this path will appeal. It is a good, strong, formal path, which is hardwearing and long-lasting. The imitation York stone flags and terracotta trim (both made from concrete) ensure a firm, non-slippery surface. The path is made up from three component parts: a basic flagstone, a Celtic knot strip, and a Celtic corner square (used in a central position in the design).

Considering the design

The pattern consists of a number of repeats, each comprising two flagstones surrounded by three strips and a single corner square. The path is 1.074 m wide. The length of the strips allows the slabs to be set in place with an all-round joint width of about 6 mm.

Getting started

Decide how long you want your path to be. Divide the total length by 612 mm to work out how many repeats you need, and then multiply the number of components in the repeat to give you the total amounts of materials required.

Overall dimensions and general notes

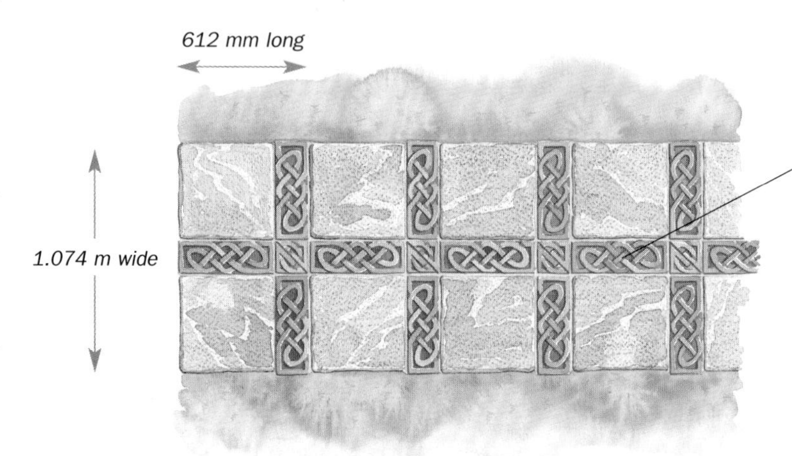
612 mm long
1.074 m wide
The design can be changed to suit your needs (the paving strips could run either side of the path instead of down the middle)

This bold, colourful path works well in many styles of garden, from minimalist modern spaces to traditional cottage plots. The design is only suitable for a straight path.

You will need

Tools

- ✔ Tape measure and straight-edge
- ✔ Pegs and string
- ✔ Spade, fork and shovel
- ✔ Wheelbarrow and bucket
- ✔ Crosscut saw
- ✔ Claw hammer
- ✔ Club hammer
- ✔ Sledgehammer
- ✔ Tamping beam: about 1.5 m long, 60 mm wide and 30 mm thick
- ✔ Bricklayer's trowel
- ✔ Spirit level
- ✔ Rubber mallet
- ✔ Pointing trowel
- ✔ Soft-bristled brush

Materials

All quantities are per 612 mm of path (1 repeat). Path is 1.074 m wide

- ✔ Reconstituted York stone paving slabs: 2 slabs, 450 mm square
- ✔ Celtic knot terracotta paving strips: 3 strips, 462 mm long, 150 mm wide and 38 mm thick
- ✔ Celtic knot terracotta corner square: 1 piece, 150 mm square and 38 mm thick
- ✔ Pine boards: length to suit your path, 150 mm wide and 20 mm thick (formwork)
- ✔ Pine battens: length to suit width of your path, 30 mm wide and 20 mm thick (expansion battens, tamping beam and formwork pegs)
- ✔ Hardcore: 2 wheelbarrow loads
- ✔ Concrete: 1 part (14 kg) cement, 3 parts (42 kg) ballast
- ✔ Mortar: 1 part (10 kg) cement, 2 parts (20 kg) soft sand
- ✔ Nails: 1 kg of 38 mm-long nails

Cut-away view of the magic knot path

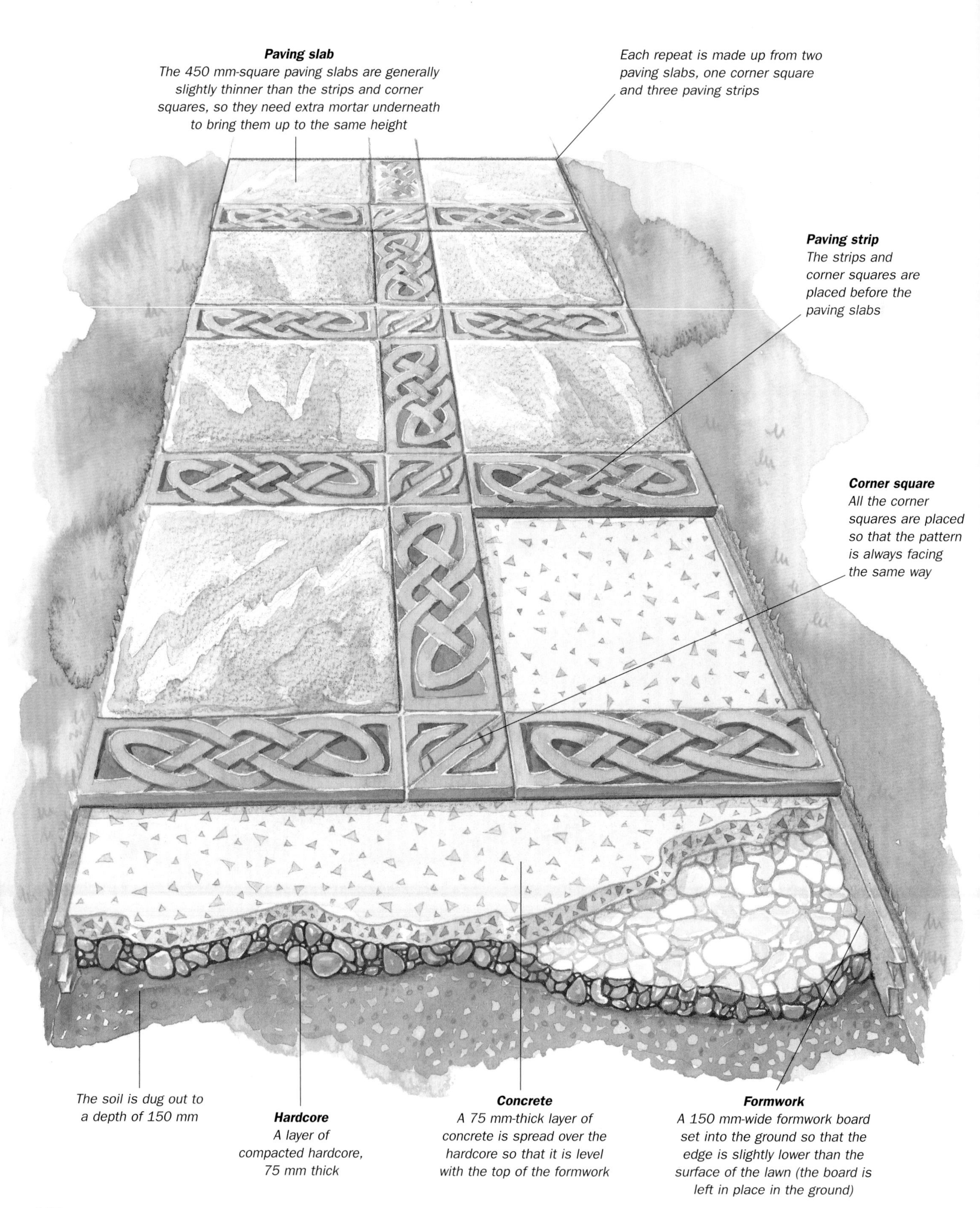
Paving slab
The 450 mm-square paving slabs are generally slightly thinner than the strips and corner squares, so they need extra mortar underneath to bring them up to the same height
Each repeat is made up from two paving slabs, one corner square and three paving strips
Paving strip
The strips and corner squares are placed before the paving slabs
Corner square
All the corner squares are placed so that the pattern is always facing the same way
The soil is dug out to a depth of 150 mm
Hardcore
A layer of compacted hardcore, 75 mm thick
Concrete
A 75 mm-thick layer of concrete is spread over the hardcore so that it is level with the top of the formwork
Formwork
A 150 mm-wide formwork board set into the ground so that the edge is slightly lower than the surface of the lawn (the board is left in place in the ground)

Making the magic knot path

1 Setting up the formwork
Mark out the path, making it 1.074 m wide. Dig out the earth to a depth of 150 mm. Put the formwork boards in the recess, nailing them with the claw hammer and fixing them in place with the formwork pegs. Compact a 75 mm layer of hardcore on the path.

2 Filling with concrete
Set expansion battens every 2–3 metres across the width of the path to allow for expansion of the concrete. Mix the concrete to a thick consistency. Shovel it over the hardcore and use the tamping beam to tamp it level with the top edge of the formwork.

3 Establishing guidelines
Use string to mark out a guideline at one side of the path. Placing the paving strips against this, set out another guideline 462 mm in from the side to mark the position of the corner squares in the centre of the path.

4 Laying the strips
Mix the mortar to a stiff, buttery consistency and lay the corner squares and paving strips down the centre of the path. Use the spirit level and rubber mallet to ensure that they are level.

5 Laying the paving slabs
Lay each York stone paving slab by setting five generous, bun-sized blobs of mortar on the path. Position the slabs so that they are level with the paving strips. Make sure that the joints are consistently 6 mm wide.

6 Pointing
Finally, mix a small amount of mortar to a dry, crumbly consistency, and brush and trowel it into the joints. Wait about four hours and then brush all surplus mortar off the path.

Japanese suiseki stone

Easy

Making time
One weekend
One day for casting the stone, and one day for arranging the stone and the cobbles

Traditional Japanese gardens make great use of stone for ornamental and symbolic purposes. One such stone is termed a *suiseki* – meaning a large, natural basin. Our suiseki combines Japanese heritage with the very English craft of making stone-like containers from hypertufa, which is a mixture of moss, sand and cement. If you like the notion of East meeting West, this project will add oriental tranquillity to your garden.

Overall dimensions and general notes

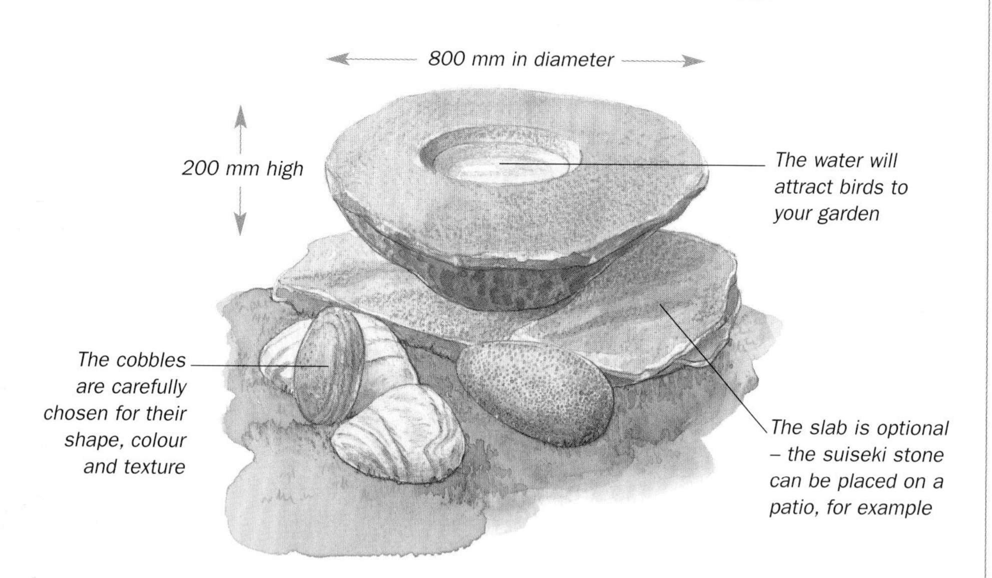
800 mm in diameter
200 mm high
The water will attract birds to your garden
The cobbles are carefully chosen for their shape, colour and texture
The slab is optional – the suiseki stone can be placed on a patio, for example

The suiseki will look good in slightly wild settings; also in a modern garden or courtyard. It is a traditional element in Japanese gardens, which are famed for their relaxing qualities.

Considering the design

This is one of the easiest projects in the book – the suiseki stone emerges after a straightforward process which really only involves pressing the hypertufa mix over an upturned bowl to create a cast basin. However, the simplicity of its creation belies the finished effect – once the basin is displayed with one or two specimen rocks and stones, and shown off against a subtle backdrop of carefully chosen plants, perhaps in a quiet and protected corner of the garden, it comes into its own as an object of surprising beauty. In a Japanese garden, the suiseki symbolizes the refreshing and purifying aspects of nature, such as dew on a leaf, or water in the cleft of a rock.

The suiseki is about 800 mm wide at the rim and 200 mm tall, and the under-cut and textured underside contrasts with the smooth and level top surface.

Getting started

Start searching for a smooth plastic or metal bowl that is wider at the rim than at the base. We used a stainless-steel bowl found in a charity shop, 300 mm in diameter at the rim, 170 mm in diameter at the base, and 100 mm in height.

You will need

Tools

- Workboard: 1 m square
- Wheelbarrow
- Shovel
- Bucket
- Bricklayer's trowel
- Tape measure and a spirit level
- Wire snips
- Paintbrush

Materials

For a suiseki stone 800 mm in diameter and 200 mm high

- Hypertufa mix:
  1 part (25 kg) cement,
  1 part (25 kg) sharp sand,
  2 parts (50 kg) sphagnum moss
- Bowl: metal or plastic, 300 mm in diameter at the rim, 170 mm in diameter at the base, and 100 mm in height
- Bar of kitchen soap
- Wire grid mesh: 25 mm mesh, about 400 mm square
- Mortar: 1 part (2 kg) cement, 3 parts (6 kg) soft sand
- Resin: about 4 cupfuls of waterproofing medium
- Cobbles for decoration

Cross-section of the Japanese suiseki stone during construction (the stone is upside-down)

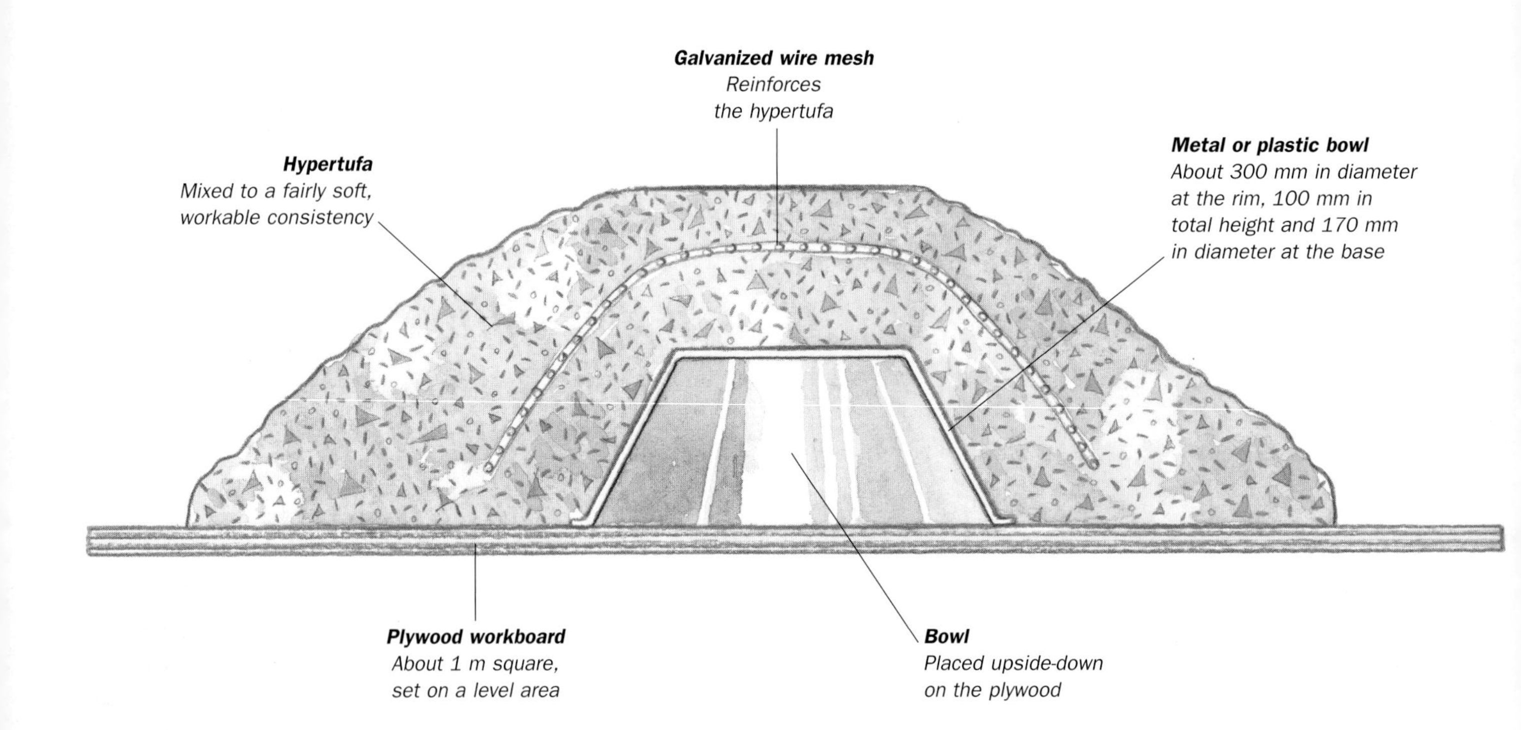
Galvanized wire mesh
Reinforces
the hypertufa
Hypertufa
Mixed to a fairly soft,
workable consistency
Metal or plastic bowl
About 300 mm in diameter
at the rim, 100 mm in
total height and 170 mm
in diameter at the base
Plywood workboard
About 1 m square,
set on a level area
Bowl
Placed upside-down
on the plywood

Cut-away view of the Japanese suiseki stone

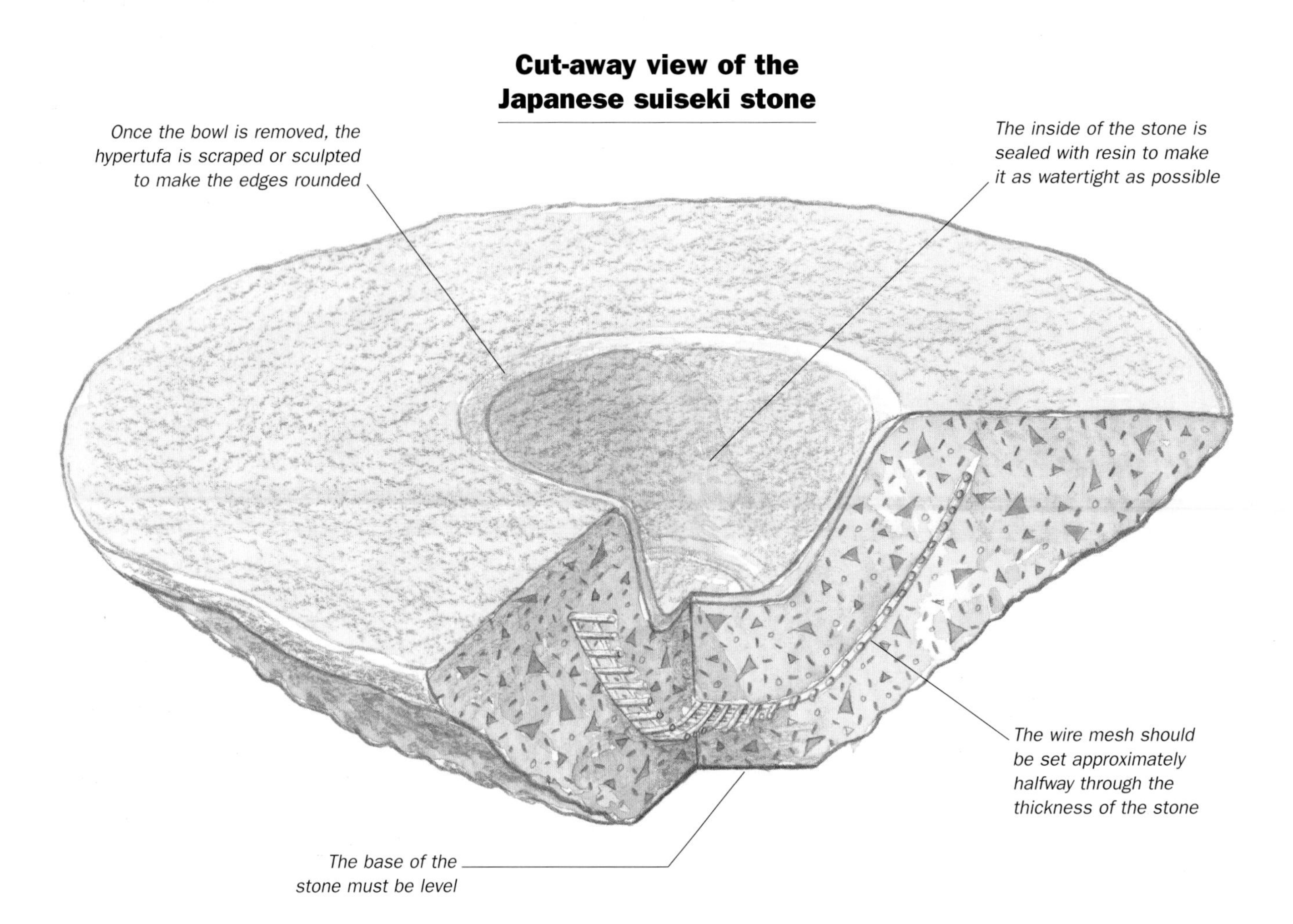
Once the bowl is removed, the
hypertufa is scraped or sculpted
to make the edges rounded
The inside of the stone is
sealed with resin to make
it as watertight as possible
The wire mesh should
be set approximately
halfway through the
thickness of the stone
The base of the
stone must be level

Making the Japanese suiseki stone

1 Mixing the hypertufa
Wipe the outside of the bowl with a small amount of water and a lot of soap, until it is slippery. Set it upside-down on the workboard. Mix the hypertufa ingredients with water to form a soft consistency, and start spreading a layer of it over the bowl.

2 Inserting the wire mesh
Build up a layer of hypertufa about 70 mm thick, then cut the wire mesh to fit over the mound and press it in. All the edges should be embedded and it must be a tight, close-hugging fit.

3 Completing the mound
Continue adding hypertufa until the wire mesh is completely covered. Aim for a mound that is irregular in shape and about 800 mm in diameter at the widest part of the rim. Run the trowel round the rim to smooth it.

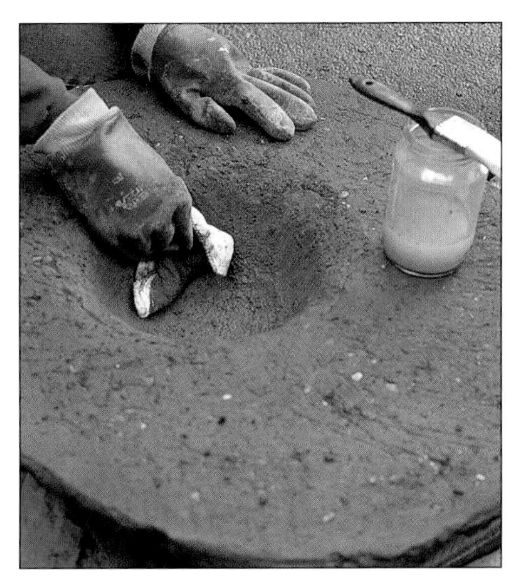

4 Texturing the surface
Level the top of the mound so that the finished basin will sit flat when it is flipped over. Use your fingers to knead and texture the surface of the sides so that it looks weathered and worn.

5 Painting with resin
When the hypertufa is dry, turn the mound over and remove the bowl. Wipe the inside of the depression with mortar. When it has dried, paint a coat of resin over the mortar to make it waterproof.

6 Setting up the suiseki
Continue to make the surface of the hypertufa look like weathered stone by scratching and scraping it. Finally, set the suiseki level on your chosen slab of stone, fill it with water, and decorate it with cobbles and plants.

Old English random paving

If you are intending to build a patio, but do not want to use identical square paving slabs or tessellating blocks, Old English random paving is a good option. It is easy to lay, functional, and the subtle repeat pattern looks good. Although the style is "Old English", the slabs are very modern reconstituted stone. This patio is 3 m square, which gives plenty of space for a table and chairs, or a couple of sun loungers.

★
Easy

Making time
One weekend
One day for setting out the formwork; one day for laying the concrete and the slabs

Considering the design

The design is based on a 300 mm grid. The patio is made from three sizes of reconstituted York stone slab: twelve large squares, eighteen half-squares, and sixteen quarter-squares. However if you wish, the emphasis of the pattern could be shifted to a different ratio of small to large squares, or the dimensions of the patio could be changed.

The ground in our site was so firm, dry and compacted that once the formwork was in place, we were able to simply fill the frame with concrete and lay the slabs. But if the ground in your garden is soft, insert a 100 mm layer of hardcore before laying the concrete.

Getting started

Once you have studied your site, draw up a 300 mm grid. If you want to vary the ratios of the three different slab sizes from those we have described, to make a different pattern, play around with the various options to work out how many of each type of slab you need.

You will need

Tools

- Tape measure and straight-edge
- Pegs and string
- Crosscut saw
- Spirit level
- Claw hammer
- Spade, fork and shovel
- Wheelbarrow and bucket
- Tamping beam: about 1.6 m long, 60 mm wide and 30 mm thick
- Club hammer
- Soft-bristled brush
- Pointing trowel

Materials

For a patio 3 m square

- Reconstituted York stone paving: 12 slabs, 600 mm x 600 mm; 18 slabs, 600 mm x 300 mm; 16 slabs, 300 mm x 300 mm
- Pine: 5 boards, 3 m long, 150 mm wide and 20 mm thick (formwork)
- Pine: 20 battens, 300 mm long, 30 mm wide and 20 mm thick (formwork pegs)
- Old boards to use as tread boards
- Concrete: 1 part (200 kg) cement, 5 parts (1000 kg) ballast
- Mortar: 1 part (20 kg) cement, 3 parts (60 kg) soft sand
- Nails: 1 kg of 38 mm-long nails

Overall dimensions and general notes

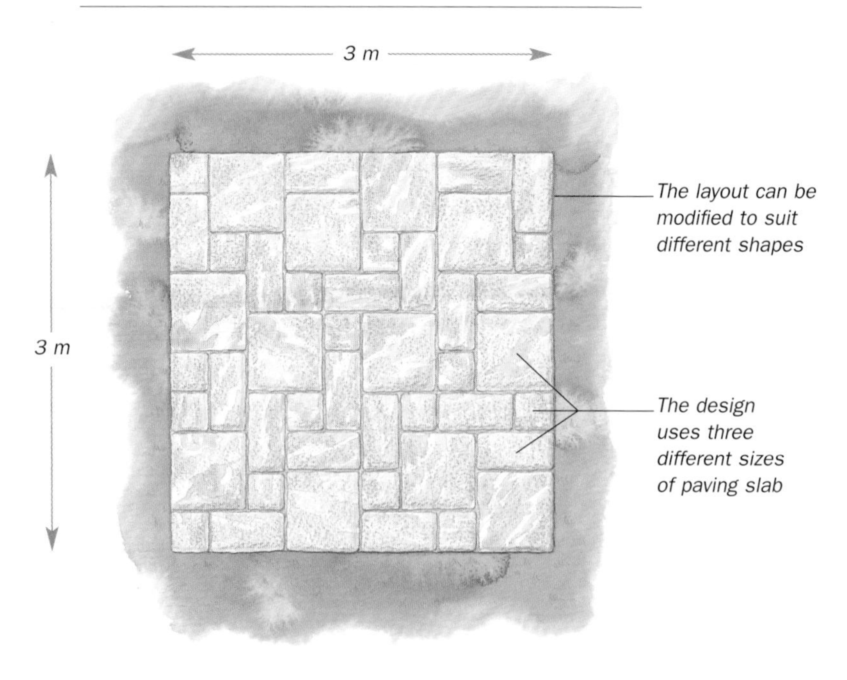
3 m
3 m
The layout can be modified to suit different shapes
The design uses three different sizes of paving slab

This patio will slot into many styles of garden successfully. The slabs are generally sold in three colours: buff, light sand and slate grey – choose a single colour or a mixture.

Cut-away view of the Old English random paving

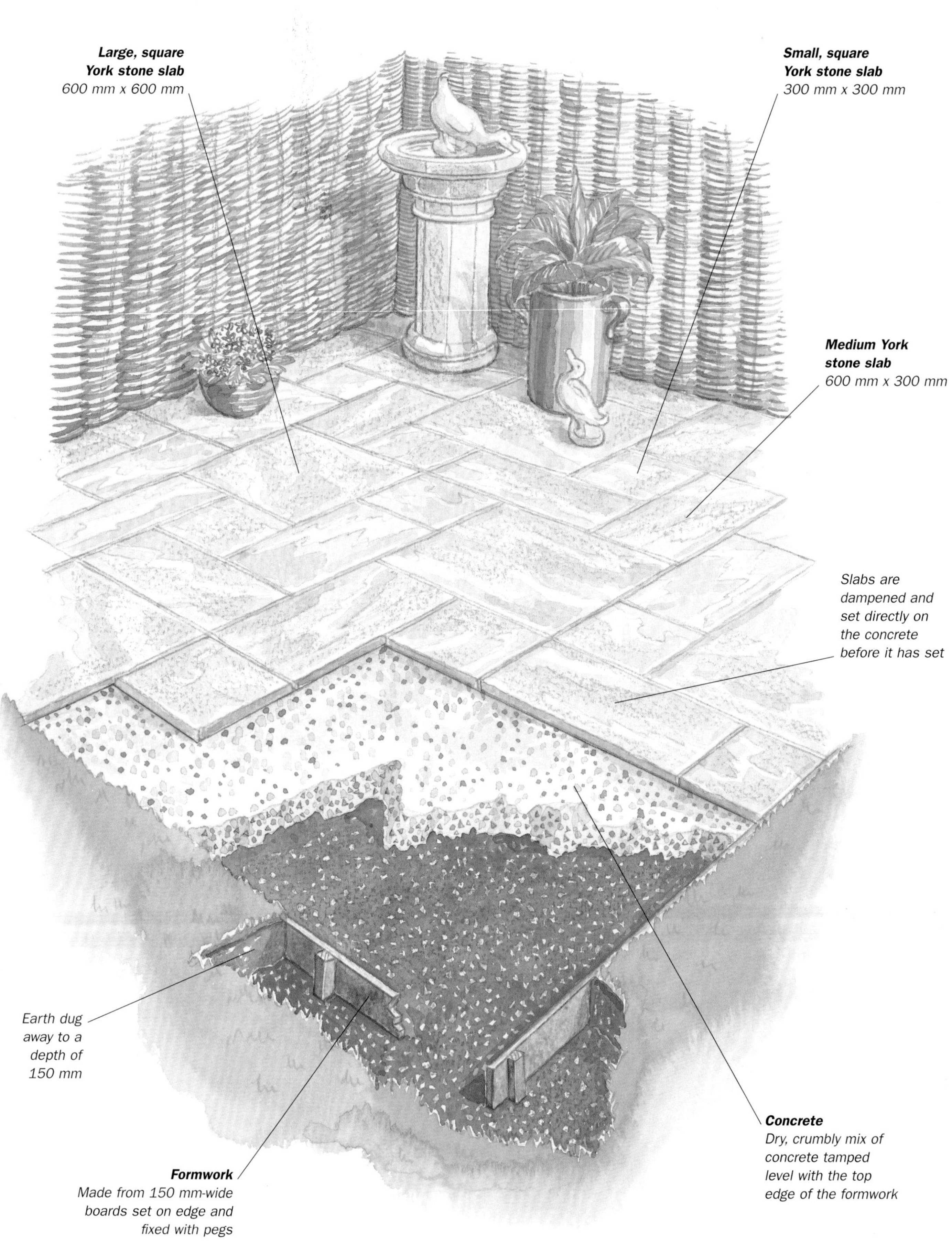
Large, square York stone slab
600 mm x 600 mm
Small, square York stone slab
300 mm x 300 mm
Medium York stone slab
600 mm x 300 mm
Slabs are dampened and set directly on the concrete before it has set
Earth dug away to a depth of 150 mm
Concrete
Dry, crumbly mix of concrete tamped level with the top edge of the formwork
Formwork
Made from 150 mm-wide boards set on edge and fixed with pegs

Making the Old English random paving

1 Building the formwork
Measure out the site and set the formwork boards in place – one on each of the four sides, and one down the middle. Level the boards and then adjust them so that there is a slight slope from one side of the site to another (for drainage).

2 Laying the concrete
Fix the formwork boards with formwork pegs and nails. Make a dry, crumbly mix of concrete and spread it over the base of the patio. Use the tamping beam to scrape the concrete level with the top edge of the formwork.

3 Laying the slabs
Dampen the back of the slabs and, very carefully, set them one at a time on the concrete. Use the handle of the club hammer to tap them level to each other.

4 Protecting the slabs
When it is necessary to walk over the slabs, cover them with the tread boards so that your weight is evenly spread, which will prevent the slabs from being knocked out of alignment. Step off the tread boards only when you are laying a slab.

5 Pointing
When the concrete has cured, mix the mortar to a dry, crumbly consistency and use the brush to sweep it between the slabs. Finally, use the pointing trowel to stroke the mortar to a smooth finish. Brush off any excess mortar.

Serpentine path

The serpentine path is a wonderful solution when you want an exciting and dynamic path to wind its way around various features in the garden. Its design also gives you the opportunity to keep your options about the precise shape and route of the path open until the last minute. It has been made from grey slabs throughout, but you could use a different colour, or even a combination of colours, if desired.

★★
Intermediate

Making time
One weekend
One day for preparation, and one day for laying the slabs and making good

Overall dimensions and general notes

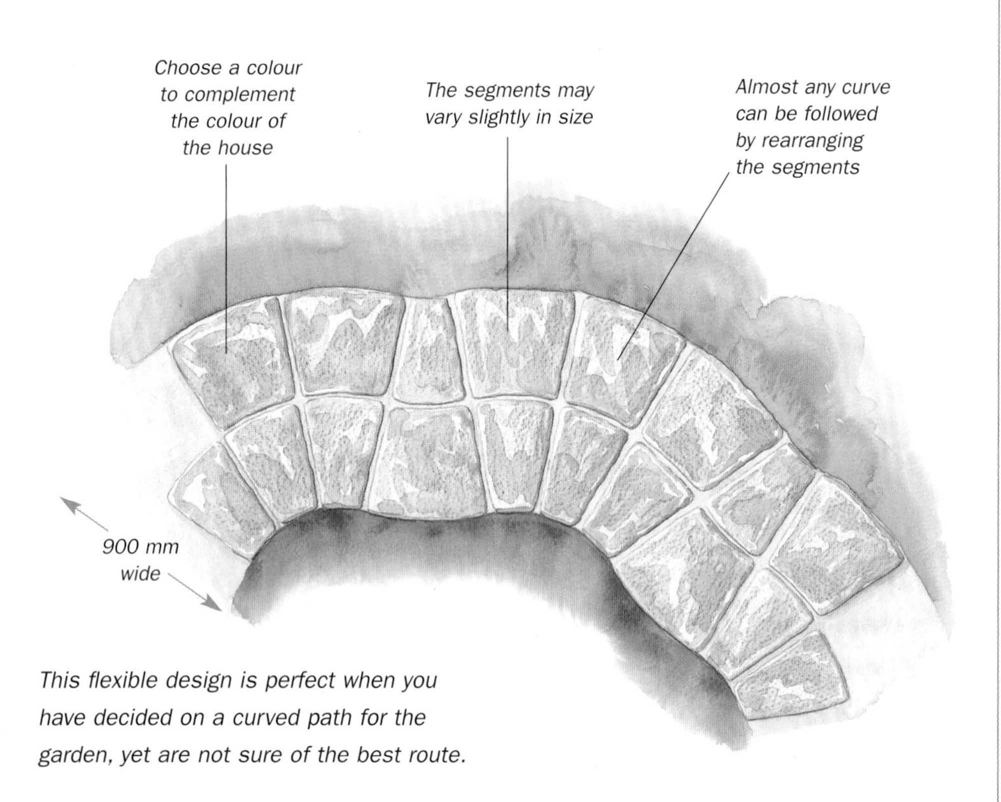
Choose a colour to complement the colour of the house
The segments may vary slightly in size
Almost any curve can be followed by rearranging the segments
900 mm wide

This flexible design is perfect when you have decided on a curved path for the garden, yet are not sure of the best route.

You will need

Tools

- Tape measure and chalk
- Spade, fork and shovel
- Wheelbarrow and bucket
- Rake and stiff-bristled broom
- Sledgehammer
- Bricklayer's trowel
- Tamping beam: about 1.5 m long, 60 mm wide and 30 mm thick
- Club hammer

Materials

For 4 m of path, 900 mm wide

- Middle segment paving slabs (reconstituted stone): 12 slabs, 450 mm radius
- Outer segment paving slabs (reconstituted stone): 12 slabs, 450 mm radius
- Sharp sand: about 400 kg
- Fine gravel: about 300 kg
- Mortar: 1 part (25 kg) cement, 2 parts (50 kg) soft sand

Considering the design

The path is made up from the middle and outer slabs in a circular patio kit. The slabs are set down in pairs to form two-slab wedges, and alternate wedges are reversed along the course of the path.

If you want the path to follow a direct route you reverse every other pair of slabs, whereas if you want it to bend to run around corners, you group the pairs in part-circle curves. The shapes of the slabs allow the path to run around bends and over bumps. Using a combination of middle segment and outer segment paving slabs, both measuring 450 mm on the radius line, the path works out to be about 900 mm wide. Quantities have been given per 4 m of path – adjust to suit your requirements.

Getting started

Take three or four paired slabs and put them on the lawn. Experiment with various arrangements in order to see how to steer the path around both gentle and sharp curves along the proposed route.

Cut-away view of the serpentine path

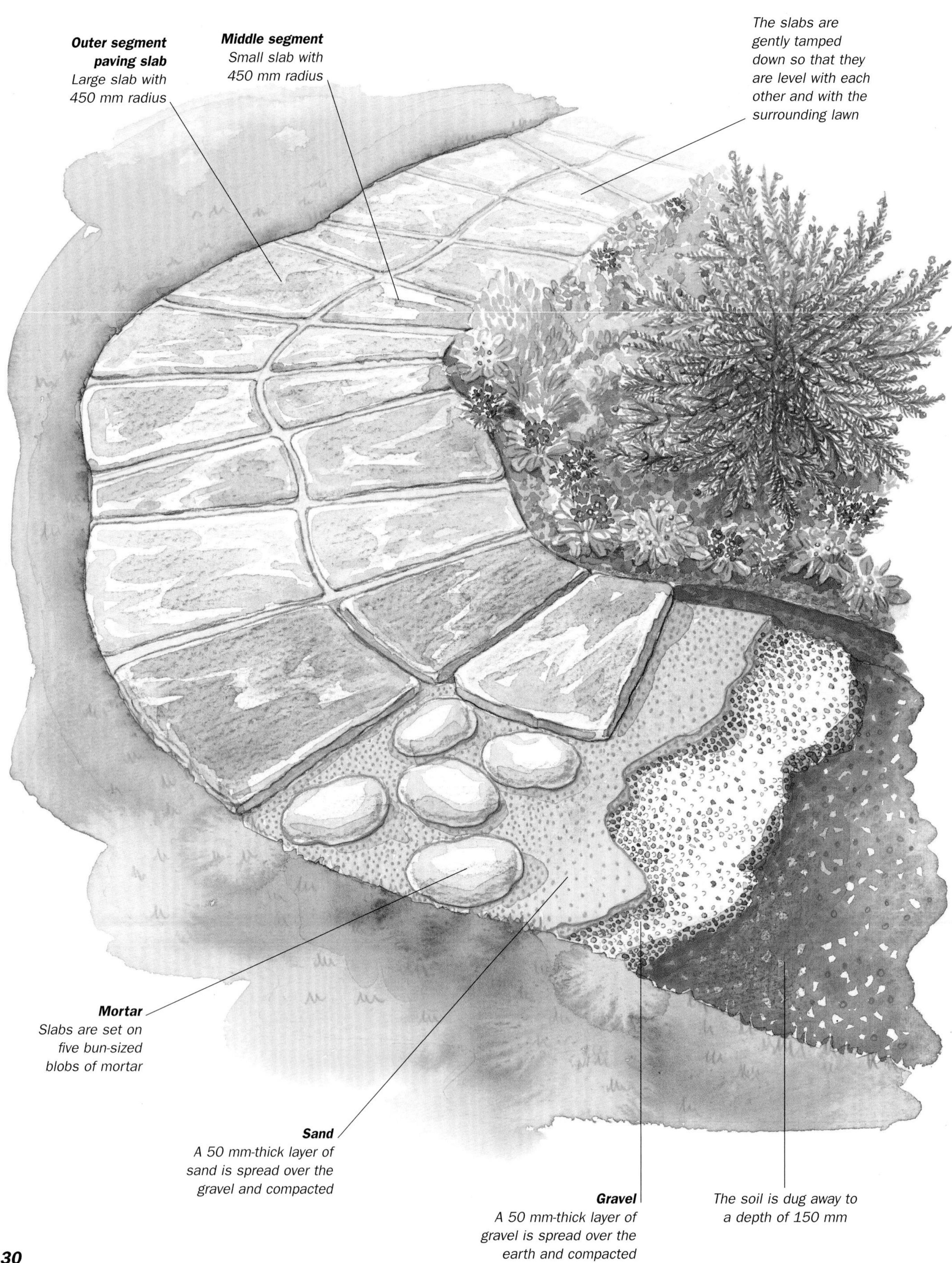
Outer segment paving slab
Large slab with 450 mm radius
Middle segment
Small slab with 450 mm radius
The slabs are gently tamped down so that they are level with each other and with the surrounding lawn
Mortar
Slabs are set on five bun-sized blobs of mortar
Sand
A 50 mm-thick layer of sand is spread over the gravel and compacted
Gravel
A 50 mm-thick layer of gravel is spread over the earth and compacted
The soil is dug away to a depth of 150 mm

Making the serpentine path

1 Setting out the slabs Set the paired middle and outer segment slabs in place on the ground. Make a swift sketch so that you know how they relate to each other. Number the slabs with chalk if desired. Slice around the arrangement with the spade and then move the slabs to one side.

2 Clearing the site Dig up the turf – you (or a neighbour) may be able to use it elsewhere. Dig out the topsoil (to a depth of about 150 mm) by slicing it into manageable squares, and use the spade, fork and wheelbarrow to remove it from the site.

3 Making the foundation Spread and rake a 50 mm layer of gravel over the earth and use the sledgehammer to stamp it down firmly. Shovel sand over the gravel and spread it out until it forms a layer 50 mm thick.

4 Laying the slabs Dampen the slabs. Set each slab on five generous blobs of mortar and use the tamping beam and club hammer to tap them level with each other and with the lawn bordering the path.

5 Pointing When the mortar has set (leave for two or three hours), sweep the rest of the sand into the joints and around the slabs. Repeat this procedure over several days until the joints feel firm.

Dry-stone border wall

Intermediate

Making time
One weekend per 4 m of wall
Half a day for the trench; rest of the time for building the wall

The technique of building dry-stone walls has evolved over many thousands of years. There are no concrete foundations or complex planning involved, just a slow and methodical procedure of studying the shapes of the field stones and then fitting them together. If you are planning to build a low raised border in your garden, and have a good source of stone, this project provides an absorbing way of constructing it.

Considering the design

The wall is three courses high, plus a course of coping stones, and built entirely from salvaged stone. We have used large blocks of rough-cut stone for the primary thick course, thin slices of roof stone to fill in the courses, and square blocks of stone for the coping. The most economical way of tackling the project is to use whatever stone is available and modify your technique accordingly.

Dry-stone walling is straightforward, but it does involve a lot of concentration and co-ordination between hand and eye. First, a trench is dug, which is filled with hardcore. The hardcore is compacted to supply a footing. The first course is laid, consisting of primary stones filled and levelled with secondary stones. Earth is raked down behind the wall, then the second course is set in place.

During construction, you will need to check the horizontal level by eye and make sure that the courses are tilted so that, to a small extent, the wall leans back against the bank of earth. Every half metre or so along the courses, the wall must be stabilized by running extra-long stones back into the earth.

Getting started

Work out how long you want your wall to be, divide it by 4 m and multiply the stated quantities accordingly. Order the stone. Ideally, you need stone that shows one straight edge and two smooth faces.

You will need

Tools

- ✔ Tape measure and straight-edge
- ✔ Pegs and string
- ✔ Spade, fork and shovel
- ✔ Wheelbarrow and bucket
- ✔ Sledgehammer
- ✔ Club hammer
- ✔ Bricklayer's trowel
- ✔ Mason's hammer
- ✔ Bolster chisel
- ✔ Old carpet: 300 mm x 600 mm

Materials

For 4 m of wall, 550 mm high

- ✔ Salvaged rough-cut stone: ½ cu. m (wall and coping)
- ✔ Salvaged roof stone: 1 wheelbarrow load
- ✔ Hardcore: 12 bucketfuls

Overall dimensions and general notes

4 m long
550 mm high

This is an ideal project when you want to create a retaining wall for a raised border. The length and height of the wall can be adjusted to suit.

Cut-away view of the dry-stone border wall

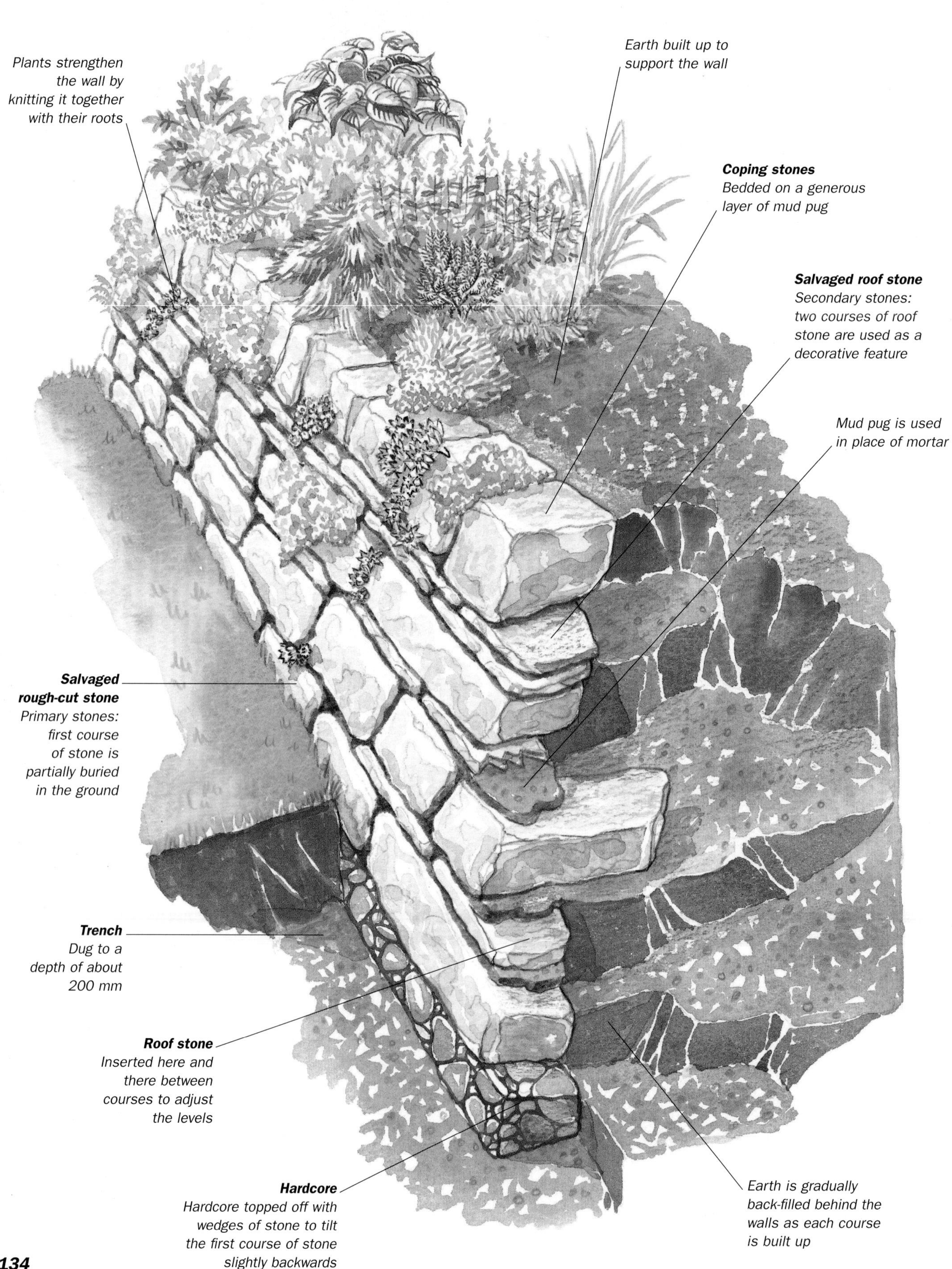
Plants strengthen the wall by knitting it together with their roots
Earth built up to support the wall
Coping stones
Bedded on a generous layer of mud pug
Salvaged roof stone
Secondary stones: two courses of roof stone are used as a decorative feature
Mud pug is used in place of mortar
Salvaged rough-cut stone
Primary stones: first course of stone is partially buried in the ground
Trench
Dug to a depth of about 200 mm
Roof stone
Inserted here and there between courses to adjust the levels
Hardcore
Hardcore topped off with wedges of stone to tilt the first course of stone slightly backwards
Earth is gradually back-filled behind the walls as each course is built up

Making the dry-stone border wall

1 Digging a foundation

Dig away the soil down to ground level to reveal the bank of earth that needs retaining. Excavate a trench 300 mm wide and 200 mm deep, and half-fill it with compacted hardcore.

2 Making mud pug

Take a bucket or so of topsoil and mix it with water until it has the consistency of mortar – this mixture is called mud pug and is used in place of mortar. Remove all the large stones.

3 Laying the first course

Lay the first course of stones on the levelled hardcore, with wedges or slivers of roof stone underneath to ensure that the course is angled slightly backwards. Rake earth down from the bank to back-fill behind the course. Compact the earth with the club hammer.

4 Levelling the course of stone

Use roof stone to bring all the stones of the first course up to the same level. Trowel a generous layer of mud pug over the top of the course and lay the roof stone (trim with the mason's hammer as necessary). Run long stones into the bank to provide extra support.

5 Building further courses

If necessary, use the club hammer and bolster chisel to cut and trim stone, resting it on the old piece of carpet. Trowel mud pug into cavities, and tap misfitting stones back into line. Adjust individual stones by banging small slivers of waste stone into the mud pug.

6 Bedding the coping stones

Continue building the wall until it is three courses high. Now trowel a layer of mud pug over the top course, and bed the coping stones in place.

Japanese rockery

Intermediate

Making time
One weekend
One day for selecting the stones, and one day for building the rockery

Traditional Japanese gardens often incorporate a bridge in their design, to symbolize our journey through life. This Japanese-inspired rockery includes a stepping-stone bridge and other symbolic features such as a lantern to represent a guiding light, and shards of weathered plum slate to depict water. If you would like to create an original rockery with a philosophical twist, this project will provide a great talking point.

Overall dimensions and general notes

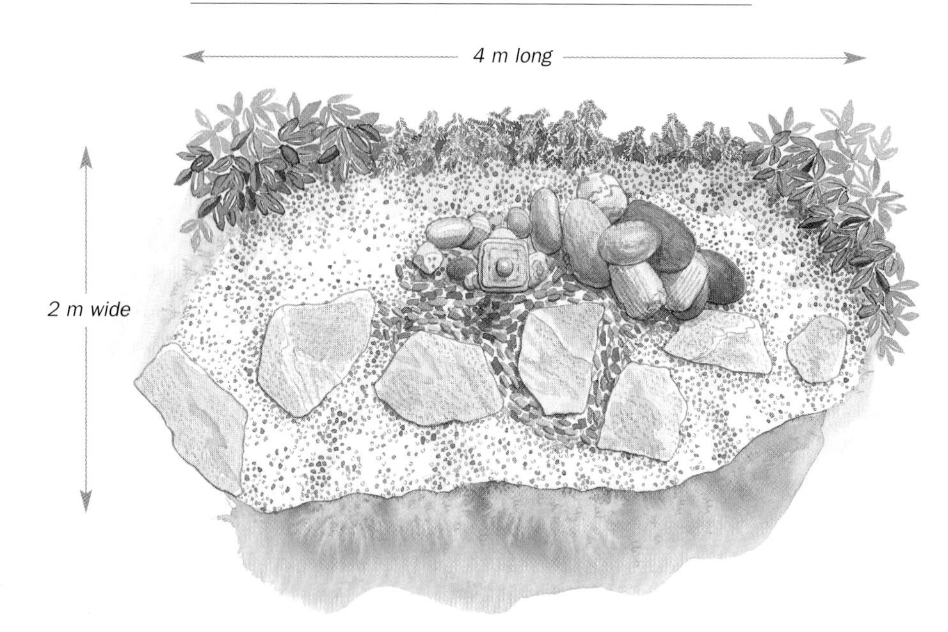
4 m long
2 m wide

This rockery is simply an arrangement of beautiful stones with a hand-built lantern as the central feature, and is suited to any modern garden. The size of the rockery can be adjusted to suit a smaller space. If you prefer, you could use a shop-bought lantern.

Considering the design

The rockery measures about 4 m long and 2 m wide. It has slate to suggest a turbulent flow of water, fine pea gravel to mark the shore at the water's edge, large sandstone slabs to form a bridge over the water, rocks that resemble mountains and symbolize barriers, and a stone lantern that indicates light, hope and guidance.

You can choose just about any stones that take your fancy for the stepping stones and the "water", but the lantern requires rocks of a certain shape and size. The main column is 400 mm long and 150 mm square, with 100 mm of its length buried in the ground. The table at the top of the column is 200 mm square, and the lantern roof is 150 mm square.

Getting started

Take a pencil, tape measure and a notebook to the stoneyard, and spend time studying what is on offer. Select stones and rocks for the various components and lay them out on the ground to see how they look together.

You will need

Tools

- ✔ Tape measure, knife, straight-edge
- ✔ Pegs and string
- ✔ Spade, fork, shovel, wheelbarrow, bucket, pointing trowel, spirit level

Materials

For a rockery 4 m long and 2 m wide

- ✔ Block of salvaged, weathered, cut stone: 400 mm long and 150 mm square (lantern column)
- ✔ Slab of salvaged, weathered, cut stone: 200 mm square and 50–60 mm thick (lantern table)
- ✔ Sandstone: 20 pieces, about 50 mm in diameter (lantern pillars)
- ✔ Slab of salvaged, weathered, cut stone: 150 mm square and 50–60 mm thick (lantern roof)
- ✔ Large feature stone: about 80 mm in diameter (finial cobble)
- ✔ Split sandstone: 7 or 8 large slices, about 300–400 mm wide (stepping stones)
- ✔ Boulders: about 6, ranging in size from 150–400 mm in diameter, in colours and textures to suit ("mountains")
- ✔ Slate, weathered: 50 kg, plum colour ("water")
- ✔ Pea gravel: 150 kg ("shore")
- ✔ Woven plastic sheet: 4 m x 2 m
- ✔ Mortar: 1 part (2 kg) cement, 1 part (2 kg) lime, 4 parts (8 kg) soft sand

Exploded view of the Japanese rockery

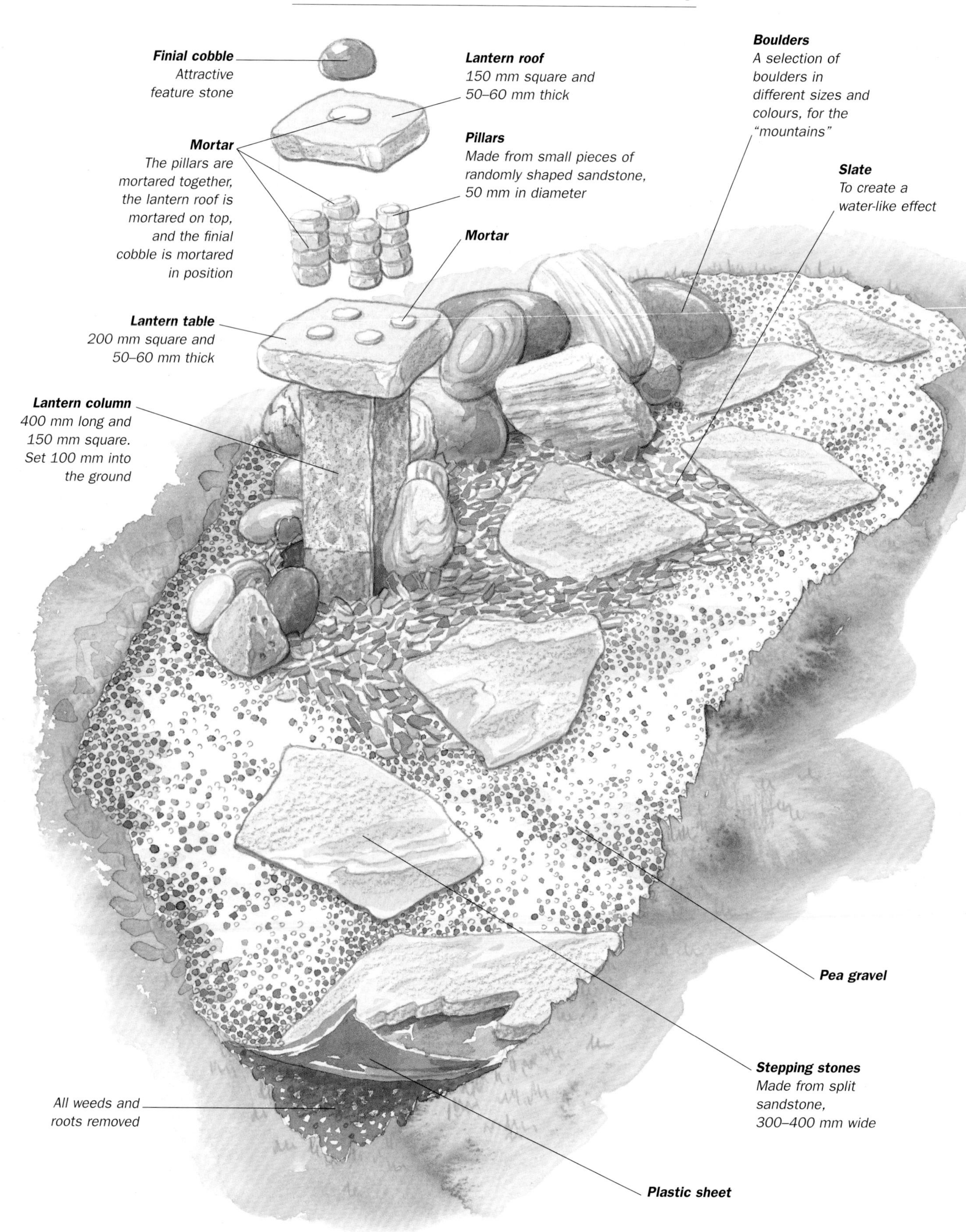
Finial cobble
Attractive feature stone
Mortar
The pillars are mortared together, the lantern roof is mortared on top, and the finial cobble is mortared in position
Lantern roof
150 mm square and 50–60 mm thick
Pillars
Made from small pieces of randomly shaped sandstone, 50 mm in diameter
Mortar
Boulders
A selection of boulders in different sizes and colours, for the "mountains"
Slate
To create a water-like effect
Lantern table
200 mm square and 50–60 mm thick
Lantern column
400 mm long and 150 mm square. Set 100 mm into the ground
Pea gravel
Stepping stones
Made from split sandstone, 300–400 mm wide
All weeds and roots removed
Plastic sheet

Making the Japanese rockery

1 Digging the column hole

Measure out the site and stand the lantern column in the most suitable position. Mark around it with the spade, move the stone and dig a hole to a depth of about 100 mm.

2 Laying the plastic

Spread the plastic sheet over the site and cut a hole in it, aligned with the hole in the ground. Lower the lantern column into the hole and check that it is upright. Fold under the outer edges of the sheet to match the shape of the site.

3 Placing the stones

Start to arrange the rockery stones – the stepping stones for the bridge over the water, and the boulders to act as the mountain range. Consider your use of shape and colour carefully.

4 Arranging the slate

Spread the plum-coloured slate in and around the stones to suggest a flow of water. Add pea gravel along its borders to create a shore. Take your time, standing back frequently to study the arrangement. Follow your own design instincts.

5 Finishing

Spread mortar on top of the lantern column and set the table stone in place. Mortar the little sandstones upon each other to make the pillars. Mortar the roof stone and the finial cobble. Spread the rest of the pea gravel over the plastic sheet, making sure it is all covered.

Stone sett and brick path

The sett and brick path is good on many counts – it makes an excellent footpath, the surface is sturdy enough for a wheelbarrow to be pushed along it, and it is perfect when you want to build a path across a lawn. The flexibility of the flow of bricks neatly does away with the need for a lot of forward planning. Best of all, you can mow straight over the whole path without damaging your lawnmower.

Intermediate

Making time
One weekend
One day for putting down the sand, and one day for laying the setts and bricks

Considering the design

Because of the firm and stony nature of the topsoil in our garden, we were able to lay the path with nothing more than a thick layer of sand as a foundation. However, if your soil is soft and boggy, you need to lay down a layer of gravel or hardcore prior to the sand.

Getting started

The quantities we have given are for a path that is 1 m wide and 3 m long. Study your lawn and consider the route for the path. Measure the length of path required, and then modify the quantities accordingly. Decide what you are going to do with the excavated turf and topsoil.

First of all, have a dry run with the setts and bricks to check the placement. Then remove the turf, compact the earth and put down the sand foundation. Position the bricks, add extra sand where the setts will go, to make up the difference in thickness between bricks and setts, and lay the reconstituted grey stone setts. Push soil into the spaces between the bricks and the setts and sprinkle with grass seed.

Overall dimensions and general notes

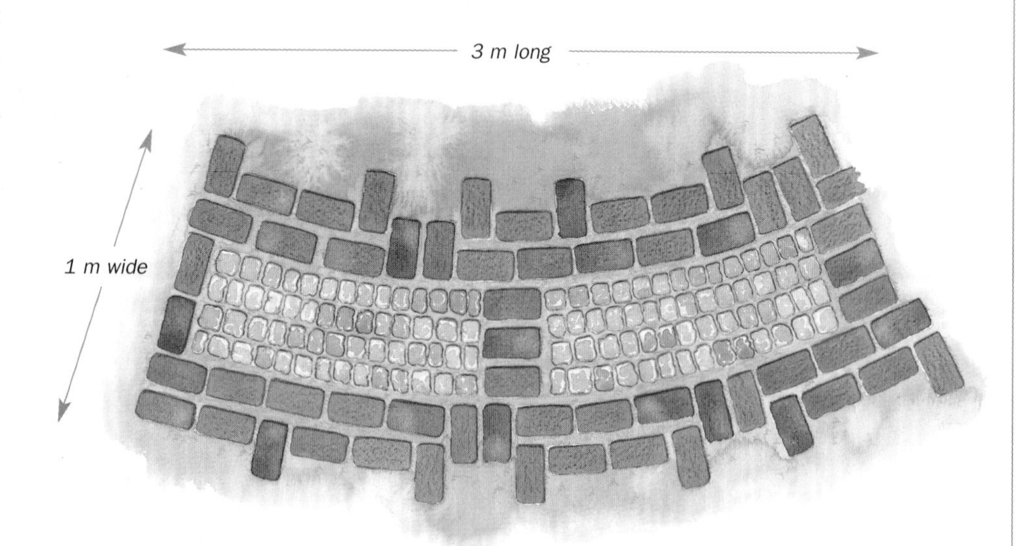
3 m long
1 m wide

A traditional path built from a mixture of bricks and stone setts. It looks especially good in a country garden setting. It is easy to build and does not use any cement, so you can take as much time as you like to lay the bricks and setts.

You will need

Tools

- Tape measure and straight-edge
- Spade, fork and shovel
- Wheelbarrow and bucket
- Rake
- Sledgehammer
- Bricklayer's trowel
- Club hammer
- Tamping beam: about 1.5 m long, 60 mm wide and 30 mm thick
- Stiff-bristled broom

Materials

For a path 3 m long and 1 m wide

- Reconstituted paving setts: 112 components 80–100 mm square and 50 mm thick, charcoal colour
- Bricks: 32 bricks, 225 mm long, 112.5 mm wide and 75 mm thick, colour and texture to suit
- Sand: about 150 kg
- Topsoil: about 75 kg
- Grass seed: about 9 good handfuls
- Wooden workboards to protect the lawn: size and number to suit your situation

Cut-away view of the stone sett and brick path

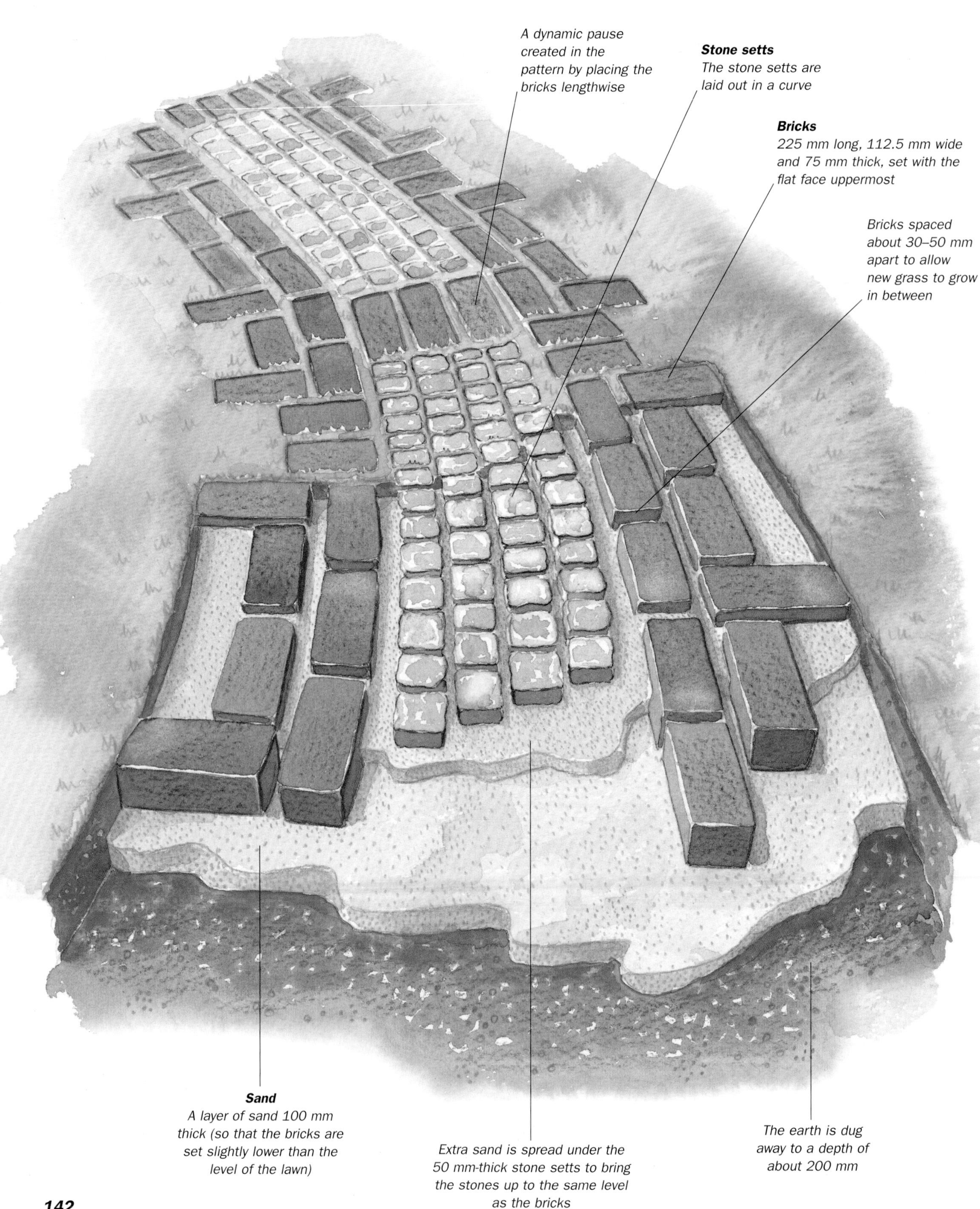
A dynamic pause created in the pattern by placing the bricks lengthwise
Stone setts
The stone setts are laid out in a curve
Bricks
225 mm long, 112.5 mm wide and 75 mm thick, set with the flat face uppermost
Bricks spaced about 30–50 mm apart to allow new grass to grow in between
Sand
A layer of sand 100 mm thick (so that the bricks are set slightly lower than the level of the lawn)
Extra sand is spread under the 50 mm-thick stone setts to bring the stones up to the same level as the bricks
The earth is dug away to a depth of about 200 mm

Making the stone sett and brick path

1 Checking the placement
Position the stone setts on the lawn and arrange the bricks so that there is a uniform spacing of about 30–50 mm between the various components. Make a swift sketch so that you know what goes where.

2 Removing the turf
Slice around the arrangement with the spade. Remove the setts and bricks, and cut the turf into manageable squares. Use the fork and wheelbarrow to remove the turf from the site.

3 Laying the sand
Rake the earth level and compact it with the sledgehammer. Spread a 100 mm-thick layer of sand over the earth and rake it so that it looks more or less level with the surrounding lawn.

4 Positioning the stones
Place the stone setts into position down the middle of the path. Place the bricks on either side of the setts, using uniform spacing of 30–50 mm. With club hammer and beam, tamp them level with each other and a bit lower than the lawn.

5 Finishing
Lay the setts on an extra layer of sand to bring them up level with the bricks and the lawn. Brush the topsoil into the joints, tamp everything level, and sprinkle grass seed in the joints.

Plinth and slab table

This table is a beautifully simple idea – just a single slab of stone set on a low plinth, and is reminiscent of Eastern garden designs. Use it for drinks or for serving afternoon tea. The beauty of this piece of garden furniture is that it is weatherproof, and doesn't have to be taken in at the end of the day. It can also double up as a display plinth, ideal for showing containers of plants or a favourite piece of sculpture.

★★
Intermediate

Making time
One weekend
One day for casting the foundation slab, and one day for building the table

Considering the design

The table is straightforward – it consists of three courses of split sandstone topped off with a massive flagstone, all mounted on a concrete foundation slab. The plinth stands about 300 mm high, and the tabletop is 650 mm x 600 mm.

Visit a stoneyard to obtain materials – the best way to make your choice is to chalk out the 450 mm x 400 mm plan view on the ground, and carefully select enough pieces of 100 mm-thick stone to complete the three courses. Allow one or two extra stones for each course (so you can choose the best fit when you get home) and include twelve good, square-cut corner stones – four for each course. Choose a single flagstone for the tabletop, which shows one good face.

Getting started

Select the site and stack the stone so that it is close to hand. Build the formwork, making the interior dimensions 400 mm long and 450 mm wide. Set it in position in your garden. Cut around the frame and remove the turf and earth to a depth of 100 mm. Level the frame in the recess.

You will need

Tools

- Tape measure, chalk, spirit level
- Crosscut saw and claw hammer
- Spade and shovel
- Tamping beam: 600 mm long, 80 mm wide and 50 mm thick
- Workboards: planks and pieces of hardboard to protect the area around the site
- Club hammer and bolster chisel
- Mason's hammer
- Bricklayer's and pointing trowels

Materials

For a table 650 mm long, 600 mm wide and 370 mm high

- Flagstone: 1 salvaged slate/sandstone/limestone flag, 650 mm long, 600 mm wide and 70 mm thick
- Split sandstone: 1 sq. m of sandstone (pieces about 120–250 mm long, 50–150 mm wide and 100 mm thick)
- Concrete: 1 part (10 kg) cement, 2 parts (20 kg) sharp sand, 3 parts (30 kg) aggregate
- Mortar: 2 parts (24 kg) cement, 1 part (12 kg) lime, 9 parts (108 kg) soft sand
- Pine: 1 piece rough-sawn pine, 2 m long, 80 mm wide and 50 mm thick (formwork)
- Nails: 4 x 100 mm-long nails

Overall dimensions and general notes

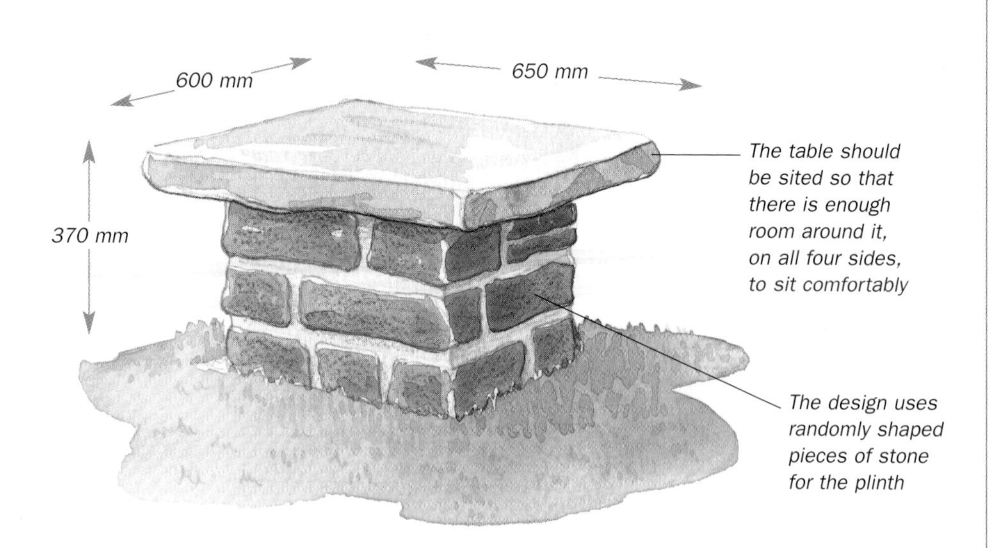
600 mm
650 mm
370 mm
The table should be sited so that there is enough room around it, on all four sides, to sit comfortably
The design uses randomly shaped pieces of stone for the plinth

This timeless design will suit almost any style and size of garden and will last a lifetime. It is constructed from natural stone rather than the reconstituted variety, and so requires a little bit of patience to select and arrange the parts into a pleasing whole.

Exploded view of the plinth and slab table

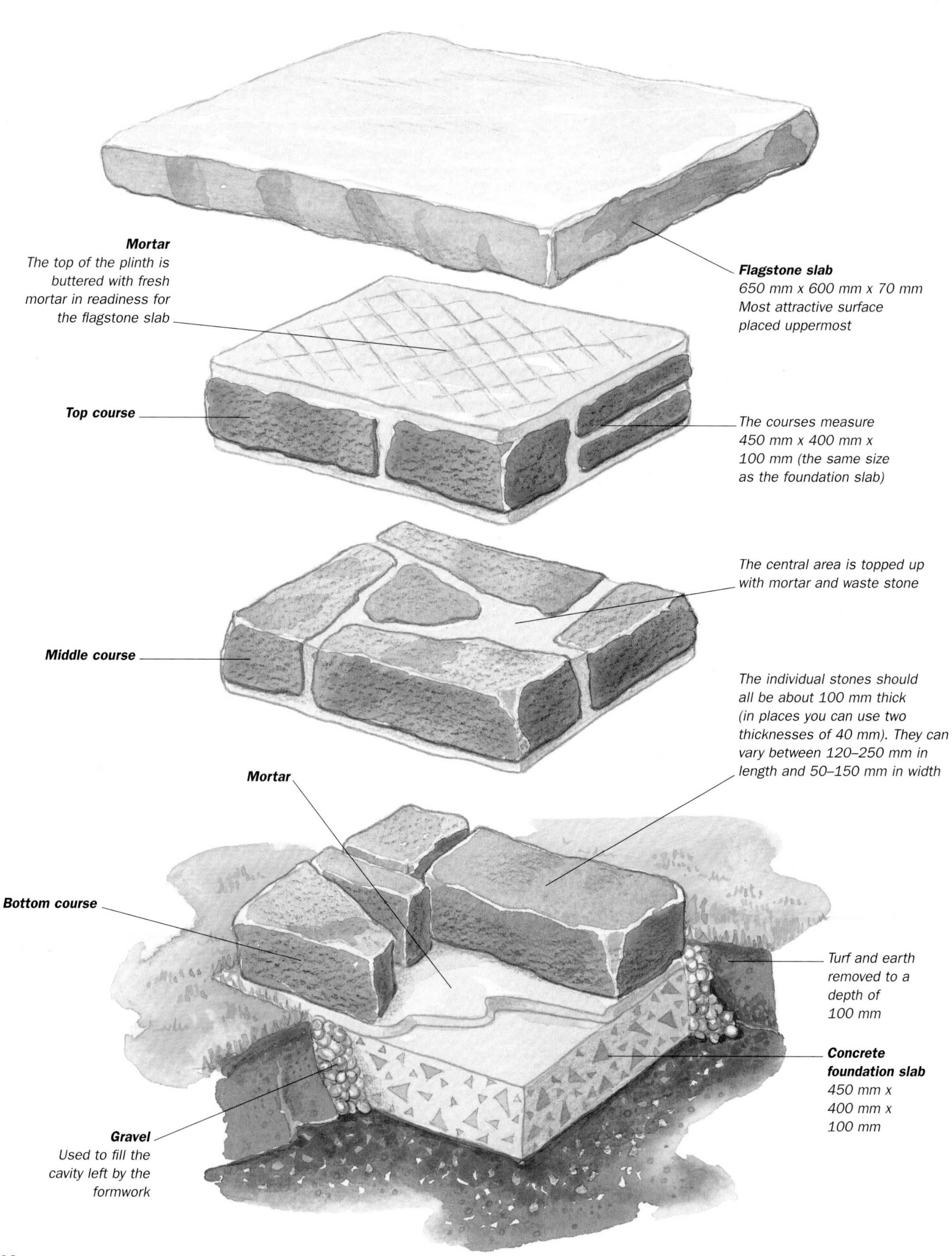
Mortar
The top of the plinth is buttered with fresh mortar in readiness for the flagstone slab
Flagstone slab
650 mm x 600 mm x 70 mm
Most attractive surface placed uppermost
Top course
The courses measure 450 mm x 400 mm x 100 mm (the same size as the foundation slab)
The central area is topped up with mortar and waste stone
Middle course
The individual stones should all be about 100 mm thick (in places you can use two thicknesses of 40 mm). They can vary between 120–250 mm in length and 50–150 mm in width
Mortar
Bottom course
Turf and earth removed to a depth of 100 mm
Concrete foundation slab
450 mm x 400 mm x 100 mm
Gravel
Used to fill the cavity left by the formwork

Making the plinth and slab table

1 Making the frame

Set the wooden formwork frame in the excavation and wedge it level with stones. Check with the spirit level. Fill the frame with concrete. Use the tamping beam to level the concrete with the top edge of the frame. Leave to set. (The formwork is removed later.)

2 Trial layout

Protect the area around the concrete foundation with workboards. Arrange the pieces of stone on the foundation, so that you have all the makings for three 100 mm-high courses. From course to course, make sure the vertical joints are staggered.

3 Breaking stone

To break a piece of stone, set the stone on the grass, position the bolster chisel firmly on the line of cut, and give it one or more well-placed blows with the club hammer. Make sure that you wear goggles and gloves. Use the mason's hammer to trim stone.

4 Laying the first course

Spread a generous layer of mortar over the foundation and lay the first course of stones. Use the weight of the club hammer to gently tap the stones level. Check with the spirit level.

5 Second and third courses

Repeat the procedure to build the other two courses. Fill the central area of the plinth with a mixture of mortar and fragments of waste stone. Use the pointing trowel to tidy up the mortar in the joints of the courses.

6 Laying the flagstone

When you have achieved a level, square pillar, spread a generous layer of fresh mortar over the top of the stack. Dampen the underside of the flagstone slab and get help to gently lower it into position. Pour gravel into the slot between the plinth and the grass.

Boulder and coping wall

Intermediate

Making time
One weekend for every 3 m of wall
One day for building the basic wall, and one day for the coping

This little wall is charming in its simplicity and directness. You don't have to engage in a lot of forward planning – you simply order a heap of random split sandstone and a limestone boulder for every metre of wall, and start building. The more challenging part is building the scalloped coping, but it is great fun to do. An added advantage is that the modest weight of the components means that the project is open to everyone.

Overall dimensions and general notes

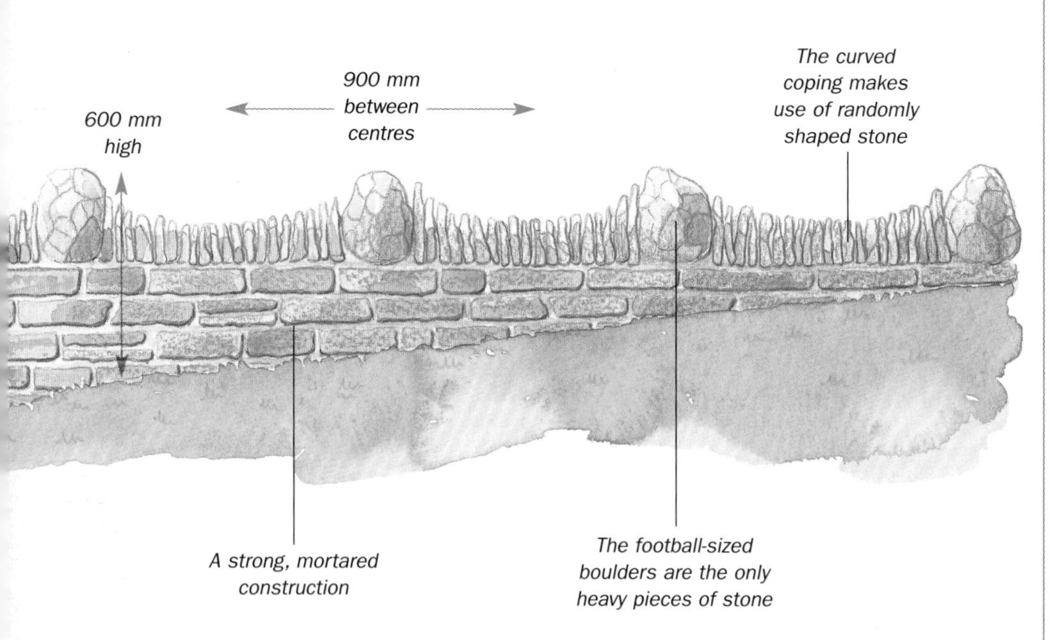
600 mm high
900 mm between centres
The curved coping makes use of randomly shaped stone
A strong, mortared construction
The football-sized boulders are the only heavy pieces of stone

The project produces a low, decorative wall. It is perfect for creating a raised bed – simply build end walls, fill with a layer of gravel for drainage, top with soil and plant up.

Considering the design

The wall is built up from just below ground level, with the first course of stone set on a layer of compacted waste stone. First you dig a shallow trench, stamp all the bits of waste stone into the bottom of it with a sledgehammer, and then set the first course in the trench so that it is just below ground level.

When the wall is about three or four courses high, the top of the wall is buttered with a generous wedge of mortar, and the boulder and stone slices for the coping are set in place. All you do is mark in the position of the boulders, and the halfway point between them. Then set the first boulder in place and arrange the coping so that the pieces descend in size up to the midway point, and then increase in size up to the next boulder.

Getting started

Work out how long you want your wall to be. The quantities given are per 1 m of wall: multiply as necessary. Visit the stoneyard, discuss what you are planning to build, and choose some attractive boulders and random split sandstone.

You will need

Tools

- Tape measure
- Pegs and string
- Spade, fork and shovel
- Wheelbarrow and bucket
- Sledgehammer
- Bricklayer's trowel
- Club hammer
- Mason's hammer
- Pointing trowel
- Old hand brush

Materials

For 1 m of wall, 600 mm high

- Sandstone: about 2 wheelbarrow loads of random stones in various sizes and thicknesses
- Limestone boulder: 1 large, football-sized stone
- Hardcore (waste stone): 9 bucketfuls
- Mortar: 1 part (25 kg) cement, 3 parts (75 kg) soft sand

Cut-away view of the boulder and coping wall

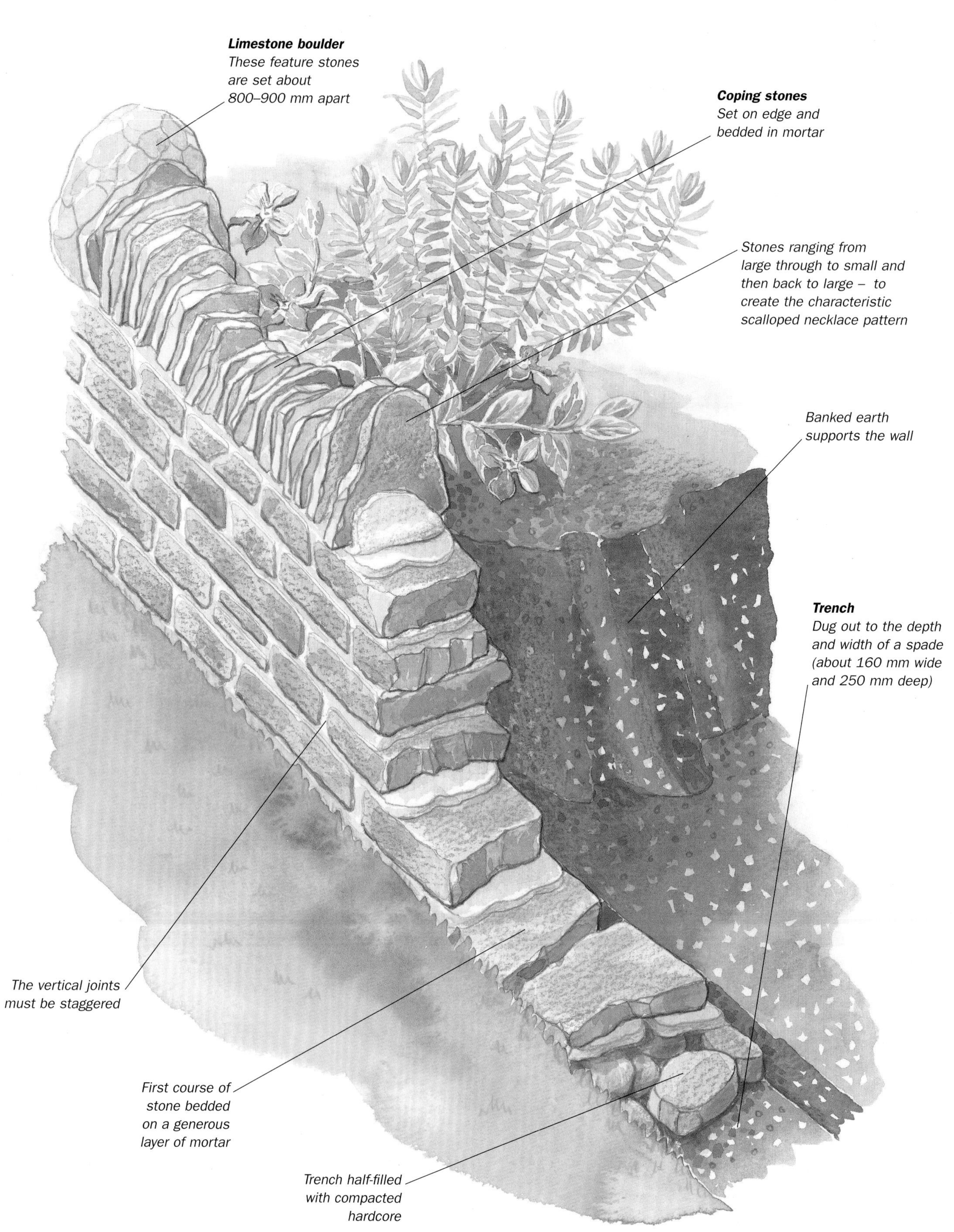
Limestone boulder
These feature stones are set about 800–900 mm apart
Coping stones
Set on edge and bedded in mortar
Stones ranging from large through to small and then back to large – to create the characteristic scalloped necklace pattern
Banked earth supports the wall
Trench
Dug out to the depth and width of a spade (about 160 mm wide and 250 mm deep)
The vertical joints must be staggered
First course of stone bedded on a generous layer of mortar
Trench half-filled with compacted hardcore

Making the boulder and coping wall

1 Marking out

Use the string and pegs to mark out the dimensions of the wall. Dig a trench to the depth and width of a spade (about 160 mm wide and 250 mm deep). Half-fill the trench with hardcore and compact it with the sledgehammer.

2 Laying the first course

Trowel a generous layer of mortar into the trench and set the first course of stone in place. Level up by eye and use the club hammer to make adjustments. Rake earth up behind the inside face of the wall to support it.

3 Adding more courses

Continue building one course upon another, all the while doing your best to ensure that the vertical joints are staggered. Fill the cavities with mortar and slivers of sandstone.

4 Placing the boulders

Generously butter the top of the wall with mortar. Mark the positions of the boulders and halfway points between them. Place the first boulder, and then range slices of stone on edge, running in a scallop pattern to the next boulder. Use the mason's hammer to trim stones.

5 Pointing

Finally, use the pointing trowel to fill the joints with mortar. Sculpt the topmost wedge of mortar, between the coping stones and the rest of the wall, so that it angles down from the coping. Tidy up the joints and brush off surplus mortar.

Inlay block steps

Advanced

Making time
One weekend
One day for getting the flight of steps into place; one day for the detailing and finishing

This is the ideal project for a minimalist. If you have a crisp, modern home with lots of glass and concrete painted in flat colours, inlay block steps in the garden will complement it perfectly. This simple flight of steps can be built with the minimum of fuss. Each step is decorated with a small amount of detailing, made up of slivers of Welsh slate arranged in an attractive basketweave pattern.

Considering the design

Each step consists of two hollow concrete blocks, making a 440 mm square. The whole flight is dug into the ground and the top step is flush with ground level. This technique negates the need both for complex measuring and for side retaining walls. Each step stands clear and separate from its neighbour. Once the blocks are in place, the hollows in them are filled with concrete, topped with mortar and studded with stone, both for decorative effect and to provide a firm footing.

Getting started

Once you have taken delivery of the blocks, play around with various arrangements until you have a clear picture of how they relate to each other. Make a sketch and take measurements.

Overall dimensions and general notes

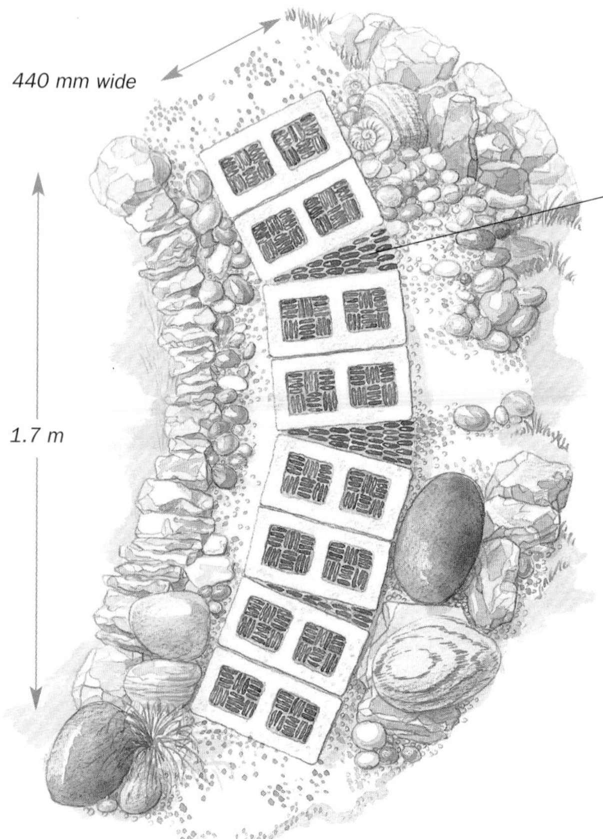
440 mm wide
1.7 m
The angles between the steps can be adjusted to suit almost any curve

These steps draw their inspiration from an architect-designed building by the sea. They are particularly easy to build and can be painted in whatever colours you wish.

You will need

Tools

- Tape measure and straight-edge
- Pegs and string
- Spade, fork and shovel
- Spirit levels: one long and one short
- Wheelbarrow and bucket
- Bricklayer's trowel
- Pointing trowel
- Soft-bristled brush
- Paintbrush

Materials

For a flight of steps about 1.7 m long and 440 mm wide

- Hollow concrete building blocks: 8 blocks, 440 mm long, 210 mm wide and 210 mm thick
- Welsh plum slate: 25 kg
- Rocks and cobbles: 2 wheelbarrow loads (to decorate the site)
- Concrete: 1 part (20 kg) cement, 5 parts (100 kg) ballast
- Mortar: 1 part (10 kg) cement, 2 parts (20 kg) soft sand
- Paint: exterior-grade flat paint in colour to suit

Exploded view of the inlay block steps

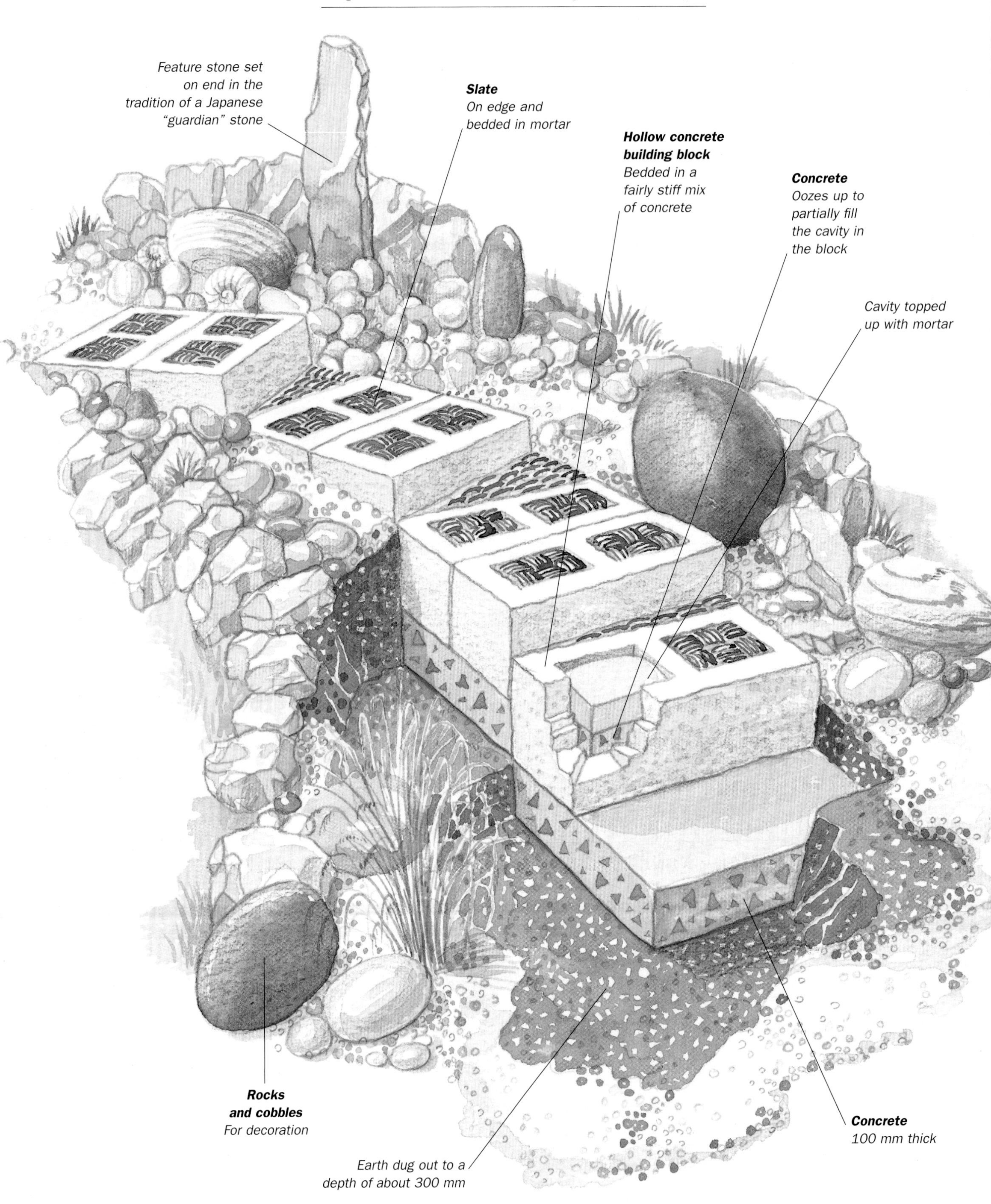
Feature stone set on end in the tradition of a Japanese "guardian" stone
Slate On edge and bedded in mortar
Hollow concrete building block Bedded in a fairly stiff mix of concrete
Concrete Oozes up to partially fill the cavity in the block
Cavity topped up with mortar
Rocks and cobbles For decoration
Earth dug out to a depth of about 300 mm
Concrete 100 mm thick

Making the inlay block steps

1 Trial arrangement
Arrange the concrete blocks in pairs along the proposed route of the path, so that each pair stands separate, and so that the total flight gradually angles to follow the route.

2 Clearing the turf
Use the spade to mark around the pairs of blocks. Remove the blocks, slice away the turf and dig individual holes to a depth of about 300 mm. Use the small spirit level to check that the bottom of the holes are level.

3 Laying the concrete blocks
Make a fairly stiff mix of concrete, spread a 100 mm-thick layer in the bottom of each hole, and set the paired blocks in place. A little concrete will ooze into the cavities. Make adjustments until the blocks are level with each other, and with the whole flight.

4 Step inlays
Trowel concrete into the cavities in the blocks, half-filling them, then add mortar to within 10 mm of the top. Set the Welsh plum slate in the mortar, forming a basketweave pattern. Check that the surface is flush with the block.

5 Painting and decoration
Brush all dust and debris from the blocks, and paint them in your chosen colour. Finally, decorate the site with rocks and cobbles.

Trough planter

Advanced

Making time
One weekend
One day for laying the foundation slab, and one day for building the walls

This planter draws its inspiration from the carved stone water troughs seen in fields in northern England. It is made from three courses of reconstituted York stone, and the top of the planter is finished with a traditional coping technique known as "spotted dick" – no doubt named after the steamed pudding popular in that part of the world. This is a good project for a formal garden.

Considering the design

Each course is made up of nine blocks, one of which has to be cut approximately two-thirds of the way along its length (it is pre-marked with registration grooves, scored round the block with a club hammer and bolster chisel). Building the coping is good fun. A generous wedge of mortar is spread on top of the finished trough, modelled to a smooth, half-round section, and then studded with small pebbles.

Getting started

Decide how long you want your trough to be. Have a trial run with the blocks so you know how the courses fit together.

Overall dimensions and general notes

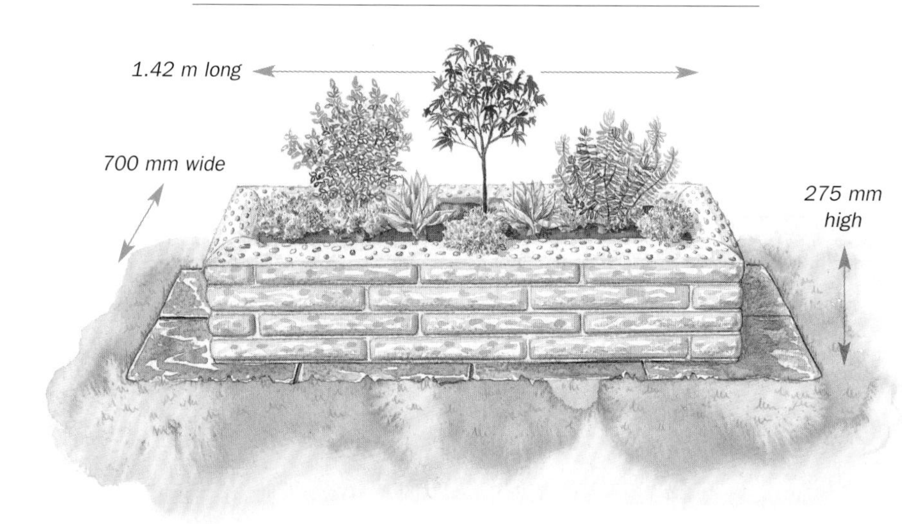
1.42 m long
700 mm wide
275 mm high

A small trough made from reconstituted stone blocks is ideal for a tiny garden. The size of the trough can be adjusted easily, and square or L-shaped configurations are possible.

You will need

Tools

- Tape measure, straight-edge and chalk
- Pegs and string
- Boards to protect the surrounding grass
- Spade, rake and shovel
- Wheelbarrow and bucket
- Crosscut saw
- Claw hammer
- Spirit level
- Sledgehammer
- Tamping beam: about 1 m long, 60 mm wide and 30 mm thick
- Bricklayer's trowel
- Club hammer
- Bolster chisel
- Pointing trowel
- Wire brush
- Soft-bristled brush

Materials

For a trough 1.42 m long, 700 mm wide and 275 mm high

- Reconstituted York stone blocks: 36 blocks, 420 mm long, 130 mm wide and 60 mm thick
- Concrete slabs: 8 slabs, 450 mm square, colour and texture to suit
- Pebbles: 1 bucketful, size and colour to suit
- Hardcore: 2 wheelbarrow loads
- Soft sand: 6 wheelbarrow loads
- Mortar: 1 part (30 kg) cement, 6 parts (180 kg) soft sand
- Pine: 6 m long, 75 mm wide and 25 mm thick (formwork)
- Nails: 1 kg of 38 mm-long nails

Exploded view of the trough planter

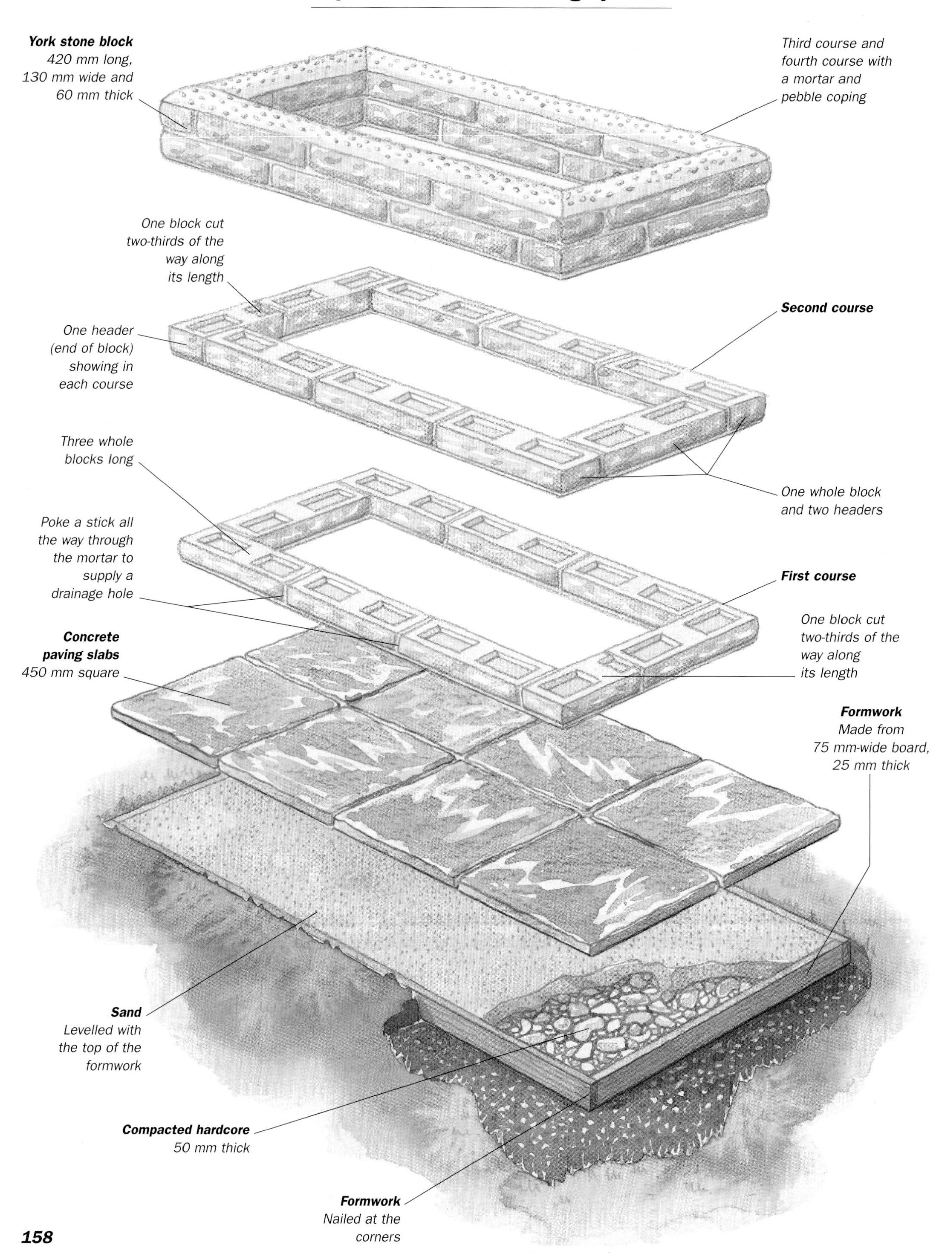
York stone block 420 mm long, 130 mm wide and 60 mm thick
Third course and fourth course with a mortar and pebble coping
One block cut two-thirds of the way along its length
Second course
One header (end of block) showing in each course
Three whole blocks long
One whole block and two headers
Poke a stick all the way through the mortar to supply a drainage hole
First course
Concrete paving slabs 450 mm square
One block cut two-thirds of the way along its length
Formwork Made from 75 mm-wide board, 25 mm thick
Sand Levelled with the top of the formwork
Compacted hardcore 50 mm thick
Formwork Nailed at the corners

Cut-away view of the trough planter

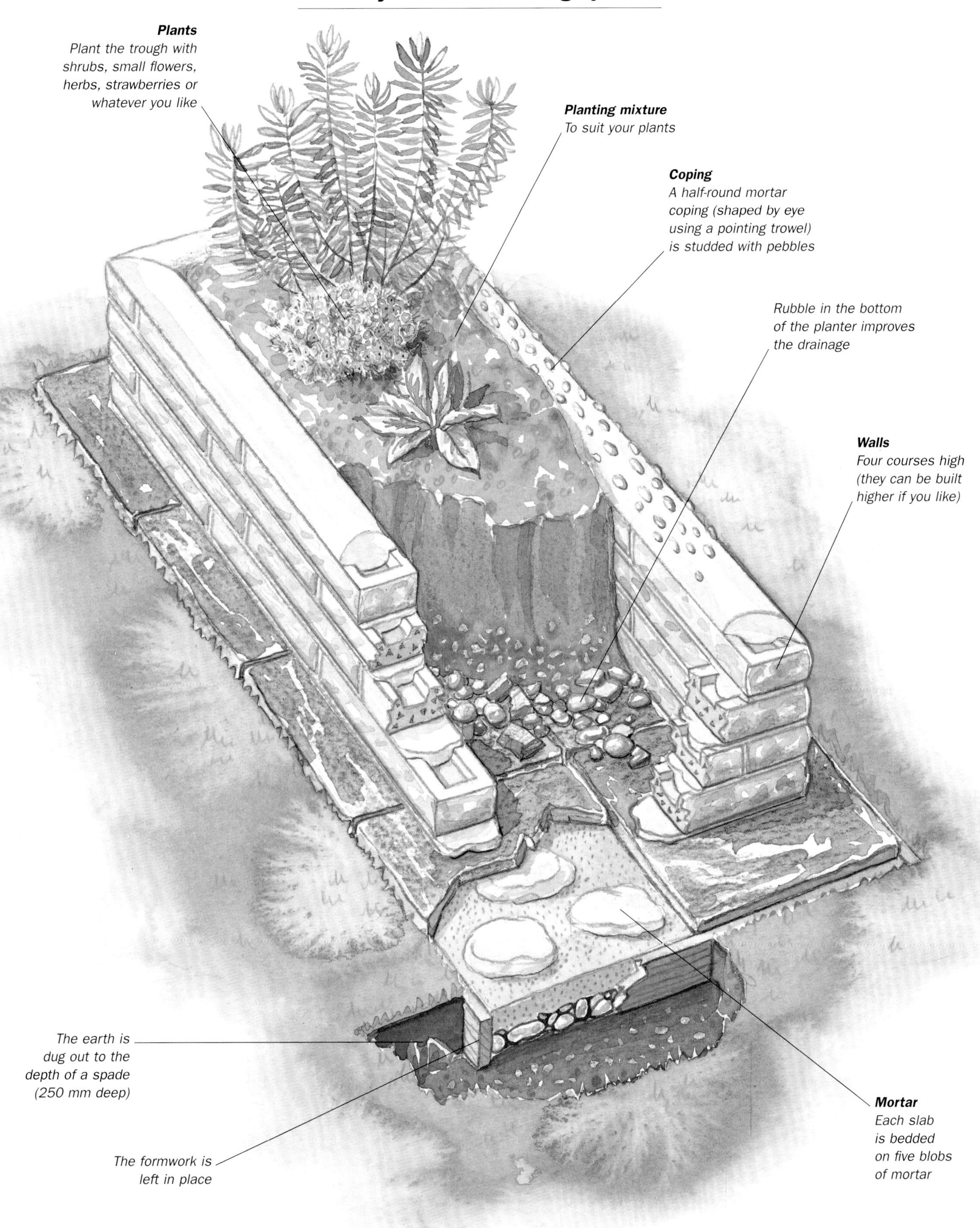
Plants
Plant the trough with shrubs, small flowers, herbs, strawberries or whatever you like
Planting mixture
To suit your plants
Coping
A half-round mortar coping (shaped by eye using a pointing trowel) is studded with pebbles
Rubble in the bottom of the planter improves the drainage
Walls
Four courses high (they can be built higher if you like)
The earth is dug out to the depth of a spade (250 mm deep)
The formwork is left in place
Mortar
Each slab is bedded on five blobs of mortar

Making the trough planter

1 Formwork
Measure out the foundation area, making it 900 mm wide and 1.8 m long. Dig out the area to the depth of the spade. Insert and level the formwork, and fix it in place with nails. Spread hardcore in the formwork frame and compact it with the sledgehammer.

2 Spreading the sand
Shovel sand over the hardcore within the frame and rake it out. Use the tamping beam to compact and level the sand. It should end up as a firm foundation, which is level with the top edge of the formwork.

3 Making the concrete slab base
Mix the mortar to a smooth, firm consistency. Put five generous, bun-shaped blobs on the sand where the first concrete slab will be positioned. Dampen the back of the slab and set it carefully in place upon the sand. Repeat with the other slabs.

4 Laying the first course
Use the tape measure, straight-edge and chalk to set out the shape of the planter on the concrete slab base. Have a dry run to place the first course of York stone blocks. Using club hammer and bolster chisel, cut one block to fit. Check that all is correct.

5 Levelling the blocks
Trowel mortar on the concrete slabs, dampen the blocks for the first course and set them in place. Use the tamping beam, club hammer and spirit level to ensure that the whole course is level. Insert two drainage holes in the mortar as shown on page 158.

6 Building the other courses
Repeat the procedure to build the other three courses. Make sure that all the joints are full of mortar, but at this stage, do not bother to remove the excess. Keep checking that a course is level before building the next course.

7 Checking with the spirit level
When all four courses are in place, use the tamping beam and spirit level to ensure that the horizontal and vertical levels are true. Tap non-aligned blocks into line with the club hammer.

8 Studding with pebbles
With the pointing trowel, lay a generous coping of mortar on the top course and sculpt it to a smooth, half-rounded finish. Press pebbles into the mortar. Use the trowel, wire brush and soft-bristled brush to create a good finish on the courses.

Bench with arch detail

Advanced

Making time
Two weekends
One day for building the basic arch, and three days for the walls and slabs

This bench is a beautifully dynamic shape, and the building procedure is very satisfying. When you have run the stone over the formwork, and then removed the formwork to see that the arch actually stands unsupported, it's a triumphal moment. If you had planned to build a bench in your garden, to sit on or perhaps to use as a table, try this project – you will amaze yourself and your friends with your stoneworking skills.

Considering the design

The bench is constructed on a base slab (or an existing patio slab). Two pillars are built and plywood sprung between them. Thin slivers of stone are worked into mortar over the plywood, the end and side walls are built up to square off the structure, and finally the structure is topped with slabs to create the seat.

Getting started

Start by searching out the stone. You need a small number of square-edged blocks for the two pillars, and a heap of thin, broken sandstone for the arch.

Overall dimensions and general notes

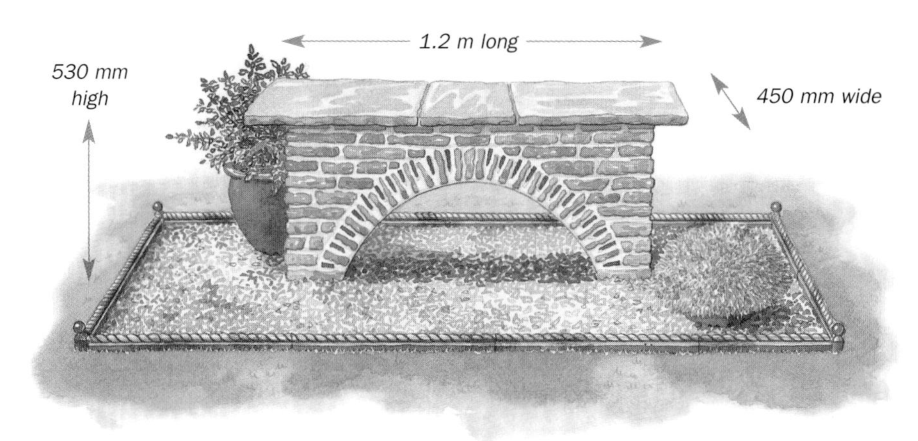
1.2 m long
530 mm high
450 mm wide

This decorative bench has been built on a specially constructed foundation slab, but can be built directly on to an existing patio. The arch is deceptively easy to make.

You will need

Tools

- ✔ Tape measure, chalk and straight-edge
- ✔ Pegs and string
- ✔ Shovel
- ✔ Wheelbarrow and bucket
- ✔ Old carpet: about 300 mm x 600 mm
- ✔ Club hammer
- ✔ Bolster chisel
- ✔ Mason's hammer
- ✔ Bricklayer's trowel
- ✔ Pointing trowel
- ✔ Spirit level
- ✔ Soft-bristled brush

Materials

For a bench 1.2 m long, 450 mm wide and 530 mm high

- ✔ Sandstone: 1 wheelbarrow load of pieces about 150 mm wide and 60–70 mm thick (pillars)
- ✔ Sandstone or salvaged roof stone: 3 wheelbarrow loads of thin split stone (arch and walls)
- ✔ Waste roof stone and broken tiles: 1 bucketful of each (arch)
- ✔ Natural or reconstituted York stone: 2 slabs, 450 mm square; 1 slab, 450 mm long and 300 mm wide (seat)
- ✔ Rope-top edging: 12 edging components, 600 mm long, 150 mm high and 50 mm thick, terracotta colour (to frame the slate infill)
- ✔ Pillar and ball posts: 4 posts, 280 mm high and 60 mm square, terracotta colour (to link the edging)
- ✔ Welsh plum slate chippings: 50 kg (decorative infill)
- ✔ Concrete blocks: 6 blocks, 450 mm long, 225 mm wide and 100 mm thick (for springing the plywood)
- ✔ Formwork or former: a sheet of thin plywood, 900 mm long, 360 mm wide and 5 mm thick (the grain must run across the width of the plywood)
- ✔ Hardcore: 8 wheelbarrow loads
- ✔ Concrete: 1 part (35 kg) cement, 2 parts (70 kg) sharp sand, 3 parts (105 kg) aggregate
- ✔ Mortar: 1 part (25 kg) cement, 3 parts (75 kg) soft sand

Exploded view of the bench with arch detail

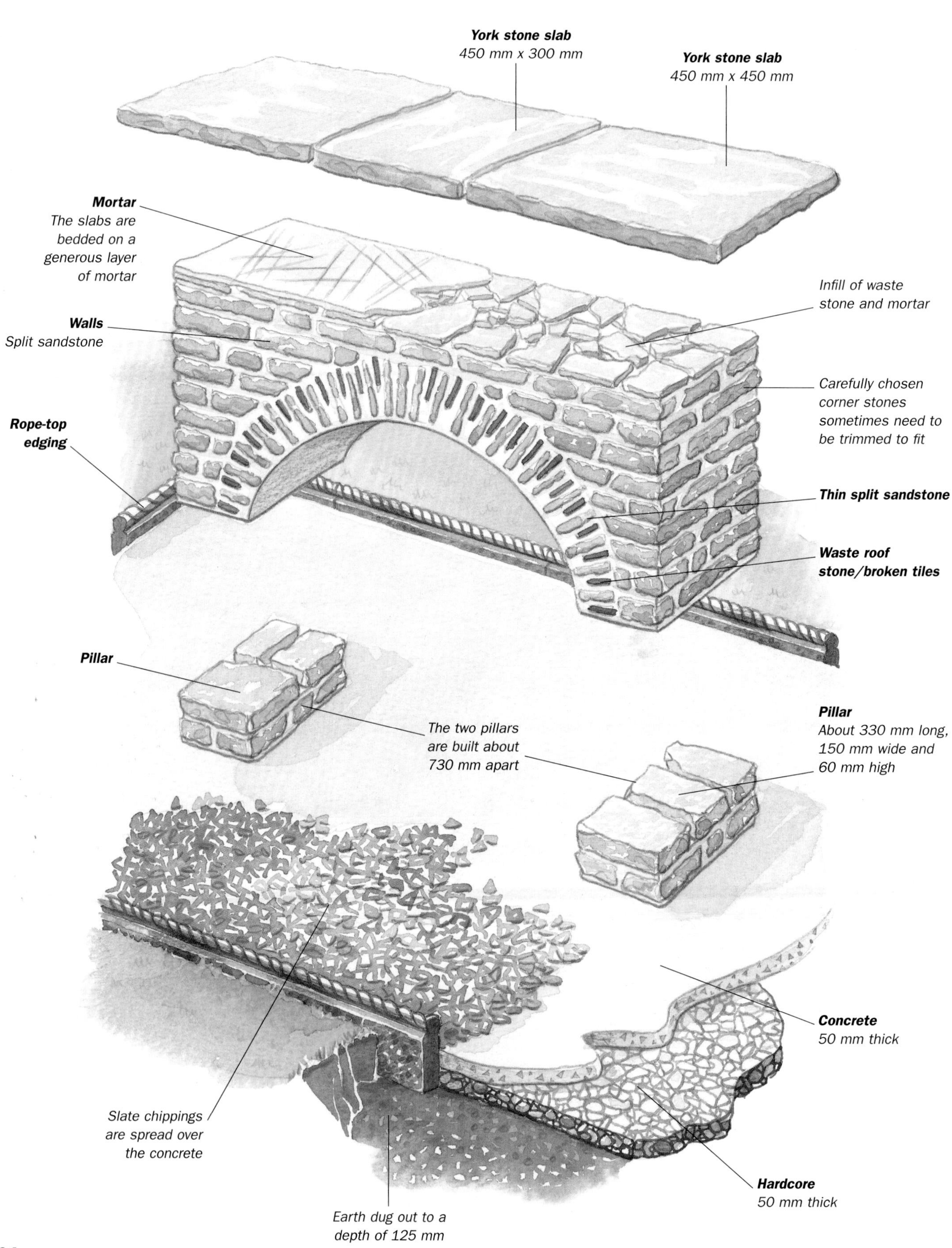
York stone slab
450 mm x 300 mm
York stone slab
450 mm x 450 mm
Mortar
The slabs are bedded on a generous layer of mortar
Infill of waste stone and mortar
Walls
Split sandstone
Carefully chosen corner stones sometimes need to be trimmed to fit
Rope-top edging
Thin split sandstone
Waste roof stone/broken tiles
Pillar
The two pillars are built about 730 mm apart
Pillar
About 330 mm long, 150 mm wide and 60 mm high
Concrete
50 mm thick
Slate chippings are spread over the concrete
Hardcore
50 mm thick
Earth dug out to a depth of 125 mm

Detail of the base of the bench

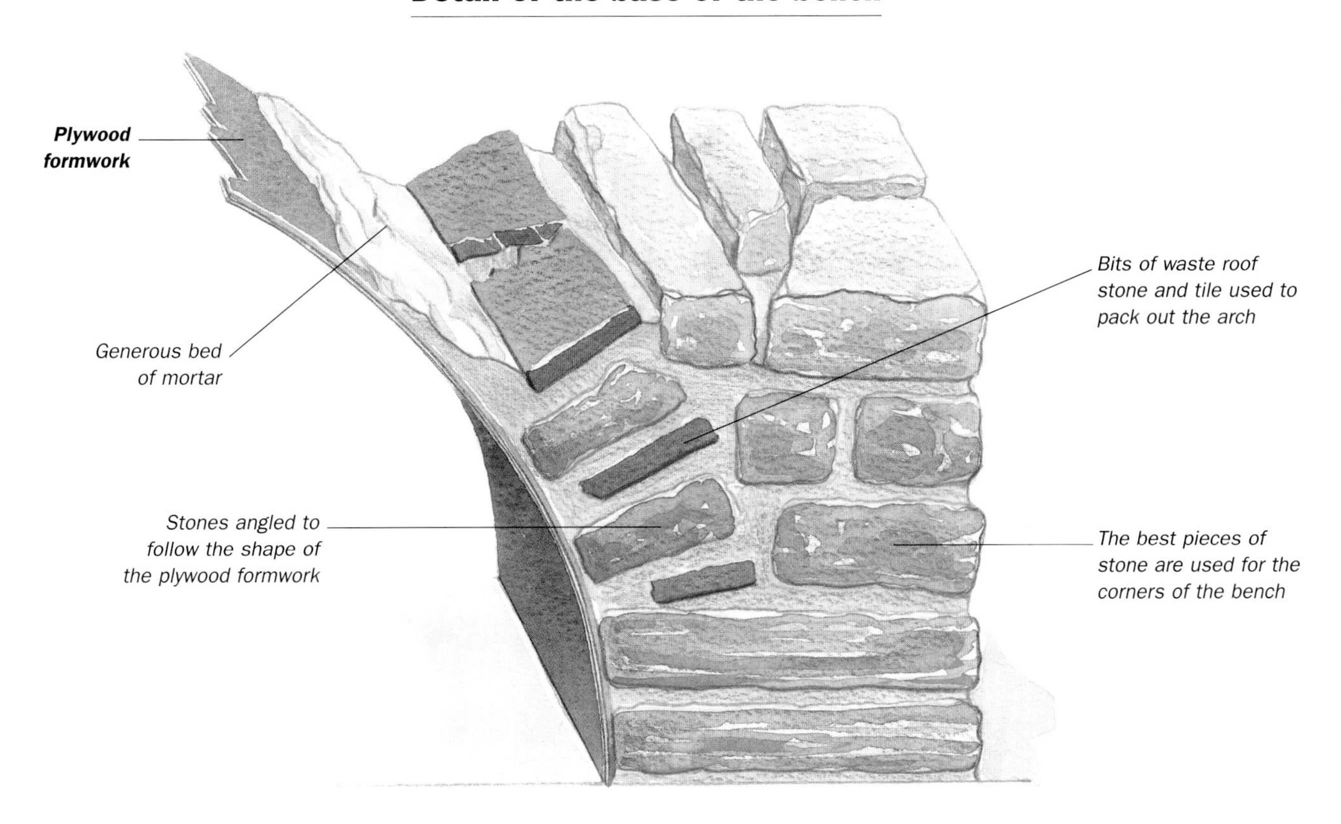
Plywood formwork
Generous bed of mortar
Stones angled to follow the shape of the plywood formwork
Bits of waste roof stone and tile used to pack out the arch
The best pieces of stone are used for the corners of the bench

Cross-section of the bench

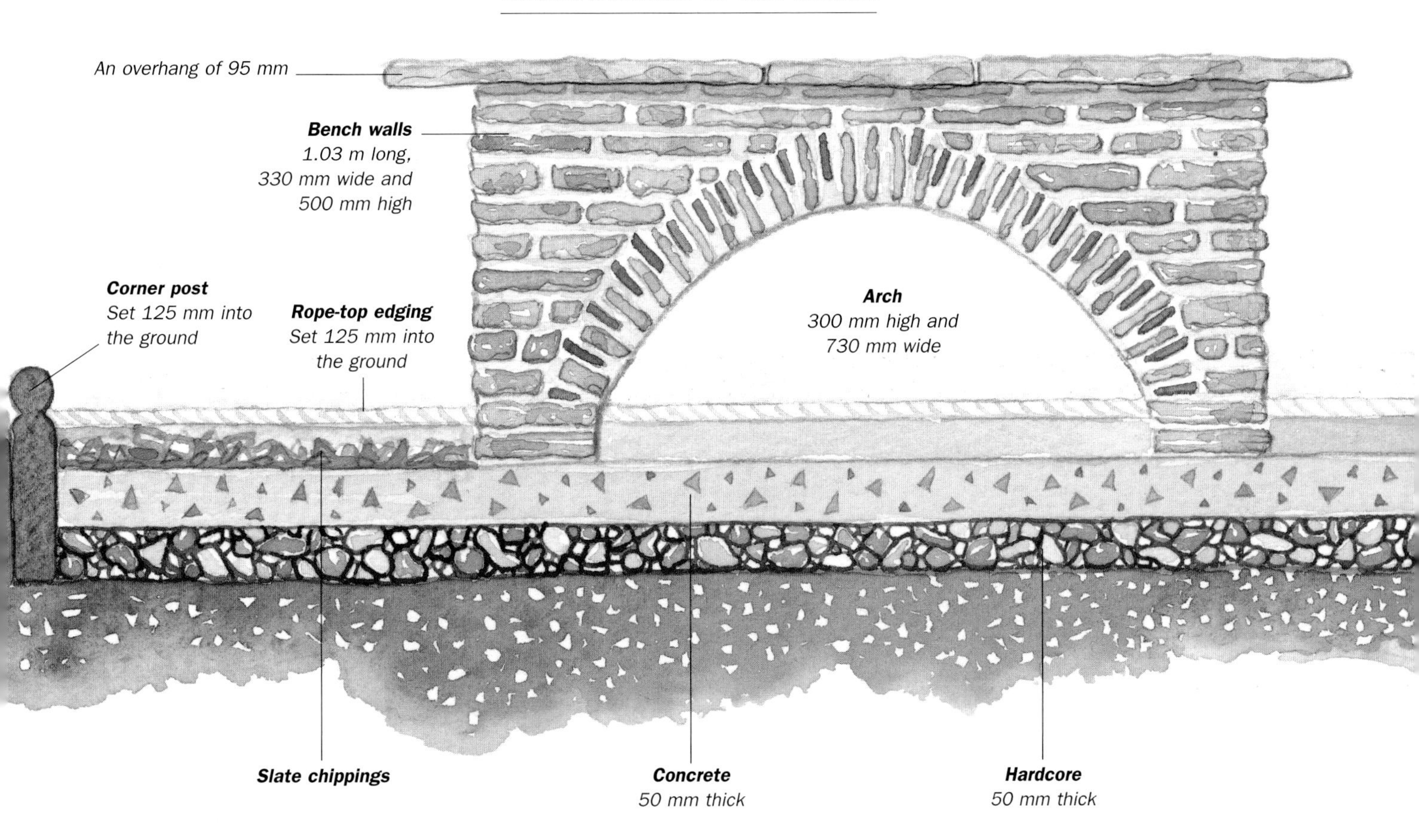
An overhang of 95 mm
Bench walls
1.03 m long, 330 mm wide and 500 mm high
Corner post
Set 125 mm into the ground
Rope-top edging
Set 125 mm into the ground
Arch
300 mm high and 730 mm wide
Slate chippings
Concrete
50 mm thick
Hardcore
50 mm thick

Making the bench with arch detail

1 Measuring out
Build a concrete base slab if needed. Dig out the earth to a depth of 125 mm and compact 50 mm of hardcore in the recess. Lay the concrete. Mark out the seat. The pillars need to measure about 330 mm long x 150 mm wide x 60 mm high, and stand about 730 mm apart.

2 Building the pillars
Build up the two pillars dry, making sure that the corners are, as near as possible, at right angles. Cut stone with the club hammer and bolster chisel, and trim it with the mason's hammer. Then build the pillars with mortar and leave to set for a few hours.

3 Arch formwork
Set the concrete blocks around the pillars and spring the sheet of plywood into an arch, so that it is supported by the concrete blocks and is just touching the inside of the pillars.

4 Making the arch
Mix the mortar to a soft, buttery consistency and lay the thin pieces of stone over the formwork. Work up from both sides in order to keep the weight equally distributed. Try to keep the sides of the arch aligned with the edge of the plywood.

5 Removing the plywood
When the mortar has set, carefully remove the plywood and the concrete blocks. Lay courses of stone on the pillars, doing your best to ensure that the corners are crisp and square.

6 Checking the structure
Every now and again as you are building the walls, stop and use the spirit level to ensure that the sides of the structure are vertically true. Use a hammer or the handle of the trowel to nudge stones into line.

7 Tidying the mortar
Wait until the mortar is crisp (after about two or three hours), and then use the end of the pointing trowel to scrape out excess mortar and reveal the edges of the stones to best advantage, giving the bench a more attractive appearance.

8 Bedding the slabs
Spread a generous layer of mortar over the top of the last course, dampen the back of the seat slabs and gently bed them in place. Make checks with the spirit level and if necessary, tamp the slabs level with the handle of the club hammer.

9 Inserting the rope-top edging
Dig a shallow trench around the base slab and set the rope-top edging and pillar and ball posts in place on a bed of mortar. Check the levels with the spirit level. Tidy up the bench with the brush. Finally, fill the area around the bench with slate chippings.

Crazy-paving steps

Advanced

Making time
Two weekends
One day for putting in the concrete foundation slab, and three days for building

If you want a low-cost flight of three or four steps, how about making stone crazy-paving steps? The design harks back to the 1920s, and uses a mixture of natural split sandstone and salvaged cut stone. The low risers make the steps easy to use for everyone, from the very young to older members of the family. The slightly rippled surface of the steps feels good underfoot and is attractive to look at.

Considering the design

The steps spring off a single concrete strip foundation slab that runs under the whole flight. The foundation slab is built first, then the first riser, side and back walls. The walls are back-filled with concrete and topped with the crazy paving to make the first tread. Then the next riser wall and related walls are built, back-filled and so on. We have used random split sandstone for the walls, but you could use limestone, or even a mixture of bricks and stone instead: it really depends on your budget and the availability of materials. The height of the riser walls and the depth of the treads are, to a great extent, governed by safety and comfort – low risers are both comfortable and safe to negotiate; however the width of the flight can be shaped to suit the size of your site and your own requirements.

Getting started

Decide how long you want the flight of steps to be. Establish the position and mark out the shape of the foundation slab. Plan how to move around the garden while the steps are being built.

Overall dimensions and general notes

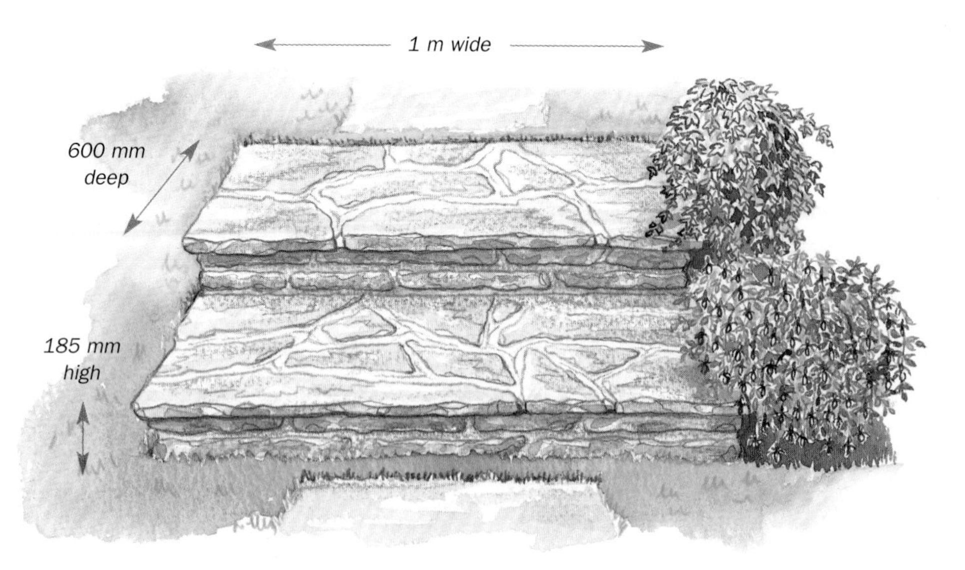
1 m wide
600 mm deep
185 mm high

A good project for a country or urban garden. The crazy paving is an attractive and practical surface for steps (it provides a lot of grip). The width, height and depth of the steps can be adjusted to suit your requirements and the slope of the site.

You will need

Tools

- Tape measure and straight-edge
- Pegs and string
- Spade, fork and shovel
- Sledgehammer
- Wheelbarrow and bucket
- Tamping beam: about 1.5 m long, 60 mm wide and 30 mm thick
- Club hammer and claw hammer
- Mason's hammer
- Bricklayer's and pointing trowels
- Spirit level
- Soft-bristled brush

Materials

For two steps, each 1 m wide, 600 mm deep and 185 mm high

- Sandstone: about 1.2 sq. m split stone in random sizes and thicknesses (amount allows for wastage and choice)
- Hardcore (builder's rubble or waste stone): about 10 wheelbarrow loads
- Pine: 8 m long, 60 mm wide and 30 mm thick (formwork)
- Concrete: 1 part (100 kg) cement, 5 parts (500 kg) ballast
- Mortar: 1 part (50 kg) cement, 3 parts (150 kg) soft sand (allows for wastage)
- Nails: 12 x 50 mm long

Exploded view of the crazy-paving steps

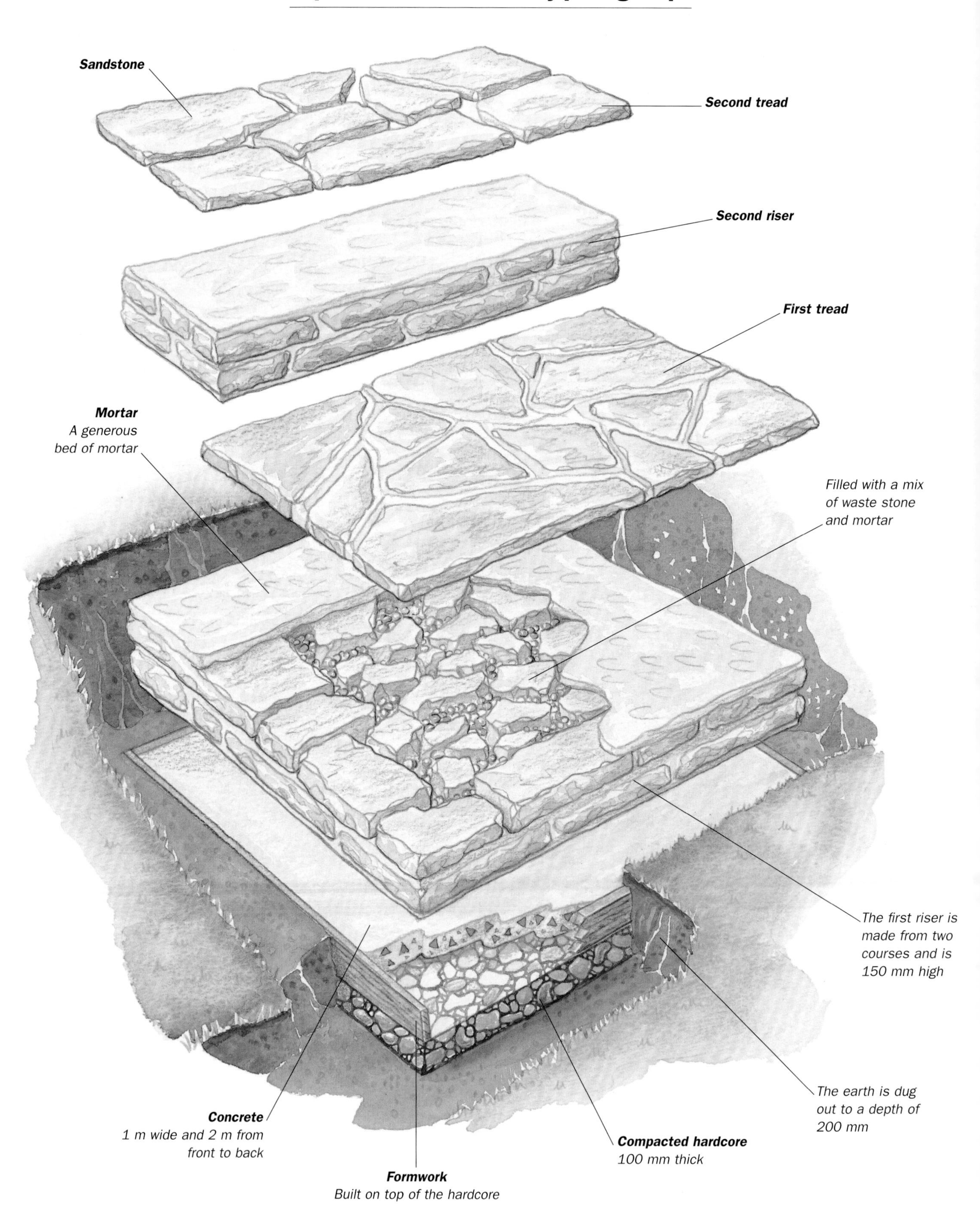
Sandstone
Second tread
Second riser
First tread
Mortar
A generous bed of mortar
Filled with a mix of waste stone and mortar
The first riser is made from two courses and is 150 mm high
The earth is dug out to a depth of 200 mm
Concrete
1 m wide and 2 m from front to back
Compacted hardcore
100 mm thick
Formwork
Built on top of the hardcore

Cut-away view of the crazy-paving steps

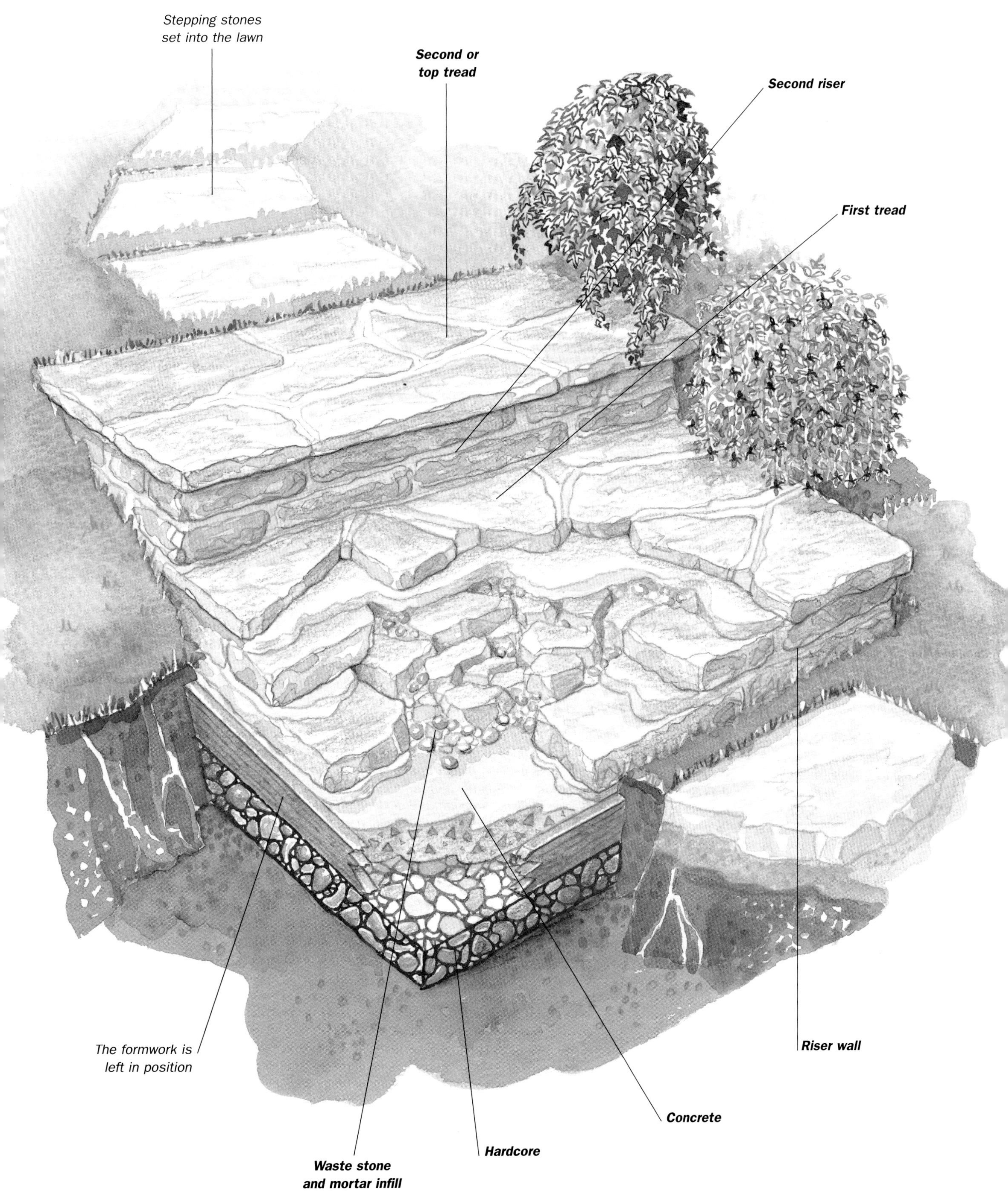
Stepping stones set into the lawn
Second or top tread
Second riser
First tread
The formwork is left in position
Riser wall
Concrete
Hardcore
Waste stone and mortar infill

Making the crazy-paving steps

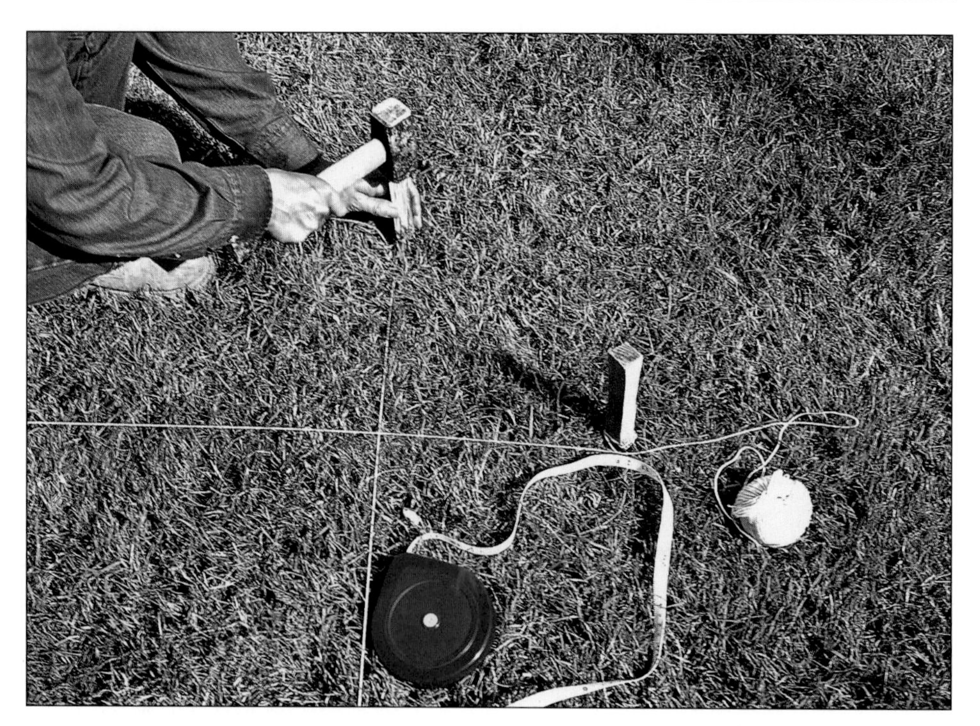

1 Marking out
Use the tape measure, pegs and string to mark out the overall size and shape of the foundation slab, which is 1 m wide and 2 m from front to back. Remove the turf, in squares, from the site (use elsewhere in the garden or give to a friend).

2 Making the foundation slab
Dig out the earth to a depth of 200 mm. Half-fill the recess with hardcore and compact it with the sledgehammer. Fix the formwork and fit it into place. Top the hardcore with a 100 mm-thick layer of concrete, levelling it with the tamping beam.

3 Setting out the first step
Use the tape measure, straight-edge and chalk to set out the position of the first riser wall, side and back walls on the concrete slab. Select stones and lay them out dry. The border is 300 mm wide. Make joints as small as possible and use right-angled stones for corners.

4 Building the first step
Mix the mortar to a buttery consistency and build the riser wall, side and back walls to a height of 150 mm. Back-fill the area within the walls with 125 mm of waste stone and leftover mortar. Top the central area with concrete and level off.

5 Bedding the crazy paving
When the concrete has set, select stones for the crazy paving and lay them on top. Trowel mortar on the concrete and bed the crazy paving in place. Arrange the stones so that there is an overhang to the tread of about 20 mm at the front and side edges.

6 Building the other steps
Measure back 600 mm from the edge of the tread, establishing the depth of the tread and the position of the riser wall for the next step. Repeat the procedure already described to build the next step. Keep checking that everything is level.

7 Selecting crazy paving
When selecting pieces of stone, place them together in different ways to achieve the best fit and reduce the need for cutting. Use the mason's hammer to cut stone. Make up a complete rectangle, the correct size for one tread, before mortaring.

8 Pointing
Use the pointing trowel and some freshly mixed mortar to tool all the courses to an angled finish. Finally, fill the joints between the crazy paving with mortar and work to a peaked finish.

Roman arch shrine

★★★
Advanced

Making time
One weekend
One day for the base slab and formwork, and one day for building the arch

Many countries have an ancient tradition of building shrines in quiet corners of the house and garden, perhaps for religious purposes or for displaying a meaningful family item. This shrine has been inspired by the little arch-topped alcoves and niches common in Italy. It would be perfect for displaying a piece of garden sculpture or a favourite container plant, or it could comprise part of a water feature.

Considering the design

The arch is constructed over a wooden former set on wedges on the base slab, with its back against a wall. Stone is set in mortar over the former, the courses are jointed, and when the mortar has set, the wedges and former are removed. The rule of thumb is the thinner and more uniform the pieces of stone, the easier it is to run them over the arch.

Getting started

Start by building the former. It's very simple – just two sheets of plywood held apart with lengths of wood, and the sides of the shape covered in plywood.

Overall dimensions and general notes

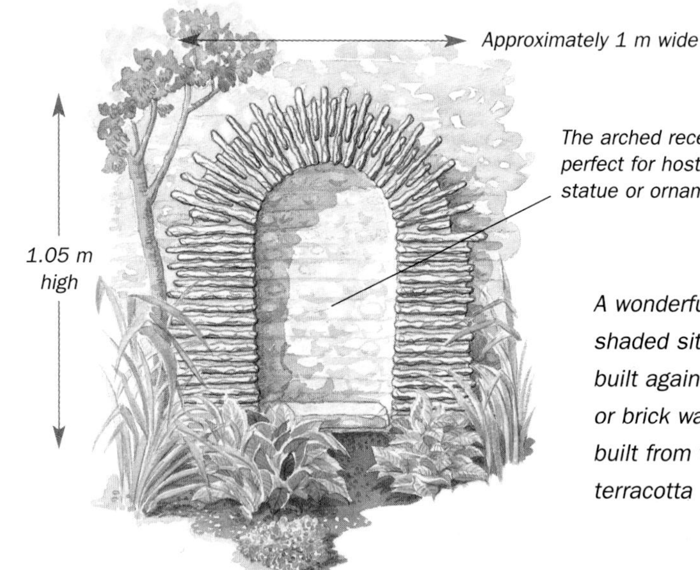
Approximately 1 m wide
The arched recess is perfect for hosting a statue or ornament
1.05 m high

A wonderful project for a shaded site. It needs to be built against an existing stone or brick wall. The arch can be built from thin stone, slate or terracotta roof tiles.

You will need

Tools

- Tape measure, straight-edge and compass
- Crosscut saw
- Electric jigsaw
- Claw hammer
- Screwdriver
- Pegs and string
- Spade and shovel
- Wheelbarrow and bucket
- Spirit level
- Sledgehammer
- Mason's hammer
- Bricklayer's trowel
- Pointing trowel
- Pliers
- Soft-bristled brush

Materials

For an arch 1.05 m high and 1 m wide

- Hardcore: about 1 wheelbarrow load
- Stone base slab: approx. 1 m long, 300 mm wide and 50 mm thick, colour and texture to suit
- Stone plinth slab: approx. 400 mm long, 150 mm wide and 75 mm thick, slightly bigger than the base of the former
- Roof stone: 2 wheelbarrow loads of thin stone, either salvaged or split
- Plywood: 2 pieces, 700 mm long, 400 mm wide and 4 mm thick; 1 piece, 2 m long, 200 mm wide and 4 mm thick (former)
- Pine: 15 pieces, 200 mm long, 35 mm wide and 20 mm thick (former joining battens and wedges)
- Mortar: 1 part (10 kg) cement, 1 part (10 kg) lime, 2 parts (20 kg) soft sand
- Screws: 50 x 25 mm-long cross-headed screws (this allows extra)
- Nails: 50 x 25 mm-long flat-headed nails (this allows extra)
- Soft galvanized wire: 600 mm

Exploded view of the former for the Roman arch shrine

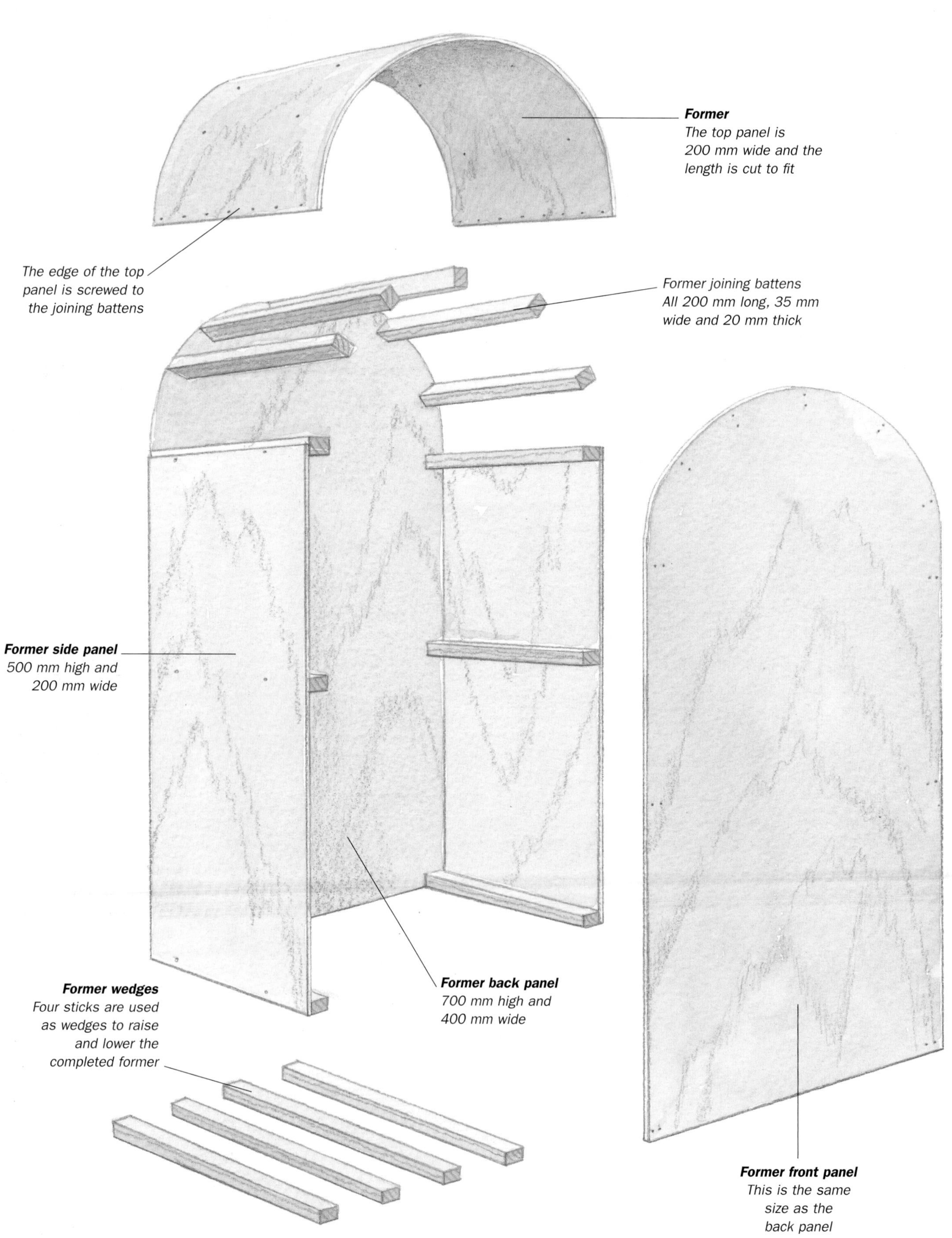
Former
The top panel is 200 mm wide and the length is cut to fit
The edge of the top panel is screwed to the joining battens
Former joining battens
All 200 mm long, 35 mm wide and 20 mm thick
Former side panel
500 mm high and 200 mm wide
Former wedges
Four sticks are used as wedges to raise and lower the completed former
Former back panel
700 mm high and 400 mm wide
Former front panel
This is the same size as the back panel

Exploded view of the Roman arch shrine

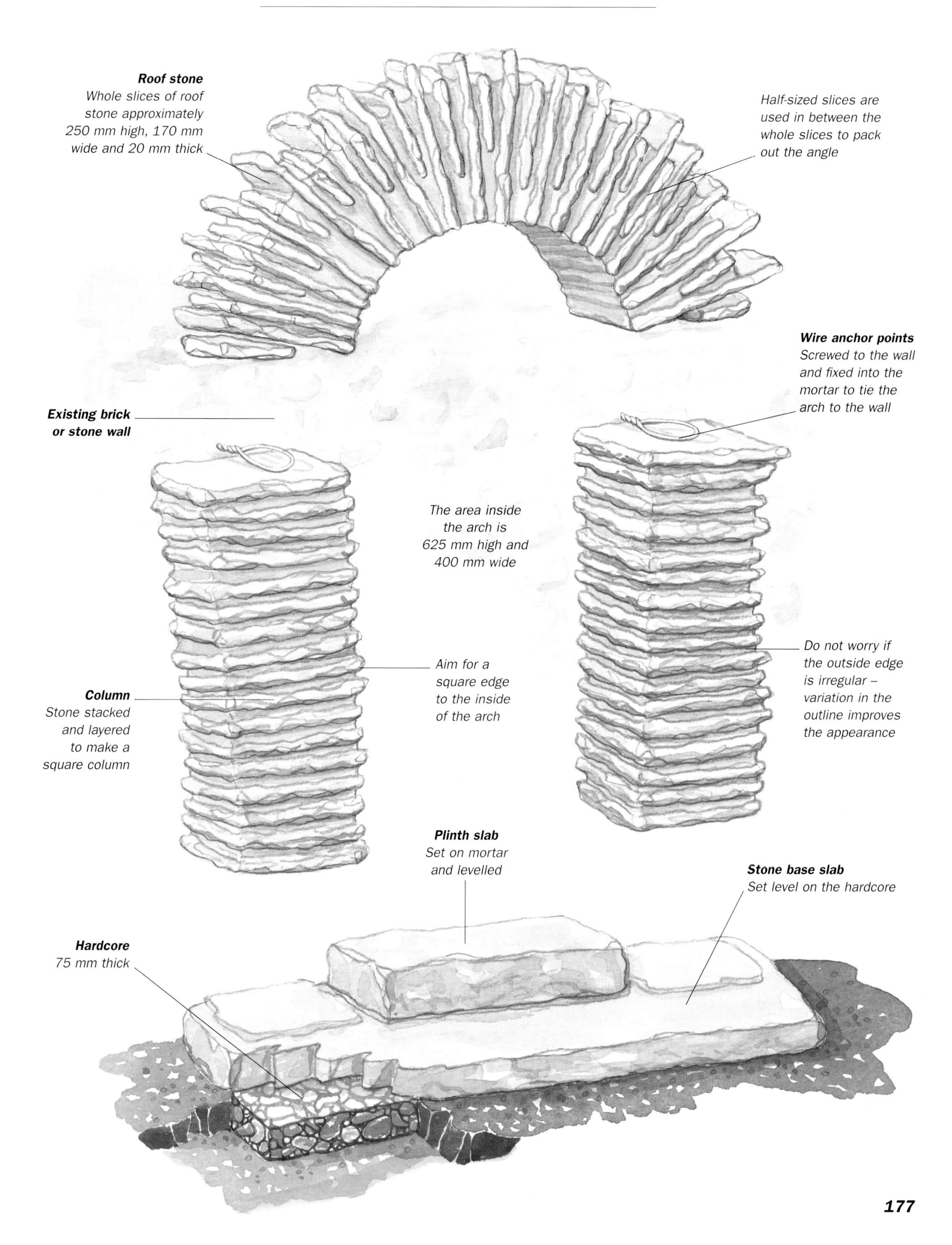

Roof stone
Whole slices of roof stone approximately 250 mm high, 170 mm wide and 20 mm thick
Half-sized slices are used in between the whole slices to pack out the angle
Wire anchor points
Screwed to the wall and fixed into the mortar to tie the arch to the wall
Existing brick or stone wall
The area inside the arch is 625 mm high and 400 mm wide
Do not worry if the outside edge is irregular – variation in the outline improves the appearance
Aim for a square edge to the inside of the arch
Column
Stone stacked and layered to make a square column
Plinth slab
Set on mortar and levelled
Stone base slab
Set level on the hardcore
Hardcore
75 mm thick

Making the Roman arch shrine

1 Making the former
Build the front and back of the former with the two sheets of plywood, setting them 200 mm apart, as shown in the working drawing. Nail or screw the plywood shapes directly to the ends of the 200 mm-long joining battens.

2 Covering the former
Cover the sides of the former with plywood. Ease the plywood over the curve and screw it to the joining battens. Use a generous quantity of screws.

3 Laying the base slab
Clear and level the site and compact the earth with the sledgehammer. Lay a 75 mm layer of hardcore and compact it with the sledgehammer. Set the base slab in place on generous blobs of mortar. Make checks with the spirit level.

4 Setting up the plinth slab
Bed the plinth slab in mortar on the base slab. Use the tape measure and spirit level to ensure that it is levelled and centred on the base slab.

5 Positioning the former
Place wedges of wood on the plinth and set the former on top of it, hard against the wall. Make sure that it is levelled and centred. Pay particular attention to the side-on view, making sure that the former is not tilting forwards (it can tilt backwards slightly).

6 Building the arch
Mix the mortar to a butter-smooth consistency and start to build layers of stone on each side of the former to make the square columns. Ensure that the stacks are both vertically and horizontally level, by making regular checks with the spirit level.

7 Anchor wires
Screw twists of wire to the wall at four or five places around the top of the arch, to provide anchor points for the stonework. As you build up the columns, insert the ends of the wire into the mortar between the slices of stone, to help hold the structure firm.

8 Forming the arch
Stack pieces of stone over the curved top of the former, setting half-slices between them to ensure a good spacing. Finally, when the mortar is dry and hard, use the pointing trowel to sculpt the mortar to reveal the edges of the stone.

GARDEN PONDS

Bryan Hirst

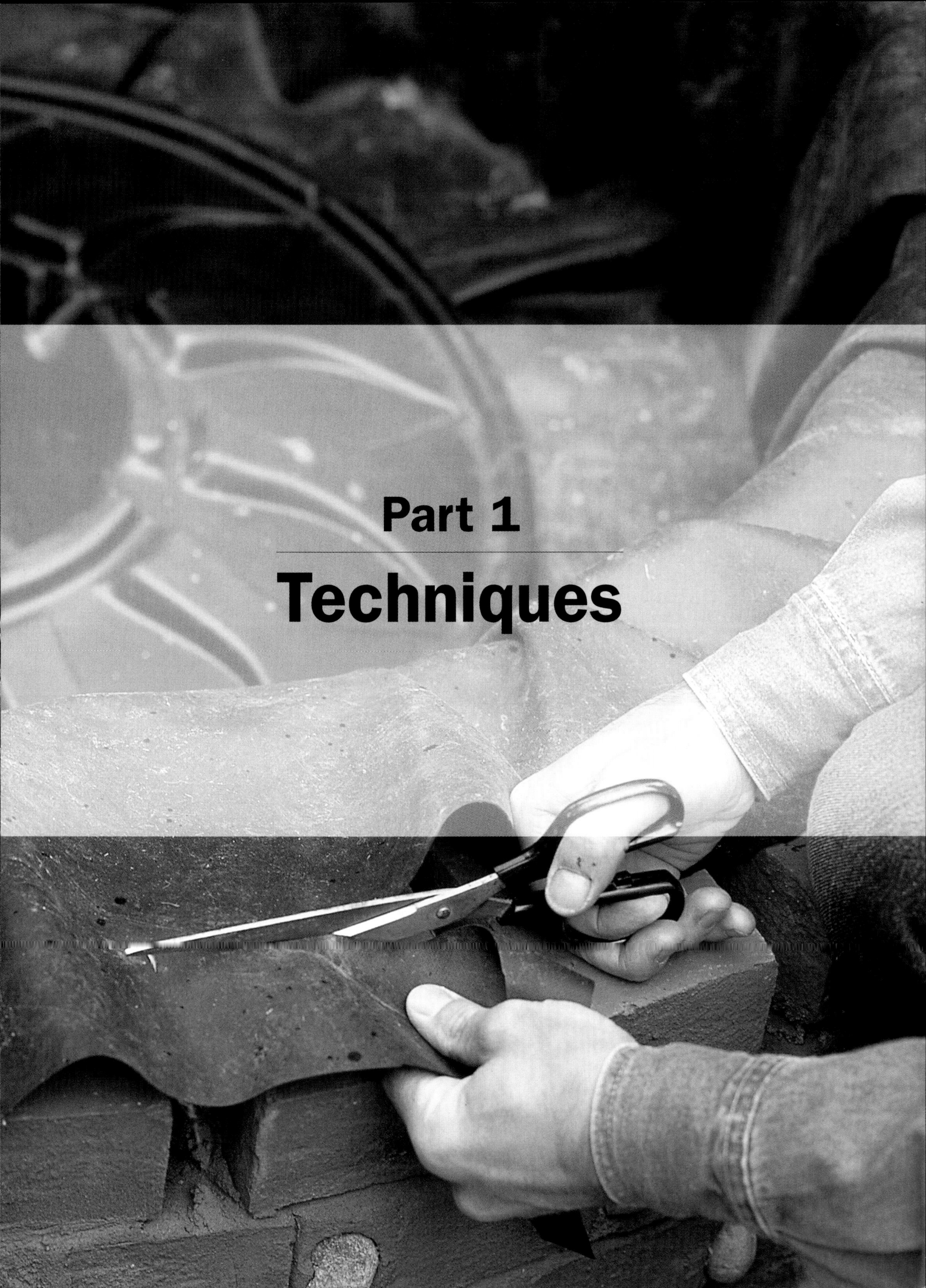

Part 1

Techniques

Designing and planning

Building a water feature is a big undertaking that involves a fair amount of hard work and as it is designed to be a permanent feature of the garden, planning is essential. The decisions to be made are based partly on what sort of pond you want, and partly on the limitations of your garden. These and the following pages suggest pond types, locations and functions to help you choose what suits your needs best.

Types of pond

Natural pond

This pond follows the forms and curves of nature, with no built-up edges, and perhaps includes an outcrop of stone or a beach. This allows for planting, where appropriate, in and at the edges of the pond and gives the impression that the water was there long before the rest of the garden and house were constructed.

Bog garden

Wet areas, often located next to ponds, support a wide range of plants that do not grow in ordinary garden conditions. Bog gardens can be built to stand alone or as part of an informal pond.

Above: For a natural-looking pond to be completely successful, the lining must be entirely hidden from view, especially at the edges. Restrained planting suitable for a natural pond is also a key feature.
Right: Include a boggy area in your pond design if you want to grow plants like this Arum lily, one of a large range of plants that will thrive with roots under water.

Above: As well as offering the delights of water lilies which will flower all summer long, this sunken formal brick pond brings the sky down to earth with constantly changing reflections and leads the eye down the full length of the pond.

Formal pond

A geometric design works best if it forms an association in materials and design with the buildings that are close to it. It may, for example, be rectangular, octagonal or linear in form, and may have a stone or paved edge that allows easy access to the water's edge. Where possible, any change of level can be exploited with small waterfalls running from the higher to the lower pond. Planting is possible in a formal pond, although this is more likely to be a few carefully chosen architectural plants, rather than a large number.

Raised pond

This is a formal pond constructed above ground level and contained by brick or stone walls. Its advantage is that it reduces the amount of spoil that needs to be removed from the site; however, this saving is usually absorbed by the increased cost of construction of the exterior walls. As they will be a major feature, they often require finishing materials that can be more expensive than hidden construction materials, where the finish is not important.

Above: If a raised pond is at a comfortable sitting height (450 mm is ideal), it is fascinating to dabble or to watch the varied life in the pond life close up whilst enjoying a drink or contemplating life.

Rill or stream

The principles of creating a stream or a rill are more or less the same. A stream is designed to appear entirely natural, whereas a rill, or channel, is a formally contained stream. You can use a slope by creating an apparently natural source of water: this is achieved by pumping water to a disguised source, giving the impression of water coming up from a spring. The character of the stream or rill will be altered by the gradient of the ground. The steeper the gradient, the greater the potential for pools and waterfalls.

This gentle stream with planting along the edges allows you to make the most of a slight gradient. If your garden is steep enough, you can have waterfalls as the water makes its way down. The stream must nestle comfortably in the ground for it to look natural.

Locations

Marking the shape

When you have worked out all the possible locations for your pond, mark them out with lengths of rope or a garden hose, or even spray paint. Marking out the pond shape and viewing it from all aspects allows you to be sure that the end shape (which is difficult and expensive to change) is exactly what you expected. If you have the technology, it is worth photographing the area with a digital camera and manipulating the image to see how this can affect reality. Should any trees be reshaped, reduced or removed? Are there any natural dips or gullies that could be made to hold water, or any slopes from which water could run from fountain to pond? Is there a vista that you can reflect in the surface of your pond?

Above: The natural lie of the land will dictate the shape and character of a pond. Gentle curves are easier on the eye than sharp bends in informal settings. Nature abhors straight lines and perfect circles. Above right: This natural looking pond makes the most of its beautiful setting, allowing the reflections of the sky to reach up to the edge of the pond and tempting you down to the water's edge. The grassy bank edging the pond is perfect for sitting by the water on summer days.

Natural advantages

The surface of a pond reflects light and all the changing humours of the weather and seasons, and the placing of what is effectively a mirror surface to gain the most from this quality is something that should be given major consideration. Studying the movement of the sun across the horizon may give you an opportunity to create a dappled effect on the ceiling or walls inside your house, and to bring more light into a shady area. Place mirrors in the intended pond area to help evaluate the effect of the reflected light.

Visibility

To get the most from your pond it is often best to site it where you can see it from inside your house – perhaps from your bedroom window or the kitchen or recreation areas – so you can enjoy its appearance changing with the time of day as well as the seasons. Remember that the perceived shape of the pond will be altered by the viewpoint: for example, an oval pond will appear round when viewed along the greater length, as the apparent length will become reduced.

Alternatively, some of the most exciting ponds are sited away from a property and require a walk to them. If your garden is large enough, try to have some part of the pond not immediately visible from the house, as this encourages the adventure of a search and exploration of the grounds to reveal the whole picture.

Child safety

Children can and sometimes do get into trouble in ponds, and it is important to consider all potential hazards. A raised pond deters children from crawling or stumbling into it, or borders can be built around the inside perimeter of the pond to keep children out of water that is more than 75 mm deep. A custom-made decorative steel grid could be used.

The design of some fountains allows stones to be placed in the basin to reduce the depth of the water; these can be removed later when children have reached a safer age. Another alternative is to delay the project until your children have reached an age when they do not need constant supervision near water.

Make sure that it is not possible to drive a car or other machinery into the water – for example, if the pond is to be near car parking areas or driveways, put up bollards, posts or raised kerbs to physically stop any runaway machines.

Ease of use

Make sure that you can approach the pond easily and that there is going to be provision for seating near the pond on a flat surface. Consider placing a pergola, barbecue or dining area near the pond.

Stepping stones sunk into a lawn will allow you to approach the pond during the winter or when the grass is wet. Make sure that the stones are well set into the ground and will not interfere with the mowing. People naturally congregate by a pond so make enough space by it.

By-products

If your pond is to be dug out, rather than raised, consider what are you going to do with the excavated material (spoil). Can you build up a bank, or should you take the spoil away, which can be expensive and difficult? If you are removing good topsoil, look at possible uses elsewhere to add to the quality of the soil, or to level another section of your property. It is easy to underestimate the amount that you will have to take away – often it bulks up and becomes up to a third more in volume than when it was in the ground.

Neighbours

If your project can be seen or heard by the neighbours, check that they have no objection to your proposed scheme. A rock waterfall, for example, will be heard by your neighbours and may cause them irritation. Excavations can affect the foundations of a neighbour's house or outhouses, fences or trees, as well as the water table or water supply to adjoining properties. If you consider that any of these factors could be a problem, consult an engineer.

Experiment with sound by adjusting the volume of water flowing over waterfalls and by positioning stones to alter the music.

Sound

For many, the sound of running water from a stream or fountain gives an enormous sense of calm and relaxation. This sound may be tuned or adjusted by altering the volume of water that is flowing, or by placing obstacles, such as stones or rocks, in the path of the water.

Obstacles checklist

- ✔ Are there underground services, which may be affected by your workings? Check with the relevant utilities companies.
- ✔ Consider the type of soil and what lies underneath it: for example, solid rock will be expensive to break up and remove, clay soil requires hard work to dig deeply and it is impossible to make clean-sided holes in sandy soil.
- ✔ Could there be the foundations of an earlier building or construction?
- ✔ Are there any large plants or trees nearby which are likely to have wide spreading roots that you need to avoid cutting through?
- ✔ Has the ground been disturbed and polluted or made unstable?

Functions

The next consideration is what you want the water feature to do for you, and how important each of your requirements is, compared to each other.

Reflections

Watching still waters reflect the changing weather patterns in the sky can be immensely enjoyable, and these reflections are radically altered if water from a fountain falls on to the surface of the pond. A waterfall will ripple the surface and break up light reflections.

Falling water is fascinating; it catches the sunlight as well as causing ripples and breaking up the surface of the pool below.

As a natural pond matures, the surface of the water will be covered with plants. Arrange in groups or stands of the same plants together as the effect is generally more pleasing and the area is easier to maintain. Below: Wildlife will come naturally to your pond. Attempts to import wildlife are unsuccessful as each habitat will support particular life.

Entertainment

Waterside entertainment has some added magical properties: decking allows you to be over the water whilst eating or relaxing; lights placed near the pond reflect in the water to add to the waterside effect; and a barbecue and dining area close to the pond could be considered.

Activity

The scale of your pond may allow boating, fishing, diving and swimming, while even sitting on the edge with your feet in the water on a hot day can give real pleasure. Children may be able to play with model boats. In the evening, floating paper boats with candles in them on the water adds charm and a sense of calm.

Plants

The quality and range of plants that can be grown in and beside the pond affect its visual characteristics enormously. Plants can be positioned in or beside the pond, either in the ground or in suitable containers.

Wildlife

This should come naturally to a pond, although it is possible to encourage certain types of wildlife, such as frogs and newts, by building a beach to allow ease of access. The size and depth of a pond will dictate the range and quantity of the wildlife that use it.

Fish

When a pond has had a year to develop, it can support a small number of fish without upsetting the delicate ecological balance. If, however, you want to keep a considerable number of ornamental fish, you will need to fit filtration and cleaning facilities. These vary in size and type, but be aware that some filtration units can take up an area of up to half the surface area of the pond. Power supplies are required and special pipework needs to be built into the pond; protection for plants must also be installed.

Birds

Ornamental ducks can become tame, and wild birds will often attempt to colonize a pond. If ornamental ducks are planned for your pond, you should build a floating island house where they can be safe from foxes and other vermin; a pebble beach should also be built where they will be encouraged to enter and leave the water, and set up an area where they can rest and be fed. This will also minimize and contain the damage that ducks can do to the surrounding flora.

Filtration should be considered to remove the added nutrients that birds add to the pond through their droppings. These nutrients encourage algae and weeds such as duckweed which can quickly make a pond unsightly.

These houses protect birds from vermin such as foxes. They are ideally placed on an island which saves you the daily task of penning and releasing your birds, as most vermin will not swim to attack ducks.

Birds can have a devastating effect on a newly established pond, as they damage young plants. If they are unwelcome, early discouragement before they start nesting should generally be effective. Herons also pose a threat to fish keepers as they will often come at first light and take fish from a pond. There are various ways to discourage them which may be used with varying success. Decoys are available as wrought iron structures that resemble herons but they are often ineffective as the real herons will notice the lack of movement and disregard them after some time. Netting is effective, if unsightly but there are some attractive metal grille options available. Herons like shallow water so a depth of water at the sides of the pond will also deter them.

Practicalities

With the basic design and planning in hand, the next move is to consider the wider effects of adding a pond to your garden – whether it would affect nearby property, for example. Consider your neighbours, talk over your plans and agree the scheme before you start work.

Costs

Undertaking a project yourself is unquestionably the most cost-effective method, as long as you have researched and designed your project well, as most of the cost of building a pond is taken up by moving materials. Costs are hugely affected by access and the difficulties of materials handling, and by hidden factors, which may only be revealed during the excavation. Labour costs can be difficult to estimate, but materials, plant hire and fuel can be more easily estimated and priced. The more you know and are able to do yourself, the lower your costs. Check your bank account before starting, as there is nothing more depressing and morale-lowering than a half-complete project awaiting funds and energy.

Disruption

Unlike interior projects, the weather and amount of rainfall during a pond project can cause problems and increase the time taken to complete it. You know the weather in your area best – however, I do not recommend the undertaking of a project if you are likely to experience frozen ground conditions, heavy rain or intense heat during the work.

Careful routing and storage of building materials minimizes disruption to your household during the works. Earth, concrete and general debris have an uncanny ability to spread themselves over the house, car, driveway, clothes and machinery, and neighbours may complain if machinery is used or work is undertaken during unsociable hours.

Removal of excess materials

A skip container or storage site, easily accessible from the road, may be required. Make sure that the relevant authorities have been informed of your plans and have given any necessary approval. Because trucks may need to unload materials, make sure that an out-of-the-way location is clearly signposted.

Works access

This may require the co-operation of neighbours and the removal of plants or fence panels, so plan carefully. The narrowest comfortable width for a wheelbarrow to pass through is 1 m; avoid sharp turns where possible, and prepare steps with wooden planks to enable loaded barrows to pass easily over them.

If you are thinking of using an excavator (see page 194), check the minimum width and height required. Note that an excavator needs additional turning space at the sides and it may damage the surface on which it skews, so protect any vulnerable surfaces with boards.

Supply of services

During construction you will need water and electricity. If the project is large, arrange a temporary supply to the key locations using extension cable and hose pipes, so that these services are not affected during the workings.

Pond liners

Until the modern development of manufactured flexible liners, ponds were lined in traditional ways and it is worth considering the possible advantages of using such materials for both aesthetic and practical reasons before making a choice for your project. Availability of materials and costs for additional work in using them can be offset against savings made in the purchase of a modern liner.

Non-flexible liners

Clay

For many years clay was the lining material used for ponds, lakes and waterways; the canals of Great Britain, for example, were mostly made waterproof with puddled clay. In some instances it is still the most cost-effective and best way to line ponds, especially where it is present in the subsoil and there is a plentiful water supply. That said, it has its limitations, as all clay ponds leak to a greater or lesser extent. This may be caused by plants, which put their roots through the clay lining, leaving fissures when the organic materials in the roots rot. It may be also caused by drought: if the water level drops the clay cracks, and when the level rises again water escapes through the cracks and erodes into channels.

Another possibility is that the clay has been mixed with some other unsuitable material that allows water to leach out. To minimize this, clay should be carefully compacted in layers. This is generally done with the tracks of excavators while the clay is still damp. In addition, it is difficult to raise the water level of a clay pond above its natural level, dictated by the surrounding land and water table.

Before applying concrete, line the pond with geotextile and butyl
Use a plywood profile to spread and shape the concrete
Once covered with concrete, the liner will remain stable and waterproof for years

Concrete makes the ideal surface for covering with tiles or a mosaic. Before the concrete is applied, the pond should be lined with layers of geotextile and butyl (see opposite).

Lead

This material is rarely used in practical ponds today, and water from a lead-lined container should not be drunk. It is, however, supremely long-lasting, as demonstrated by the Roman baths at Bath, England which were made with a 19 mm layer of lead, dressed with stone – there is no record of this ever leaking. Lead is now available in rolls for roof work and can be used, when appropriate, to cover vulnerable or unattractive materials at the water's edge. After a few years it takes on a stable, mellow and attractive finish.

Steel

This is little used, but may have appeal if you are near a shipbuilding centre, where it is readily available. It can be used to create attractive curves and natural shapes, and if good-quality steel is used and the pond is kept full of water, it should have an extended life.

Concrete

Until the arrival of butyl and other flexible membranes, concrete was the favoured material for the building of most garden ponds. It is rarely used today, as it is expensive and has a tendency to crack after some years and leak. When using concrete, it is important to reinforce it with a skeleton of steel and to ensure that the concrete is well prepared and vibrated to make sure that no air gaps are left in the fabric. Specialist contractors undertake this type of work. It is possible to repair concrete ponds under some circumstances, but the repairs are often unsatisfactory and difficult to make permanent.

Fibreglass

Using the same technology as that employed to make boats and certain car bodies, fibreglass can be an attractive option for small ponds where the shape and size are difficult to construct using a flexible liner. The material can also be dyed to any colour required. It is important that sufficient layers of fibreglass are laid down, and that the final gel coat is waterproof. Using fibreglass is an expensive option and is best undertaken by a specialist firm or experienced craftsman.

When fitting a premoulded liner make sure that the voids underneath are carefully filled with sand. Back-fill around the pond, checking the levels as you go.

Preformed pond liners

These come in different shapes and qualities and are best used in very small-scale ponds where the shape is ideal for your purpose – which is rarely the case. When these are used it is important that there are no voids left between the liner and the sand in which it is buried, as these voids lead to stresses which can make the liner crack and leak. Large, irregularly shaped units with different depth zones are difficult to support properly and are more likely to fracture.

Flexible liners

Butyl

Flexible liners have made a huge difference to pond construction. One of the first flexible liners and still the best is butyl rubber, which is used for a wide range of applications, from car windscreen sealant to tyres, each made to a different formulation, principally using petroleum products. Butyl for pond liners is rather like the inner tubes of bicycle tyres in appearance and characteristics, and while it is extremely flexible and stretches without breaking, it is very vulnerable to piercing with sharp objects (again like bicycle tyres). Butyl, therefore, needs to be protected from objects such as flints, sharp stones or gardener's forks. It can, however, be repaired if punctured by cleaning carefully and fitting with a butyl rubber patch. Although it has a very long life, it can be damaged if exposed to ultraviolet light and should be protected with geotextile at all times, especially during construction.

Do not walk on the liner unless you remove your shoes

Put just enough water in to hold the liner stable

Pull the liner up the sides and arrange any folds neatly

After you have positioned the butyl liner, pour some water into the bottom as this will help in neatly arranging any folds or tucks. Adjust any folds as necessary as the water level rises. The pond can be left for a day or two to allow for further settling.

PVC and other flexible liners

These liners are slightly cheaper than butyl, but they share its vulnerability and have none of the benefits of flexibility and reparability. They tend to become brittle in a very few years, and rarely give a satisfactory long-term lining.

Geotextiles

These blanket-like materials – which are not waterproof – are used to stop flexible liners being penetrated by sharp stones and the like. Old carpet or underlay, if non-organic and non-rotting, can be used for the same purpose when savings have to be made. Geotextile is available in various strengths, which are indicated by the weight of material per square metre. Generally, the greater the weight, the stronger and safer the product.

Lay the underlay smoothly. Duct tape can be used to join the underlay and hold it in position while the liner is fitted.

Pumps, pipework and lighting

Pumps are used for fountains, streams and waterfalls and may be powered by solar- or mains-generated electricity. Part of the challenge when designing and building a pond is working out how to conceal and protect the electricity supply and water delivery pipes. Remember that water and electricity are a lethal combination. If you are in any doubt about fitting a pump or light, consult a professional.

Submersible electric pumps

These are ideal for most garden pond applications. Silent and invisible when placed at the bottom of a pond or in a balancing chamber, they comprise a sealed electric motor, generally run at mains voltages, and an impeller in a single casing. There are a large number available on the market, of all sizes.

Factors to be considered in choosing submersible pumps are:

- ✔ The length of the guarantee, now often three years or more.
- ✔ The effectiveness of the anti-clogging filtration system supplied. Generally, the larger the surface from which the water for the pump is drawn, the less quickly it will become clogged up.
- ✔ The volume of water pumped and the height to which it can be supplied. Check with your dealer when you have made the calculations.
- ✔ If the flow of water from a pump is too restricted it can heat up and damage the coils. Make sure that there is a bypass system fitted which allows the pressurized water to flow back into the pond. These are supplied with most pond pumps.

Non-submersible electric pumps

These are mainly used in industrial situations where large quantities of water are to be moved long distances. Easily maintained, they have the disadvantage of being noisy and require soundproofed housings which are liable to flood if placed below ground level.

Ram pumps

Where there is a natural flow of water near your pond, you may consider the use of ram pumps, which were widely used in the 19th and early 20th centuries. Using the force of a downward running stream, they force a small quantity of water up an incline. Still occasionally used today, they have the disadvantage of making a sharp tapping noise, and are best used where electricity or solar power are not available to run a modern pump.

Pipework

Where conduits are required for filters or a balancing chamber, good quality preformed pipework should be used – the pipework used for drainage in domestic situations is inexpensive and readily available. Use the largest practical bore for the pipework, as it is less likely to block up and create problems for maintenance. Always test the joints and couplings as, when the pond is filled, the joints will be under considerable strain, (more than in a drainage situation), caused by the head of water attempting to expand and burst the joints.

For land drainage or allowing water to drain away, use flexible plastic pipes perforated with many small holes. These pipes should ideally be buried in gravel, which will allow water to percolate through and run off (see page 198).

Lighting

A large number of lights are available for both exterior and underwater use. These are generally low voltage and have a transformer. All cables should be carefully hidden and protected from damage by gardening implements such as pronged forks. Underwater lamps should be placed so that the lenses do not become covered with detritus in the water, or if that is not possible, position them so that they can easily be cleaned. Water diffuses light, so place lenses close to the surface of the water.

Controls

Lighting and pumps can be controlled remotely from the pond, ideally from a situation where you can see the pond. However it is important to protect the controls from the weather. In planning electrical controls, it is wise to consult an electrician at an early stage. Modern contact breakers and RCD units should be fitted to any external electrical units, and any power supplies should be conducted in armoured cables capable of handling the required amperage without difficulty. All external fittings should be of a waterproof or weatherproof approved standard.

Water supply

This is usually taken from the mains supply or a natural source such as a spring or stream. When an automatic topping-up system such as a ballcock is to be used, fit a non-return valve into the system in order to make it completely impossible for water to flow back from the pond into the mains supply (see page 199).

Pumps, pipes and lights

There is a large range of pumps available; generally the more you pay the better the quality. Your retailer will advise and ask two key questions: what amount of water is required and what height is it to be raised. Measure the height from the water surface to the outlet and explain the type of display you wish to achieve. Some outdoor light fittings can be used either around the edge of the pond, or as underwater lights.

Fountainhead Some are adjustable like the nozzle on a garden hosepipe
Telescopic outlet pipe Extends telescopically to suit different depths
Pipe reducer For fitting different size fountain heads
Push-fit connector Check that this is suitable for your set-up
Screw-fit connector Ensures secure joints
T-junction Facility for a tap and a second outlet pipe
Integral adjuster Rotates to restrict flow
Reinforced garden hosepipe
Flexible armoured pipe
Flexible clear plastic pipe
Domestic drainage pipe
Perforated land drainage pipe
Joint for domestic drainage pipe (various angles available)
Order a spare bulb when you buy any lamps
Take care not to damage the liner when fixing the light
Cable outlet
Underwater light
The glass features a structured surface which breaks the light
A bracket allows the light to be turned up to 180°
A garden spike can easily be attached to the bracket
Exterior light
Power selector
Pump and filter housing
Submersible pump
Fixing plate

Construction materials

In general, the fewer the number and type of materials involved in the construction of a pond and surrounding area, the more pleasing it is to the eye. If any particular type of brick or stone is used near the pond, make sure that you will be able to obtain replacements at a later date, in case any of them are damaged. Where possible use local materials. Architectural salvage yards are always worth investigating.

Concrete and mortar

Concrete

Used to form solid foundations and footings, the strength of concrete is dictated by the ratio (by volume) of sand and stones (ballast) to cement powder. For most pond construction work a ratio of 4 parts ballast to 1 part cement is ideal, but if large areas are to be concreted, it is worth considering reinforcing the concrete with steel mesh. Most cement manufacturers will be happy to advise you.

The amount of water used in a concrete mix affects its handling properties: the more water used, the sloppier the concrete. Too much water will affect the strength of the cured concrete. For most practical pond work the concrete should stand rather like stiff mashed potatoes, and it should be used quickly after it has been mixed, before it stiffens up. There is a range of proprietary additives that affect its properties, but these are expensive and can affect the strength, and I would suggest avoiding them unless unusual circumstances prevail.

Concrete should not be mixed or used when frost or below-freezing temperatures are expected, as they make concrete crumble and become useless. If there is a possibility of frost once you've laid the concrete, protect it with sacking or insulating material which stop it from freezing. Equally, if high temperatures are anticipated, protect concrete from drying out too quickly, using plastic sheeting, damp hessian cloths or sacking.

Mortar

This is the sand-and-cement mixture that is used to bond bricks and blocks together. It can be made in a variety of types and strengths: for building brick walls a mixture of 3 parts builders' sand to 1 part cement is standard. This can be coloured if required, using readily available colorants.

Caution

The cement powder used to make concrete and mortar is corrosive. Always wear a dust-mask, gloves and goggles. If you get cement on your skin wash it off immediately with plenty of water.

Other materials

Gravel

Gravel is used for under-liner drainage as it allows water to pass through, and can also be used for beaches, paths and level areas. It is available in many grades, from fine pea gravel to gravel the size of a small egg. It can be bought washed or unwashed – the latter is cheaper.

Soil

Clay loam for putting in ponds should ideally be sterilized to kill any weed seeds that may be in it. Aquatic nurseries can supply small amounts; use sterilized, screened topsoil for large amounts.

Wood

Wood can be used for bridges, decking and garden buildings – and even as a surround for a formal pond. It is generally classified as either hardwood or softwood. Hardwood is slow-grown wood from deciduous trees such as oak, elm or ash, while softwoods are usually from pine or other evergreen trees. Most softwoods should be treated in order to stop them from rotting – especially if they are to be in contact with water. Check with the manufacturer that the treatment will not affect the fish or wildlife and avoid anything that has loose knots or splits.

Each type of tree has its own characteristics for strength, ease of handling and cutting, and resistance to water. Freshly cut oak (known as green oak), for instance, is ideal for decking applications as it lasts in water for more than 25 years. It takes on a lovely silver-grey colour, and is relatively inexpensive and easy to work. Avoid beech wood and most other hardwoods unless you have checked its resistance to rotting in water. Carpenters or your wood supplier will advise you.

Use stainless steel, brass or galvanised bolts and screws as others will corrode and damage the wood.

Walling materials

Generally walling which will be seen ("facing work") is more expensive than hidden materials. Often walls have a backing of inexpensive bricks or blocks with a facing of high-quality bricks or stonework. Natural materials should be used wherever possible. Stone generally ages better than pre-moulded materials although these are often less expensive and easier to work with. If you are in doubt, a builder's merchant will advise you.

Concrete blocks are generally weatherproof; however, some bricks are not resistant to water and frost and will fail if used in pond or exterior construction.

Calculating quantities

- ✓ Allow 10% over the calculated quantities to allow for wastage.
- ✓ Talk to your merchant before quantifying: some materials are measured in face square metres, some by weight and some by number of units.
- ✓ Concrete and mortar quantities quoted in this book refer to volumes (parts) and weights, eg. 1 part cement (25 kg) and 4 parts sand (100 kg). The weights are only a rough guide to ordering; always mix by volume.

Paving materials

A vast range is available at widely differing prices, with natural stone the most expensive. If purchasing natural stone to edge a pond, remember that, unlike in most other situations, the depth of the stone is important because the edges of the pavers will be seen, so consistency in depth should be specified.

Manufactured pavers, made to look like natural stone, are also available. The better ones age well and become indistinguishable from natural stone when lichens and other materials age them. Others lose their colour quickly and can become an eyesore, so choose carefully.

Construction materials

General DIY stores, builders' merchants and architectural salvage yards will have a wide range of bricks, stone, wood and fixings. Explain the purpose and use as some may be adversely affected by water. You will find variations in price so check with different manufacturers. Sometimes you can reduce costs by changing the design.

Brick
Boulder
Natural stone paving
Gravel
Manufactured paving
Slate
Coach bolt, washer and nut
Galvanised steel nail
Cobbles
Coated screw
Softwood post, plank and other useful sections
Sleeper

Tools

Tools are one of the main keys to successful pond-building. Although the best tools are no substitute for enthusiasm and determination, carefully chosen, top-quality tools will ensure that each and every task is accomplished with minimum effort and maximum efficiency, in the shortest possible time. It is fine to begin by using your existing tools for the projects – buy new ones if and when the need arises.

Level

Because water levels are flat it is vital that the edge of a pond is also built flat. The easiest way to achieve this is to use a long spirit level (1–2 m long is suitable) which can also be used in conjunction with a straight beam of wood. For large ponds (5 m in diameter or more) a number of wooden pegs can be hit in the ground and levelled with each other. A surveyor's level will give improved accuracy.

Excavator

Depending on the scale of your project and the availability of access, you can rent a tracked excavating machine, with or without an operator. The size and type of mechanical digger required for a job is related to the amount of work to be done – generally a 360-degree tracked excavator, ranging in size from 1 to 32 tons, is suitable. Your hire shop will be able to make recommendations when you outline the size of the excavations and your needs for handling material. If you are hiring a dumper truck, make sure it is not too small for the job; again, advice from the hire company will be helpful.

Try to plan the work so that you do not disturb more ground than is necessary, starting in one area and working your way out. Precision with levels is important, as replaced subsoil is not as structurally sound as the virgin ground. Keep others well outside the danger areas where you are working.

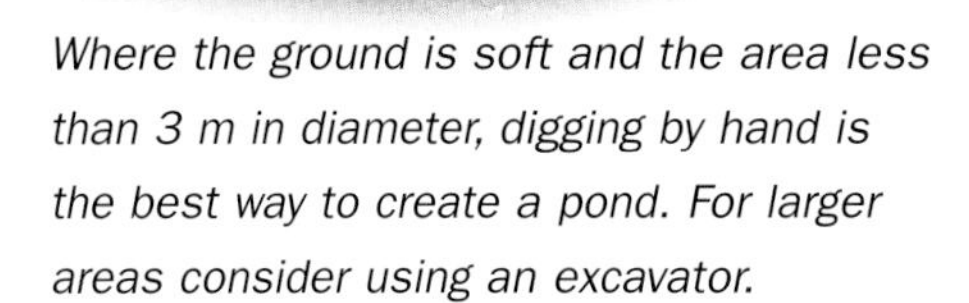

Where the ground is soft and the area less than 3 m in diameter, digging by hand is the best way to create a pond. For larger areas consider using an excavator.

Hand digging tools

Chose your tools with care – a well-chosen, quality tool is a worthwhile investment. A good spade is particularly important if you are excavating the pond manually. For very hard ground you will need a spade with a narrow cutting edge but if the soil is friable you may approach with a shovel. Most hardware stores carry a good range. Generally metal tools are less expensive and more durable than wood or plastic handled tools. Gently does it if you are not in the habit of digging. You will use muscles unused to work so half an hour is the maximum you should work on the first outing; build up carefully after that. A sturdy wheelbarrow is an essential tool that will make lifting and carrying easier. Make sure you get the right size of wheelbarrow for the job: one that can be handled easily when full but is still large enough to be useful.

Concrete mixers

Although small quantities of concrete can be mixed by hand, the work is much eased by using a powered concrete mixer. These are generally powered by electricity or a petrol engine. If electricity is available close to the workings, an electric mixer should be your preferred option as they are quieter and cheaper to run. Make sure you have a circuit breaker plugged into the power socket to protect you from electric shock if an accident occurs.

It is important to wash out the mixer thoroughly after each load is used up as otherwise the mortar or concrete will set in the drum and reduce efficiency as well as incur a cleaning cost when the machine is returned to the hirer.

Safety equipment

- ✔ Sturdy boots with steel toecaps, available at builder's merchants, are necessary for all pond construction.
- ✔ Gloves are vital during work with concrete, as your skin may react if in contact with concrete or mortar.
- ✔ Goggles are required if you are operating any grinding equipment, as is ear protection if you have to hire noisy machines.
- ✔ If you are involving an excavator, wear a hard hat.
- ✔ Make sure you have the number of the local hospital handy, and keep a first-aid kit close to hand.

A basic tool kit

A good set of tools makes pond building easy and the right tool can save you a lot of time. For the projects in this book, you will need a bucket, a wheelbarrow and some of the tools shown below. All of these can be bought from a local general DIY superstore, or hired. Some specialist tools, such as a pick or mattock for hard ground are not shown but hire shop staff can advise on what you might need. A wooden board of about 500 mm square will be helpful for placing mortar on for brick laying. Rubble bags and a broom will be necessary for tiding up.

Gloves
Large tape measure
Spirit level
Spade
Pegs and string
Scissors
Fork
Line set
Mortar trowel
Shovel
Sledgehammer
Pointing trowel
Bolster chisel
Rake
Grinder
Club hammer
Tape measure
Square
Carpenter's pencil
General saw
Drill bit
Drill
Claw hammer
Adjustable spanner
Cordless driver

Caution
Power tools

Electricity, early-morning dew, buckets of water and wet hands are a potentially dangerous combination. When you use a power tool or an electric cement mixer, make sure that you use it in conjunction with an electricity circuit breaker and switch off the power when not in use.

Basic techniques

Pond building can be good fun especially when you have a clear understanding of the basic techniques such as marking out, laying concrete and building brick walls, and when you can handle the tools and materials with confidence. If you have never made garden projects before, start with something small and simple. If you need encouragement why not plan a big pond and get some friends to help?

Getting started

Dress right for the job

Old clothes are fine, as they will get dirty, however overalls are readily available and have many useful pockets. A sound pair of boots is essential, personally I favour boots which have a steel toecap and are easy to get on and off. Gloves should be worn if your hands are soft or you are dealing with materials like concrete, which can irritate the skin.

Take plenty of breaks

Stop for at least ten minutes every hour to assess your progress, have a pause and plan the next stage. Do your calculations and order materials when you are fresh and take photographs of each stage of the progress; you will be able to show them proudly in years to come. Take your time, and bring in help if some part of the job will over stretch you. If you come across obstacles like huge rocks consider keeping them as part of your design.

Measuring and marking

Use the carpenter's maxim "measure it twice and cut it once" and always make a note of your measurements.

Keep a good-quality carpenter's pencil handy for marking out on wood.

When ordering bricks, blocks, sand and concrete allow 10% for wastage.

Road marking paints of various colours are available from builders' merchants and are ideal for marking out lines. Clear the nozzles after each use.

A taut string
line will ensure
accurate digging

Before proceeding be absolutely confident in your setting out. Do not hurry this stage as any mistake will be difficult and costly to rectify and require fruitless labour.

Foundations

The purpose of foundations is to provide a level and stable base on which to build. Foundations should generally be twice as wide as the wall that is to be built on them. The depth of the foundations varies but for most pond work 250 mm is deep enough; however if the base material is unstable, or liable to crack and heave such as clay, it is wise to err on the side of caution and dig down to 500 mm. Fill the majority of the void with hardcore and compact it by beating it down with a heavy hammer or by using a vibrating compaction machine before filling up to the required depth with concrete.

Foundations need to be
level; pegs set at the
same level can be used
as a guide to spreading
the concrete
This trench will
be filled with a
layer of hardcore
and topped off
with concrete

Most ponds require foundations and these are either "footings" (a narrow strip of concrete) or a slab. If you don't build foundations the pond may quickly disintegrate.

Laying concrete

Always wear gloves as splashes can irritate and burn the skin. If you do get concrete on your skin wash it off with plenty of water immediately.

When you are moving the concrete from the mixer to the point of laying, do not overfill the barrow, as any slops will be unsightly, kill grass and be difficult to clean up afterwards. Also a heavy wheelbarrow full of liquid can be hard to control over uneven ground.

Start in one corner and work backwards, achieving the finished level with your float or tamping bar before moving on to the next section. In the same way as you would ice a cake, put an appropriate amount of concrete in the middle and then spread and manipulate the concrete making sure that you have sufficient before pushing it down to the final level. Work only in one direction at a time and do not leave any unfinished sections before moving on. Do not be rushed by the person delivering the concrete to you (if you are so lucky) and leave it in the barrow until you are ready to receive it.

When you have finished laying a section, immediately clean all your tools and put the unused concrete to good use. Never be tempted to bury it.

Use a piece of wood to "tamp" the concrete level

Make sure that you have prepared the area before you start pouring concrete. Building a level wooden frame called "formwork" is sometimes the easiest option.

Brick work

The main thing is to build the wall upright, in the right place and with all the layers or courses of brick or block horizontal with staggered vertical joints.

The key to success is in the mixing of the mortar, which ideally should have the consistency of stiff mashed potatoes; if it is too dry the bricks will not readily bond to it. However, if it is too wet, the bricks will slide about. If possible watch a bricklayer at work and try to emulate his mortar. Be careful not to add too much water at the end of the mixing process as if the mix becomes too wet the only way to stiffen it up is to add more sand and cement, which can easily result in the over filling of the mixer.

Trial and error is the only way to learn, however once you have got it right once it is easy to do the same thing again, a bit like riding a bicycle.

Use a string line to show where the bricks should be laid by wrapping the string around a brick, pulling the line over another and pulling the ends apart until the line is straight. Do a dry run without any mortar just touching (or kissing) the line with the bricks without moving the line.

Allow for a 15 mm bed of mortar below the bottom brick and carefully reset the line so that the top edge of the brick will kiss the line.

Remove the bricks and lay down the mortar so that the entire bottom of the brick is on mortar. Place each brick frog uppermost on to the mortar and bed it down until it is in the correct position. Place some mortar on the ends of each brick before placing it so that you will have a 10 mm joint between each brick. If a brick is too low, lift it from the mortar bed, add fresh mortar and re-bed it.

Do not hurry the early process, it will rapidly become easier. Once laid a brick should not be touched again as that movement will break the seal between the brick and the mortar; if this happens the brick must be removed and the mortar and the brick replaced. So be careful not to knock any new brickwork. Do not begin laying the next brick until you are completely satisfied that the last one is correctly positioned.

When a row of bricks is complete, remove the excess mortar by slicing it off with the trowel.

The pattern of the brickwork is called the bond and it is this decorative arrangement of bricks that gives a wall its strength; it is important that the vertical joints do not occur near each other, as it weakens the wall and looks unsightly.

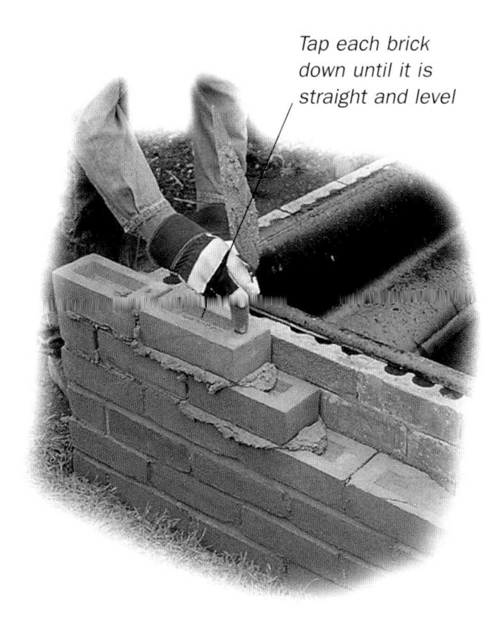
Tap each brick down until it is straight and level

Bricks and mortar are the ingredients for a classic raised pond. Position the bricks carfully, avoid smearing them with mortar, and do a nice job of finishing the joints.

Preparing the pond area for lining

Because butyl and other liners are damaged by sharp objects such as flints it is critical that during the building of a pond they are protected. Old carpet (of a synthetic, non-rotting type) can be used as an underlay, although modern geotextiles are readily available and easier to work with in a secure way (see page 189).

Consider the subsoil where the pond is to be. If it is naturally draining and is not affected by the local water table, no further action need be taken; however, if the subsoil may hold some water (such as clay or shale for example) or the natural water table may come up during the winter, you will need to create an escape for any water that might accumulate under the liner. Dig a trench 300 mm wide by 300 mm deep from the lowest point in the excavation, following the contours of the excavation towards the (downhill) lowest side of the site. End the trench 800 mm outside the excavated area. Place a 100 mm perforated land drain in the trench and fill with 10 mm gravel.

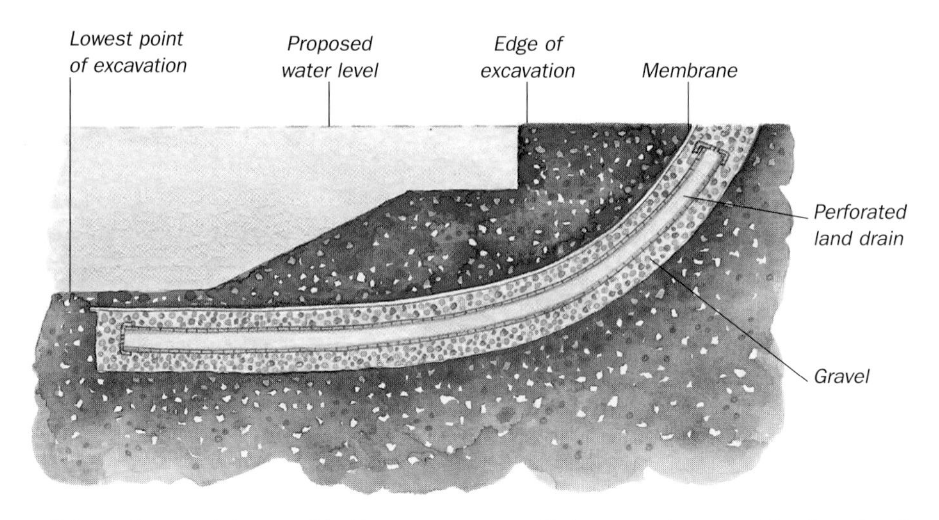
Lowest point of excavation
Proposed water level
Edge of excavation
Membrane
Perforated land drain
Gravel

If the soil around the pond holds some water or if the natural water table rises in winter, a water escape trench will help deal with the water accumulating under the liner.

Pond lining

Positioning a flexible liner

With the liner roughly in place, take an edge in both hands and raise and lower it sharply. This produces a cushion of air between the liner and the geotextile and allows the liner to be drawn towards you. Repeat until the liner is correctly positioned, checking that the geotextile has not been dislodged during the process. Stop further wind affecting the liner by weighing it down at the sides, taking care not to allow any sharp objects to come into contact with the liner. Fill the pond with enough water to hold the bottom securely, and tug at the edges to minimize any creases and folds (see page 189).

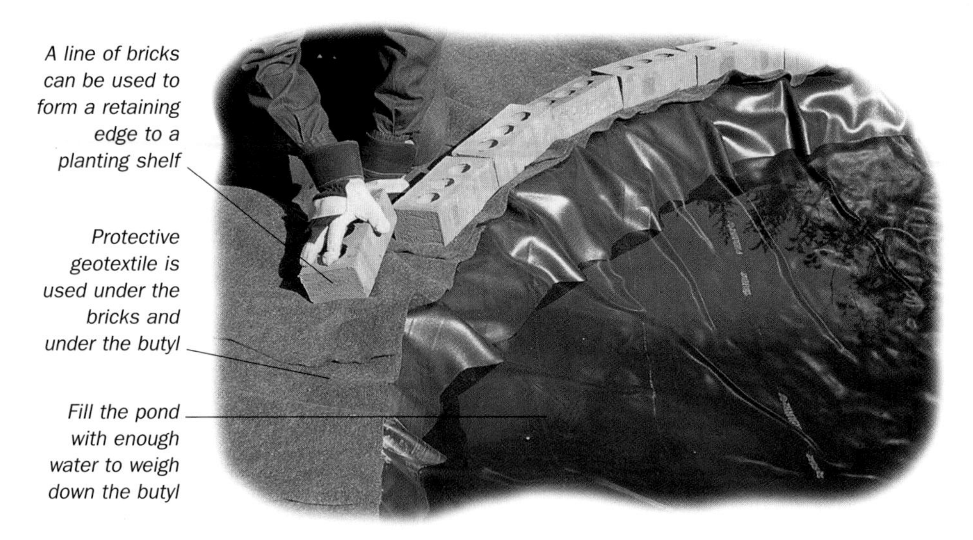
A line of bricks can be used to form a retaining edge to a planting shelf
Protective geotextile is used under the bricks and under the butyl
Fill the pond with enough water to weigh down the butyl

A flexible liner such as butyl is suitable for any pond shape and should be laid on top of soft geotextile. Additional geotextile is used wherever there is risk of damaging the butyl.

Fitting a non-flexible liner

The important thing is not to leave any voids beneath the liner, as when it is filled with water it will be strained and may crack. Try to dig the hole to match the shape of the shell, allowing for at least 25 mm of sand all round. When you have achieved this, shovel a small amount of sand all around the excavation. By placing and removing the shell you will be able to see all the places where the sand has touched the shell allowing you to build up the sand in areas where it has not touched. By repeating this procedure of adding and removing sand, the bottom section of the shell should sit evenly on a bed of sand. When you are satisfied that no more can be done by this method finally place the shell and fill up the voids at the side using a stick to push the sand and compact it. When the edges are nearly full put a hosepipe into the sand and when the area is soaking compact the sand where you can to fill any remaining voids. It is then safe to fill the pond.

Repairing leaks in a flexible liner

Butyl liners can leak either because something is penetrating the liner or because it is undergoing stress brought about by stretching. In either case ensure that the cause is dealt with before undertaking the repair. The main difficulty lies in exposing the hole and making sure the surrounding area is clean and dry before you begin repairing the hole. A patch is made by attaching joining tape to a pre-sized piece of butyl, leaving the waxed paper on the tape until the last possible moment. Although this is a fairly straightforward job it can be challenging on a muddy wet construction site, especially as cleanliness is essential to make permanent waterproof joints. Offer up the liners for joining making sure that the join will not be under strain when complete. Wash away any earth or materials that have stuck to the liner and clean an area at least 100 mm around where the join is to be made. Use petrol to further clean the surfaces to be joined. Make sure the surfaces are dry with no rucks or pleats before taping together. Place the double-sided rubber tape between the cleaned surfaces. Using a blowlamp, warm the joined area by constantly moving the heat source so as not to burn the surface. When an area of about 300 mm is warmed up turn off the blowlamp and wearing light gloves knead the join to ensure complete adhesion to both surfaces. Repeat the process on the next section of the join until the join is complete. Using scissors trim off any material left over next to the completed join. Carry out any repairs on a hot dry day.

Automatic top-up system

During dry summer months, the level of water in a pond may drop considerably. It can easily be topped up using a hose pipe, however, on butyl-lined ponds an automatic system can be built into the pond during construction. This uses the mains water supply to keep the water level in the pond continually at the optimum level. This is particularly useful when the pond has fountains, streams or waterfalls which increase water evaporation.

Once you have excavated your pond, but before it has been lined, you will need to select the position for the automatic top-up chamber. This should be on rising ground ideally not more than 2 m from the edge of the pond. Buy a multibase drains inspection unit and enough 100 mm rigid pipe to reach from the chamber into the pond. These are available from most builders' merchants.

Excavate a hole large enough to contain the chamber and set it so that the top rim is at least 100 mm above the proposed water level in the pond. Stop up any unused pipe penetrations into the chamber. I use clear silicon around the clean stopper as an additional measure.

Dig a trench which leads from the chamber to the pond and attach the rigid pipe to the chamber so that it leads into the pond. Backfill around the chamber and pipe using soft sand.

When you come to line the pond you will need to cut a hole in the liner to allow the pipe to penetrate through without allowing water out. You can do this by buying a purpose-made penetration sleeve from the supplier of the butyl. This can be attached to the liner using double-sided tape and heated to ensure a watertight joint. Bury flexible water pipe from the source of supply to the chamber. In colder climates this should be trenched in not less than 500 mm below ground to stop it from freezing during the winter. Connect the water supply to the mains. When the pond is filled the water level in the chamber will be at the same level as the pond. Affix to the side of the pond a domestic ballcock adjusted so that the supply is turned off when the pond is full but turned on when the water level falls.

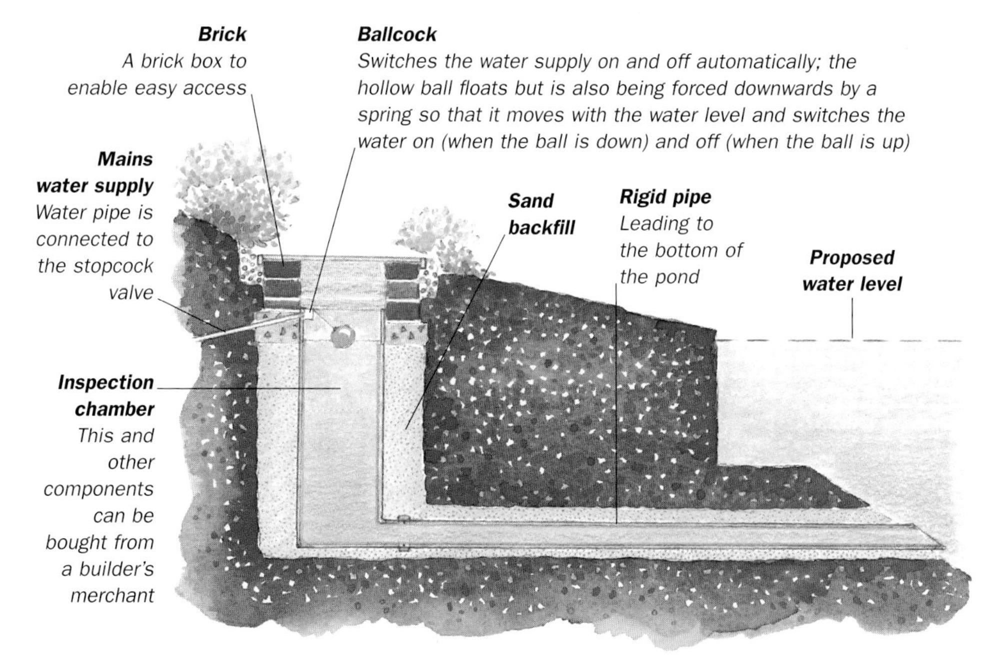
Brick
A brick box to enable easy access
Ballcock
Switches the water supply on and off automatically; the hollow ball floats but is also being forced downwards by a spring so that it moves with the water level and switches the water on (when the ball is down) and off (when the ball is up)
Mains water supply
Water pipe is connected to the stopcock valve
Sand backfill
Rigid pipe
Leading to the bottom of the pond
Proposed water level
Inspection chamber
This and other components can be bought from a builder's merchant

An automatic top-up system like this one can be used for large ponds where there is a concern that the water level may drop rapidly in periods of hot dry weather.

Planting and development

The planting of a pond is, like the furnishing and decorating of a house, entirely a matter of personal taste. You may prefer an immediate complete scheme or to plant very simply and develop the project over a number of years, with each change or addition holding some personal significance or reflecting changing personal taste. The main thing is to find a knowledgeable plant supplier with a good range of stock.

Choosing plants

A mature pond with well established plants, rather in need of some routine maintenance and thinning. The ideal is to have one third of the surface of the water covered with plants as too much shaded area lowers the oxygen levels of the pond. Overcrowded plants are more prone to pests and diseases.

Plants can be moved easily, and the scheme can be altered as the various plants develop. Bold clumps with just a few classic plants generally have a more pleasing effect than a large number of different species. Simpler is generally better although your choice of plants will depend on the style of your pond.

Many aquatic plants are available by mail order. There are five categories:

- ✔ Submerged, also known as oxygenators or pondweeds
- ✔ Floating
- ✔ Floating-leaved
- ✔ Emergent or bog
- ✔ Waterside

Submerged plants (oxygenators or pondweeds)

These are the first plants that should be put into a newly completed pond for two reasons. First, they start putting oxygen into the water and grow rapidly during the growing season; and second, they generally have secondary forms of pond life in them, such as water fleas and daphnia which, as long as there is no competition, rapidly reproduce, creating a richer environment that encourages other forms of beneficial pond life.

It is worth visiting your local pond shop to see what oxygenators they have available, but take care that they are native to your environment, as some imported plants can grow rampantly and are unable to provide food or shelter for native forms of pond life.

Weigh down oxygenators with small metal collars (which can be obtained from aquatic supply shops) so that they take root at the bottom of the pond. Excessive amounts of pondweed should be thinned out during the summer months, by hand or using a plastic rake.

Floating plants

These obtain their nutrients from fine root hairs that they suspend in the water. It is important that floating plants are not allowed to cover too much of the surface of the pond, as they can stifle the submerged plants that depend on light filtering down through the water. If they become over-vigorous, they can be raked out. Some plants are liable to frost damage and should be brought indoors during periods of extreme cold.

Floating-leaved plants

One of the most popular floating-leaved plants are water lilies with round or oval leaves, which are suitable for any depth of water up to 1.75 m deep. There is a wide range available with a variety of leaf sizes, and if you live in a tropical region, a more exotic range is available.

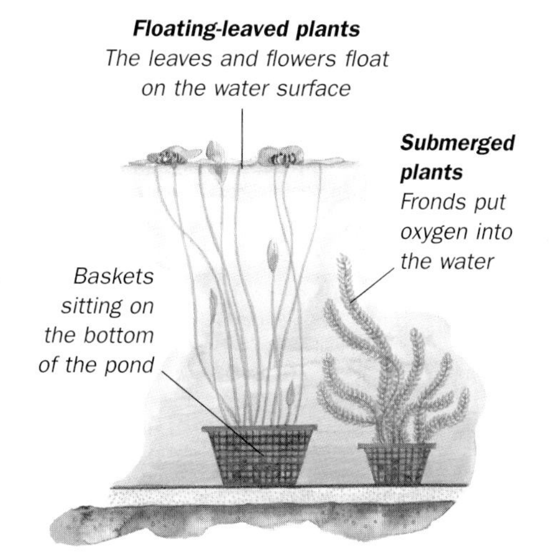
Floating-leaved plants
The leaves and flowers float on the water surface
Submerged plants
Fronds put oxygen into the water
Baskets sitting on the bottom of the pond

Submerged plants and floating-leaved plants both need to be rooted at the bottom of the pond (refer to plant labels).

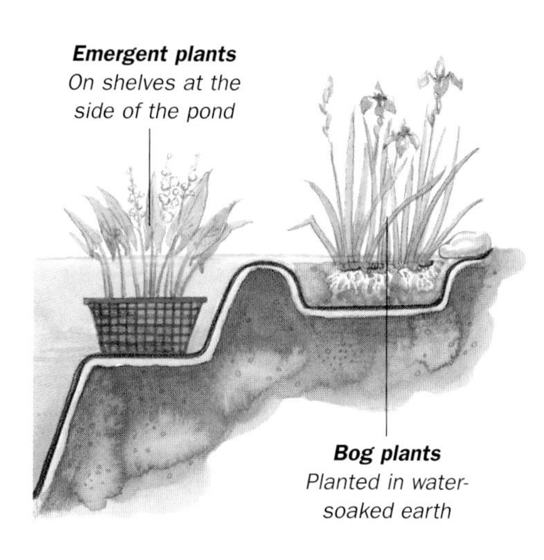
Emergent plants
On shelves at the side of the pond
Bog plants
Planted in water-soaked earth

Emergent and bog plants have very different needs – read the plant labels and ask for advice before purchasing them.

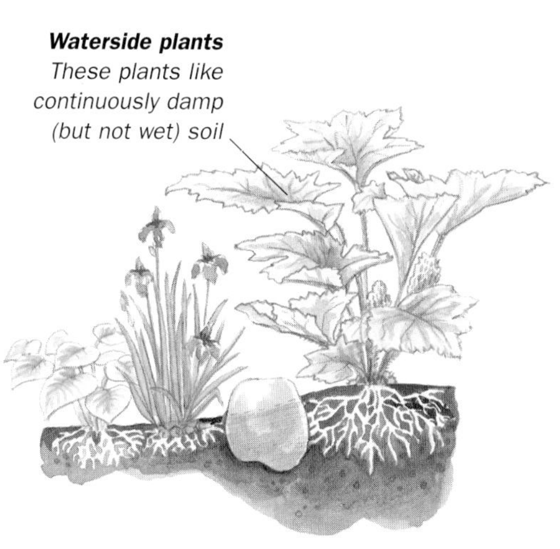
Waterside plants
These plants like continuously damp (but not wet) soil

Waterside plants require frequent watering until they are established. Choose larger species for a dramatic effect.

Floating-leaved plants should be grown in pots placed upright on the bottom of the pond at levels to suit. Remove excess and dying leaves, cutting the stems as low as practical in the water.

Lilies need to be thinned and divided after a number of years. Lift the plants in their baskets to the side of the pond and, using pruning shears, cut the corms into two sections, making sure that both halves have roots, flower heads and leaves. Cut back long or damaged roots and replant in clay or aquatic soil in perforated pots with the corm just showing above the soil, and cover with gravel to hold the earth in place.

Emergent and bog plants

Planted on planting shelves, bog areas or in containers at the edge of a pond, perennial emergent plants grow up quickly in the spring and die down in the autumn. Some forms of plants, such as rushes and grasses, which remain standing in the winter, will provide colour and form during the winter months. They should be divided in the autumn after two or three years. Some plants require different care and conditions so read the labels carefully and plant accordingly.

Waterside plants

These may be much larger than the emergent and bog plants that grow at the water's edge. During the winter months they offer contrasting scale, colour and form, and may produce reflections off the water. It must be remembered that, although they are next to the pond, they are outside the wet area and are unable to take water from the pond so that they may require additional watering during the early years while they establish themselves and develop. Be aware that while some plants might be described as waterside plants – like some species of bamboo – they are so fast growing that the sharp roots can damage a flexible pond lining. You should build a barrier or avoid them.

Maintenance

The hard slog of building the pond may be over, but regular, simple maintenance is vital if it is both to look its best and attract the wildlife that develop a working ecosystem (see page 204). But what could be better on a bright spring day than to put on rubber boots and splodge around in water and mud? Take this opportunity to inspect pumps and pipework, clean out clogged filters and make necessary repairs.

Pond maintenance

Every pond will need some kind of maintenance, although deep ponds tend to remain cleaner than shallow ones. Most of the jobs are quick and easy to do and are aimed at removing obvious debris like leaves and twigs, checking the balance of plant life which may entail raking away algae, weeding out over-dominant plants and reducing the number of fish. Occasionally you will need to change the water and repair any damaged liner (see page 199).

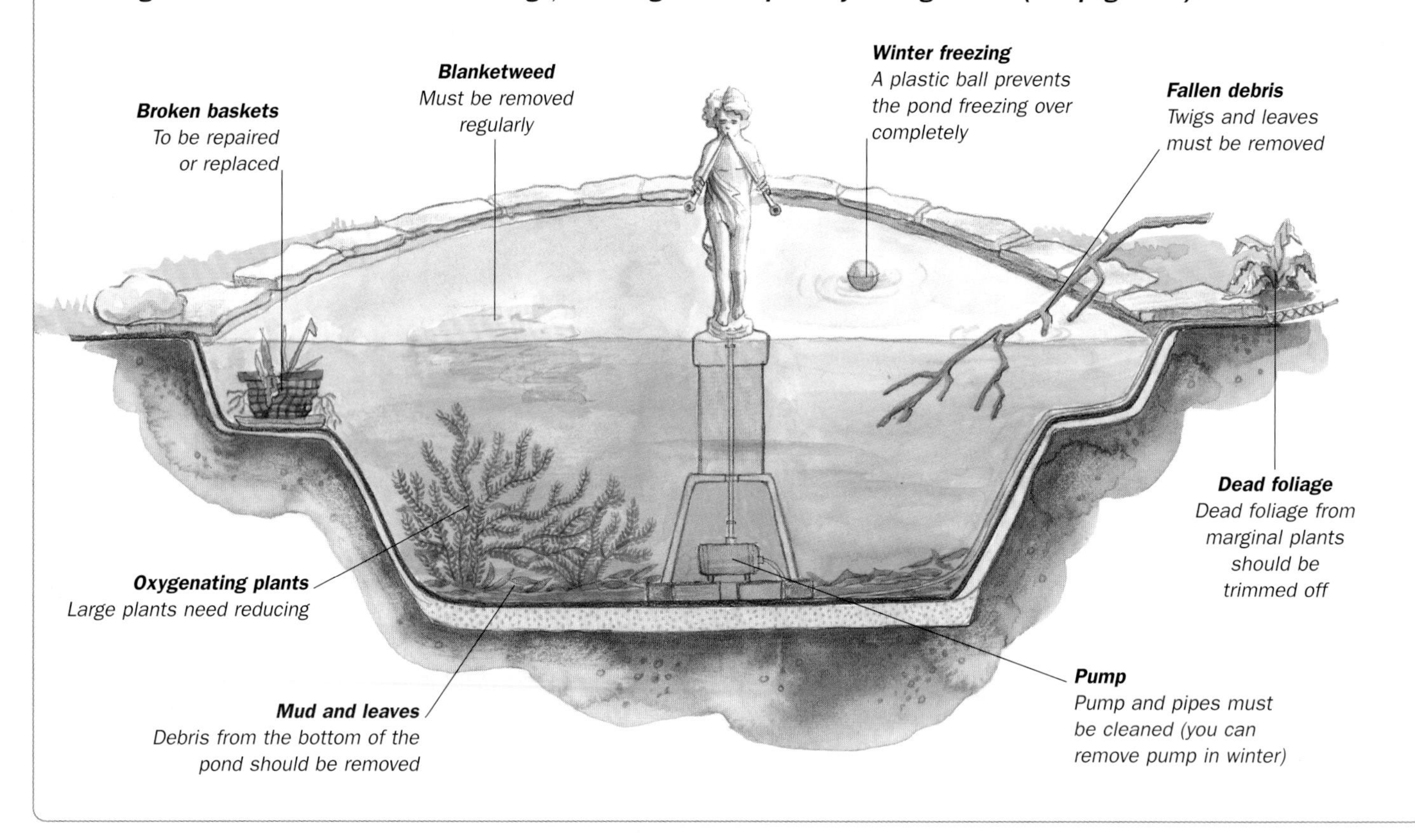
Broken baskets
To be repaired or replaced
Blanketweed
Must be removed regularly
Winter freezing
A plastic ball prevents the pond freezing over completely
Fallen debris
Twigs and leaves must be removed
Dead foliage
Dead foliage from marginal plants should be trimmed off
Oxygenating plants
Large plants need reducing
Mud and leaves
Debris from the bottom of the pond should be removed
Pump
Pump and pipes must be cleaned (you can remove pump in winter)

Routine maintenance

Controlling algae

Algae, particularly blanketweed, often proliferates on a garden pond, particularly when it is new and has not achieved a balanced ecosystem or is overstocked with fish. While there are a large number of preparations and suggestions for controlling algae, many of these have detrimental long-term effects. During the spring and early summer, remove algae on a frequent basis, using a plastic garden rake. As the growing season progresses and the pond's ecosystem develops, algae will grow with less vigour.

Plant maintenance

Controlling plants, so that one species does not dominate and inhibit other plants, can be done throughout the growing season as need dictates. In particular, floating-leaved plants should be watched carefully. Weeding unwanted species should be done little and often on a weekly basis, especially during the spring.

Fallen leaves floating on the pond surface sink in time and add to the detritus that accumulates at the bottom of a pond. In order to delay the time when a pond needs clearing out, these should be raked off and removed. For a small pond a net, spread over the pond's surface during the autumn, will facilitate this task.

Cut back and remove dead plant life during the autumn or, if you prefer, late in winter, just before the spring growing season. If the pond has a liner avoid using sharp-pronged metal tools and generally take care not to cause damage.

Care of fish

Remove and re-site fish if they have bred and their numbers and size are greater than originally planned. They are easiest to catch in the autumn, as the water temperature lowers and they become sluggish. If a pond is overstocked, fish become prey to disease and stresses. It is no kindness to the fish to allow them to breed and grow without control.

Occasional maintenance

When to clean out

Because of the constant input of detritus into ponds, all need cleaning out from time to time, otherwise you will notice after some years that the characteristics of the pond become altered – the water becomes dark and cloudy, and the plants and wildlife that used to thrive start to die out. Cleaning work is generally best done in the spring or early summer, not least because the water is warmer and more pleasant to deal with.

Clearing and cleaning the pond

Start by pumping out the pond, using a submersible pump with a flexible hose, taking care to run the water into a drain or somewhere it can percolate away slowly without doing damage. Take care to preserve the fish or wildlife that you find as the water level drops, transferring the fish to a temporary container (a clean plastic dustbin is suitable), making sure that the water in it is well provided with oxygen, or the fish may suffocate. Putting an air pump into the holding container generally takes care of this problem.

Once the pump has taken out all the water that it can without becoming blocked, remove the rest of the detritus using a bucket and soft scoop. There is a real danger of damaging pond liners whilst they are unprotected by water, so make sure that no metal or sharp objects are used in this operation; also make sure that no sharp stones are trapped in the soles of boots. Do not be tempted to use any detergents or cleansing agents.

Remove the majority of the detritus – but not all. It is important to allow a certain amount to remain, as it contains enough of the microscopic pond life to recolonize the pond. Cleared detritus should be allowed to dry beside the pond and then be removed in sacks or placed on a compost heap, where it will rot down to provide an excellent compost.

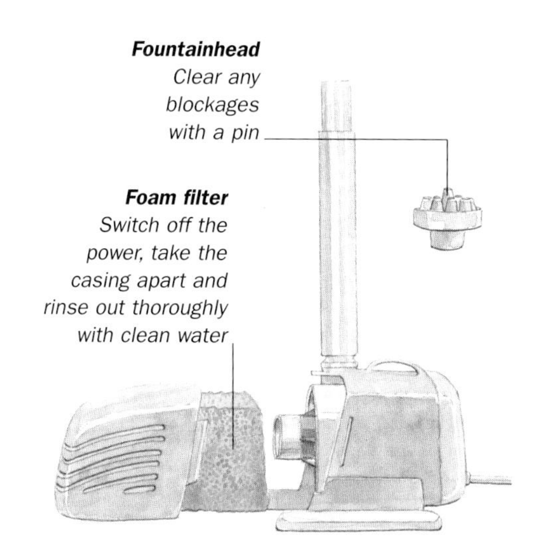
Fountainhead
Clear any blockages with a pin
Foam filter
Switch off the power, take the casing apart and rinse out thoroughly with clean water

Clean your pump regularly. If dirt and weed build up in the filter, the pump will fail.

Now is an excellent time to carefully assess the plants and divide any whose root systems are now accessible.

Any pumps and pipes should be carefully inspected and cleaned or replaced.

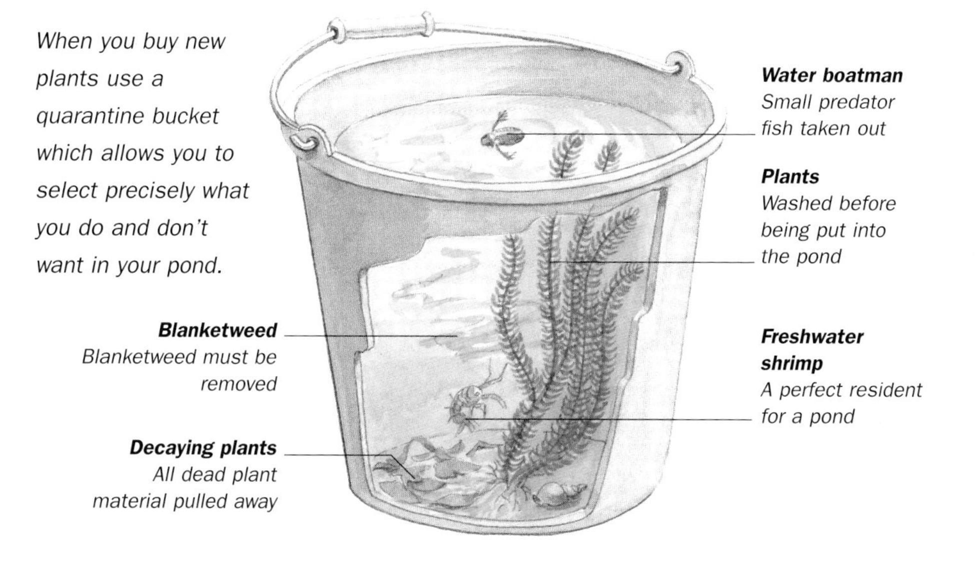
Water boatman
Small predator fish taken out
Plants
Washed before being put into the pond
Freshwater shrimp
A perfect resident for a pond
Blanketweed
Blanketweed must be removed
Decaying plants
All dead plant material pulled away

When you buy new plants use a quarantine bucket which allows you to select precisely what you do and don't want in your pond.

Restocking the pond

The pond can be refilled with water from a hosepipe or, in ideal circumstances, with stored rainwater. Consider the number of fish that you have taken out of the pond and re-site some if necessary. Allow as long as possible before reintroducing fish into the pond to allow the water temperature to stabilize and give the ecosystem a chance to re-establish.

Balancing the ecosystem

Natural life will come quickly to your pond, and the ecosystem within it will start to develop as soon as it is filled. It is important not to disrupt this development by prematurely introducing fish or birds that short-circuit the ongoing development of the life of the pond. For a natural-looking pond you should choose plants and fish that are native to your area and avoid adding too many plants in the first instance.

Developing an ecosystem

The speed and development of the pond life are affected by three major factors relating to the water: nutrients, temperature and oxygen. These can be gradually manipulated through design, planting, stocking and maintenance to achieve the desired effect.

Nutrients in the water

These arrive in water, from the air, from rotting and dying plant material and from the excretions of fish and birds. If there are too many nutrients, the natural cycles which cope with the detritus break down, the water becomes entirely opaque and the system starts to smell unpleasant. In addition, nutrients in the water and high water temperature encourage the growth of algae, especially in the spring before pond plants have developed to absorb the excess nutrients.

This pond requires some basic maintenance (see page 202). The plants could be reduced, there is a lot of detritus that needs removing and surface weed that can be removed.

Problems with algae are best avoided rather than cured. This can be done in a number of ways:

- ✔ Design the pond so that water that may have fertiliser dissolved in it does not run into it.
- ✔ Make the pond deep and large enough so that the water temperature does not rise too high.
- ✔ Plant shade-providing and nutrient-absorbing plants in and around the pond.
- ✔ Do not overstock with fish or birds.
- ✔ Provide consistent maintenance (see page 202).
- ✔ Inject oxygen into the water to aid the breaking down of nutrients.

Water temperature

This is to a great extent dictated by the weather and ambient temperature; however, the deeper the pond, the less immediately responsive it will be to day-to-day changes in the weather, and the more stable it will become. There is a natural cycle, rather like the weather, in which water circulates, bringing oxygen in the water to all parts, encouraging plants and wildlife, and helping with the breaking

down of nutrients. It is principally for this reason that it is worth digging a pond as deep as is practical. Although you may be tempted to reduce costs by saving in depth, in the long term this always leads to a reduction in stability and to increased maintenance costs. Something of the same effect of depth of water can be achieved by pumping oxygen into the water; however, as with all artificial environments, it can never be as desirable or stable as an environment that works simply with nature.

Oxygen in the water

As for us, oxygen provides life in a pond: it is absorbed by the water from air passing over it, water spilling through air, and by the photosynthesis of plants in the water. The more oxygen there is in pond water, the healthier it will be and the more life it will sustain. It also aids the decomposition of detritus in the pond, helping to keep the environment healthy and dynamic.

Oxygen can be injected into water to aid the breaking down of nutrients. This can be done either by using an air pump to pump air to the bottom of the pond, as we see with domestic fish tanks, or by throwing the water into the air, as with fountains and waterfalls.

Water filtration for fish

If a pond is designed for wildlife it will be able to sustain a small number of ornamental fish without upsetting the ecology and appearance of the pond. If however, fish are to be the predominant life in the pond, and there is no freshwater supply, you will need to install a filtration system. Filtration systems, often housed in a specially constructed unit adjacent to the pond – remove nutrients in suspension or solution in the water by passing the water over a series of filters before being returned to the pond. They are usually made up from a sponge or filter to remove sizeable solids from the water and a biological filter which works in the same way as a sewage plant by passing the water over a large surface area containing bacteria which absorb and convert nutrients into a non toxic form. In addition, an ultraviolet light kills bacteria growing in the water.

In addition to filtration, air may be pumped into the water to add to its oxygen content. If you fancy adding a dramatic feature to the pond then a waterfall, cascade or fountain also keeps the water oxygenated and fresh.

A beautiful example of a natural-looking pond. Clear water, thriving plants (maybe some of the plants could be reduced), the presence of fish, frogs, gnats, water snails and dragonflies, all suggest that the ecosystem of the pond is well balanced.

Part 2

Projects

Natural Pond

★
Easy

Making time
3 weekends
Three days for digging the hole and three days for lining and building the edges

Perhaps the simplest and least expensive type of pond to create, a natural pond will fit in almost anywhere where there is a lawn or flat area in the garden. Carefully sited, it can offer stunning reflections, bringing the sky down to the earth as well as the delights of plant life both on and below the surface of the water. Once planted, wildlife will quickly come, be it frogs, newts, dragonflies or water beetles.

Considering the design

If you have decided that this is the pond for you, consider the impact it will have on your garden. Ideally you need a completely flat, level surface but it can be positioned where there is a slight slope, as we did. As long as your foundation trench is level, it doesn't matter if part of your pond edge wall is above ground level; simply fill the area behind the wall. A good idea is to mark out the area of pond (as large as possible) and imagine what you would do in your garden with the pond in place. Only once you are convinced of the practicality and correct siting of the pond should you proceed. Consider what you are going to do with the spoil, how you are going to move it and by what route and tell the neighbours of your plans.

Getting started

Assemble your materials and equipment. Choose a dry day but make sure that you have somewhere to store your cement (off the ground and covered with waterproof material) should it suddenly rain while the work is in progress. Remember the final shape and depth of your pond will alter any quantities given.

You will need

Materials

- Concrete: 1 part cement (150 kg) and 4 parts ballast (600 kg)
- Sand: 1000 kg
- Geotextile: 46 sq metres
- Butyl: 1 piece 6 m x 6 m
- Bricks: 200
- Mortar: 1 part cement (25 kg) and 3 parts sand (75 kg)

Tools

- Tape measure, spray marker and pegs
- Wheelbarrow and bucket
- Spade, fork and shovel
- Club hammer
- Spirit level
- Pickaxe or mattock
- Rake
- Scissors
- Bricklayer's trowel

Overall dimensions and general notes

The design results in a completely natural-looking pond with no lining visible at the sides
The pond is approximately 4 m long and 3.3 m wide

Up to a third of the water's surface may be covered with plants once the pond has matured. Keep at least one aspect of the pond free for marginal planting.

Cross-section detail of the natural pond

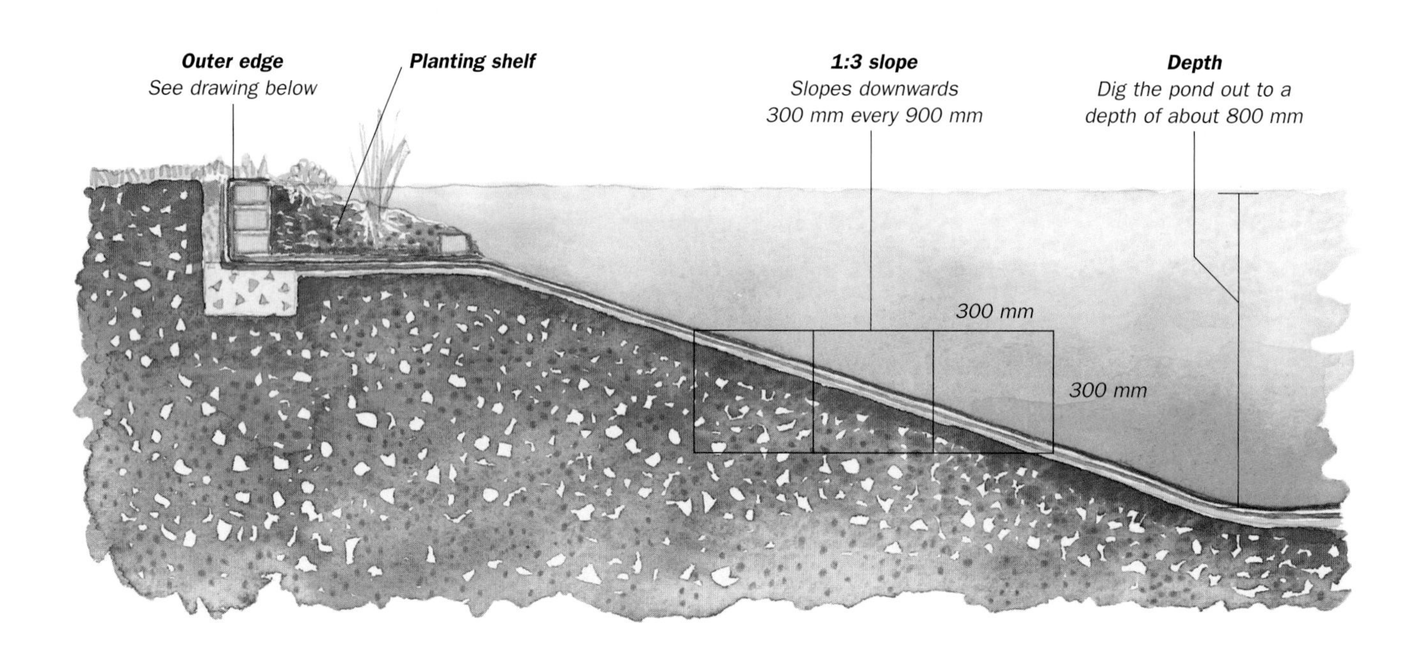
Outer edge
See drawing below
Planting shelf
1:3 slope
Slopes downwards
300 mm every 900 mm
Depth
Dig the pond out to a
depth of about 800 mm
300 mm
300 mm

Cut-away detail of the natural pond

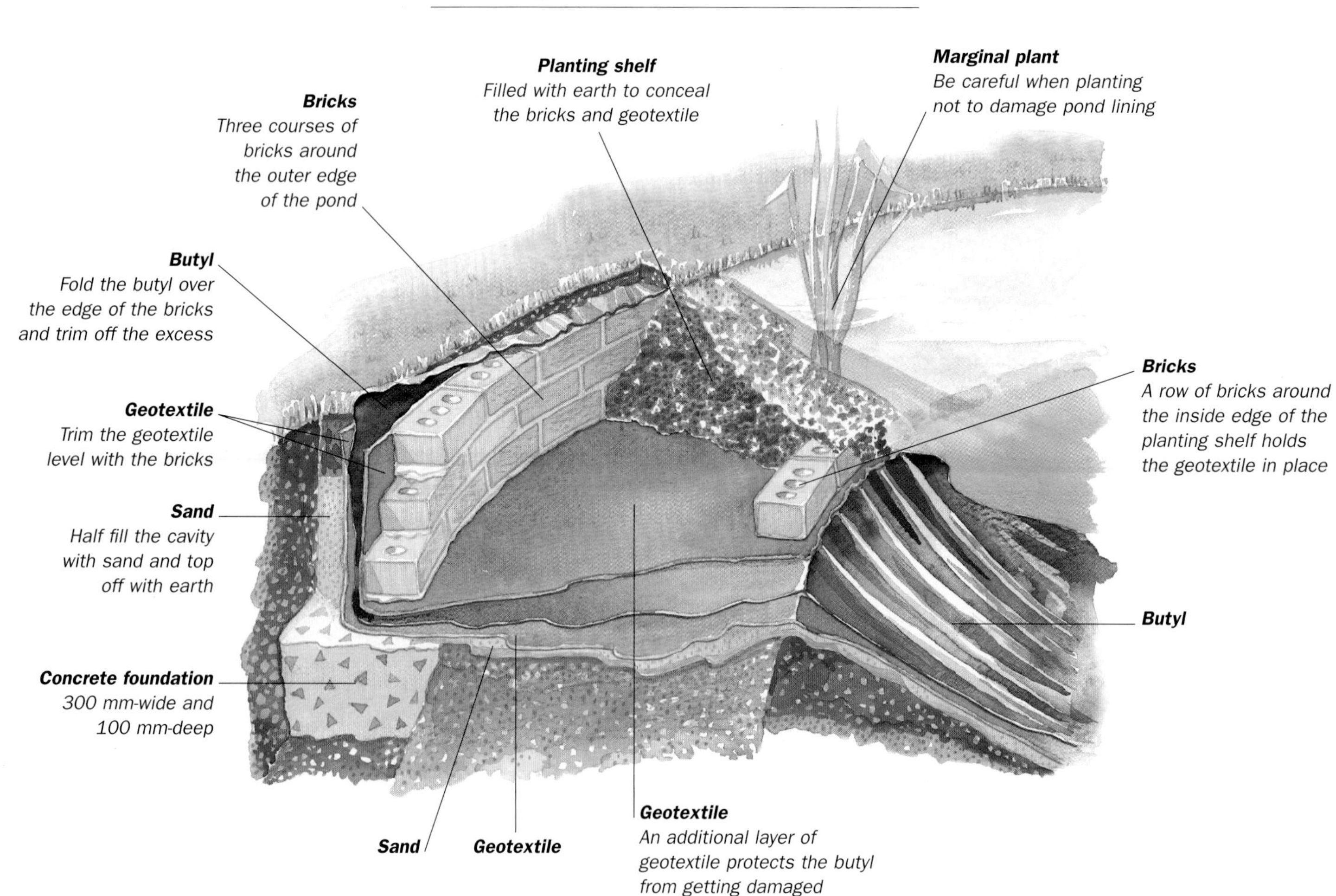
Planting shelf
Filled with earth to conceal
the bricks and geotextile
Marginal plant
Be careful when planting
not to damage pond lining
Bricks
Three courses of
bricks around
the outer edge
of the pond
Butyl
Fold the butyl over
the edge of the bricks
and trim off the excess
Geotextile
Trim the geotextile
level with the bricks
Sand
Half fill the cavity
with sand and top
off with earth
Concrete foundation
300 mm-wide and
100 mm-deep
Bricks
A row of bricks around
the inside edge of the
planting shelf holds
the geotextile in place
Butyl
Sand
Geotextile
Geotextile
An additional layer of
geotextile protects the butyl
from getting damaged

Cut-away plan view of the natural pond

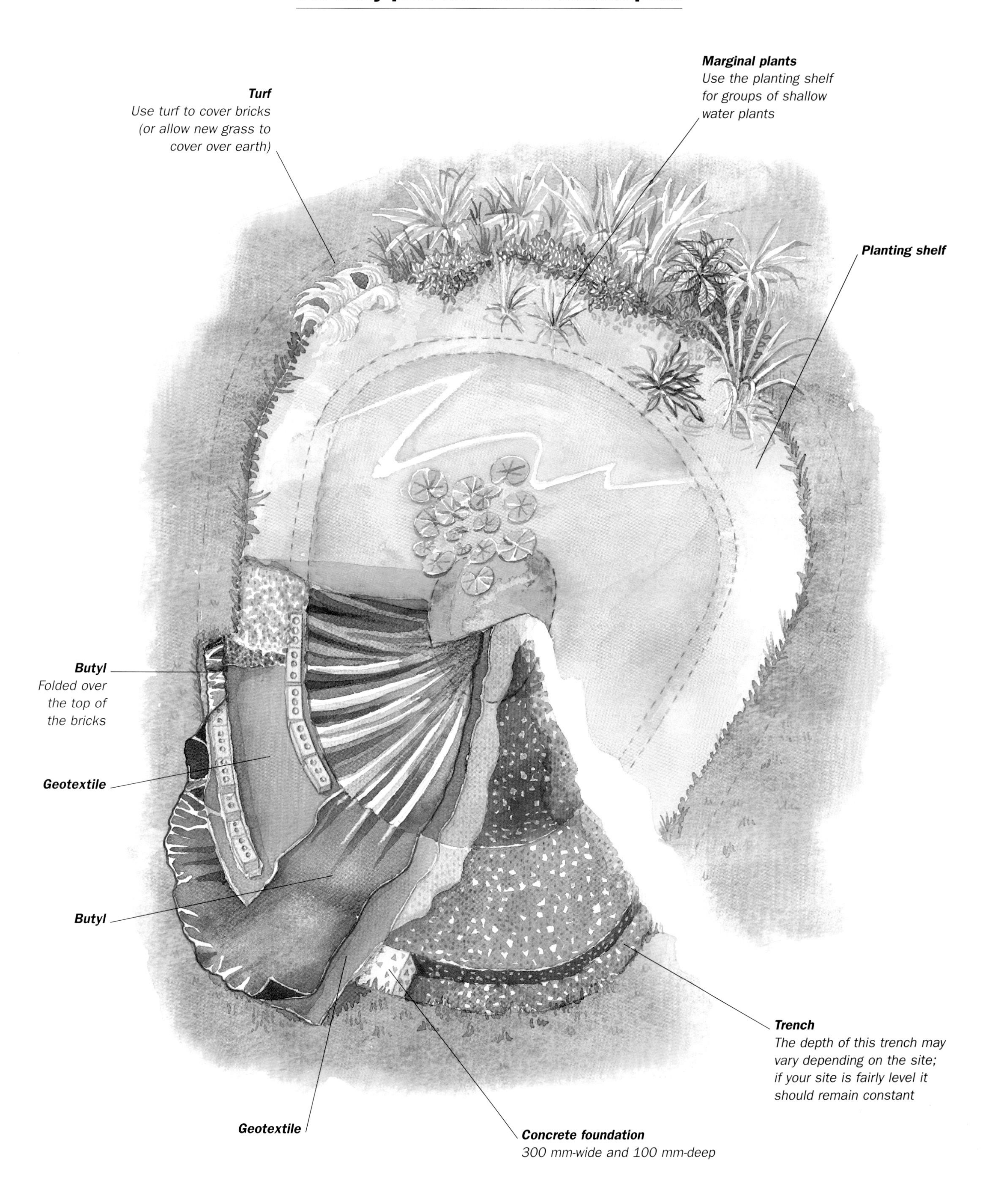
Turf
Use turf to cover bricks (or allow new grass to cover over earth)
Marginal plants
Use the planting shelf for groups of shallow water plants
Planting shelf
Butyl
Folded over the top of the bricks
Geotextile
Butyl
Trench
The depth of this trench may vary depending on the site; if your site is fairly level it should remain constant
Geotextile
Concrete foundation
300 mm-wide and 100 mm-deep

Making the natural pond

1 Digging the foundation trench
Use the tape measure and spray marker to set the shape of the pond out on a level area of ground. Use the spade to dig a narrow trench to a level depth of about 300 mm all around the pond. If your site does slope ensure the trench is a minimum of 300 mm deep.

2 Setting out a level footing
Check that the bottom of your trench is roughly level all around. Hammer in a series of wooden pegs approximately 800 mm apart so that they poke above the ground by 100 mm and the tops of the pegs are all exactly level with each other.

3 Filling the trench
Fill the trench with concrete up as far as the level of the top of the wooden pegs. The level brick wall will go on top of this concrete so make sure that you have spread the concrete evenly. A slightly sloping site may require building up with earth after the wall is built.

4 Excavating the pond
Using the pickaxe or mattock, spade and shovel, dig the pond out to a maximum depth of about 800 mm – complete with a planting shelf and a 1:3 slope (refer to the drawings on page 210).

5 Laying the geotextile
Remove all loose earth and sharp stones and cover the entire surface with a bed of raked sand. Cover the sand and the foundation with geotextile.

6 Laying the butyl
Carefully spread the butyl liner over the whole pond (see page 198 for useful tips), ensuring you have at least 300 mm of liner overlapping the edge of the pond all around. Pour a small quantity of water into the pond to hold the liner in place.

7 Edging the planting shelf
Cover the planting shelf with scraps of geotextile. Lay a row of bricks (without mortar) around the inner edge of the planting shelf to hold the geotextile in place. Do not worry about these bricks being visible – they will soon get covered in mud.

8 Building the pond edge wall
Lay three courses of mortared bricks around the outer edge of the pond, checking the level with each course. Add a mixture of mud and waste mortar in blobs around the inner edge of the dry bricks.

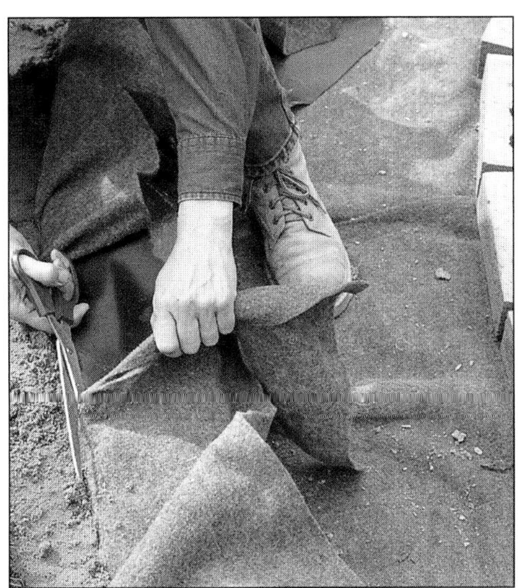

9 Trimming the lining
Fold the geotextile and butyl sandwich up and over the outer wall towards the middle of the pond. Fill the cavity between the wall and the surrounding earth with sand (do not use sharp tools). Trim the geotextile layers level with the top of the wall.

10 Finishing
Fill the planting shelf with earth, dig in your plants and top up with water. If the wall stands above the level of the ground, build up the area behind it with soil. Leave the butyl overlapping the wall and cover the exposed edge of the pond with spare topsoil or new turf.

Planted stream

Easy

Making time
3 weekends
4 days for digging and lining and a weekend to complete

Where there is sloping ground, a natural-looking planted stream is an option. This can lead down to a pond (one like the natural pond on page 208 is suitable) from which water can be pumped. It can meander with pools and eddies if the slope is a gentle one, or have waterfalls if the ground is steeper. The sound of the water can add to the delight of an environment that a wide range of interesting plants will thrive in.

Considering the design

The slope will affect the nature of your stream and the lie of the land; remember that water cannot run uphill! Study natural streams to see how a stream runs between obstacles and runs faster where the ground is steeper. If there are any natural clefts or gullies in your garden make use of them or move them to where you want your stream to be. Make sure the stream sits in, rather than on the surrounding landscape. Most problems arise when the stream is running and the water rises above the butyl at the edges! You will need constant power and water supplies for this project. Remember that a toddler can drown in as little as 10 mm of water so even a shallow stream like this one can pose a potential danger. Never leave children unsupervised.

Getting started

Plan the route of your stream and establish that the starting point is higher than the finishing point, that the sides of the liner will be at least 100 mm higher than the finished water level (even when the stream is running) and that this is below the ground level around the stream. Where rocks are to be placed to form a pool and waterfall the water will rise up to 50 mm above the obstruction.

Overall dimensions and general notes

Stones constrict the flow of the water and make more splash
Fish are drawn towards the bubbling oxygen-rich water as it enters the pond

Run the stream into an existing pond or build a new one (see the natural pond on page 208) about 2 m in diameter or larger. The materials listed will make a stream about 10 m long and 600 mm wide.

You will need

Materials

- Flexible armoured pipe: 50 mm x 12 m long
- Geotextile liner: 36 sq metres
- Duct tape
- Butyl: 1 piece 10 m x 1.8 m
- Concrete: 1 part cement (120 kg) and 4 parts ballast (480 kg)
- Mortar: 1 part cement (40 kg) and 3 parts sand (120 kg)
- Stones: 1 cu metre
- Land drainage pipe: 2 m long
- Submersible pump
- Mastic

Tools

- Tape measure and spray marker
- Spade, fork and shovel
- Hacksaw
- Scissors
- Bricklayer's trowel

Cut-away view of the planted stream

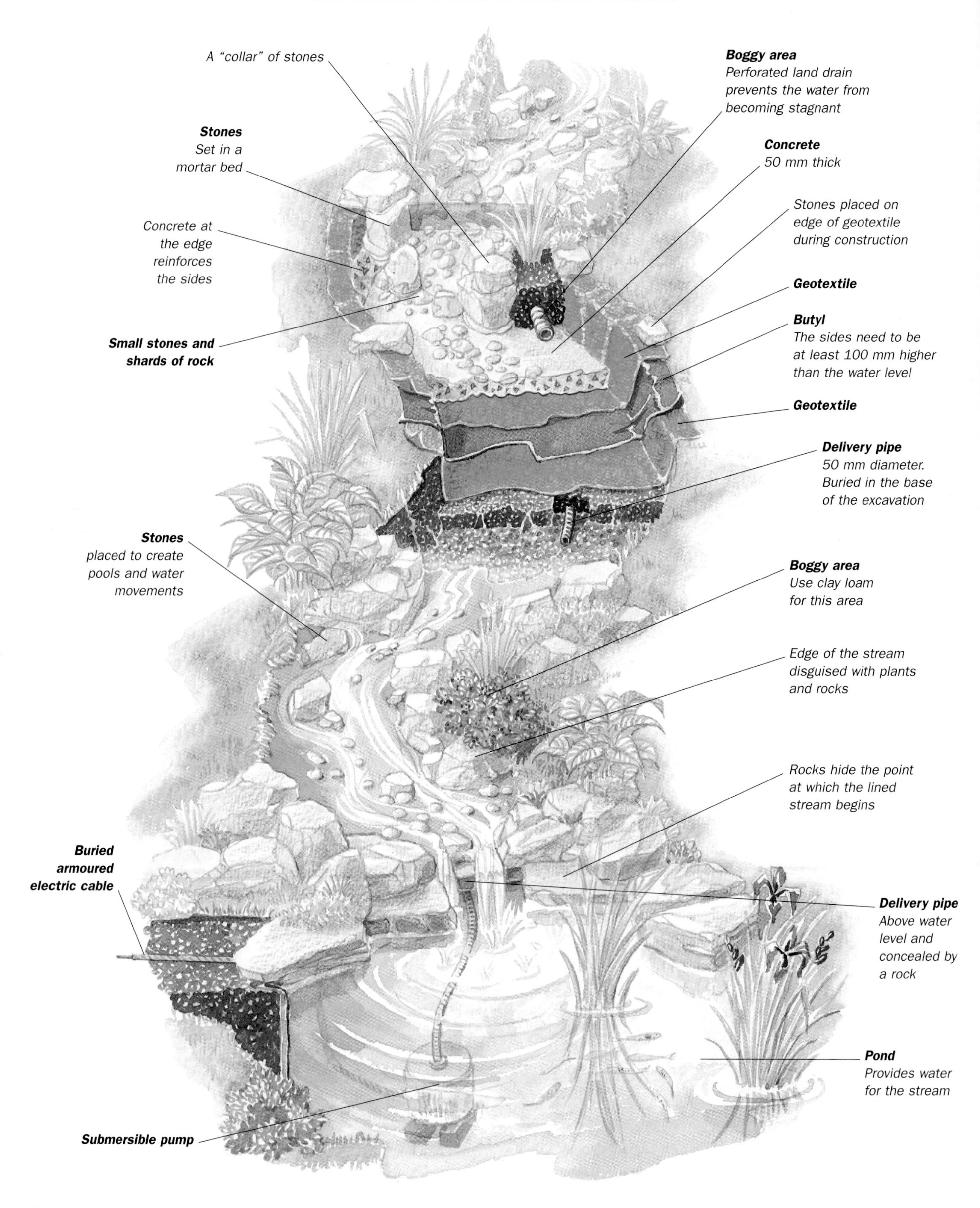
A "collar" of stones
Stones Set in a mortar bed
Concrete at the edge reinforces the sides
Small stones and shards of rock
Boggy area Perforated land drain prevents the water from becoming stagnant
Concrete 50 mm thick
Stones placed on edge of geotextile during construction
Geotextile
Butyl The sides need to be at least 100 mm higher than the water level
Geotextile
Delivery pipe 50 mm diameter. Buried in the base of the excavation
Stones placed to create pools and water movements
Boggy area Use clay loam for this area
Edge of the stream disguised with plants and rocks
Rocks hide the point at which the lined stream begins
Buried armoured electric cable
Delivery pipe Above water level and concealed by a rock
Pond Provides water for the stream
Submersible pump

Making the planted stream

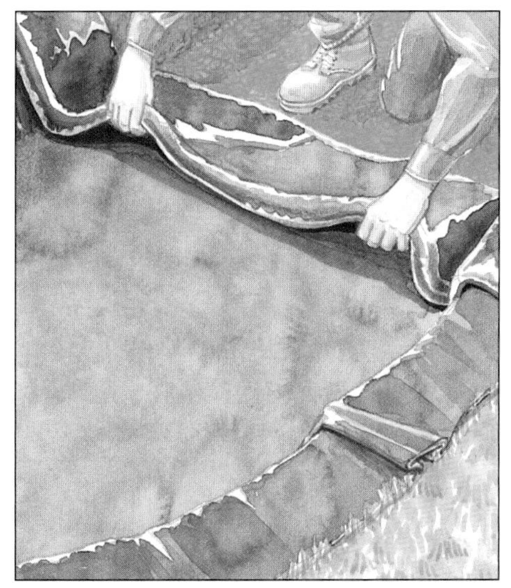

1 Excavating

Dig out the entire area to a depth 100 mm below the projected stream bed. Put in the 50 mm flexible pipe which will deliver the water from the pump to the source, and bury it in the base of the excavation.

2 Laying the liner

Remove any sharp objects from the bed of the excavation, then cover with a layer of geotextile, securing any joins with duct tape. Line the stream area with butyl, ensuring that at least 100 mm remains above the predicted water level where the stream will run.

3 Spreading the concrete base

Cover the lined area with another layer of geotextile followed by a 50 mm thick layer of concrete. Do not worry too much about creating a perfectly smooth finish as stones will cover most of the area. Leave to cure overnight.

4 Sculpting the watercourse

Lay down a mortar bed, shaping the watercourse as required and covering the stream bed with stones before the mortar has cured. A clay loam is ideal for the bog garden area. For a natural look, use one type of rock. In the boggy areas, perforated land drain should be placed in the deepest part to stop the water from becoming stagnant.

5 Installing the pump

Make sure the delivery pipe is above water level and disguise it with a one or more rocks. Attach a submersible pump and an adjustable valve to the lower end of the pipe and immerse it in the pond. Run the stream at the maximum possible ensuring there is no spillage over the sides of the butyl.

6 Trimming and finishing

Cut away any excess geotextile and butyl, covering the edge with earth or stones and hiding the point where the lined stream begins. Reduce the water flow to the desired pace and plant the bog areas. If you modify the stream at a later date check the liner sides again!

Kidney-shaped pond

Because the size and shape of this project are easily adjustable this pond can fit most gardens. The smart brick edging allows you to walk around the pond throughout the year without getting muddy or wet shoes and it could easily fit into a patio scheme or be surrounded by grass, gravel or a sweeping brick path. When you mark out the organic kidney shape try to avoid it getting too narrow at any point.

★
Easy

Making time
6 weekends
Three days for excavating the hole and the remaining time to complete

Overall dimensions and general notes

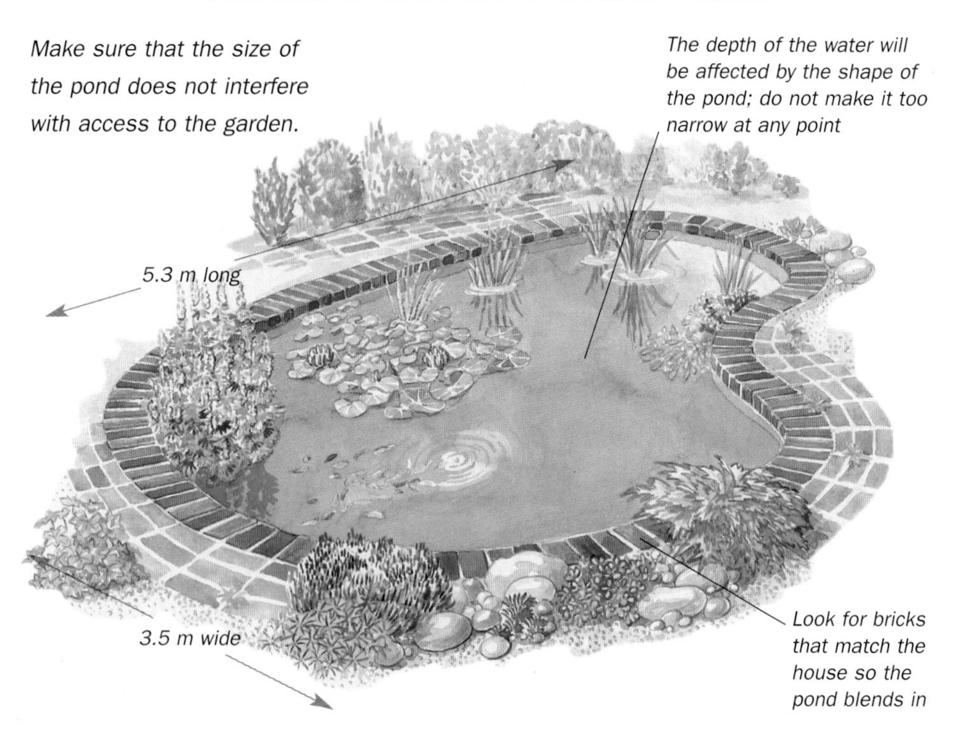
Make sure that the size of the pond does not interfere with access to the garden.
The depth of the water will be affected by the shape of the pond; do not make it too narrow at any point
5.3 m long
3.5 m wide
Look for bricks that match the house so the pond blends in

Considering the design

This pond can be shaped to suit the garden where a formal or geometric shaped pond is not required. The edges can be marked out with a garden hose, and viewed from all sides before the final shape is chosen. Remember that the further away from a round shape that the pond finally forms, the more difficult it will be to get an adequate depth of water. Deep water will, in the long term, reduce maintenance requirements and aid the pond's ecology, reducing blanketweed, for example. Never leave children unsupervised near a pond.

Getting started

Trim back or remove any existing plants that may be affected by the works. Consider what you are going to do with the spoil, how you are going to move it and by what route and tell your neighbours about your plans. Assemble your materials and equipment. Choose a dry day but make sure that you have somewhere to store your cement (off the ground and covered with waterproof material) should it suddenly rain while the work is in progress. Remember the final shape and depth of your pond will alter the quantities given above.

You will need

Materials

- ✔ Geotextile: 54 sq metre
- ✔ Duct tape
- ✔ Butyl sheet: 1 piece 7.8 m x 6 m
- ✔ Concrete: 1 part cement (180 kg) and 4 parts ballast (720 kg)
- ✔ Mortar: 1 part cement (40 kg) and 3 parts sand (120 kg)
- ✔ Bricks: 210 for the retaining walls and 120 for the coping
- ✔ Sand: 350 kg

Tools

- ✔ Tape measure, 15 m long hosepipe (for marking shape), spray marker and peg
- ✔ Spirit level
- ✔ Club hammer
- ✔ Spade, fork and shovel
- ✔ Scissors
- ✔ Bricklayer's trowel
- ✔ Pointing trowel

Cut-away detail of the kidney-shaped pond

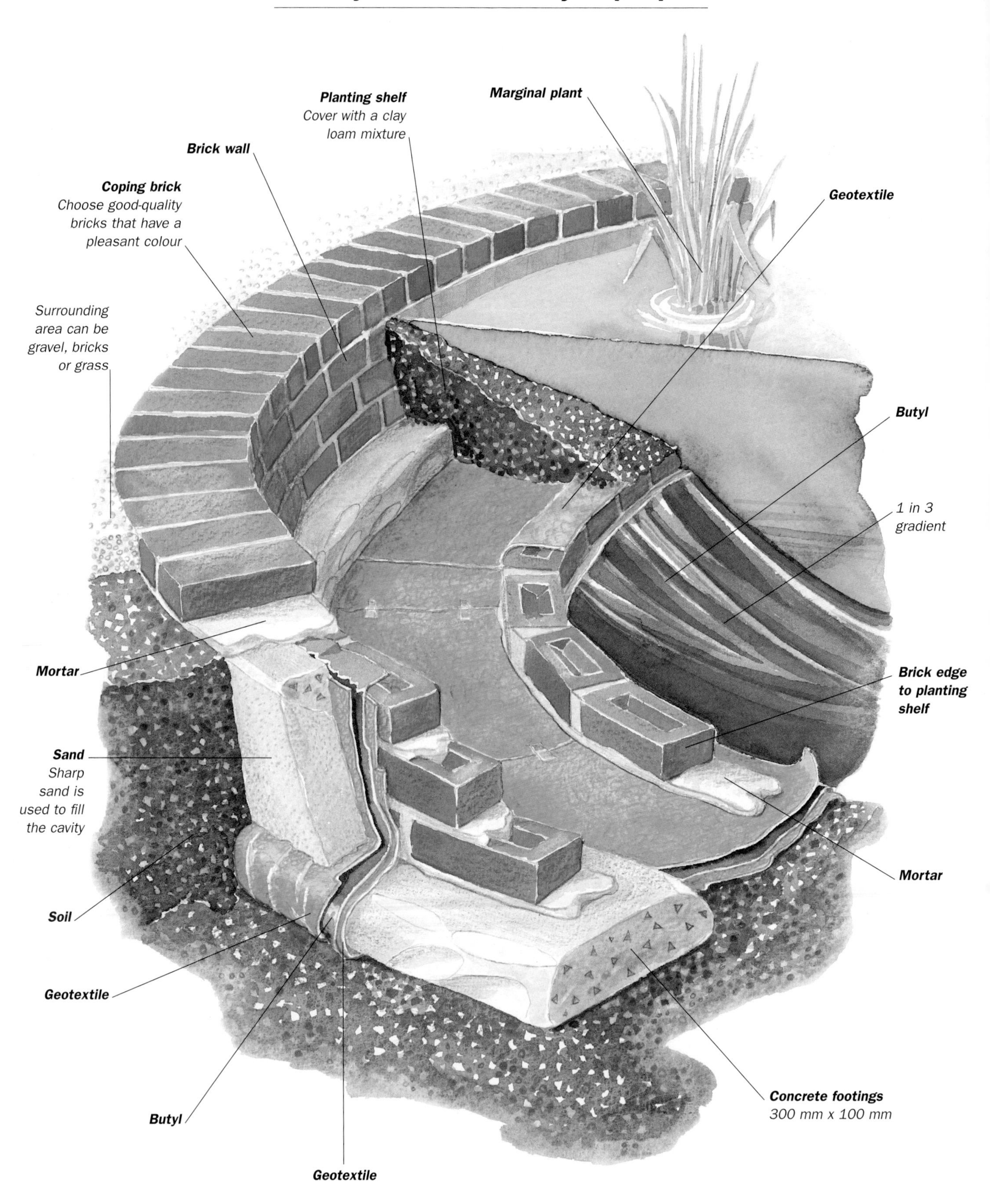
Planting shelf
Cover with a clay loam mixture
Marginal plant
Brick wall
Coping brick
Choose good-quality bricks that have a pleasant colour
Geotextile
Surrounding area can be gravel, bricks or grass
Butyl
1 in 3 gradient
Mortar
Brick edge to planting shelf
Sand
Sharp sand is used to fill the cavity
Mortar
Soil
Geotextile
Concrete footings
300 mm x 100 mm
Butyl
Geotextile

Exploded view of the kidney-shaped pond

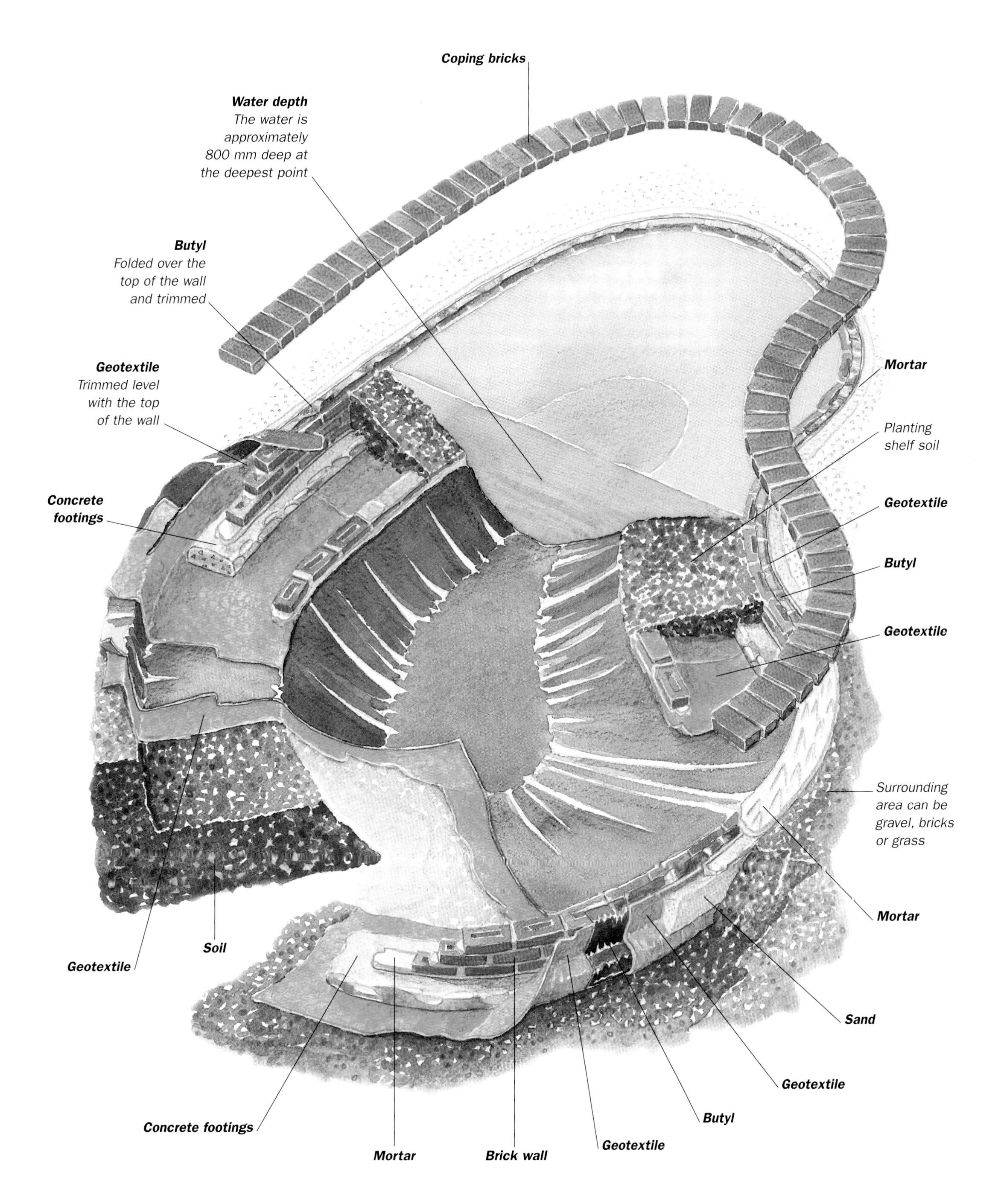
Coping bricks
Water depth
The water is approximately 800 mm deep at the deepest point
Butyl
Folded over the top of the wall and trimmed
Geotextile
Trimmed level with the top of the wall
Concrete footings
Mortar
Planting shelf soil
Geotextile
Butyl
Geotextile
Surrounding area can be gravel, bricks or grass
Mortar
Sand
Geotextile
Butyl
Geotextile
Brick wall
Mortar
Concrete footings
Geotextile
Soil

Making the kidney-shaped pond

1 Setting out the pond

Clearly mark out the area of the pond plus 300 mm all round, marking the intended water level with a peg set outside the working area. Dig the entire area, to a level depth of 300 mm. Mark the final shape of the pond, using marker spray on the levelled ground.

2 Digging out the pond

Where planting shelves are to be built into the sides of the pond, mark out where you want them to be. Dig out the central area of the pond allowing for a 1 in 3 gradient from the marked areas. Remove any sharp stones.

3 Lining the excavation with geotextile

Unroll the geotextile (which usually comes in 2 m wide rolls) to cover the entire excavation allowing 100 mm overlaps. Using short lengths of duct tape join the sides of the geotextile together at 1 m intervals.

4 Lining the excavation with butyl

Make sure that no stones or sharp objects have fallen into the excavation, unroll the butyl liner and spread it ensuring that there is at least 300 mm of liner overlapping the edge of the pond all around. Avoid treading on the liner but take off your boots if you have to.

5 Protecting the liner

Where the liner will come into direct contact with the concrete footings or brick-built sides of the pond, cover it with a further layer of geotextile, being careful that no stones or other objects come between the liner and the geotextile.

6 Building the footings and edges On the flat ledge within the excavation, build a concrete footing 100 mm deep by 300 mm wide, making sure it is flat and level. Smooth the sides with a finishing trowel and leave to cure overnight. Build up the interior edge to the pond with three courses of bricks.

7 Filling the cavity Gently fold the liner and geotextile over the top of the brick edging and fill the cavity between the wall and the earth with sharp sand. Compact the sand with your feet to avoid later subsidence. Do not try compacting the sand with sharp tools.

8 Preparing the planting shelves Where the level shelf has been extended into the pond to create a planting shelf, lay a single course of bricks bedded in mortar to keep the soil from falling into the bottom of the pond. Fill the planting area with soil – a clay loam mixture is ideal.

9 Trimming the lining Cut away the visible edges of the geotextile (any that pokes above the bricks). Leave 50 mm of butyl above the bricks and cut off the remainder. Lay this on top of the bricks.

10 Laying the coping bricks Lay the brick edging on a bed of mortar. Ensure that you trap the butyl between the bricks and maintain even-looking gaps all around. Allow the mortar to dry for a few days before filling with water.

Circular pond

Intermediate

Making time
3 weekends
A weekend for digging the hole and two weekends to complete

Filled with submerged and floating-leaved plants and their attendant wildlife, this unobtrusive, classical shape adds wonderful mirror reflections as well as beauty and interest on both the surface of the water and below it. The paved surround is perfect for sitting on when the sun is out and allows easy access to the pond, especially when the time comes to do some maintenance work on it.

Considering the design

You may wish to build this pond as part of a patio using matching stone pavers, or it could simply stand alone where it has the appearance of a well. As with all pond projects, consider the safety of children at all times (see page 185).

Getting started

Once you have chosen a level site, mark it out with pegs and string and "live with it" for a few days so that you can be sure it is in the best place for your garden. Try to complete the excavation and lining quickly, as the unsupported sides will start to collapse if there is rain during its construction.

Overall dimensions and general notes

2.78 m square
The pond is 1.5 m in diameter and is surrounded by a reconstituted stone paving kit

Ideal for a small formal garden, this circular pond would look good either as an extension to an existing patio or set in a lawn. You could use real stone crazy paving or bricks for the surround.

You will need

Materials

- Paving kit: 38 mm thick pavers forming a 2.78 m square with a 1.5 m diameter hole in the middle
- Geotextile: 37 sq metres
- Butyl liner: 1 piece 4.3 m square
- Wood: 1 piece 1.9 m x 90 mm x 60 mm and 2 pieces 1.2 m x 90 mm x 30 mm (tamping beam), 1 piece 200 mm x 75 mm x 75 mm and 1 piece 1.1 m x 35 mm x 25 mm (tramel), and 1 piece 1.84 m x 90 mm x 30 mm (beam for checking level)
- Plywood: 1 piece 500 mm square
- Nails: 5 at 60 mm long
- Concrete: 1 part cement (72 kg), and 4 parts ballast (288 kg)
- Bricks: 220
- Mortar: 1 part cement (50 kg) and 3 parts sand (150 kg)
- Builders sand: 1500 kg
- Hardcore: 0.5 cu metre

Tools

- Pegs and string
- Club hammer
- Tape measure and spray marker
- Spade, fork and shovel
- Wheelbarrow and bucket
- Scissors
- General-purpose saw
- Claw hammer
- Bricklayer's towel
- Pointing towel
- Spirit level
- Sledgehammer

Cross-section of the circular pond

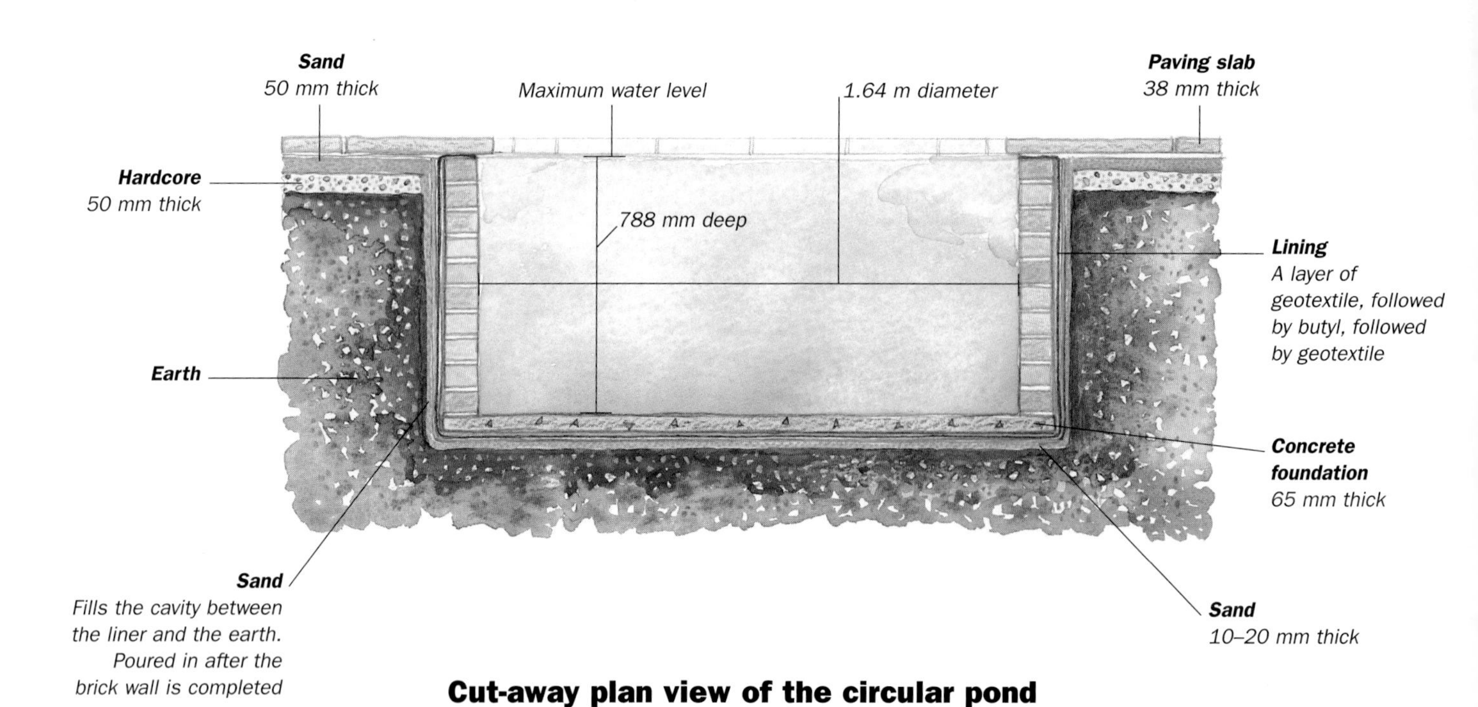
Sand
50 mm thick
Maximum water level
1.64 m diameter
Paving slab
38 mm thick
Hardcore
50 mm thick
788 mm deep
Lining
A layer of geotextile, followed by butyl, followed by geotextile
Earth
Concrete foundation
65 mm thick
Sand
Fills the cavity between the liner and the earth. Poured in after the brick wall is completed
Sand
10–20 mm thick

Cut-away plan view of the circular pond

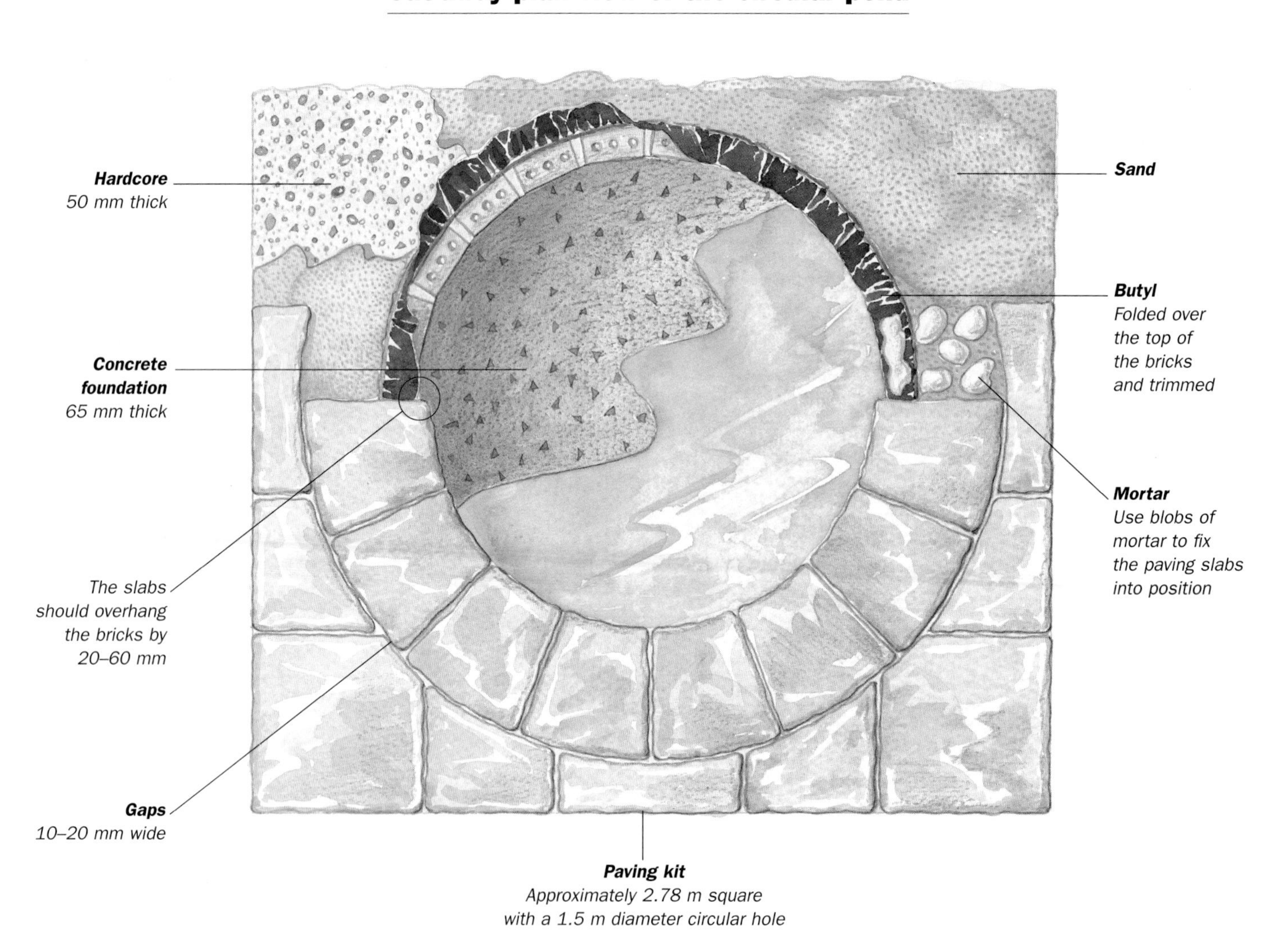
Hardcore
50 mm thick
Sand
Butyl
Folded over the top of the bricks and trimmed
Concrete foundation
65 mm thick
Mortar
Use blobs of mortar to fix the paving slabs into position
The slabs should overhang the bricks by 20–60 mm
Gaps
10–20 mm wide
Paving kit
Approximately 2.78 m square with a 1.5 m diameter circular hole

Exploded view of the circular pond

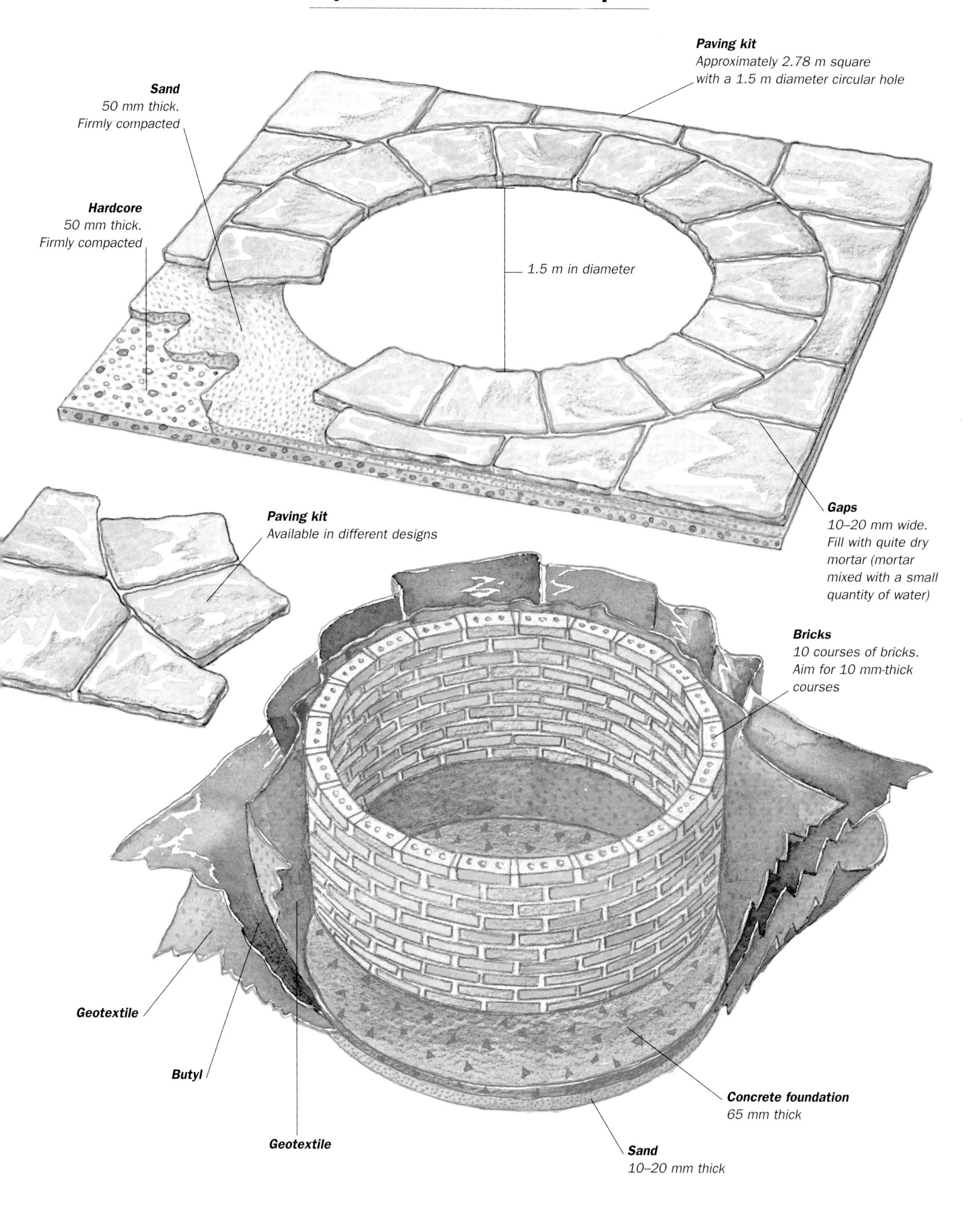

Paving kit
Approximately 2.78 m square
with a 1.5 m diameter circular hole
Sand
50 mm thick.
Firmly compacted
Hardcore
50 mm thick.
Firmly compacted
1.5 m in diameter
Paving kit
Available in different designs
Gaps
10–20 mm wide.
Fill with quite dry
mortar (mortar
mixed with a small
quantity of water)
Bricks
10 courses of bricks.
Aim for 10 mm-thick
courses
Geotextile
Butyl
Geotextile
Concrete foundation
65 mm thick
Sand
10–20 mm thick

Making the circular pond

1 Setting out the slabs
Set the paving slabs down and try them for position. Live with them for a few days. Check the dimensions of the whole square and the diameter of the circle as kits may vary slightly in size. Aim for the slabs to overhang the brick walls of the pond by 20–60 mm.

2 Marking the area
Use a tape measure, pegs, string and a spray marker to draw a circle 2 m in diameter. If your earth is crumbly it can be difficult to dig an accurately-sized hole so start by marking out a larger circle – one 2.6 m in diameter, for example.

3 Excavating the hole
Remove the turf with the spade and fork and start digging. You may wish to save the topsoil for another area of the garden and discard the rest. Make a hole 2 m in diameter and 860 mm deep, making sure it is clean-sided.

4 Lining with geotextile
Remove all sharp stones and spread a 10–20 mm layer of sand over the bottom of the hole. Cover the base and sides of the hole with geotextile, allowing for generous overlaps of at least 100 mm. Leave it overlapping until step 11.

5 Lining with butyl
Cover the geotextile with the 4.3 m square sheet of butyl. You will find this easier if you have someone to help. Take time arranging the creases so that they end up evenly distributed and weigh down the edges with bricks. Do not put any water in at this stage.

6 Laying the concrete slab
Reline the hole with geotextile (this protects the top side of the butyl) and weigh that down with bricks. Lay a 65 mm thick slab of concrete in the hole. Use the saw and nails to build the tamping beam and ask someone to hold the other end while you work.

7 Using the trammel
Use the plywood, stick, block, and nails to make a trammel (this works like the minute hand on a clock) that scribes a radius of 820 mm. Centre the trammel on the concrete base, weigh it down with bricks, and use it to indicate the correct position of each brick.

8 Building the wall
Build the circular wall with 10 mm thick mortar joints and stagger each course as shown. After completing each course, you can continue using the trammel by raising it upward by 75 mm each time, or you can simply check the brickwork is vertical using a spirit level.

9 Checking the levels
Check the level every two courses using the 1.84 m long piece of wood and the spirit level. Bear in mind that the pond must be completely level otherwise it will not look right. Continue building until you have completed the 10 courses.

10 Packing with sand
Use sand to fill any spaces between the sides of the hole and the geotextile. Dig out the surrounding earth down to a depth of 100 mm below the bricks. Spread 50 mm of hardcore and make sure that it is firmly compacted using the sledgehammer.

11 Trimming the lining
Pack the top of the cavity with concrete. Cut the geotextile off level with the bricks. Flap the butyl over the top of the wall and trim off the excess.

12 Putting down the paving
Spread a 50 mm layer of sand over the hardcore and compact this so it finishes level with the top of the bricks. Bed the paving slabs on blobs of mortar and when that has set, fill the joints with a quite dry mortar (mixed with less water so that it is still crumbly).

Formal canal

Intermediate

Making time
4 weekends
2 weekends for making the foundation and 2 weekends to complete

This beautiful design by John Brookes is part of a formal arrangement and takes the formality of the house out into the garden. It is both simple and classic and the long strip of still water reflects the sky. The brickwork edge finishes flush with the surrounding brick, gravel and lawn, making it smart and practical. This design is easy to reduce down in size for a smaller garden or courtyard.

Considering the design

As with any formal water feature, the most important thing is to make the scheme fit the environment, so make sure that your canal allows for easy access to all areas of the garden and does not act as a "moat" to discourage use of parts of the garden. Where young children are about it is dangerous as they may crawl or walk into the canal and not be able climb out. If you have young children it is better to wait a few years for them to grow up before building a pond or if you are expecting children to visit you may consider putting up some form of temporary barrier (see page 185). In order for the water plants to flourish it is important that the depth of water is not reduced below 600 mm. It is important that the water level and the level of the patio are carefully considered so that no more steps than are necessary from the house to the pond are incorporated in the design, which is elegant and requires little maintenance.

Getting started

At nearly 5 m long this is a big excavation so you do need to consider where you are going to put the spoil. You could pay to have it removed or why not plan a rockery or other feature that requires a quantity of soil?

Overall dimensions and general notes

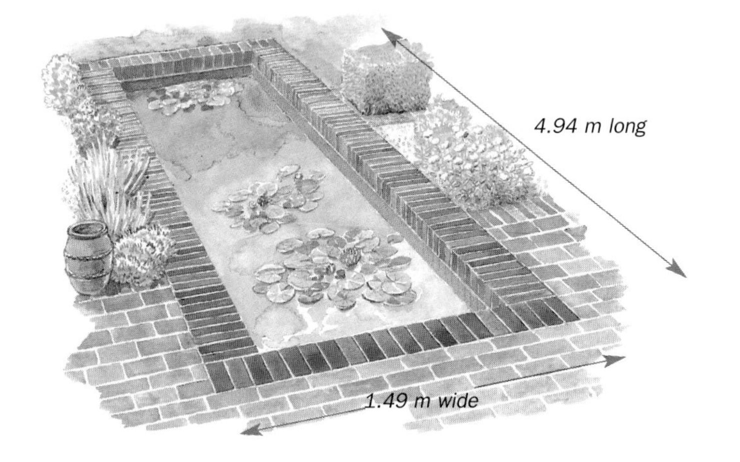
4.94 m long
1.49 m wide

This canal is suited to classic still water plants, such as water lilies.

You will need

Materials

- ✔ Hardcore: 0.7 cu metres
- ✔ Wood: 26 metres of 100 mm x 20 mm section (foundation frame and tamping pieces), 26 pieces 300 mm x 35 mm x 20 mm (foundation frame pegs)
- ✔ Plywood: 1 piece 500 mm square x 13 mm (general use)
- ✔ Nails: 34 at 38 mm long
- ✔ Concrete: 1 part cement (650 kg) and 4 parts (2600 kg) ballast
- ✔ Blocks: 143
- ✔ Bricks: 183 for the walls and 160 for the coping
- ✔ Mortar: 1 part (90 kg) cement and 3 parts (270 kg) sand
- ✔ Geotextile: 60 sq metre
- ✔ Duct tape
- ✔ Butyl: 1 piece 7.5 m x 4 m

Tools

- ✔ Tape measure, pegs, string, and a piece of chalk
- ✔ Club hammer
- ✔ Spade, fork and shovel
- ✔ Sledgehammer
- ✔ General-purpose saw
- ✔ Claw hammer
- ✔ Spirit level
- ✔ Line set
- ✔ Bricklayer's trowel
- ✔ Pointing trowel

Cut-away detail of the formal canal

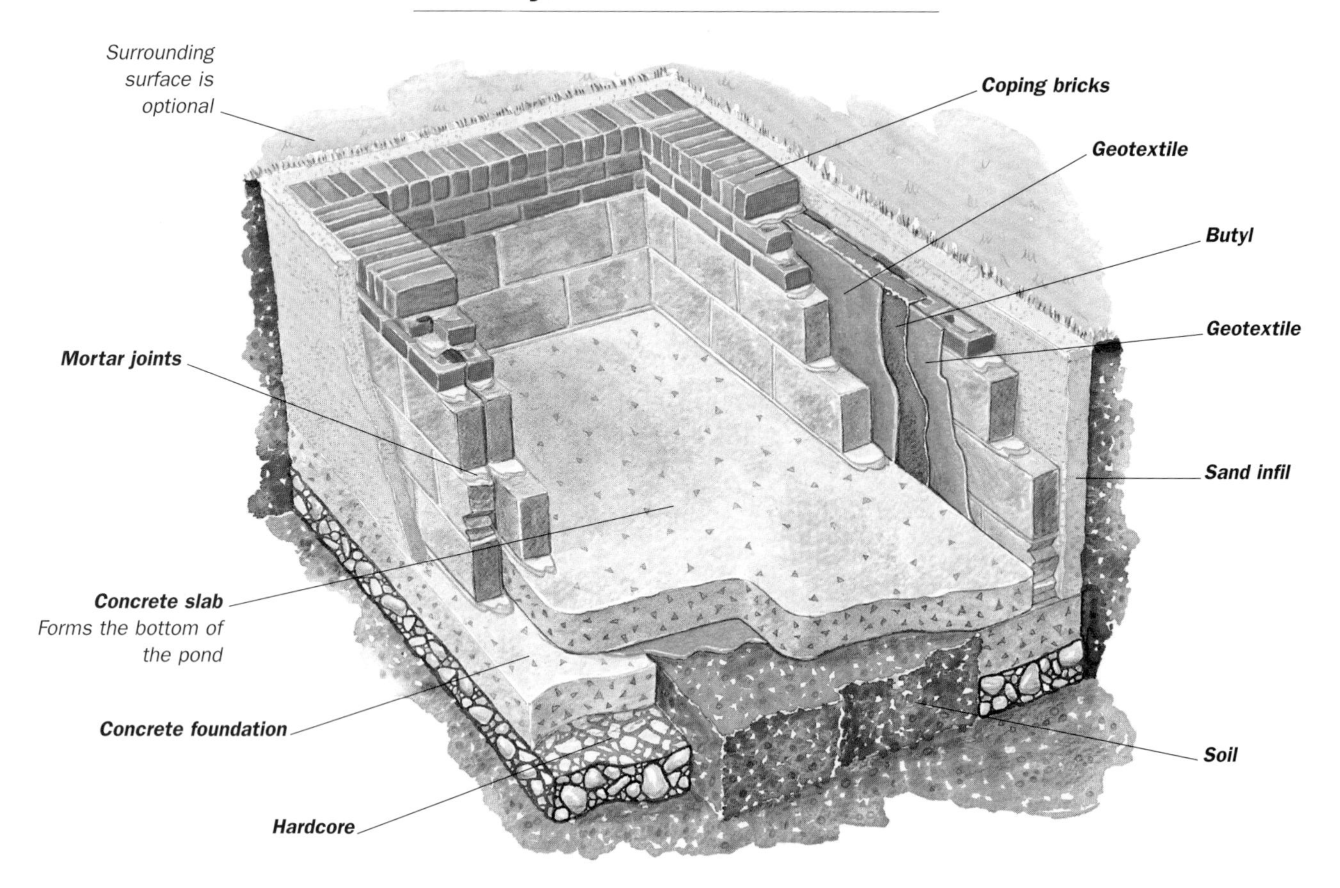
Surrounding surface is optional
Coping bricks
Geotextile
Butyl
Geotextile
Mortar joints
Sand infil
Concrete slab
Forms the bottom of the pond
Concrete foundation
Soil
Hardcore

Cross-section detail of the formal canal

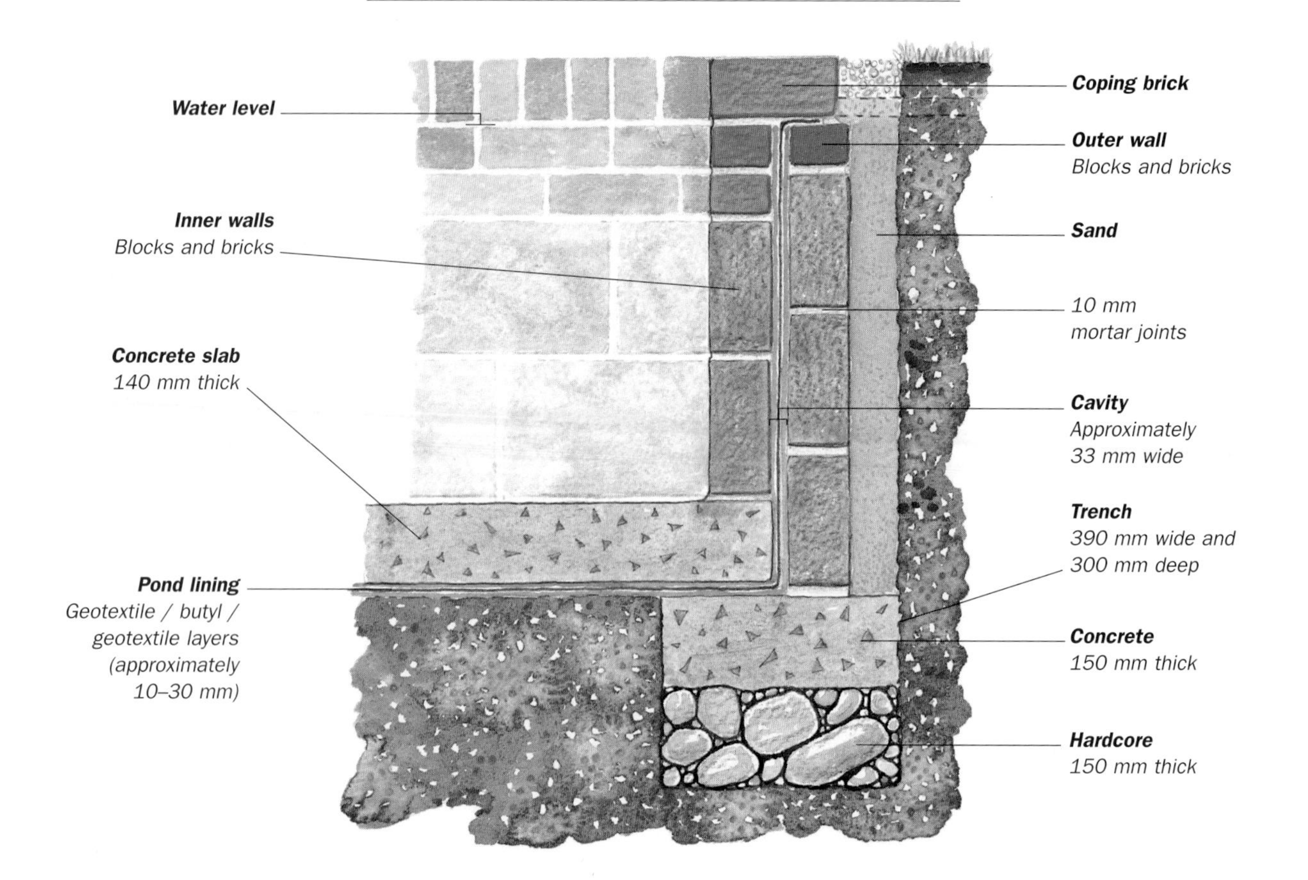
Water level
Coping brick
Outer wall
Blocks and bricks
Inner walls
Blocks and bricks
Sand
10 mm
mortar joints
Concrete slab
140 mm thick
Cavity
Approximately
33 mm wide
Trench
390 mm wide and
300 mm deep
Pond lining
Geotextile / butyl / geotextile layers (approximately 10–30 mm)
Concrete
150 mm thick
Hardcore
150 mm thick

Exploded view of the formal canal (coping bricks not shown)

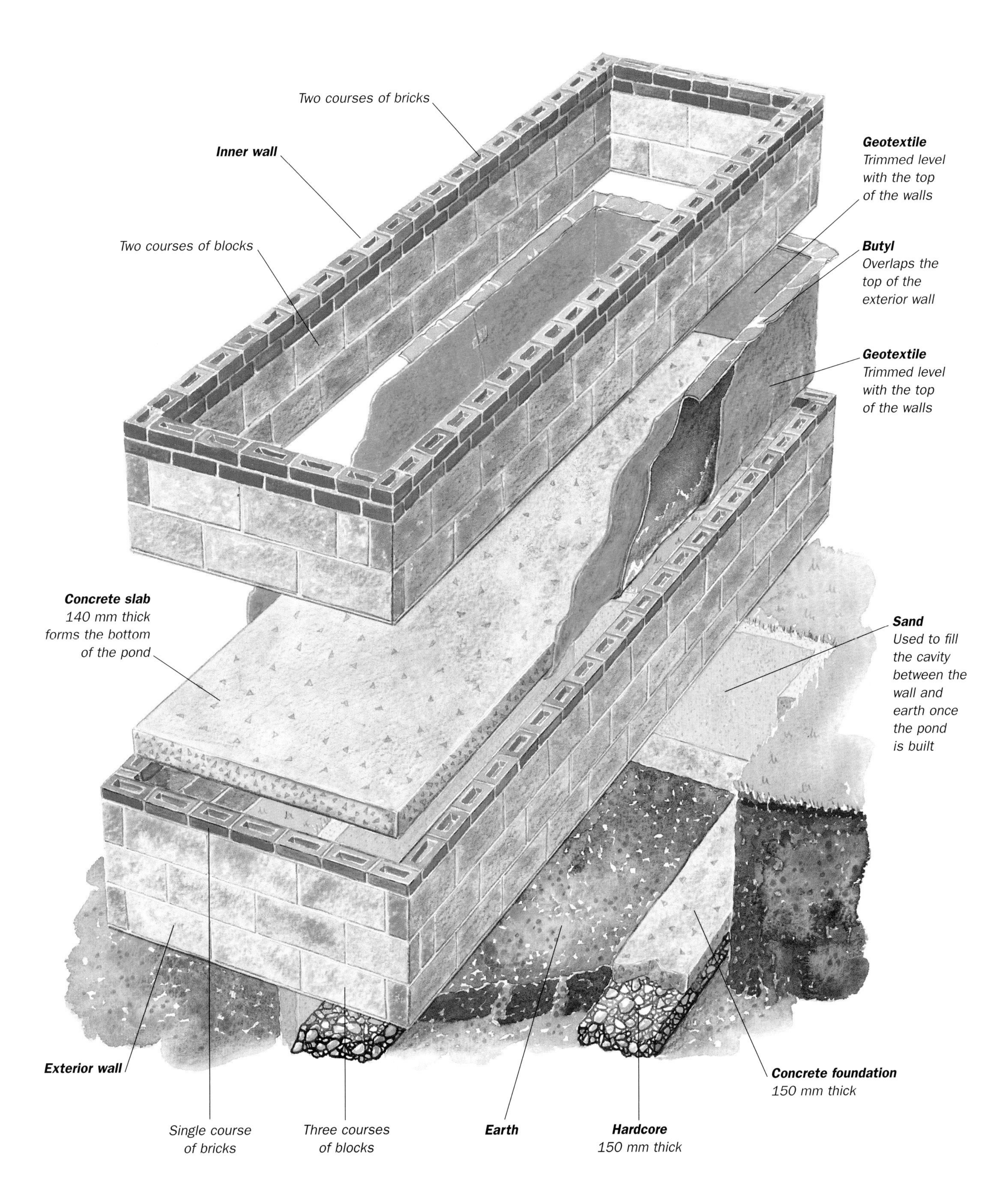
Two courses of bricks
Inner wall
Two courses of blocks
Geotextile
Trimmed level with the top of the walls
Butyl
Overlaps the top of the exterior wall
Geotextile
Trimmed level with the top of the walls
Concrete slab
140 mm thick forms the bottom of the pond
Sand
Used to fill the cavity between the wall and earth once the pond is built
Exterior wall
Concrete foundation
150 mm thick
Single course of bricks
Three courses of blocks
Earth
Hardcore
150 mm thick

Making the formal canal

1 Excavating the area
Clearly mark out an area 5.1 m x 1.7 m and remove all materials in it to a depth of 863 mm. Mark out a 390 mm-wide foundation trench into the bottom of the hole and remove the earth to a depth of 300 mm.

2 Laying the foundation
Fill the trench with hardcore to a depth of 150 mm. Use pegs and wood to form a level frame and fill this with concrete. Tamp the concrete level with the frame using a piece of spare wood. Leave to set overnight.

3 Building the exterior wall
Remove the wood frame and mark out the position of the outside edge of the exterior wall on the concrete using the chalk (4.99 m x 1.54 m).

4 Lining with geotextile
Carefully line the entire area with geotextile right to the top, folding or cutting away the darts that are formed at the corners. Use duct tape to join the pieces together.

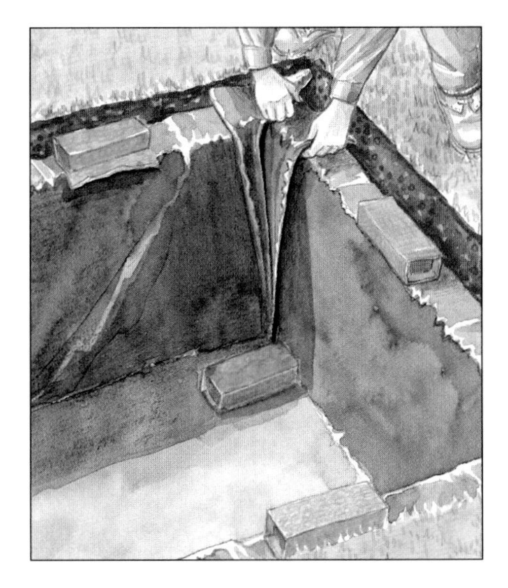

5 Lining with butyl

Place the butyl liner into the lined area, ensuring the sides reach the top all round. Use bricks wrapped in geotextile to push the liner into the corners, fold and tape the darts that rise from each corner. Cut away the liner 100 mm above the top of the bricks.

6 Laying the concrete slab

Reline the hole with more geotextile. Make a tamping frame from the spare wood and use it to cover the bottom of the hole with a level layer of concrete about 140 mm deep. Allow to dry overnight.

7 Building the inner wall

Use the chalk to mark out the inside edge of the inner wall (4.5 m x 1.06 m). This leaves a cavity of about 33 mm to accomodate the lining. Build up two courses of blocks followed by two courses of bricks.

8 Putting on the coping bricks

Trim the geotextile layers level with the top of the cavity wall and weigh down the butyl so that it overlaps the top of the exterior wall. Lay coping bricks on a bed of mortar and finish by filling the cavity between the wall and the earth with sand.

Pond with bridge and beach

Intermediate

Making time
4 weekends
2 weekends for digging the hole and 2 weekends for finishing

An informal wildlife pond provides interest all year round and fascinates children and adults alike. A wide range of pond life quickly grows up and newts, frogs and toads often appear as if by magic. A natural-looking beach and imaginative planting with lilies, iris and primroses complete the picture. The simple plank bridge gives a sense of adventure and can also save you walking all the way around the pond!

Overall dimensions and general notes

A 4 m long bridge spans the narrowest point of the pond
The best all-round advice is to go for the biggest pond that money, time and space allows.
The pond is approximately 8 m long and 5 m wide
An area of natural-looking beach

Considering the design

This pond can be built anywhere in the garden and is often away from the house in a quiet spot with wild flower and native species planting. It is often appropriate to put a bench or seat nearby for quiet contemplation. Be sure to make it as large as possible as plant growth on the water will soon make it appear smaller than it actually is. Make sure that you leave a clear area on one side so that you can walk up to it and see it clearly. People will be drawn to it if they can see a reflection or shimmer from the house. A pebble "beach" provides an attractive edge to the pond (see inset). As always, consider child safety (see page 185).

Getting started

See if you can find a place to put the earth from the excavations elsewhere in the garden (build a rockery for example), as this can be expensive to remove.

You will need

Materials

- Geotextile: 115 sq metres
- Duct tape
- Butyl: 1 piece 11 m x 8 m
- Concrete: 1 part cement (450 kg) and 4 parts ballast (1800 kg)
- Bricks: 315
- Mortar: 1 part cement (50 kg) and 3 parts sand (150 kg)
- Wood: 3 pieces, 490 mm x 100 mm x 100 mm (bridge frame horizontals), 6 pieces 700 mm x 100 mm x 100 mm (bridge frame verticals), 2 pieces (natural irregular edge is optional) 4 m x 250–300 mm x 50 mm (bridge planks)
- Bolts: 12 at 180 mm x M12 each with 1 nut and 2 washers, galvanised (bridge frames)
- Nails: 12 at 130 mm long, galvanised flat headed
- Plywood: 1.22 m x 600 mm x 26 mm (general work board)
- Sand: 700 kg

Tools

- Tape measure, hosepipe or rope (30 m long, for marking pond shape), spray marker and peg
- Club hammer and claw hammer
- Spade, fork and shovel
- Wheelbarrow and bucket
- Spirit level
- Rake
- Scissors
- Bricklayer's trowel and pointing trowel
- General-purpose saw
- Drill and 12 mm diameter bit

Cross-section detail of the bridge

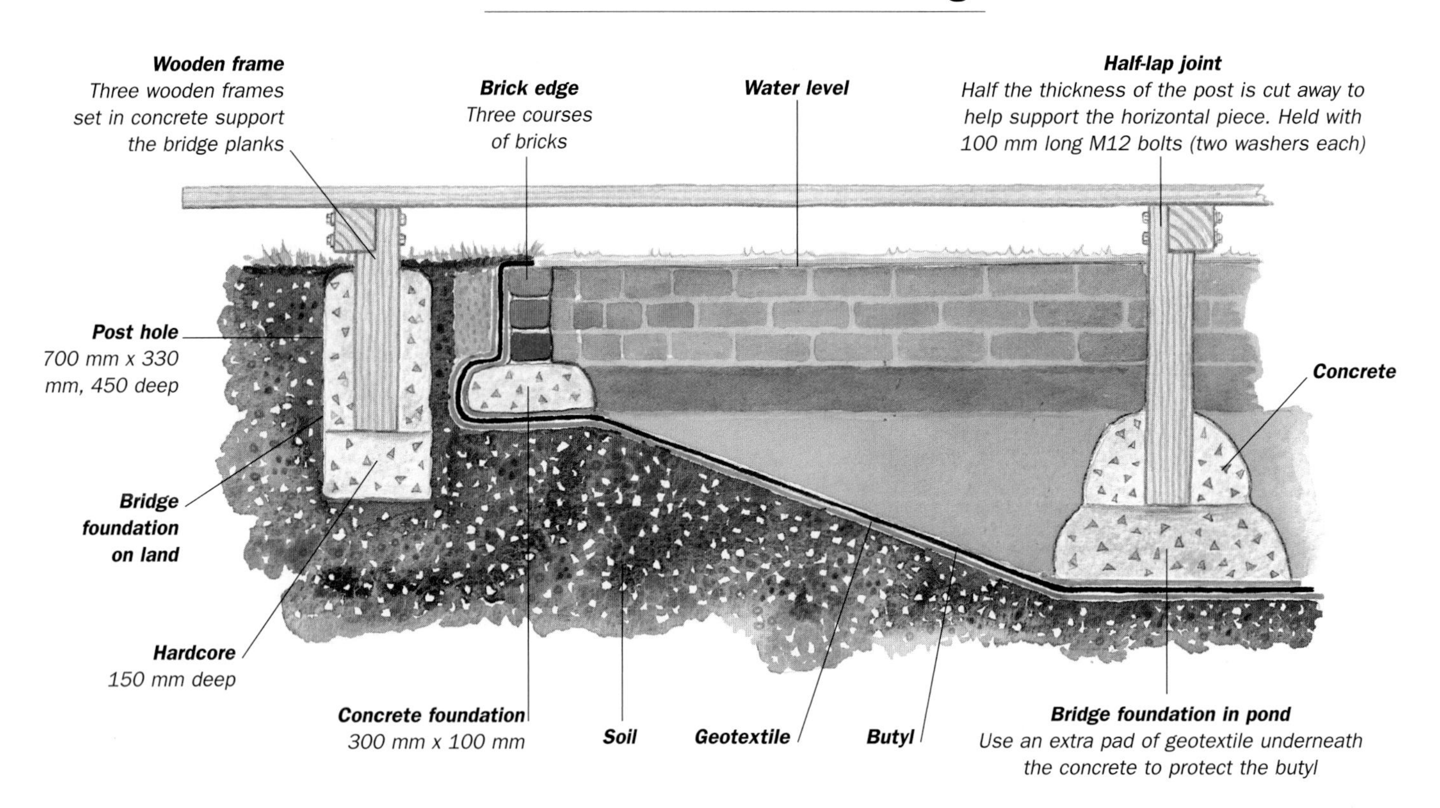
Wooden frame
Three wooden frames set in concrete support the bridge planks
Brick edge
Three courses of bricks
Water level
Half-lap joint
Half the thickness of the post is cut away to help support the horizontal piece. Held with 100 mm long M12 bolts (two washers each)
Post hole
700 mm x 330 mm, 450 deep
Concrete
Bridge foundation on land
Hardcore
150 mm deep
Concrete foundation
300 mm x 100 mm
Soil
Geotextile
Butyl
Bridge foundation in pond
Use an extra pad of geotextile underneath the concrete to protect the butyl

Cross-section detail of the pond showing beach (bridge not shown)

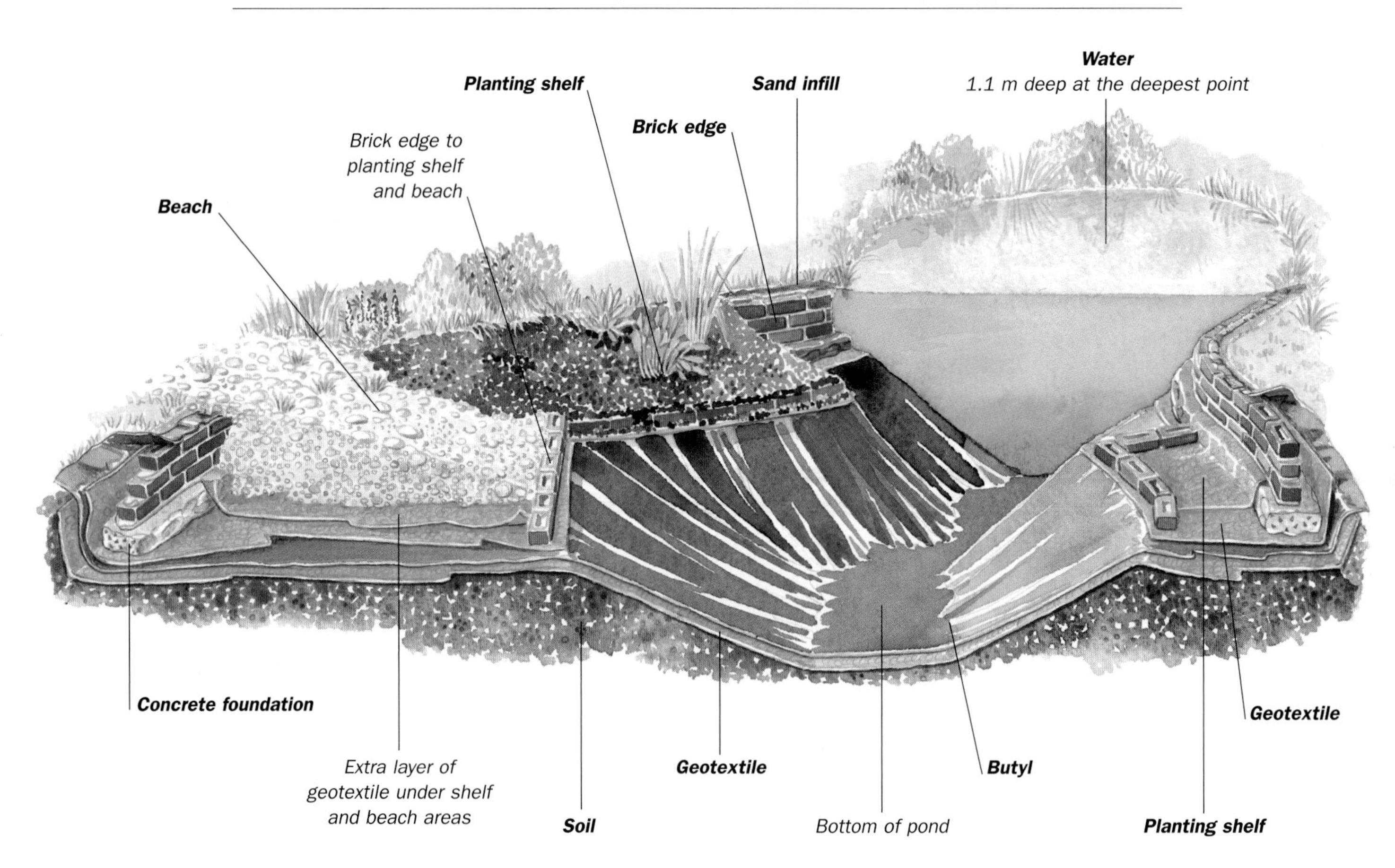
Water
1.1 m deep at the deepest point
Planting shelf
Sand infill
Brick edge
Brick edge to planting shelf and beach
Beach
Concrete foundation
Geotextile
Extra layer of geotextile under shelf and beach areas
Geotextile
Butyl
Soil
Bottom of pond
Planting shelf

Exploded view of the pond with bridge and beach

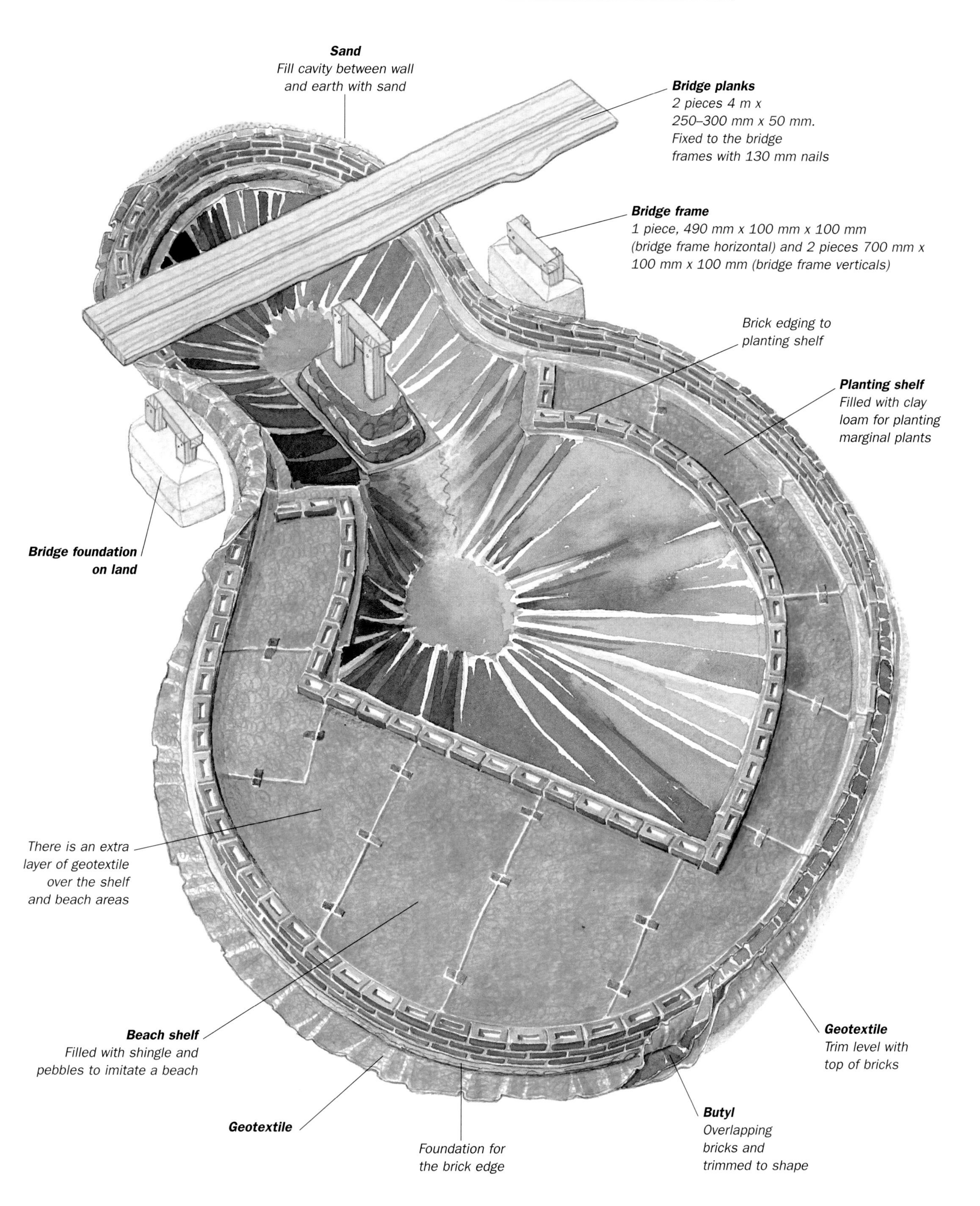
Sand
Fill cavity between wall and earth with sand
Bridge planks
2 pieces 4 m x 250–300 mm x 50 mm. Fixed to the bridge frames with 130 mm nails
Bridge frame
1 piece, 490 mm x 100 mm x 100 mm (bridge frame horizontal) and 2 pieces 700 mm x 100 mm x 100 mm (bridge frame verticals)
Brick edging to planting shelf
Planting shelf
Filled with clay loam for planting marginal plants
Bridge foundation on land
There is an extra layer of geotextile over the shelf and beach areas
Beach shelf
Filled with shingle and pebbles to imitate a beach
Geotextile
Foundation for the brick edge
Butyl
Overlapping bricks and trimmed to shape
Geotextile
Trim level with top of bricks

Making the pond with bridge and beach

1 Excavating the area
Mark out the area of the pond. Near the pond but outside the workings drive in a wooden marker peg so the top is at the intended water level. Dig the area to 300 mm below that level and mark out planting shelf areas. Dig out the remaining earth to finish the hole.

2 Measuring and raking
Allow at least 300 mm extra on both length and width. Rake over the excavation removing any sharp objects which could damage the liner.

3 Lining the excavation
Cover the entire excavation with geotextile, allowing for 100 mm overlaps. Spread the butyl over the geotextile ensuring that it extends beyond the water level all round when the pond is filled. Rearrange creases so that they are distributed evenly.

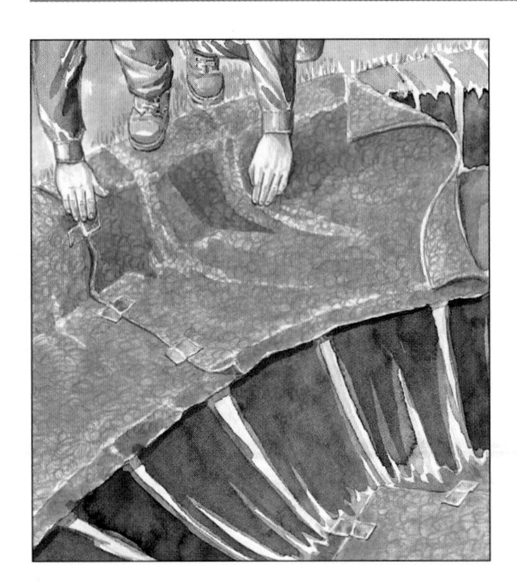

4 Laying extra geotextile
Make sure that no stones or sharp objects have fallen into the excavation and then lay extra geotextile over the planting shelf and beach areas. Use short lengths of duct tape to join the 1 m wide sheets of geotextile.

5 Building the footings and edges
On the flat ledge within the excavation build a concrete footing 100 mm deep by 300 mm wide, ensuring it is level and flat. Smooth all the sides with a finishing trowel and leave to cure overnight. Build up the interior edge to the pond with 3 courses of bricks.

6 Building the bridge frames
Establish the finished height of your bridge and prepare the bridge frame components accordingly. Mould a concrete pad for supporting the central frame. Hold it upright while you spread a mound of concrete around the bottoms of the wooden posts.

7 Completing the bridge

Dig holes either side of the pond and set the other two frames in concrete so that they are vertical and also levelled and aligned with the central frame. Once the concrete has set, fix the bridge planks to the tops of the frames using nails.

8 Backfilling behind the lining

The geotextile needs to be trimmed level with the top of the bricks and the butyl should overlap the bricks and then be trimmed. Fill the cavity behind the wall with sand. Compact the sand with your feet to avoid later subsidence but take care to avoid damaging the liner.

9 Preparing the planting shelves

Where the level shelf has been extended into the pond to create a planting shelf, check that you have adequate geotextile protecting the butyl and then lay a line of bricks along the edge (mortar is not required). Fill the planting shelves with clay loam.

10 Creating the beach and finishing the pond

Fill the beach area with a mixture of shingle and differently sized pebbles. Use a board to protect the edge of the pond while you work. When the pond is filled with water, cover the tops of the bricks with turf, cutting the turf at the edge of the water. Alternatively, cover with soil and sow grass seed.

Raised pond

Intermediate

Making time
4 weekends
A weekend to make the foundation and 3 weekends for completion

Ideal for a small garden or patio area, the coping allows for seating close to the water where you can see into the water as well as looking at the reflections of the sky and seasons. It is adaptable and takes up little space and, where there are children around it is safer, as they are less likely to stumble into the water. Placed where it can be seen from the house, it will give interest and delight throughout the year.

Considering the design

This little pond can be square or rectangular in shape and should be as large as possible, allowing for access around the area. The coping stone is 526 mm above the ground and this is just about low enough to make a comfortable seating place. Place it where it can be seen from inside the house from a much-used vantage point. Use materials that closely match those that form your house. Consider the reflections that you will see from your vantage point; placing a mirror (horizontally) where the water level will ultimately be will give you a good idea of the end result. Consider any services (water, drainage, TV, electricity, gas, or sewerage) that may be underneath the proposed site and alter the scheme accordingly. Note how the pond butts against the wall; a good option if you are short of space.

Getting started

Make a drawing showing the size that you have chosen. Use this to order the material that you will want. Allow 10% over on all materials. If materials have to be carried through the house remove or protect vulnerable things.

Overall dimensions and general notes

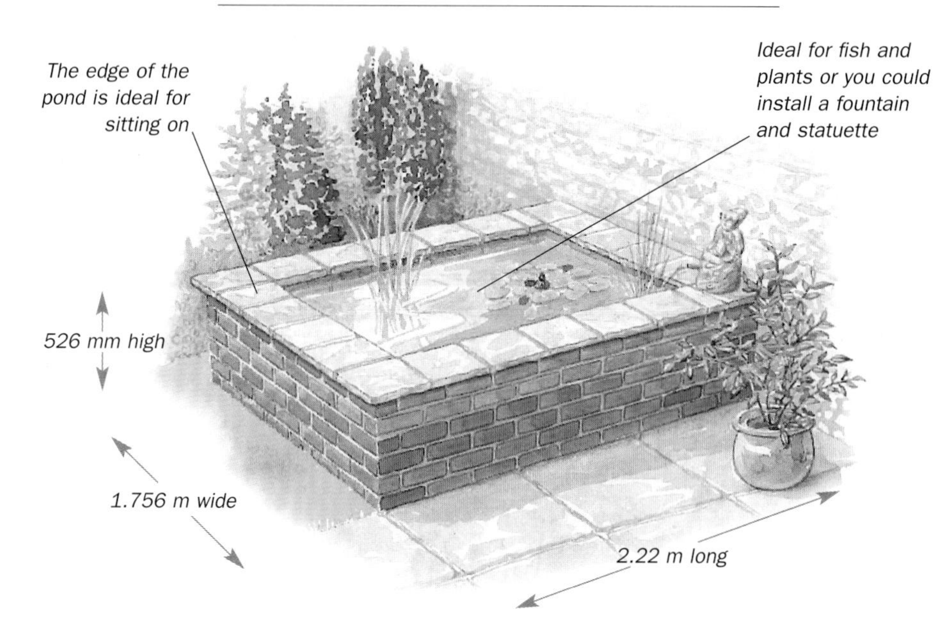
The edge of the pond is ideal for sitting on
Ideal for fish and plants or you could install a fountain and statuette
526 mm high
1.756 m wide
2.22 m long

This pond structure is built around a pre-formed rigid liner, so purchase the liner to suit your space first, and then adjust the material quantities accordingly.

You will need

Materials

- ✔ Concrete: 1 part cement (30 kg) and 4 parts ballast (120 kg)
- ✔ Wood: 1.5 m x 70 mm x 30 mm (tamping beam)
- ✔ Bricks: 196 bricks and 180 handmade irregular bricks (approximately 228 mm x 102.5 mm x 67 mm)
- ✔ Mortar mix: 1 part cement (75 kg) and 3 parts sand (225 kg)
- ✔ Plywood: 1.22 m x 610 mm x 9 mm (general workboard)
- ✔ Rigid liner: 1.8 m x 1.3 m (at outer rim) and 508 mm deep
- ✔ Stone slabs: 22 tiles, 295 mm square and 35 mm thick

Tools

- ✔ Tape measure, pegs, string and a piece of chalk
- ✔ Club hammer
- ✔ Spade, fork and shovel
- ✔ Wheelbarrow and bucket
- ✔ Spirit level
- ✔ Line set
- ✔ Bricklayer's trowel and pointing trowel
- ✔ Angle grinder

Plan view of the raised pond showing first courses of brick wall

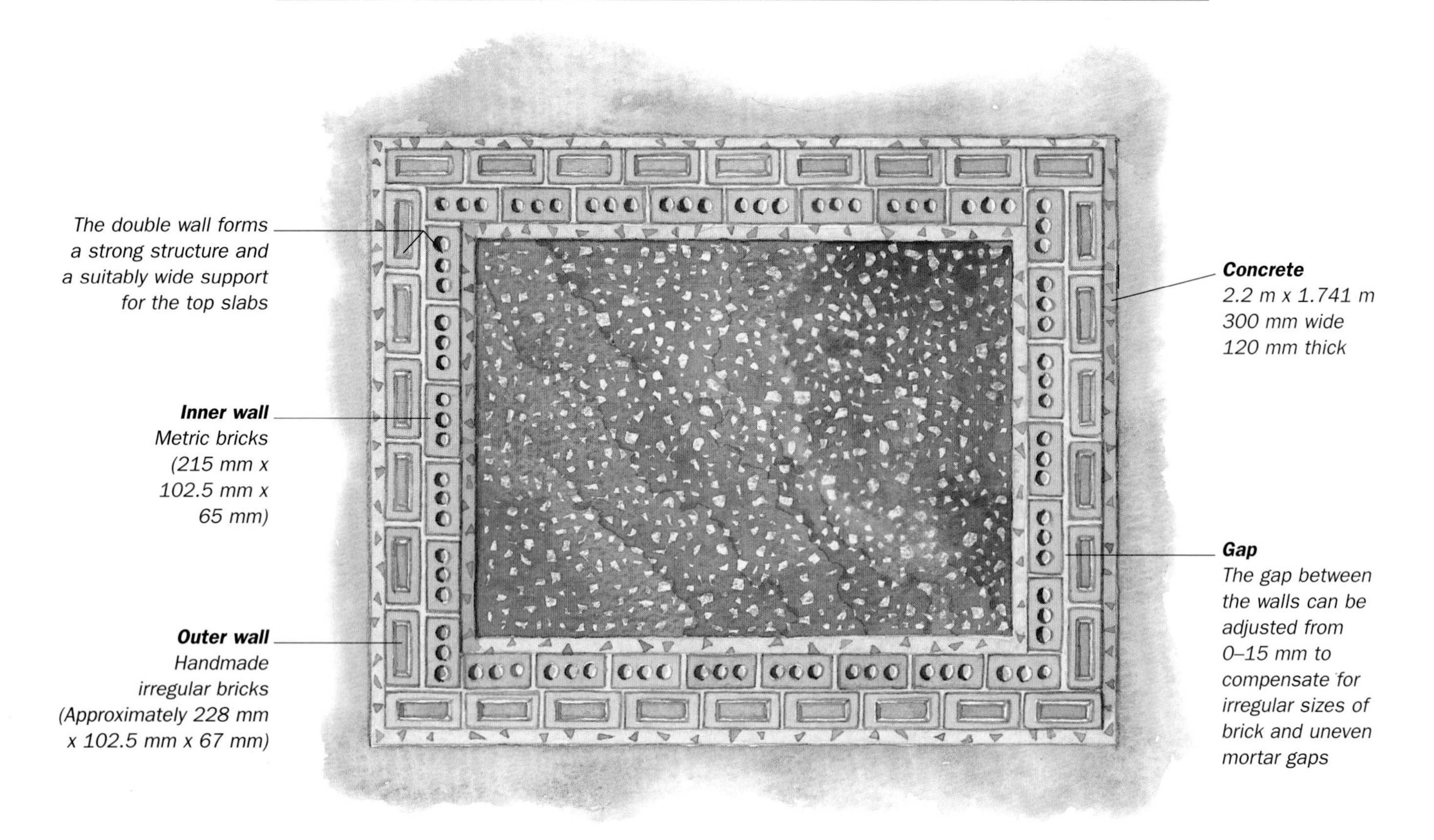
The double wall forms
a strong structure and
a suitably wide support
for the top slabs
Inner wall
Metric bricks
(215 mm x
102.5 mm x
65 mm)
Outer wall
Handmade
irregular bricks
(Approximately 228 mm
x 102.5 mm x 67 mm)
Concrete
2.2 m x 1.741 m
300 mm wide
120 mm thick
Gap
The gap between
the walls can be
adjusted from
0–15 mm to
compensate for
irregular sizes of
brick and uneven
mortar gaps

Cross-section of the raised pond

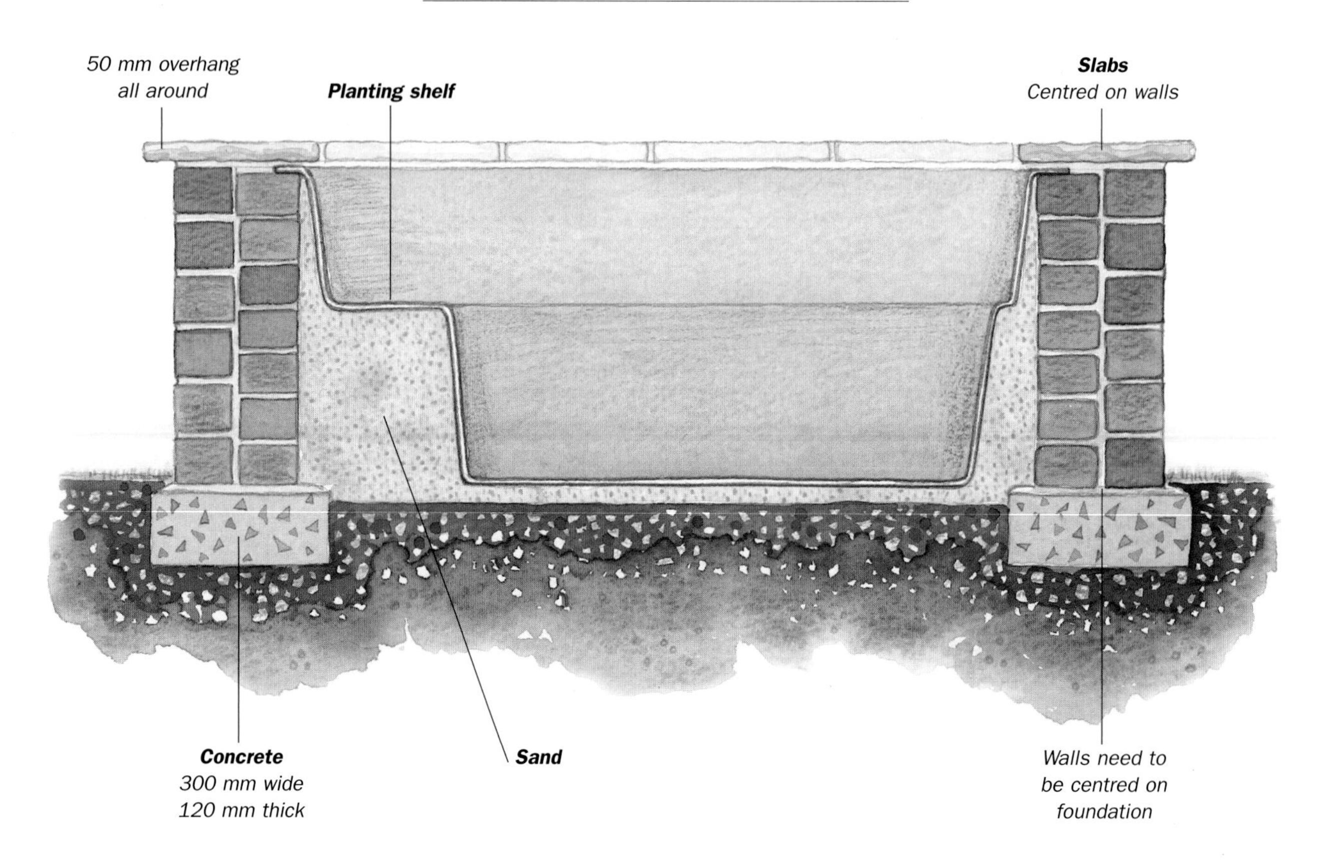
50 mm overhang
all around
Planting shelf
Slabs
Centred on walls
Concrete
300 mm wide
120 mm thick
Sand
Walls need to
be centred on
foundation

Exploded view of the raised pond

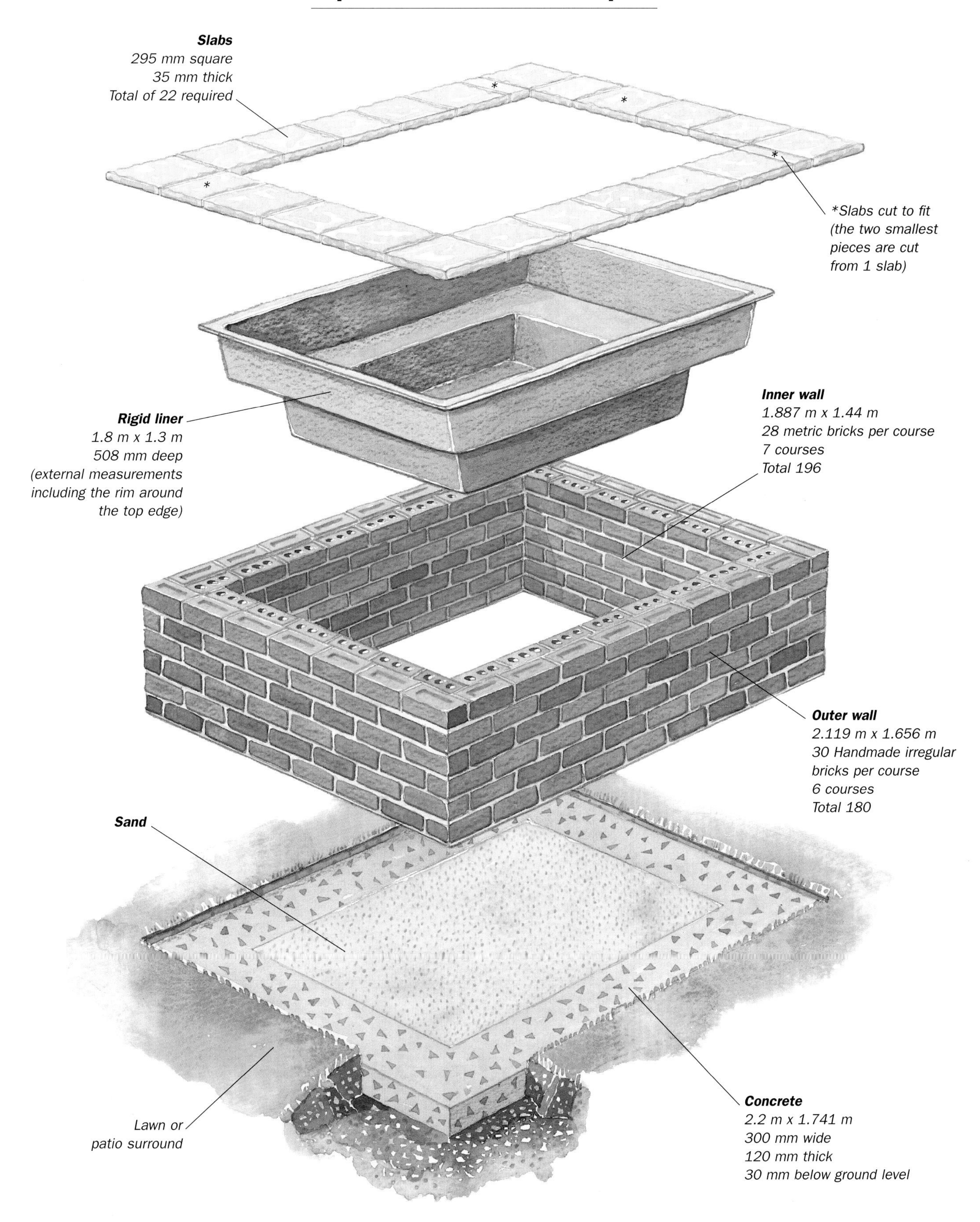

Slabs
295 mm square
35 mm thick
Total of 22 required
*
*
*
*
*Slabs cut to fit
(the two smallest
pieces are cut
from 1 slab)
Rigid liner
1.8 m x 1.3 m
508 mm deep
(external measurements
including the rim around
the top edge)
Inner wall
1.887 m x 1.44 m
28 metric bricks per course
7 courses
Total 196
Outer wall
2.119 m x 1.656 m
30 Handmade irregular
bricks per course
6 courses
Total 180
Sand
Lawn or
patio surround
Concrete
2.2 m x 1.741 m
300 mm wide
120 mm thick
30 mm below ground level

Making the raised pond

1 Marking out
Using the tape measure, pegs and string, set out the shape of the foundation on the grass – 2.2 m long and 1.741 mm wide. Remove the turf.

2 Positioning the levelling pegs
Dig out the foundation trench, 300 mm wide and 150 mm deep. Hammer in a series of wooden pegs to establish a level about 30 mm lower than the lawn.

3 Tamping the concrete
Fill the foundation trench with concrete up to the level of the wooden pegs. (Note the workboard to protect the lawn.)

4 Practise laying the bricks
Set out the first course of bricks without using mortar so that you can see how the pattern works. Arrange the ordinary bricks on the inside and the larger handmade bricks on the outside. Try to avoid cutting bricks.

5 Building the walls
Build up the inside walls to a height of six courses, and check both the vertical and horizontal levels. Use the line set to help you lay the bricks in accurate straight lines.

6 Fitting the rigid liner

Sit the plastic liner in the brick box so that the rim is resting on top of the wall. Fill the cavity between the liner and the wall with sand. Avoid leaving any gaps as these can cause the liner to distort or break over time (see page 198).

7 Cleaning the mortar joints

Build up the outside wall at the corners so that the top course is slightly higher than the level of the inner wall. Use the handle of the trowel to rake the courses to a clean finish while the mortar is still workable.

8 Finishing the brickwork

Continue laying up the courses until you have finished the exterior wall. Keep checking with the spirit level and making adjustments as necessary.

9 Laying the coping slabs

Practice arranging the slabs around the top of the pond allowing for a 50 mm overhang all around. Try to avoid cutting slabs where possible. Trowel a generous layer of mortar on top of the walls and bed the coping slabs in place. Check that they are level.

Pond with decking

Decking over a pond invites you to step over the water on to a different world. To look down in the gaps between the boards adds to the sense of adventure like being on a pleasure pier, a boat or raft. A railing is a good idea – made from metal or wood – and will stop young children falling in and will give you somewhere to rest your elbows and feel secure while looking down into the pond and observing the wildlife.

Advanced

Making time
4 weekends
A weekend for digging the hole and 2 weekends for construction

Considering the design

Decking can disguise the point at which the land stops and the pond starts so this combination has a lot of potential. You can alter the size and shape of the decking to suit your requirements.

The deck boards need to be strong and resistant to rotting. Preserved pine (stained or painted) is suitable but untreated bare oak is even better. If you have railings, they need to be strong, well supported and about 1 m high.

Getting started

If you require a deck of a different size and shape or are working with an existing pond, start by planning it out on paper.

Overall dimensions and general notes

Decking boards made from preserved pine or bare oak
An irregular shaped pond with a natural-looking edge, 5.3 m x 3.5 m
2.27 m wide
3.356 m long

The size and shape of the decking can be altered to suit your needs but be sure to provide adequate supports. Wood or metal railing is a sensible option.

You will need

Materials

- Geotextile: 54 sq metres
- Duct tape
- Butyl: 1 piece 7 m x 6 m
- Concrete: 1 part cement (225 kg) and 4 parts (900 kg) ballast
- Bricks: 210
- Mortar: 1 part cement (38 kg) and 3 parts sand (114 kg)
- Sand: 400 kg
- Hardcore: 0.1 cu metre
- Tanking paint: 5 litres
- Wood: 10 pieces, 350 mm x 100 mm x 100 mm (posts), 2 pieces 2.2 m x 100 mm x 100 mm (deck frame horizontals, long), 2 pieces 1.2 m x 100 mm x 100 mm (deck frame horizontals, short), 6 pieces 3.356 m x 200 mm x 50 mm (deck boards, long) and 5 pieces 1.364 m x 200 mm x 50 mm (deck boards, short)
- Plywood: 1.5 m x 50 mm x 6–7 mm (strip to set deck board gaps)
- Bolts: 20 at 180 mm x M12 each with 1 nut and 2 washers, galvanised
- Nails: 68 at 130 mm long, galvanised

Tools

- Tape measure, 20 m of rope or hosepipe (for marking shape of pond), peg and spray marker
- Spade, fork and shovel
- Spirit level
- Scissors
- Bricklayer's trowel and pointing trowel
- General-purpose saw
- Spanner (to fit nuts)
- Claw hammer

Exploded view of the pond with decking

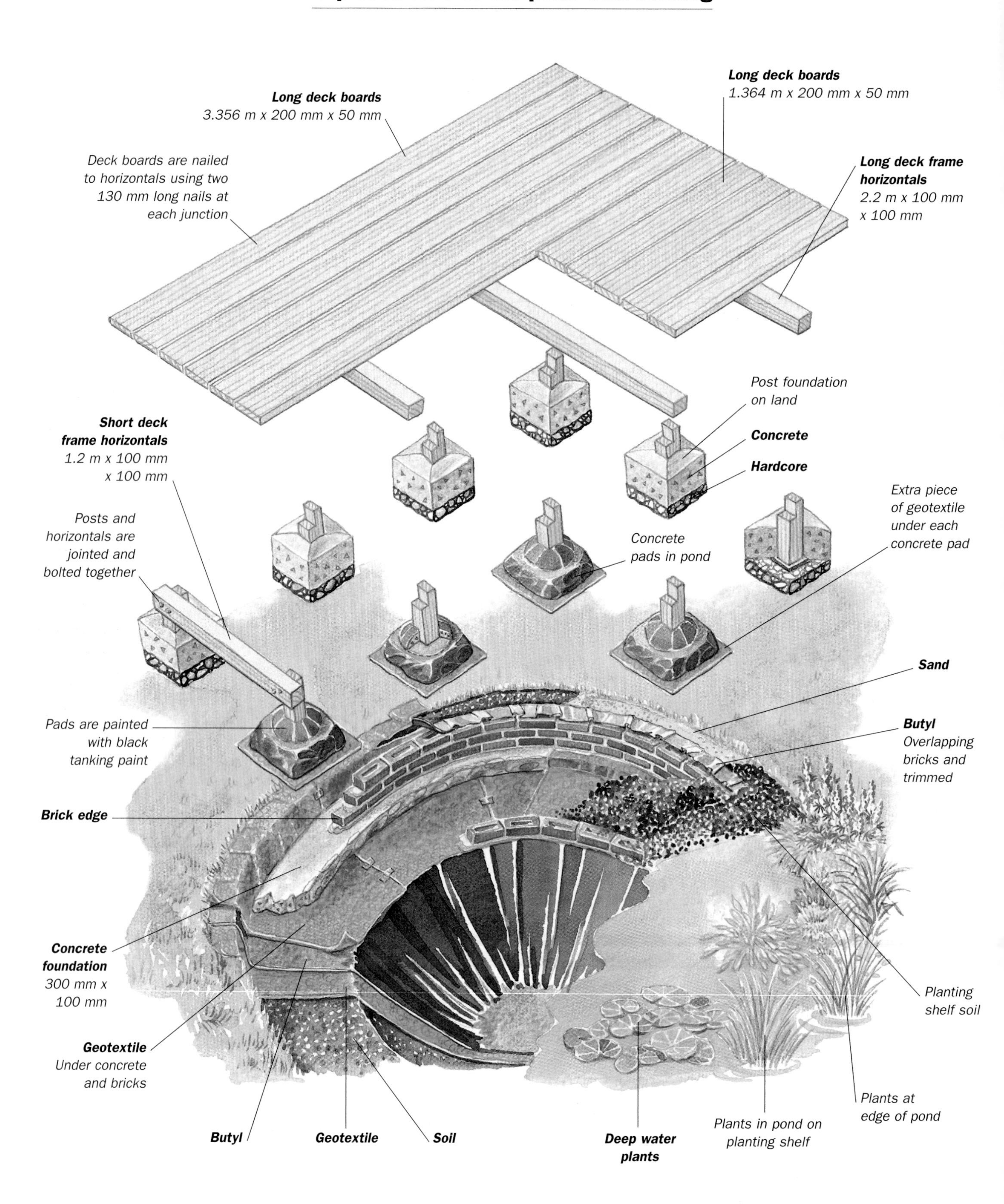
Long deck boards
3.356 m x 200 mm x 50 mm
Long deck boards
1.364 m x 200 mm x 50 mm
Deck boards are nailed to horizontals using two 130 mm long nails at each junction
Long deck frame horizontals
2.2 m x 100 mm x 100 mm
Post foundation on land
Concrete
Hardcore
Short deck frame horizontals
1.2 m x 100 mm x 100 mm
Extra piece of geotextile under each concrete pad
Posts and horizontals are jointed and bolted together
Concrete pads in pond
Sand
Pads are painted with black tanking paint
Butyl
Overlapping bricks and trimmed
Brick edge
Concrete foundation
300 mm x 100 mm
Planting shelf soil
Geotextile
Under concrete and bricks
Plants at edge of pond
Plants in pond on planting shelf
Butyl
Geotextile
Soil
Deep water plants

Cut-away detail of the pond with decking

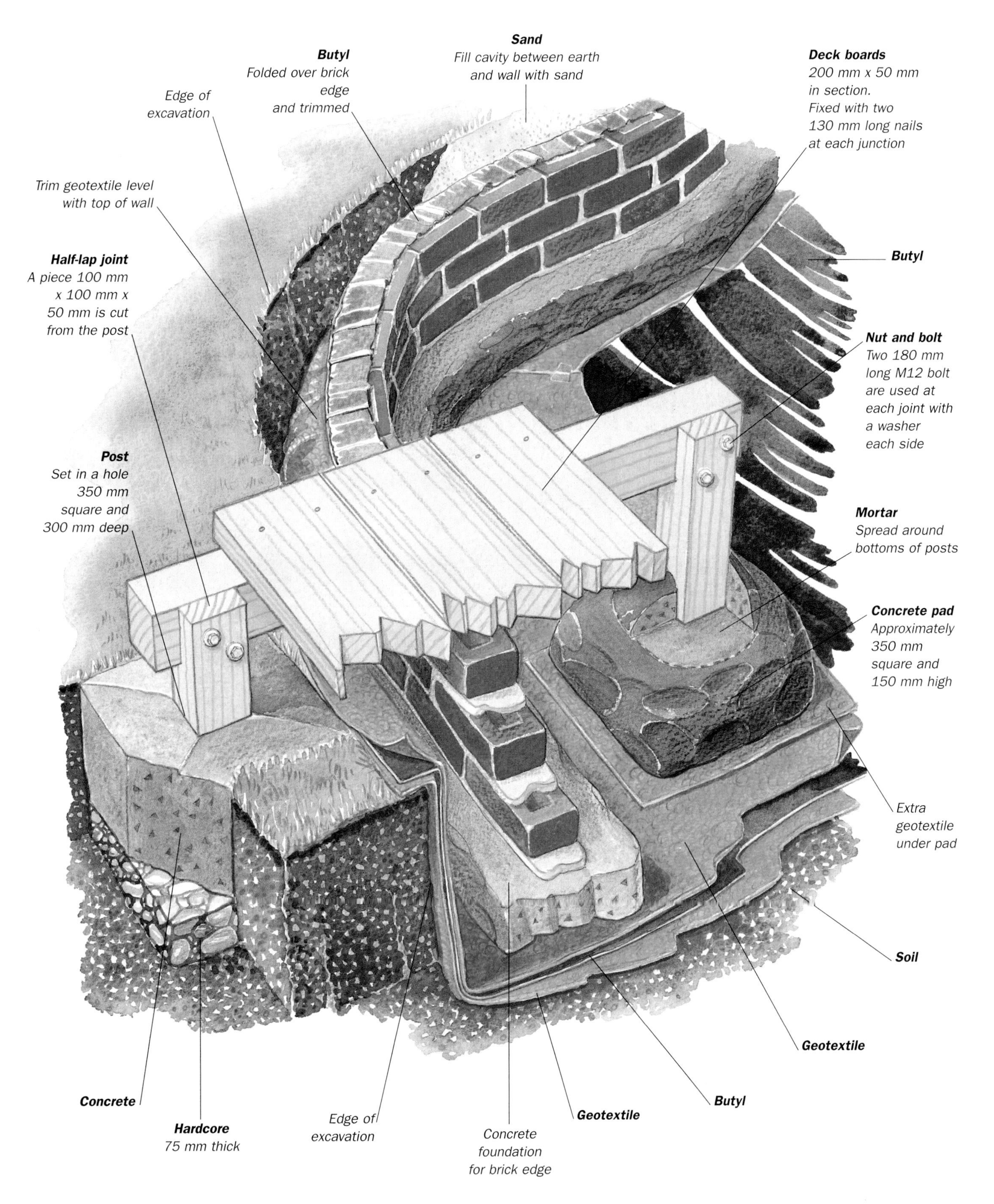
Sand
Fill cavity between earth and wall with sand
Butyl
Folded over brick edge and trimmed
Edge of excavation
Deck boards
200 mm x 50 mm in section.
Fixed with two 130 mm long nails at each junction
Trim geotextile level with top of wall
Half-lap joint
A piece 100 mm x 100 mm x 50 mm is cut from the post
Butyl
Nut and bolt
Two 180 mm long M12 bolt are used at each joint with a washer each side
Post
Set in a hole 350 mm square and 300 mm deep
Mortar
Spread around bottoms of posts
Concrete pad
Approximately 350 mm square and 150 mm high
Extra geotextile under pad
Soil
Geotextile
Concrete
Hardcore
75 mm thick
Edge of excavation
Concrete foundation for brick edge
Geotextile
Butyl

Making the pond with decking

1 Marking out and excavating
Clearly mark out the area of the pond plus 300 mm all round and dig to a depth of 350 mm. Mark out the final shape of the pond. Where planting shelves are to be built in to the sides of the pond, mark out the shelves and then finish digging out the pond.

2 Lining the pond
Remove any sharp objects from the hole. Cover the entire excavation with geotextile allowing 100 mm overlaps. Use duct tape to join the sides together at 1 m intervals. Unroll the butyl liner and lay it over the area, ensuring it extends beyond the intended water level.

3 Building the footing
Protect the liner with another layer of geotextile on the shelf areas. On the flat ledge within the excavation build a concrete footing 100 mm deep by 300 mm wide ensuring it is level and flat. Smooth all the sides with a finishing trowel and leave to cure overnight.

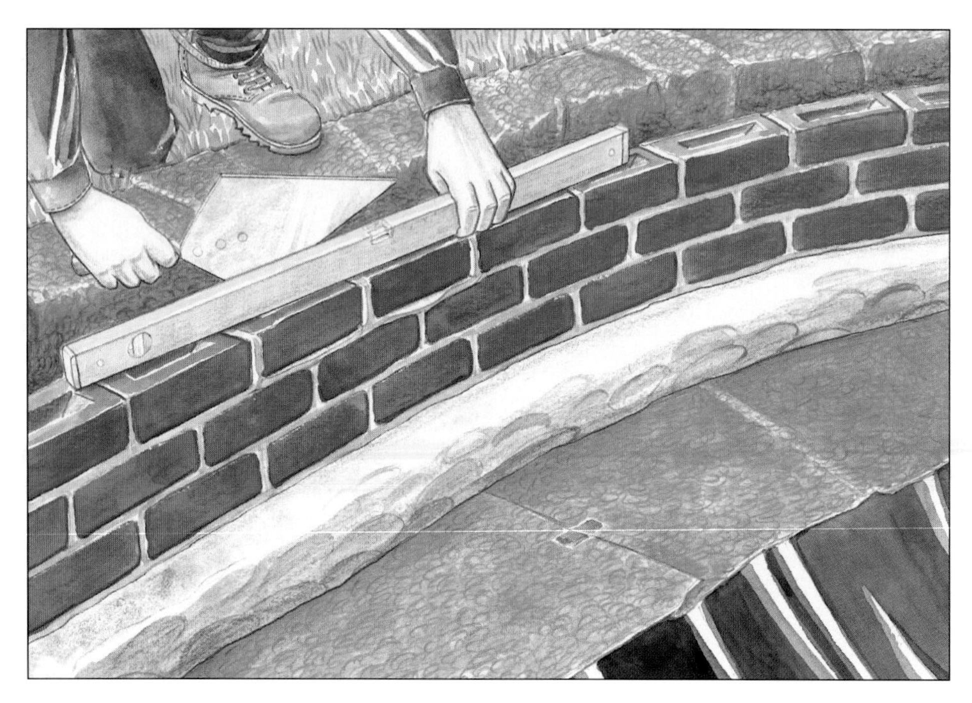

4 Building the edges
Build the interior edge to the pond with 3 courses of bricks. Check the horizontal level with the spirit level. Clean the wall with the edge of the trowel so that it is free from sharp bits of mortar.

5 Making the planting shelves
Fill the area behind the wall with sand, compact it with your feet to avoid later subsidence and trim the geotextile and butyl. Lay bricks along the edge of the planting shelves and fill these recesses with soil for planting.

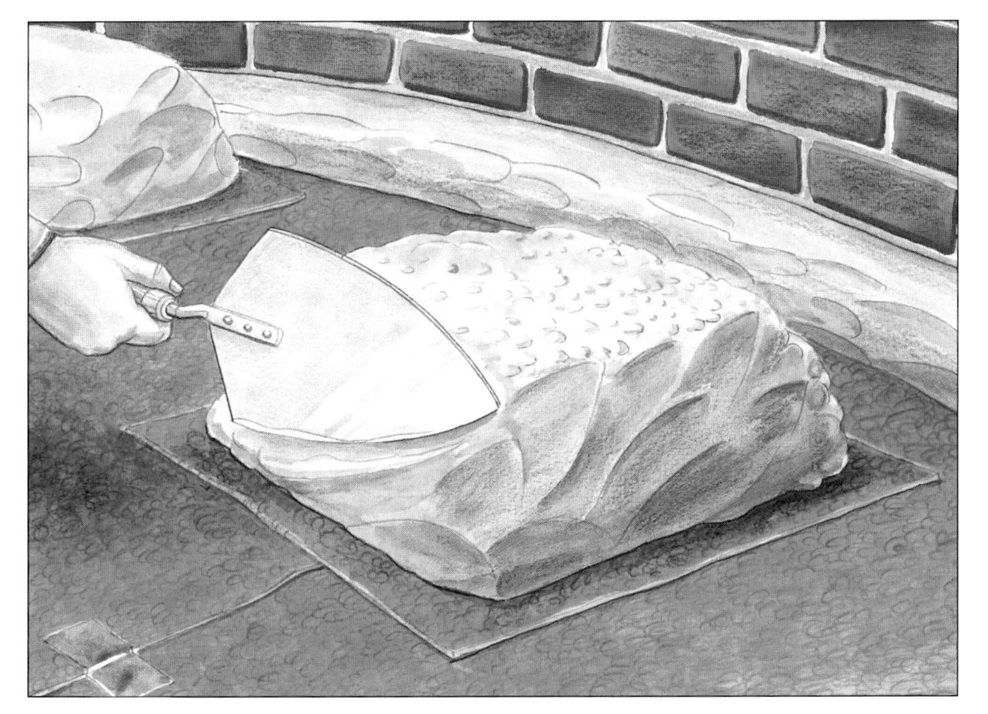

6 Locating the deck posts
Establish where the deck posts need to be. For those to the side of the pond dig holes and set them in concrete, and for the ones in the pond make up concrete pads 350 mm square and 150 mm deep. Position on top of an extra layer of geotextile.

7 Finishing the deck frame
Fix the horizontal framework to the posts at the side of the pond so that they are all level with each other. Cut the remaining posts to length, rest them on the concrete pads and bolt them to the horizontals.

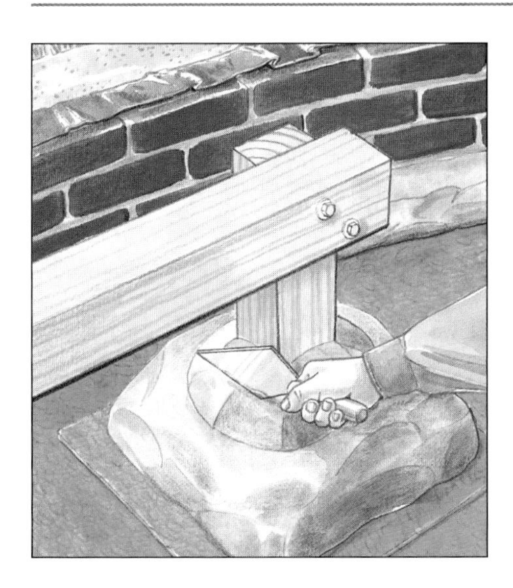

8 Haunching with mortar
Ensure that the posts on the concrete pads are haunched with mortar to stop any possible horizontal movement. Trowel the mortar to a smooth finish. Once set, paint the pads with black tanking paint.

9 Fixing the deck boards and completing the pond
Carefully nail on the decking boards using the strip of plywood to set gaps of 6–7 mm and two nails at each junction. Cover the brick wall and exposed edge of the lining with turf or soil and plant grass seed.

Mosaic pond

Ideal for a small garden or courtyard, this elegant circular fountain pond will both cool the air and make the music of water. Its timeless, classical shape will fit in any outdoor room. The mosaic design is a special touch that adds style to your water feature and gives you the opportunity to be creative; if you don't like the fish shapes, look for other images, colours, shapes and patterns that inspire you.

★★★
Advanced

Making time
3 weekends
A weekend for making the foundation and 2 weekends to complete

Considering the design

The only limiting factor in this design is the size of the plastic sump. Make sure that you can get one the right size. If you want to keep the mosaic bright, you will need to keep the water sparkling and sterile. Use bromine tablets available from a swimming pool supply company. As always, consider child safety (see page 185).

Getting started

Once you have decided where to site the pond, consider how you are going to get electrical power to it. You are creating a work of art so do not hurry – enjoy it.

Overall dimensions and general notes

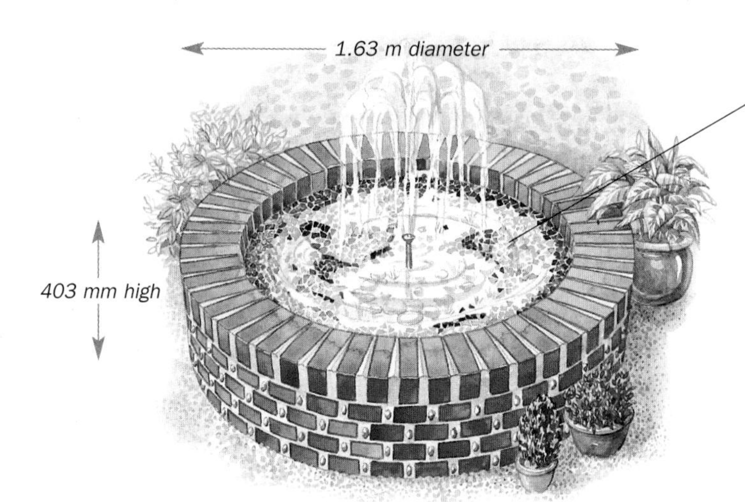
1.63 m diameter
403 mm high
Lined with concrete and covered in a bold mosaic design

The pond can be increased in size but it should not be made any smaller, as the joints between the bricks become too wide.

You will need

Materials

- Wood: 2 pieces 1.74 m x 80 mm x 20 mm, 2 pieces 1.7 m x 80 mm x 20 mm, 4 pieces 702 mm x 80 mm x 20 mm, 2 pieces 540 mm x 80 mm x 20 mm and 2 pieces 500 mm x 80 mm 20 mm (for the formwork), 1 piece 660 mm x 35 mm x 35 mm (tramel arm), 1 piece 150 mm x 70 mm x 70 mm (tramel block)
- Nails: 36 at 70 mm long
- Concrete: 1 part cement (100 kg) and 4 parts ballast (400 kg)
- Plywood: 1 piece 500 mm square x 6 mm thick (trammel base) and 1 piece 1.4 m x 590 mm x 10 mm (concrete former)
- Bricks: 192
- Mortar: 1 part cement (50 kg) and 3 parts sand (150 kg)
- Cobbles: 140 for decorating the wall and 100 kg to fill the sump
- Rigid plastic sump: 895 mm in diameter (380 mm diameter sump) and 185 mm deep
- Butyl: 1 piece 2.3 m square
- Plastic pipe (length to suit your site)
- Duct tape
- Thin card: 1 piece 400 mm square
- Glazed tiles: 30, in an assortment of colours (see page 257)
- Waterproof tile cement and grout
- Pump

Tools

- Tape measure, pegs, string, piece of chalk and a spirit level
- Club hammer and claw hammer
- Spade and shovel
- Wheelbarrow and bucket
- General-purpose saw and hacksaw
- Bricklayer's towel and pointing trowel
- Scissors
- Brick hammer
- Jigsaw

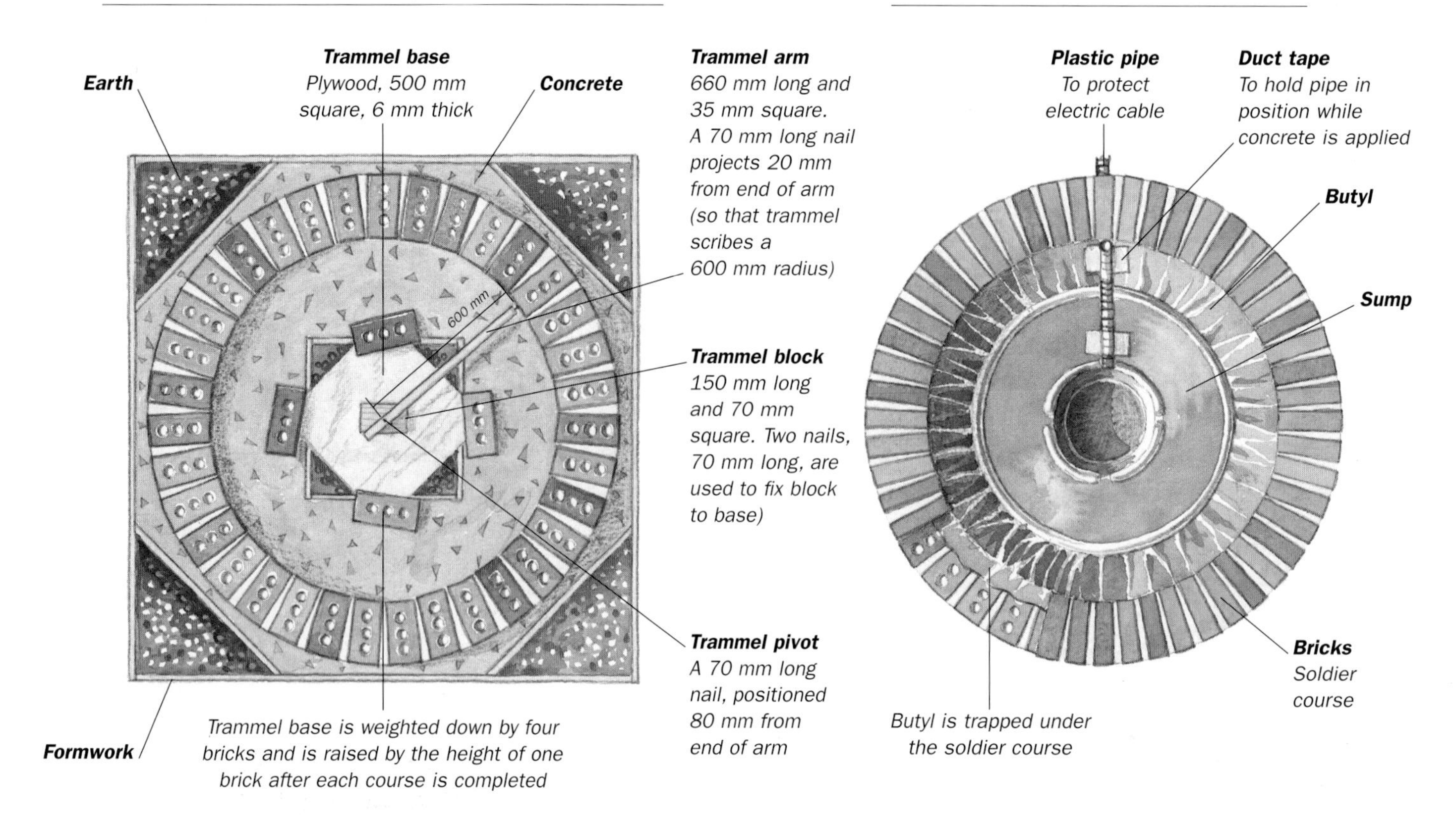

Plan view showing foundation formwork and method of laying bricks
Earth
Trammel base
Plywood, 500 mm square, 6 mm thick
Concrete
Trammel arm
660 mm long and 35 mm square. A 70 mm long nail projects 20 mm from end of arm (so that trammel scribes a 600 mm radius)
600 mm
Trammel block
150 mm long and 70 mm square. Two nails, 70 mm long, are used to fix block to base)
Trammel pivot
A 70 mm long nail, positioned 80 mm from end of arm
Formwork
Trammel base is weighted down by four bricks and is raised by the height of one brick after each course is completed
Cut-away plan view (before concrete is applied)
Plastic pipe
To protect electric cable
Duct tape
To hold pipe in position while concrete is applied
Butyl
Sump
Bricks
Soldier course
Butyl is trapped under the soldier course

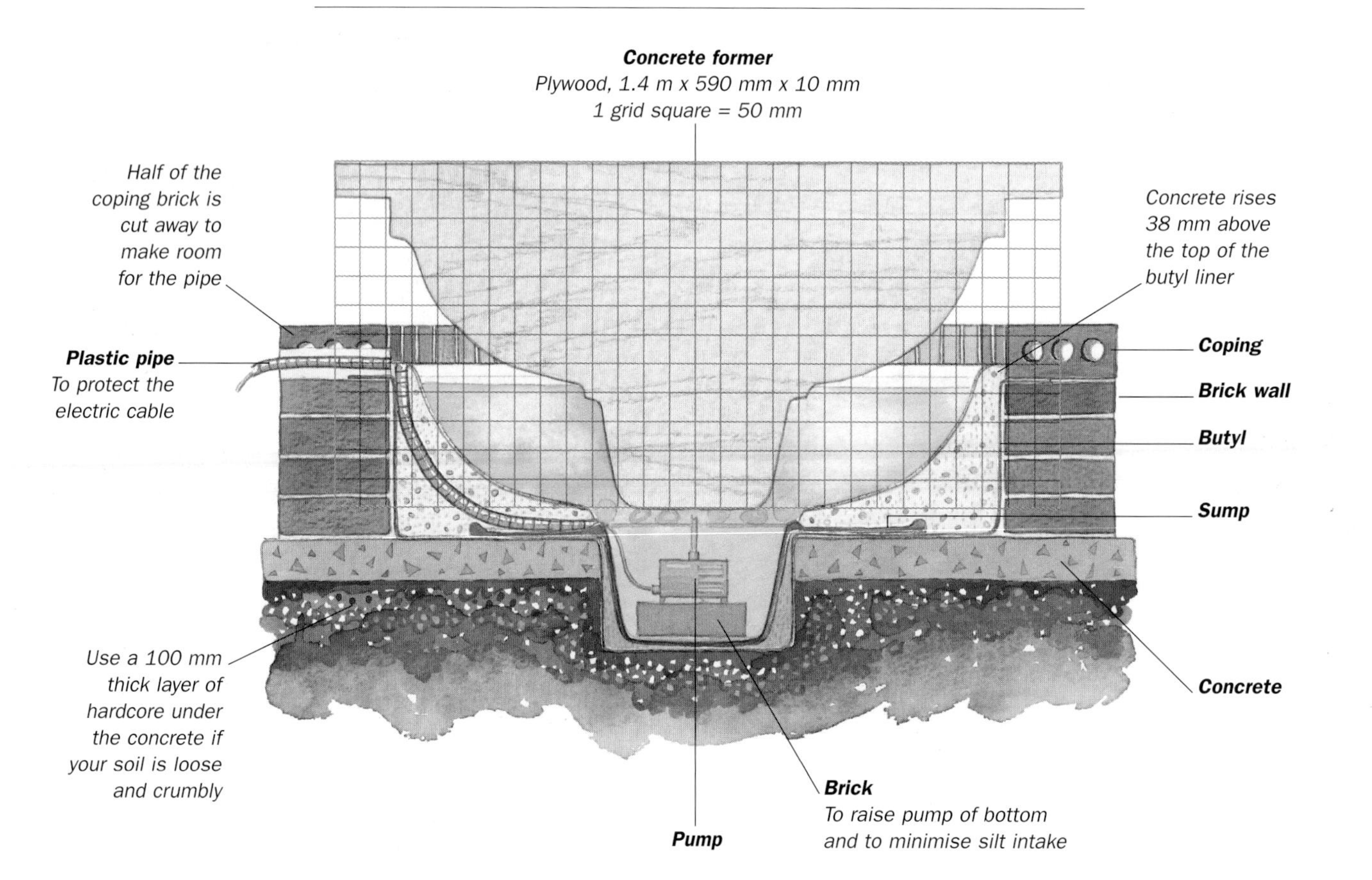

Cross-section showing method of applying concrete
Concrete former
Plywood, 1.4 m x 590 mm x 10 mm
1 grid square = 50 mm
Half of the coping brick is cut away to make room for the pipe
Plastic pipe
To protect the electric cable
Concrete rises 38 mm above the top of the butyl liner
Coping
Brick wall
Butyl
Sump
Concrete
Use a 100 mm thick layer of hardcore under the concrete if your soil is loose and crumbly
Pump
Brick
To raise pump of bottom and to minimise silt intake

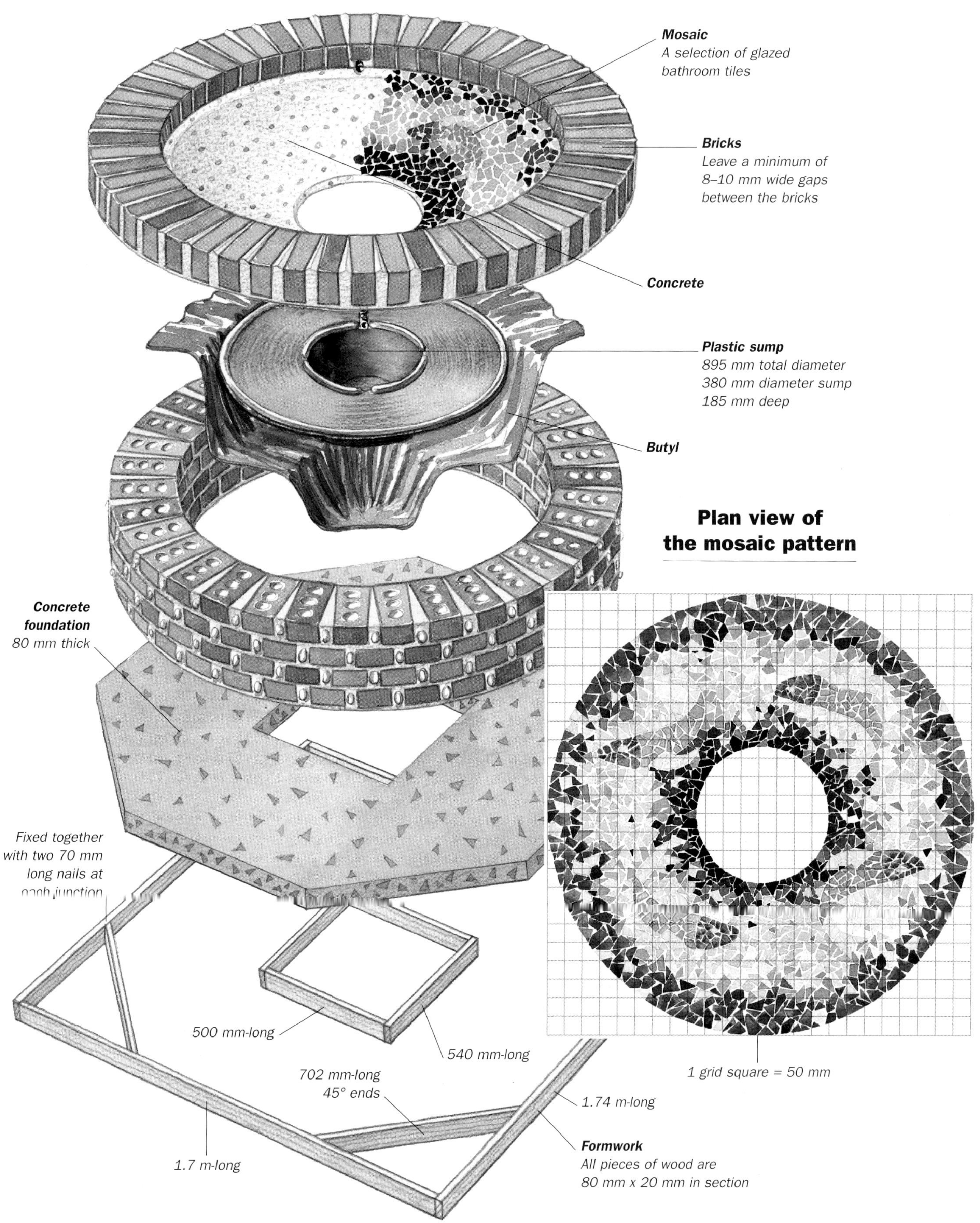
Exploded view of the mosaic pond
Mosaic
A selection of glazed bathroom tiles
Bricks
Leave a minimum of 8–10 mm wide gaps between the bricks
Concrete
Plastic sump
895 mm total diameter
380 mm diameter sump
185 mm deep
Butyl
Plan view of the mosaic pattern
Concrete foundation
80 mm thick
Fixed together with two 70 mm long nails at each junction
500 mm-long
540 mm-long
702 mm-long 45° ends
1.74 m-long
1.7 m-long
Formwork
All pieces of wood are 80 mm x 20 mm in section
1 grid square = 50 mm

Making the mosaic pond

1 Laying the concrete
Cut the 80 mm x 20 mm wood to size and build the formwork. Dig out the foundation to a depth of 200 mm, set the formwork in place and check it is horizontal using the spirit level. Pour in concrete and tamp it level with the top of the frame using an offcut.

2 Setting out the first course
Build the trammel so that it scribes a 600 mm radius and use this to help you position the bricks. Bed the bricks on mortar, and check them with the spirit level. Build three more staggered courses of brick raising the trammel for each course.

3 Placing the decorative cobbles
Fill each of the angled joints with mortar and decorate with cobbles. Carefully select the cobbles for best effect.

4 Putting in the sump
Dig the earth out from the centre of the foundation slab and set the plastic sump in place to make sure it fits.

5 Fitting the butyl
Remove the plastic sump, drape the butyl over the whole pond and arrange it so that the folds are evenly distributed. Replace the sump and trim the butyl ensuring you leave a generous overlap on top of the wall.

6 Laying the coping bricks
Lay the top layer of soldier bricks (the coping) around the edge of the pond using the trammel to guide you. Take extra care to space the bricks evenly and check each one is horizontal using the spirit level. Leave out one of the bricks at the back (see step 7).

7 Fitting the pipe
Lay a short length of pipe for taking the electric cable under the last brick of the soldier course (cut the brick in half). Run more pipe from the edge of the sump to the level of the coping bricks and hold it in position with short lengths of duct tape.

8 Tamping the concrete
Use the jigsaw to cut the profile board to shape. Make sure the profile allows for an adequate thickness of concrete as illustrated in the diagram on page 256. Trowel a thick, dry concrete mix inside the pond and use the board to assist in spreading it smoothly.

9 Applying the mosaic
Cut out a fish shape from the card and use this to mark out the design. Break the tiles into small pieces and stick them down. When completed, wipe grout into the gaps and allow to dry. Position the pump in the sump and cover with cobbles.

Split-level pool

★★★
Advanced

Making time
5 weekends
1 day planning, 4 days to dig and lay the foundation and 5 days to complete

If you have a sloping or terraced area in your garden it is a good idea to take advantage of the changes in level and build a stream (see page 214) or split-level pools like these. Plan the project so you can see and hear the waterfall while sitting in your favourite spot. The spray from the waterfall will stain the surrounding brickwork and algae will grow on the brick. Over years this will look more and more attractive.

Considering the design

Remember that the water will splash outwards as far as it has fallen, so do not make the bottom pond too small or you will have damp and slippery areas outside the pond as well as lose considerable amounts of water. When you have a waterfall you also get a fair amount of evaporation so you will want to consider an automatic top-up system.

Getting started

There will be a good deal of spoil generated in the excavation of this project, so make sure you have planned where it is to go before you start work.

Overall dimensions and general notes

This split-level design takes a lot of planning but is certainly worth achieving. It is a great way of combining fish, still-water plants and a classic waterfall feature.

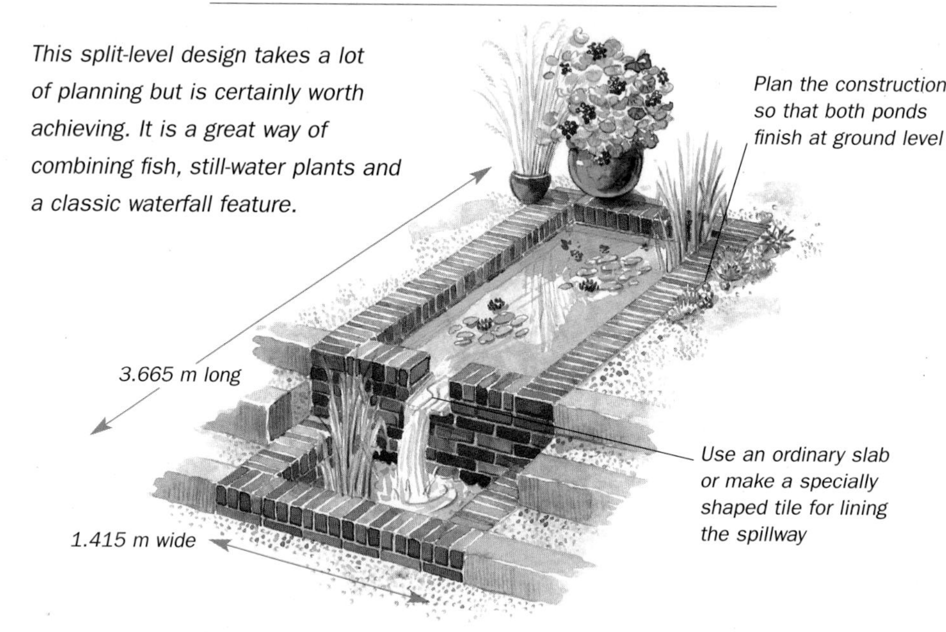
Plan the construction so that both ponds finish at ground level
3.665 m long
Use an ordinary slab or make a specially shaped tile for lining the spillway
1.415 m wide

You will need

Materials

- Hardcore: 0.5 cu metres
- Concrete: 1 part cement (750 kg) and 4 parts ballast (3000 kg)
- Blocks: 35
- Bricks: 134 (coping) and 432 (brick spacing and walls)
- Tile: 235 mm x 200 mm x 35 mm (for spillway), can be a flat tile or a specially made ceramic or concrete shape
- Mortar: 1 part cement (150 kg) and 3 parts sand (450 kg)
- Geotextile: 33 sq metres
- Glue: quick drying (for sticking geotextile to wall)
- Duct tape
- Butyl: 1 piece 4 m x 2.6 m and 1 piece 2.3 m x 2.6 m
- Plastic pipe: 1 piece 4 m long (delivery pipe) and 1 piece to protect electric cable (length to suit your site)
- Tanking paint: 16 sq metre coverage
- Pump

Tools

- Tape measure, pegs, string and a piece of chalk
- Spade, fork and shovel
- Spirit level
- Line set
- Brick hammer
- Bricklayer's trowel and pointing trowel
- Scissors
- Hacksaw
- Float
- Paint brush

Cross-section of the split-level pool

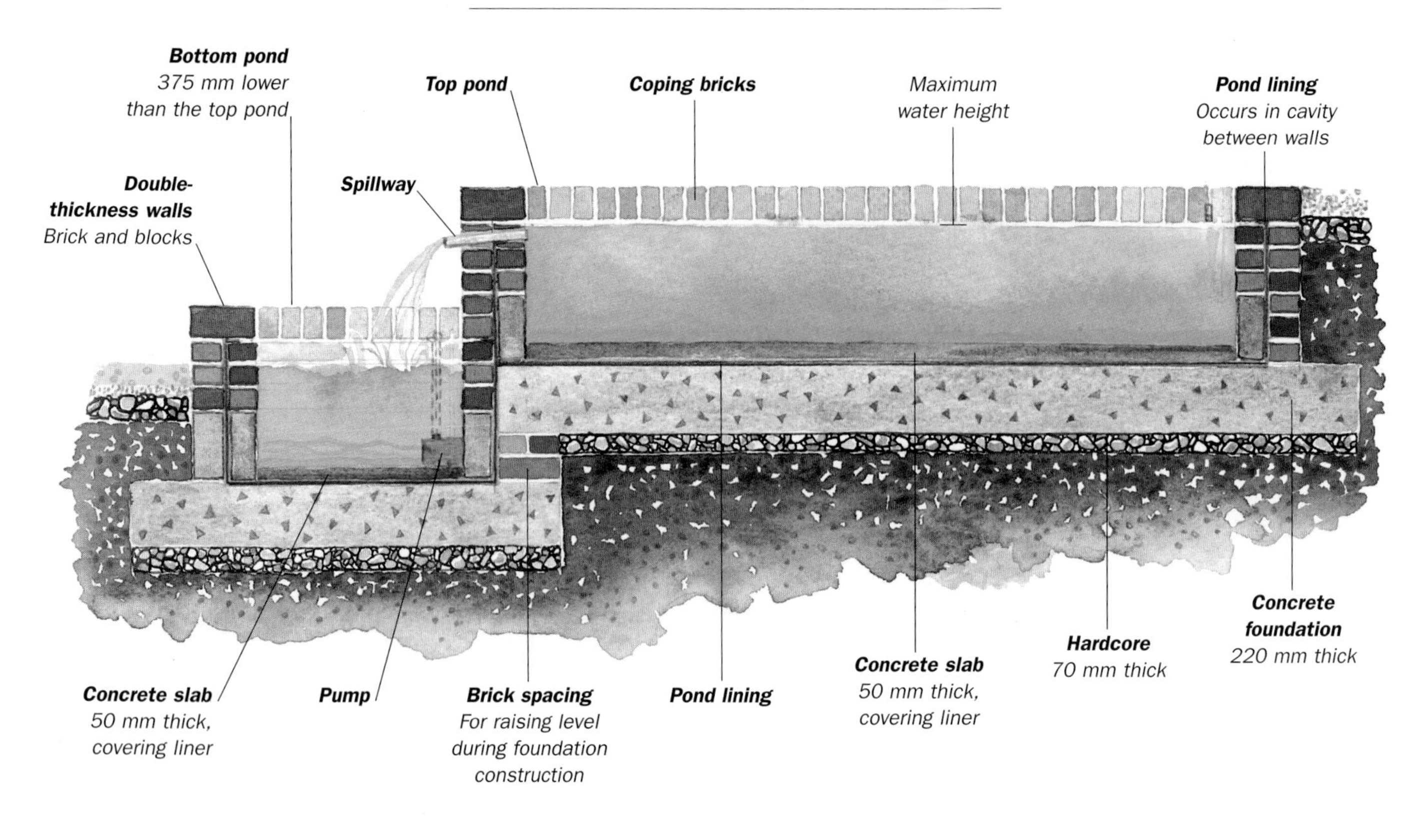
Bottom pond
375 mm lower than the top pond
Top pond
Coping bricks
Maximum water height
Pond lining
Occurs in cavity between walls
Double-thickness walls
Brick and blocks
Spillway
Concrete slab
50 mm thick, covering liner
Pump
Brick spacing
For raising level during foundation construction
Pond lining
Concrete slab
50 mm thick, covering liner
Hardcore
70 mm thick
Concrete foundation
220 mm thick

Plan view of the split-level pool

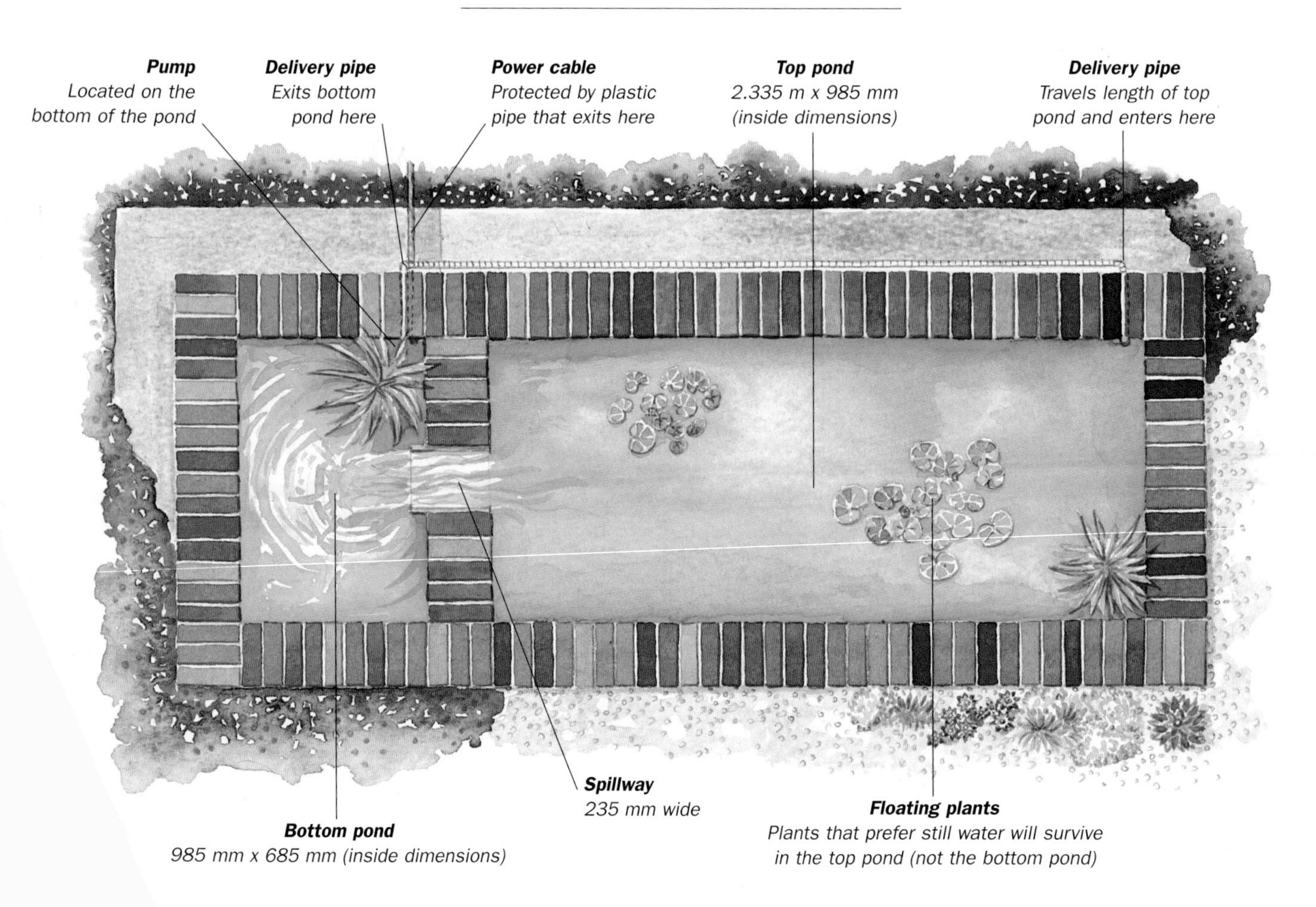
Pump
Located on the bottom of the pond
Delivery pipe
Exits bottom pond here
Power cable
Protected by plastic pipe that exits here
Top pond
2.335 m x 985 mm (inside dimensions)
Delivery pipe
Travels length of top pond and enters here
Bottom pond
985 mm x 685 mm (inside dimensions)
Spillway
235 mm wide
Floating plants
Plants that prefer still water will survive in the top pond (not the bottom pond)

Exploded view of the split-level pool (lining not shown)

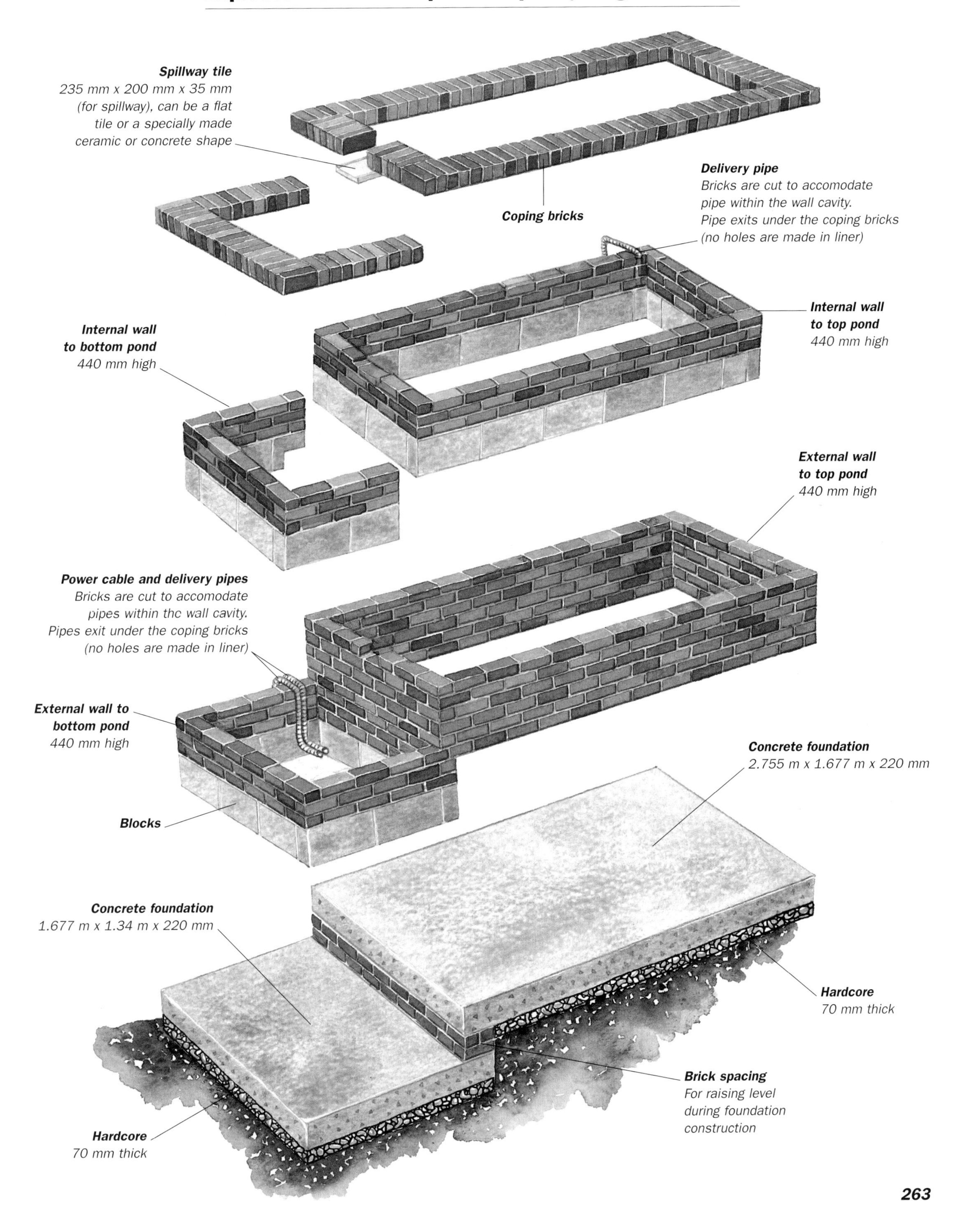
Spillway tile
235 mm x 200 mm x 35 mm (for spillway), can be a flat tile or a specially made ceramic or concrete shape
Coping bricks
Delivery pipe
Bricks are cut to accomodate pipe within the wall cavity. Pipe exits under the coping bricks (no holes are made in liner)
Internal wall to bottom pond
440 mm high
Internal wall to top pond
440 mm high
External wall to top pond
440 mm high
Power cable and delivery pipes
Bricks are cut to accomodate pipes within thc wall cavity. Pipes exit under the coping bricks (no holes are made in liner)
External wall to bottom pond
440 mm high
Blocks
Concrete foundation
2.755 m x 1.677 m x 220 mm
Concrete foundation
1.677 m x 1.34 m x 220 mm
Hardcore
70 mm thick
Brick spacing
For raising level during foundation construction
Hardcore
70 mm thick

Making the split-level pool

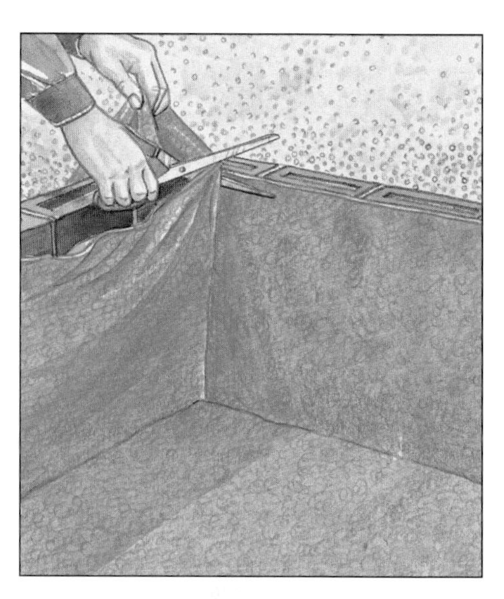

1 Excavating
Mark out the area of the foundation slabs for both ponds. Dig down to a depth of 852 mm. Spread hardcore in the bottoms of the holes, compact it to a thickness of 70 mm with a sledgehammer and cast the 220 mm thick concrete slabs.

2 Building the exterior walls
Mark out the size and positions of the exterior walls. Build up the exterior walls to a height of 440 mm using blocks for the first course and bricks for the rest. Clean up all the joints between the bricks that will remain visible.

3 Lining with geotextile
Remove or flatten any sharp objects and carefully line the entire area with geotextile right to the top, folding or cutting away darts formed at the corners, and sticking it to the walls with quick-drying glue. Trim off any geotextile that rises above the top of the walls.

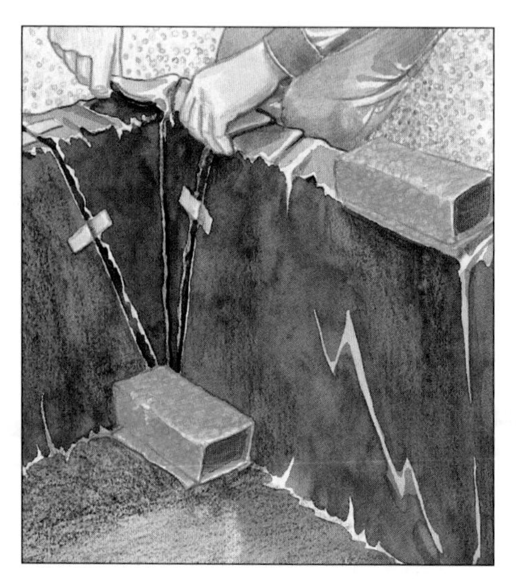

4 Lining with butyl
Position the butyl liner over the geotextile, and use bricks wrapped in geotextile to push the liner into the corners. If necessary refold the creases to make them even and use tape to hold the butyl in place. Trim the liner 100 mm above the top of the bricks.

5 Fitting the pipework
Install a pipe to carry water from the pump in the bottom pond to the far end of the top pond. The second pipe is for the power cable. The pipes do not pierce the liner; they travel up the wall (in the cavity) and over the top (under the coping).

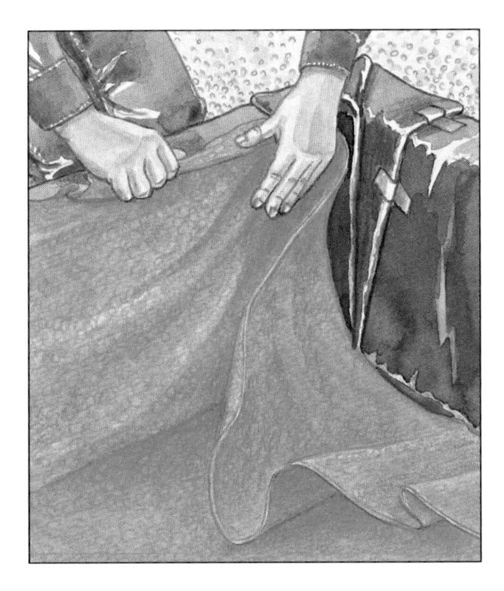

6 Laying more geotextile

Remove the wrapped bricks and reline the hole with a second layer of geotextile as before taking great care not to damage or pierce the butyl. Hang the liner over the top of the butyl at the top of the brickwork.

7 Building the interior walls

Use more blocks and bricks to build interior walls allowing for a 10 mm cavity and making a combined wall thickness of 215 mm. Finish at the same height as the exterior wall. You will need to cut blocks and bricks to accomodate the plastic pipes.

8 Fitting the coping bricks

Trim the geotextile level with the top of the walls and trim the butyl again leaving just 50 mm for folding over. Lay the coping bricks around the edge on a bed of mortar. You will need to cut a few bricks to accomodate the plastic pipes.

9 Laying the concrete bottom

Lay a 50 mm thick concrete slab over the liner in the bottom of the pond. After it has set paint the interior of the pond with black tanking paint and allow to dry completely. Fit the tile in the spillway and install the pump. Let everything dry before filling with water.

Glossary

Aligning
Setting one component part against another and obtaining a good fit or alignment of the two.

Back-filling
Filling a space that exists around a foundation or wall with earth. Filling post holes with hardcore and/or concrete in order to stabilize the posts. Also to fill the area surrounding the post to bring it up to the desired level.

Bedding
The process of setting (and levelling) a stone in a bed or layer of wet mortar.

Bracing
Minimizing any sideways or skewing movement in a structure by adding a secondary member to triangulate it.

Buttering
Using a trowel to spread a piece of stone with wet mortar, just prior to setting it in position, for example in a wall.

Butting
Pushing one component part hard up against another in order to obtain a good, flush fit, with both faces touching.

Centring
Marking and placing a component in the centre of another. Also measuring from the centre of one component to the centre of another.

Cladding
Covering a frame with decking boards.

Compacting
Using a hammer or roller to squash down a layer of sand, earth or hardcore.

Coursing
Bedding a number of stones in mortar in order to build a horizontal course.

Curing time
The time taken for mortar or concrete to become firm and stable. "Part cured" means that the mortar or concrete is solid enough to continue work.

Dressing
Using a hammer, chisel or trowel to trim a stone to size; alternatively to create a textured finish on its surface.

Dry run
Putting part of a project together without nails, screws or bolts, in order to see whether or not the components are going to fit, and to make sure that the design is going to work out successfully.

Finishing
The final procedure, at the end of a project, of sanding, painting, staining, oiling or washing down, in order to complete the project.

Floating
Using a metal, plastic or wooden float to skim wet concrete or mortar to a smooth and level finish.

Framing
Fixing horizontal joists and beams to vertical posts.

Jointing
The procedure of fixing one length of wood to another by means of screws, nails, bolts, or a traditional cut woodworking joint.

Levelling
Using a spirit level to decide whether or not a component part is horizontally parallel to the ground or vertically at right angles to the ground, and then going on to make adjustments to bring the component into line.

Marking out
Variously using a tape measure, straight edge, square, compass, chalk, a pencil or pegs and string to draw lines on a piece of wood or stone, or mark out an area on the ground, in readiness for cutting or otherwise taking a project forward.

Planning and designing
The whole procedure of considering a project, viewing the site, making drawings, and working out amounts and costs, prior to actually starting work.

Pointing
Using a trowel or a tool of your choice to fill, shape and texture mortar joints.

Raking out
Using a trowel to rake out some mortar in a joint in order that the edges of a stone are more clearly revealed.

Sawing to size
Taking sawn wood (meaning wood that has been purchased ready sawn to width and thickness) and cutting it to length.

Sighting
To judge by eye, or to look down or along a wall or a length of wood, in order to determine whether or not a cut, joint or structure is level or true.

Siting
Making decisions as to where – in the garden or on the plot – a structure is going to be positioned.

Sourcing
The process of questioning suppliers by phone, visit, letter or e-mail, in order to ascertain the best source for materials.

Squaring
The technique of marking out, with a set square and/or spirit level, to make sure that one surface or structure is at right angles to another.

Squaring a frame
Ensuring squareness (90° corners) in a rectilinear frame by measuring across the diagonals and making adjustments until both diagonals are identical – at which point the frame is square.

Tamping
Using a length of wood to compact and level wet concrete.

Trial run
Running through the procedure of setting out the components of a structure without using concrete or mortar, or trying a technique, in order to find out whether it will be successful.

Trimming
Using a hammer, chisel, the edge of large trowel, or a tool of your own choosing to bring the edge of a piece of stone to a good finish. It is very similar to Dressing (see opposite).

Watering or damping
Wetting a stone before bedding in on mortar, to prevent the stone sucking the water out of the mortar.

Wedging
Using small pieces of stone to wedge larger pieces of stone so that they reach a desired level.

Wire brushing
Using a wire-bristled brush to remove dry mortar from the face of a stone.

Suppliers

Consult the telephone directory for details of your local garden centre, builder's, stone and timber merchant.

UK

Timber and decking

Andrew's Timber
387 Blackfen Road
Blackfen, Sidcup
Kent DA15 9NJ
Tel/fax: (020) 8303 2696
www.andrews-timber.co.uk
(Timber, decking, accessories)

Sandalwood Gates & Timber Products
Elvington Industrial Estate
York Road, Elvington
York YO4 5AR
Tel/fax: (01904) 608542
www.sandalwoodgates.co.uk
(Fencing, timberwork and decking products)

South London Hardwoods
390 Sydenham Road
Croydon, Surrey
CR0 2EA
Tel: 020 8683 0292
www.slhardwoods.co.uk
(Large range of timber products)

Travis Perkins Trading Co. Ltd
Head Office:
Lodge Way House
Lodge Way
Harlestone Road
Northampton NN5 7UG
Tel: (01604) 752424
www.travisperkins.co.uk
(Builders' merchants supplying timber and decking products; branches nationwide)

Brick and stone

The Brick Warehouse
176 York Way
London N1 0AZ
Tel: (020) 7833 9992
(Brick and stone products)

Buffalo Granite (UK) Ltd
The Vestry
St Clement's Church
Treadgold Street
London W11 4BP
Tel: (020) 7221 7930
(Stone merchant)

The Natural Stone Co.
Elm Cottage
Ockham Road
North Ockham
Woking, Surrey
GU23 6NW
Tel: (0845) 066 5533
(Natural stone merchant)

Pinks Hill Landscape Merchants
Off Broad Street
Wood Street Village
Guildford
Surrey GU3 3BP
Tel: 01483 571620
(Large range of natural and reproduction stone products, including feature stones, boulders, flags, rockery and walling stone, Japanese lanterns and statues)

Tarmac TopPave Ltd
Millfields Road
Ettingsfield
Wolverhampton
West Midlands
WV4 6JP
www.toppave.co.uk
(08702) 413450
(Block pavers, decorative pavers, kerbing and edging blocks)

The York Handmade Brick Co. Ltd
Forest Lane, Alne
York YO61 1TU
Tel: (01347) 838881
Fax: (01347) 838885
www.yorkhandmade.co.uk
Southern sales office: (01909) 540680
(Handmade bricks, pavers and terracotta floor tiles)

Tool manufacturers

Black & Decker
Caswell Road
Brackmills Industrial Estate
Northampton
NN4 7PW
Tel: (01604) 768777

Stanley UK Ltd
The Stanley Works
Woodside
Sheffield, Yorkshire
S3 9PD
Tel: (0114) 276 8888

Tool retailers

Industrial Tool Supplies
607–617 High Road
Leyton
London E10 6RF
Tel: 020 8539 2231
www.itslondon.co.uk

S J Carter Tools Ltd
74 Elmers End Road
Anerley
London SE20 7UX
Tel: (020) 7587 1222

Tilgear
Bridge House
69 Station Road
Cuffley, Hertfordshire
EN6 4TG
Tel: (01707) 873 434

Pond equipment

Forsham Cottage Arks
Goreside Farm
Great Chart
Ashford
Kent TN26 1JU
Tel: (01233) 820229
www.forshamcottages.co.uk
(Duck houses)

Freshfields Water Gardens and Aquarium
Moss Side, Formby
Liverpool L37 0AE
Tel: (01704) 877964
(Water garden specialist with large selection of pools, pumps, liners, fish)

Hozelock Ltd
Thame Road
Haddenham, Aylesbury
Buckinghamshire
HP17 8JD
Tel: (01844) 291881
www.hozelock.com
(Pumps, filtration systems and lighting)

Lotus Water Garden Products
Lodge Road
Cow Lane
Burnley
Lancashire BB11 1NN
Tel: (01282) 420771
(Manufacturers of self-contained water features and fountain ornaments)

Mickfield Water Garden Centre
Debenham Road
Mickfield, Stowmarket
Suffolk IP14 5LP
Tel: (01449) 711336
www.watergardenshop.co.uk
(Garden centre selling liners, pumps, plants etc.)

Midland Butyl Ltd
Windmill Farm
Biggin Lane
Nr Hulland Ward
Ashbourne
Derby DE6 3FN
Tel: (01335) 372133
www.midlandbutyl.co.uk

OASE (UK) Ltd
OASE House
2 North Way
Walworth Industrial Estate
Andover
Hampshire SP10 5AZ
Tel: (01264) 333225
www.oase-uk.co.uk

General DIY/ garden stores (outlets nationwide, phone for details of nearest branch)

B & Q plc
Head Office:
Portswood House
1 Hampshire Corporate Park
Chandlers Ford
Eastleigh
Hampshire SO53 3YX
Tel: (023) 8025 6256

Focus (DIY) Ltd
Head Office:
Gawsworth House
Westmere Drive, Crewe
Cheshire CW1 6XB
Tel: (0845) 600 4244

Homebase Ltd
Beddington House
Railway Approach
Wallington
Surrey SM6 0HB
Tel: (0845) 077 8888
www.homebase.co.uk

Wickes
Wickes House
120–138 Station Road
Harrow, Middlesex
HA1 2QB
Tel: (0870) 6089001
www.wickes.co.uk

AUSTRALIA

ABC Timber & Building Supplies Pty Ltd
46 Auburn Road
Regents Park,
NSW 2143
Tel: (02) 9645 2511

BBC Hardware
Head Office: Bld. A
Cnr. Cambridge and Chester Streets
Epping, NSW 2121
Tel: (02) 9876 0888

Bowens Timber and Building Supplies
135–173 Macaulay Road
North Melbourne
VIC 3051
Tel: (03) 9328 1041

Bunnings Building Supplies
Head Office:
152 Pilbara Street
Welshpool, WA 6106
Tel: (08) 9365 1555

Finlayson Timber and Hardware Pty Ltd
135 Wellington Road
East Brisbane
QLD 4169
Tel: (07) 3393 0588
(07) 3244 1200
www.finlayson.com.au
(Timber and full hardware range)

Pine Rivers Landscaping Supplies
93 South Pine Road
Strathpine, QLD 4500
Tel: (07) 3205 6708

Sydney Stone Yard
1/3A Stanley Road
Randwick, NSW 2031
Tel: (02) 9326 4479

Sydney Stone Company
Mona Vale Road
Mona Vale, NSW 2103
Tel: (02) 9979 9458
(Sandstone and bluestone)

Melocco Pty Ltd
849 Princes Highway
Springvale, VIC 3171
Tel: (03) 9546 0211
www.melocco.com.au
(Sandstone, granite, bluestone)

Gosford Quarries
300 Johnston Street
Annandale, NSW 2038
Tel: (02) 9810 7555
www.gosfordquarries.com.au
(Sandstone and granite)

International Sandstone and Granite
11 Old Pacific Highway
Yatala, QLD 4207
Tel: (07) 3383 6999
www.isandstone.com.au

Mitre 10 Australia Ltd (Head Office)
122 Newton Road
Wetherhill Park
NSW 2164
Tel: (02) 9725 3222
www.mitre10.com.au
Customer Services:
1800 777 850
(DIY stores nationwide)

NEW ZEALAND

DIY stores

Mitre 10
Head Office:
182 Wairau Road
Glenfield, Auckland
Tel: (09) 443 9900
(Branches nationwide)

Placemakers Support Office
150 Marua Road
Private Bag 14942
Panmure, Auckland
Tel: (09) 525 5100

Timber

Rosenfeld Kidson
513 Mt. Wellington Highway
Mt. Wellington
Auckland
Tel: (09) 573 0503
Fax: (09) 573 0504

Timpan City Ltd
21 Walls Road
Penrose
Auckland
Tel: (09) 571 0020

South Pacific Timber
Cnr. Ruru and Shaddock Streets
Auckland City
Tel: (09) 379 5150

McConnochie Milling and Treatment
47–51 Hinemoa Street
Paraparaumu
Tel: (04) 297 2787

Lumber Specialties
117 Main South Road
Upper Riccarton
Christchurch
Tel: (03) 348 7002

Wilson Bros Timber
71 Foremans Road
Hornby
Tel: (03) 688 2336

Masonry

Firth Industries
Branches nationwide
Freephone: 0800 800 576
(Masonry)

Placemakers
Branches nationwide
Freephone:
0800 425 2269
(Masonry)

Stevenson Building Supplies
(Branches throughout Auckland)
Freephone: 0800 610 710
(Blocks, bricks, paving, concrete)

Southtile
654 North Road
Invercargill
Tel: (03) 215 9179
Fax: (03) 215 7178
Freephone: 0800 768 848
www.southtile.co.nz
(Tiles and bricks)

SOUTH AFRICA

Dunrobin Garden Pavilion
Old Main Road
Bothas Hill, Durban
Tel: (031) 777 1855
Fax: (031) 777 1893

Lifestyle Garden Centre
DF Malan Drive
Randpark Ridge
Northcliffe
Johannesburg
Tel: (011) 792 5616
Fax: (011) 792 5332

Radermachers Garden and Home Centre
Kraaibosch
National Road
George
Tel: (044) 889 0075/6
Fax: (044) 889 0071

Safari Garden Centre
Lynwood Road
Pretoria
Tel: (012) 807 0009
Fax: (012) 807 0350

Showgrounds Nursery
Showgrounds
Currie Avenue
Bloemfontein
Tel: (051) 447 5523
Fax: (051) 447 5523

Starke Ayres
322 Kempston Road
Sydwill, Port Elizabeth
Tel: (041) 451 0389
Fax: (041) 451 0393

Stodels
Eversdal Road
Bellville, Cape Town
Tel: (021) 919 1106
Fax: (021) 919 9324

Stoneage Concrete Industries
126 Crompton Street
Pinetown, Durban
Tel: (031) 701 2411
Fax: (031) 701 6842

Index

R

S

T

W

Acknowledgments

Decks and Decking and Stonework

AG&G Books would like to thank Garden and Wildlife Matters Photographic Library for contributing the photographs used on pages 18-23 and 104-109.

Garden Ponds

The vision and skill of Rosemary Wilkinson made this book possible. Clare Sayer ably realised and edited the work and, with the help of the Bridgewaters, has produced a work of which we can all be proud.

I found the space between concept and reality something of a curate's egg and could not have persisted without Clare's charming prompts, Jane, David and the support and help of many who shall remain nameless.

Anthony Archer-Wills first inspired me as to the mysteries of water whilst I was at Merrist Wood College, tutored by Paul Colinridge, Tony Begg, Pauline May and Geoff Ace. The demands of workmates, students and clients with the knowledge and pain gained working with Anthony made necessary this primer about ponds.

My gratitude to the above as well as, to name a few: Mr and Mrs A D Allanson, Mr and Mrs J Ashpool, Mr and Mrs D Bradbury, Mrs P Brenan, Mr and Mrs P Corbett, Ms X Coventry, Mr and Mrs H Davies, P G Jeeves, Mr and Mrs I Keith, Mr David Kiff and Berkeley Homes, Mr and Mrs P Graves, Harveys, Hirsts, Lulubelle for inspiration, Mr and Mrs W Matthews, Mr and Mrs G David Neame, Mr and Mrs W Nicholson, Ms Poppy Totman, Robbie and Rosina, Mr and Mrs J Simon, Sonya, Toby Wear, Véronique and the pond makers of England.

I would also like to thank the following people for letting us photograph their ponds: Major L Cave (pages 186 and 204), Mrs J Isaacs (page 215), Gillian Harris (page 219), Anne-Marie Bulat/John Brookes (pages 231 and 236), Camilla Hyde (page 237) and Mr and Mrs Shepard Walwyn (page 248).

New Holland Publishers would like to thank the following companies for supplying pictures: Forsham Cottage Arks (page 191) and OASE (page 191, bottom right: lights). See Suppliers on page 268 for further details.